Cats

500 Purr-fect Portraits to Brighten Your Day

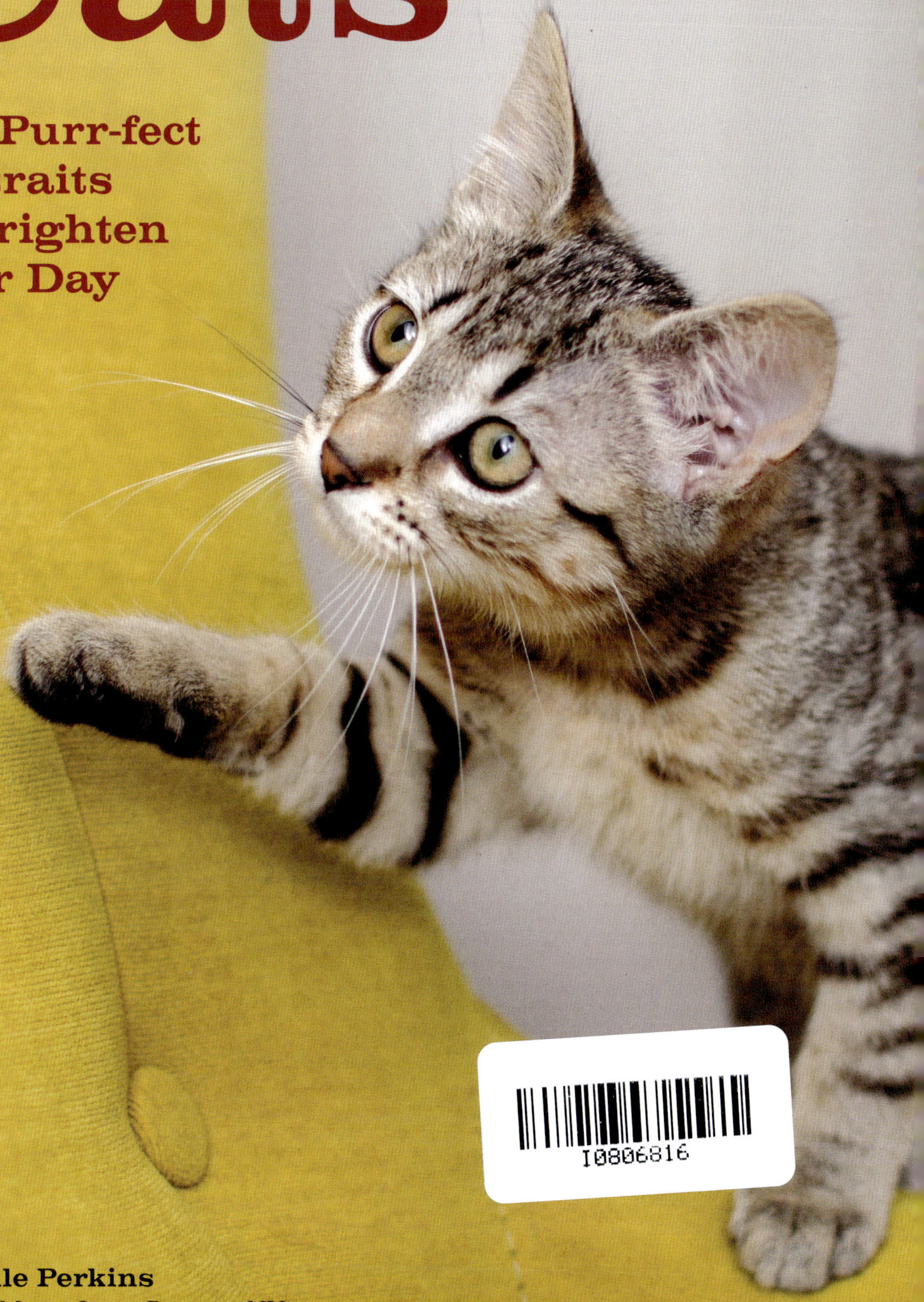

Michelle Perkins

Amherst Media, Inc. ■ Buffalo, NY

This book is dedicated to animal lovers everywhere—but especially to pet rescue volunteers and veterinary care providers. Thank you for making the world a happier, healthier place for our animal companions!

Published by:
Amherst Media, Inc., P.O. Box 538, Buffalo, N.Y. 14213
www.AmherstMedia.com

Publisher: Craig Alesse
Senior Editor/Production Manager: Michelle Perkins
Editors: Barbara A. Lynch-Johnt, Beth Alesse
Acquisitions Editor: Harvey Goldstein
Associate Publisher: Katie Kiss
Editorial Assistance from: Roy Bakos, Carey A. Miller, Rebecca Rudell, Jen Sexton
Business Manager: Sarah Loder
Marketing Associate: Tonya Flickinger

ISBN-13: 978-1-68203-378-4
Library of Congress Control Number: 2018936013
Printed in The United States of America.
10 9 8 7 6 5 4 3 2 1

Notice of Disclaimer: The information contained in this book is based on the author's experience and opinions. The author and publisher will not be held liable for the use or misuse of the information in this book.

www.facebook.com/AmherstMediaInc
www.youtube.com/AmherstMedia
www.twitter.com/AmherstMedia

Introduction

Ask any cat lover: cats and kittens are the best thing ever! Cats lift our moods, lower our blood pressure, and improve our sense of well-being. In fact, people who have pets in their lives even live longer! In this book, we've collected five hundred photos that capturing the beauty and personality of a wide range of felines from around the world—and wide variety of cats' favorite activities, from lazy naps to spirited exploration. Inspirational quotes about cats and their honored roles in our lives and homes add another level of optimism and love. This book is perfect for moms, grandparents, teachers, kids, or anyone who might need a little lift. Just a few minutes with these adorable kitty faces provides a boost that will last all day!

Contents

1. Friends and Family

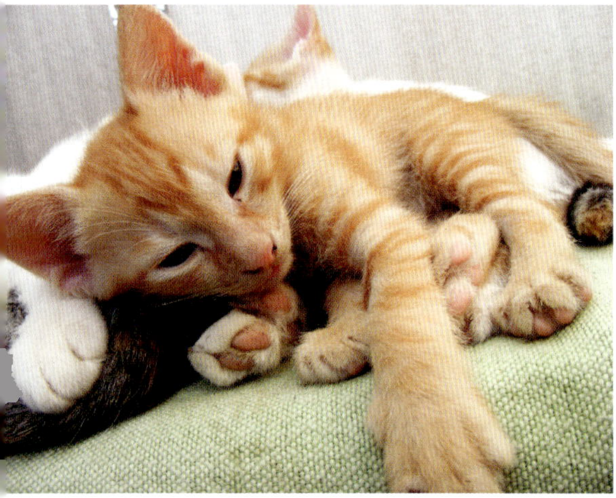

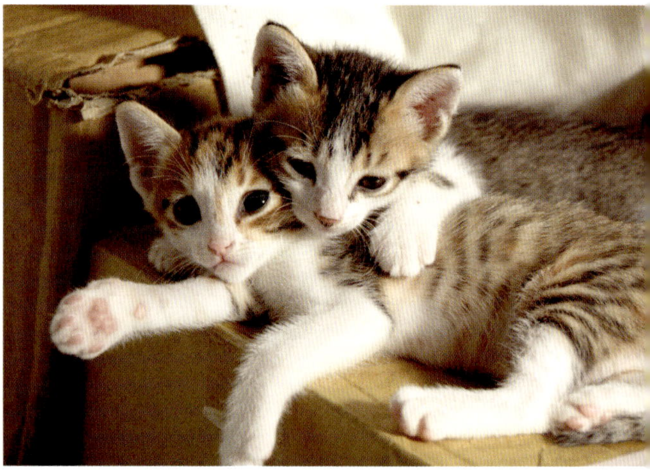

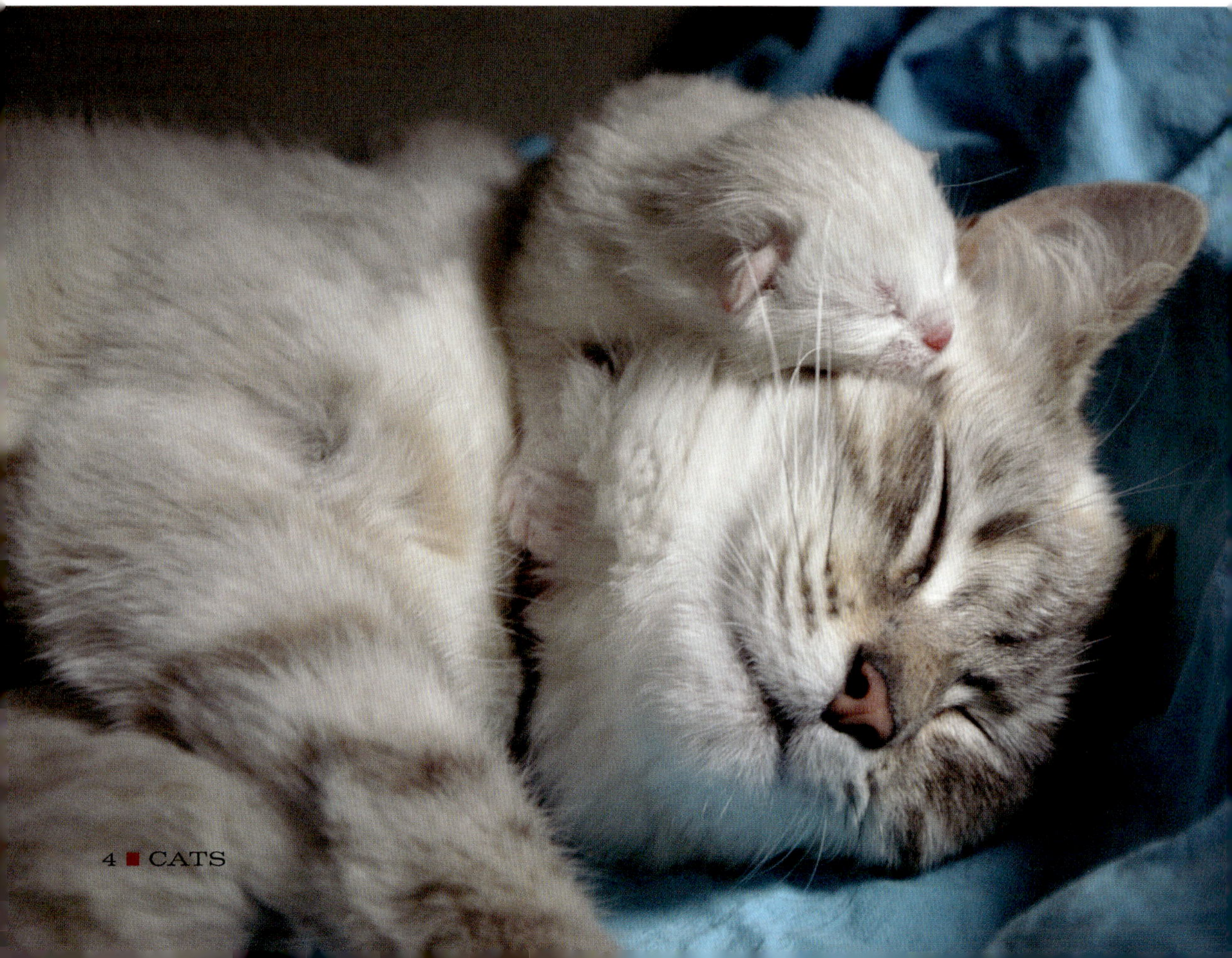

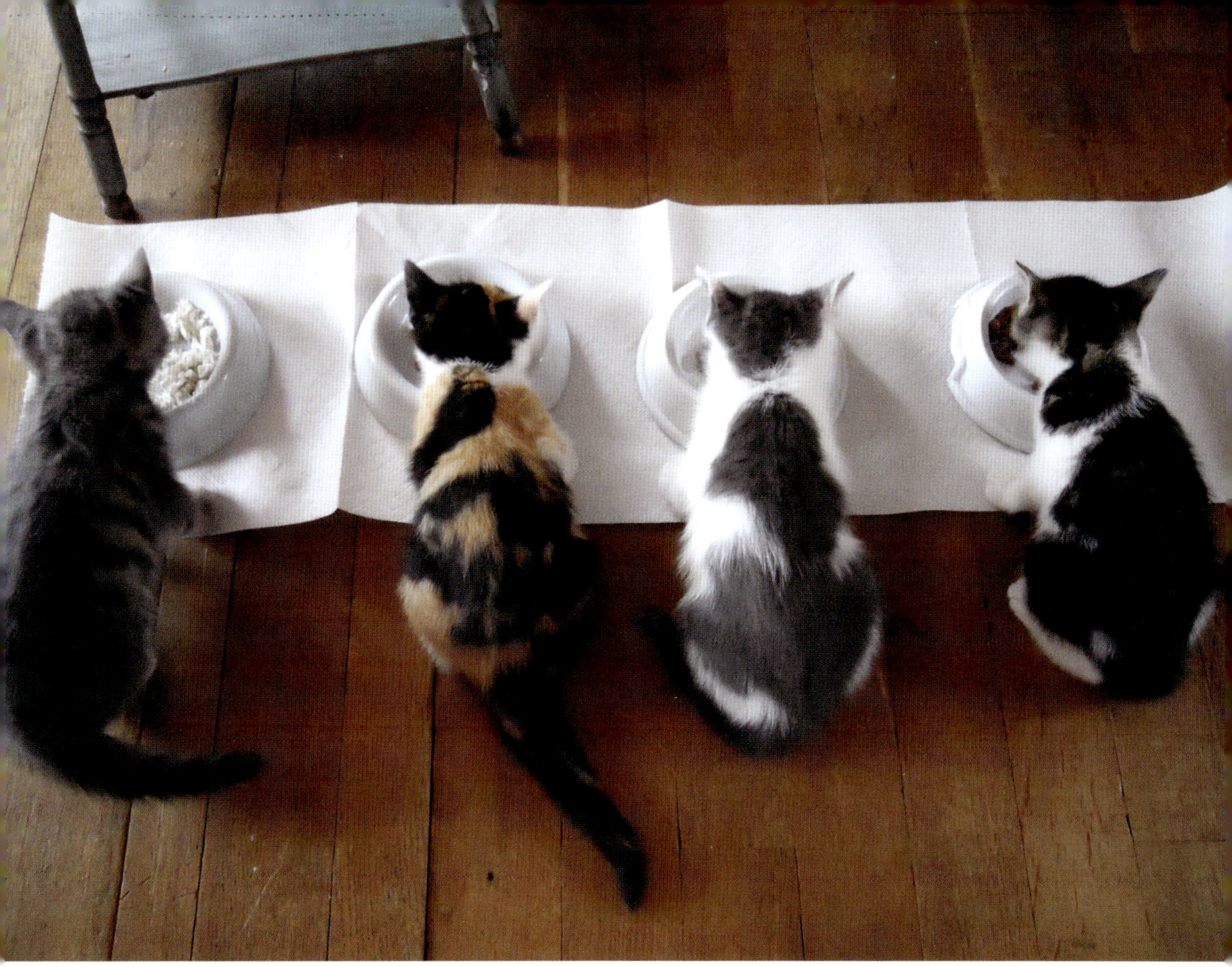
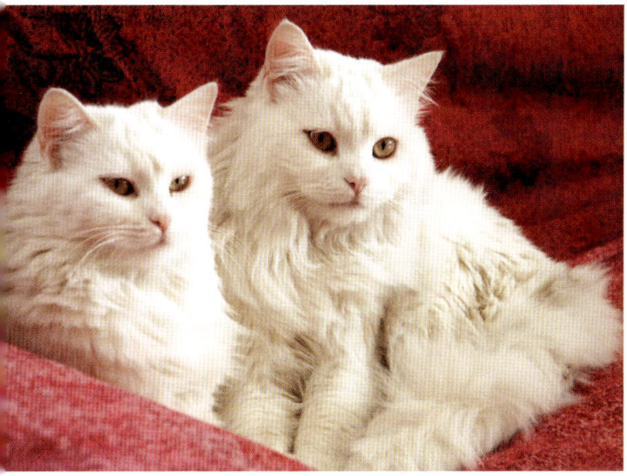
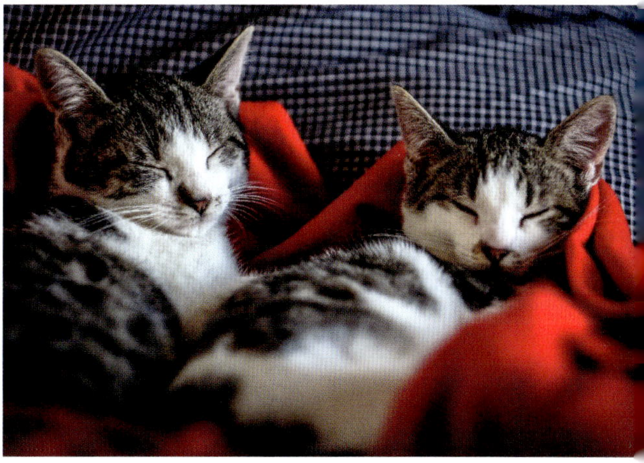
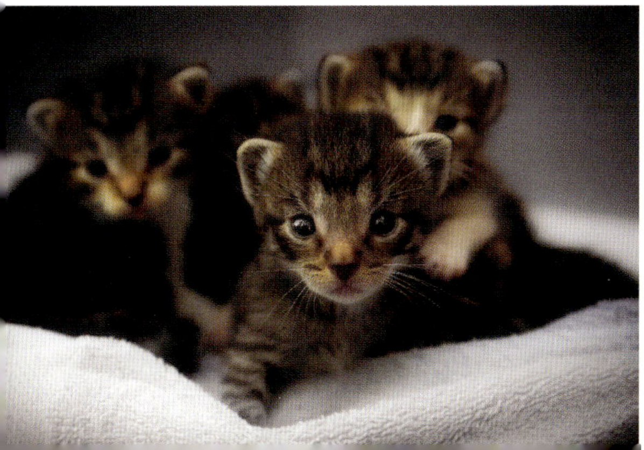
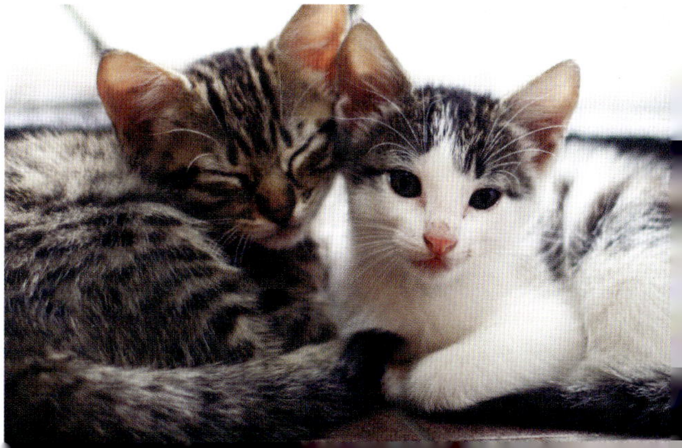

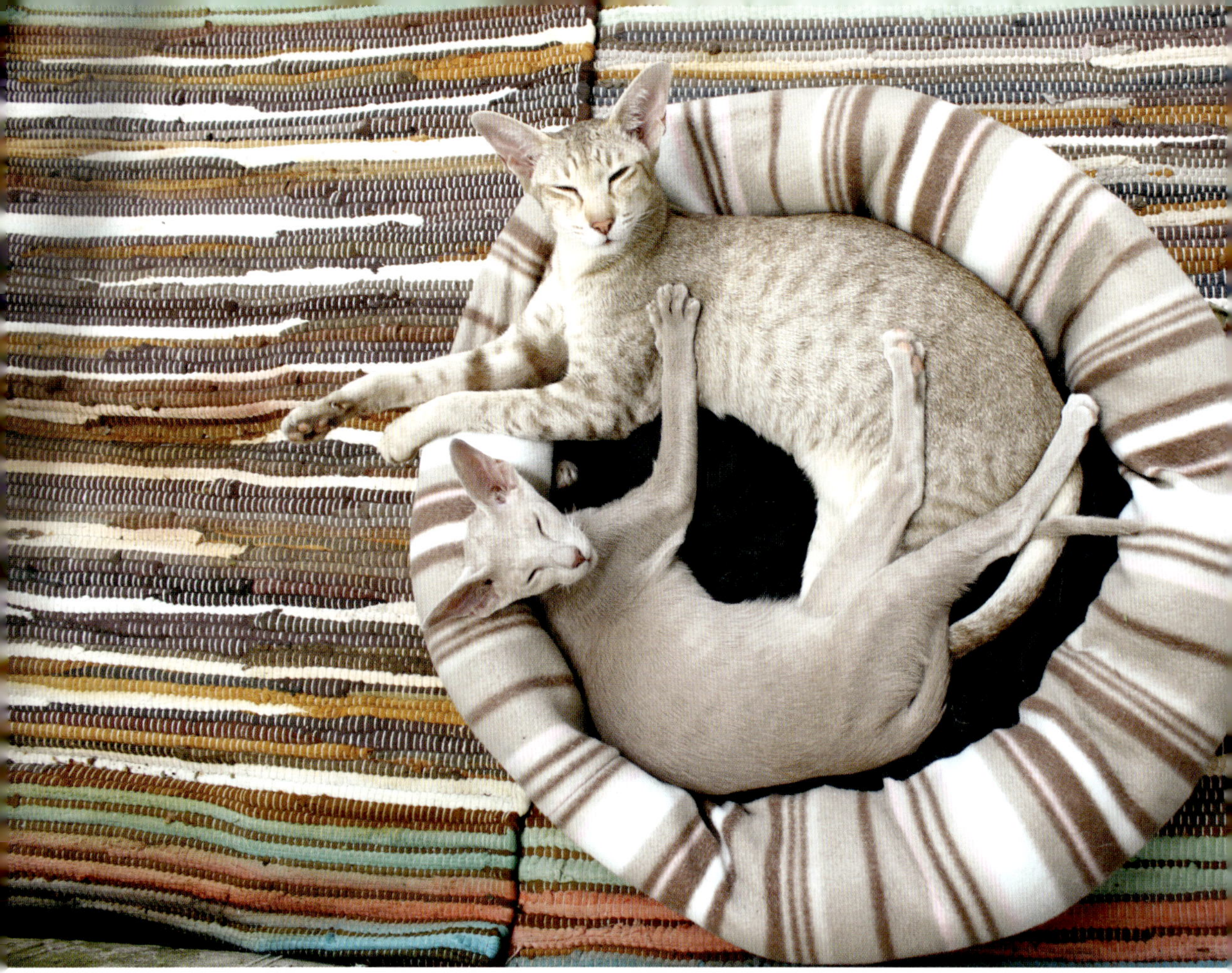

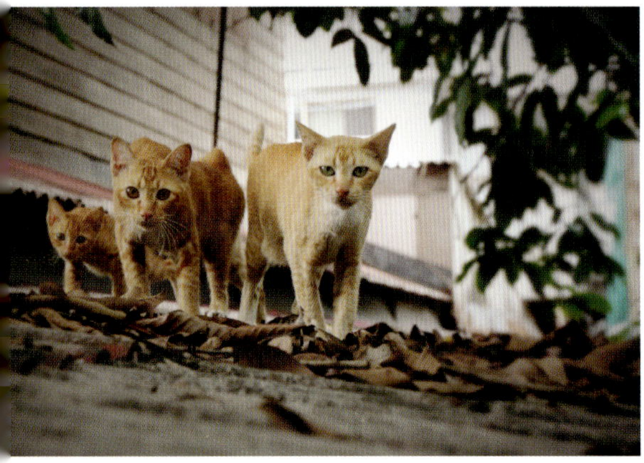

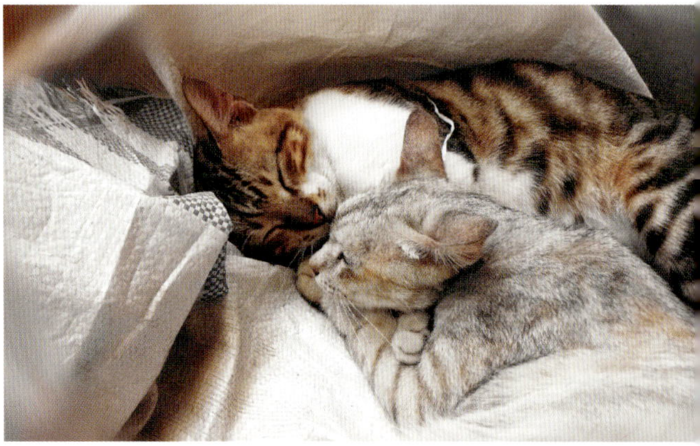

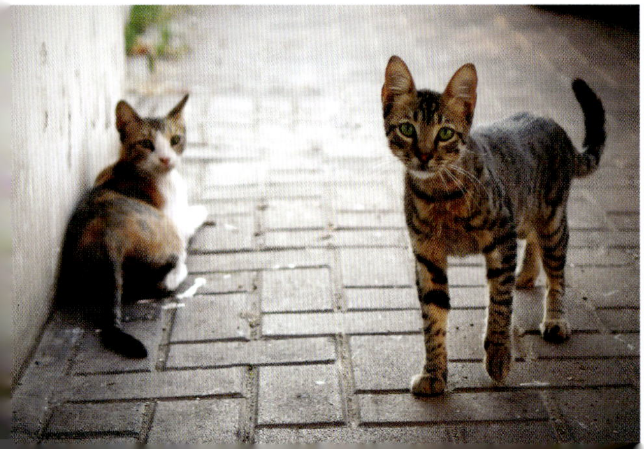

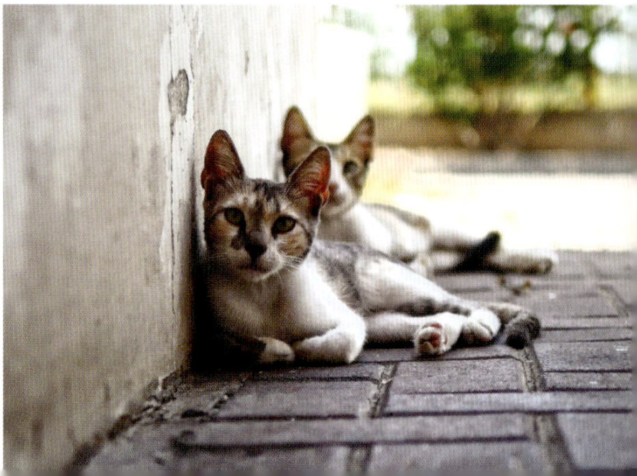

"Cats have it all—admiration, an endless sleep, and company only when they want it."

—Rod McKuen, poet and songwriter

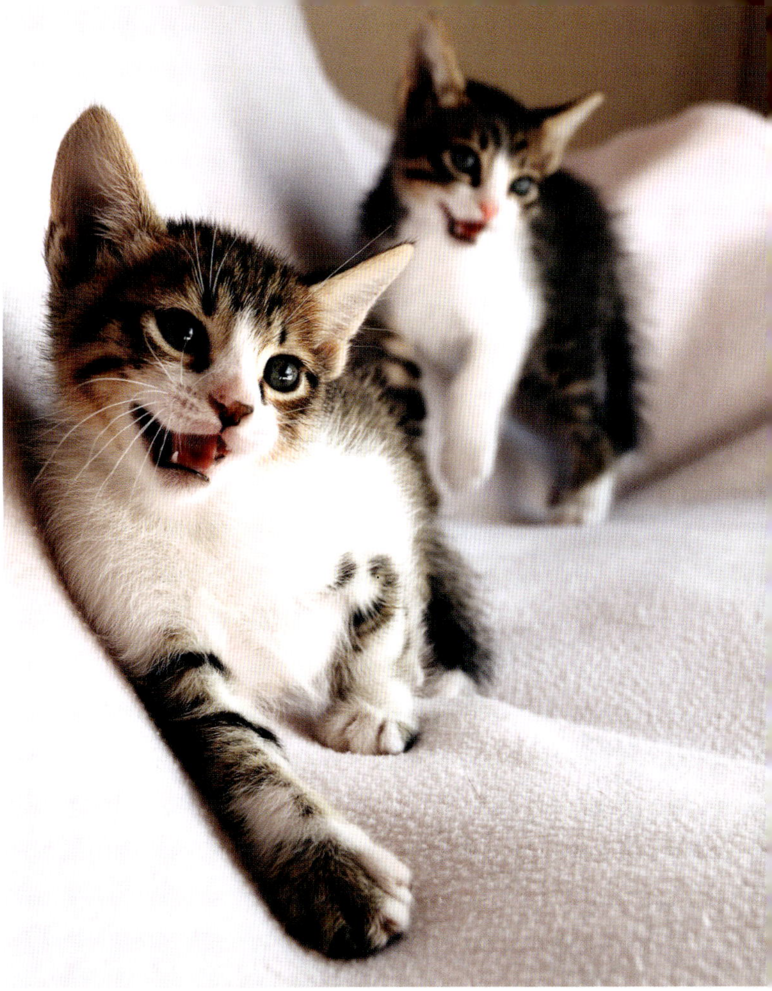

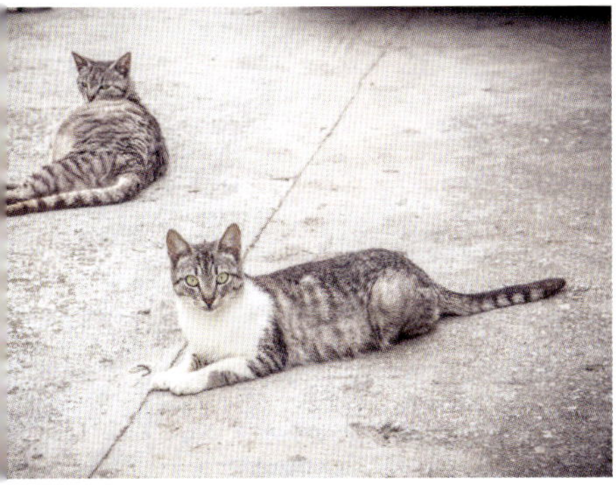

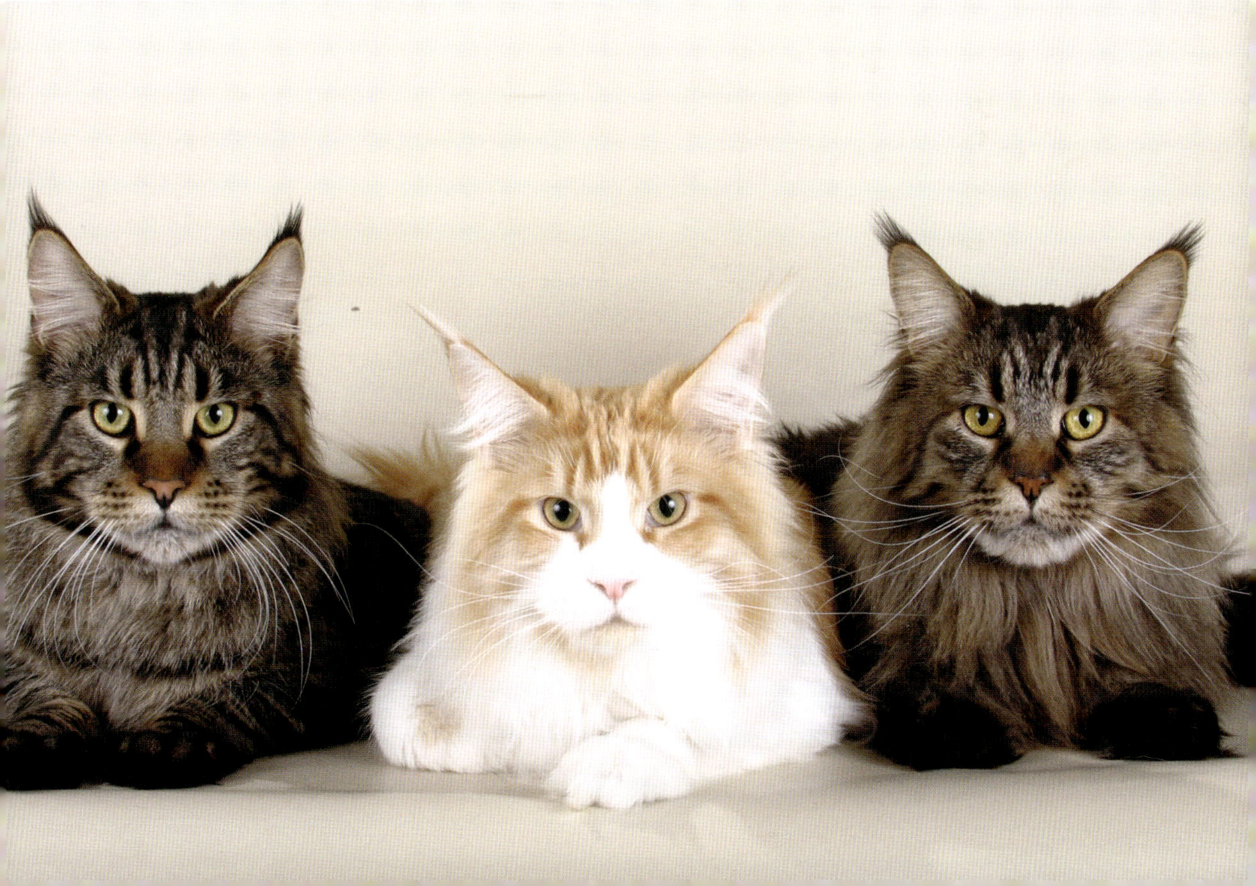

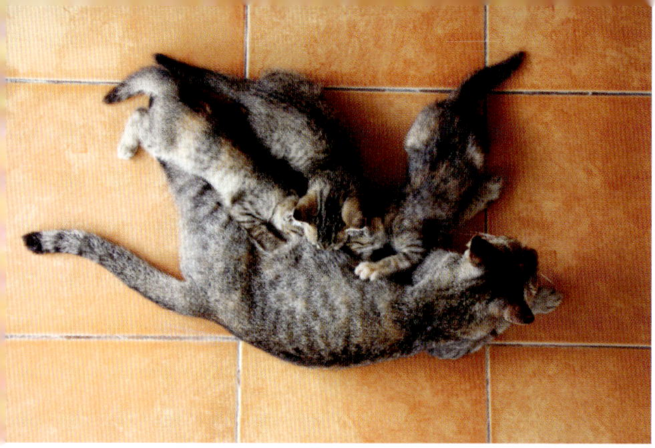
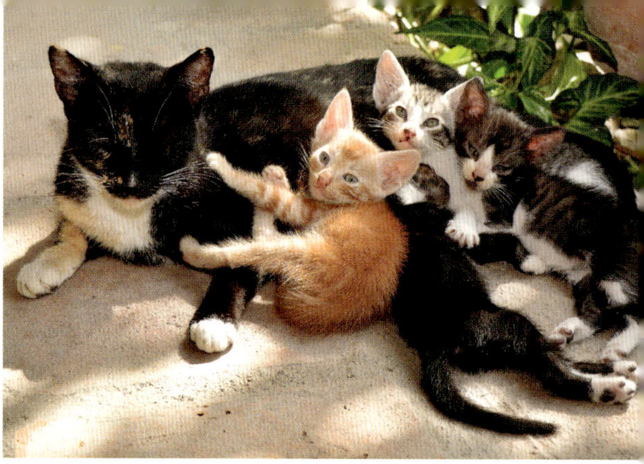
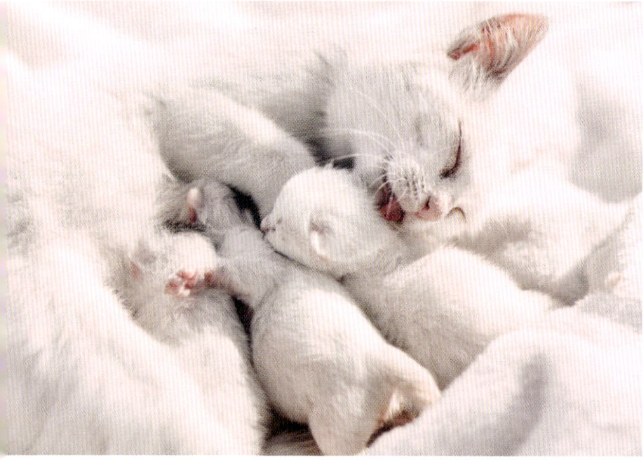
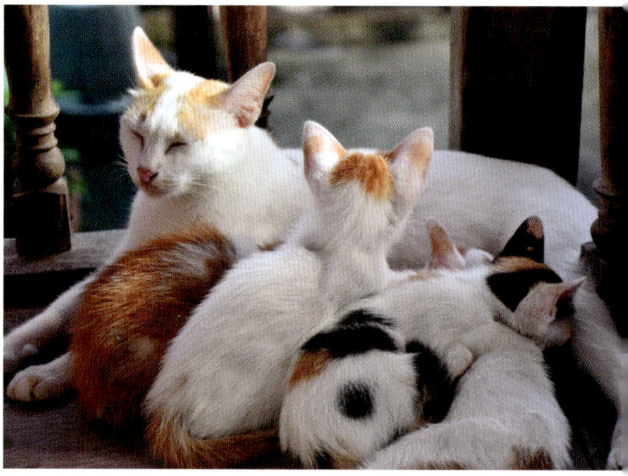
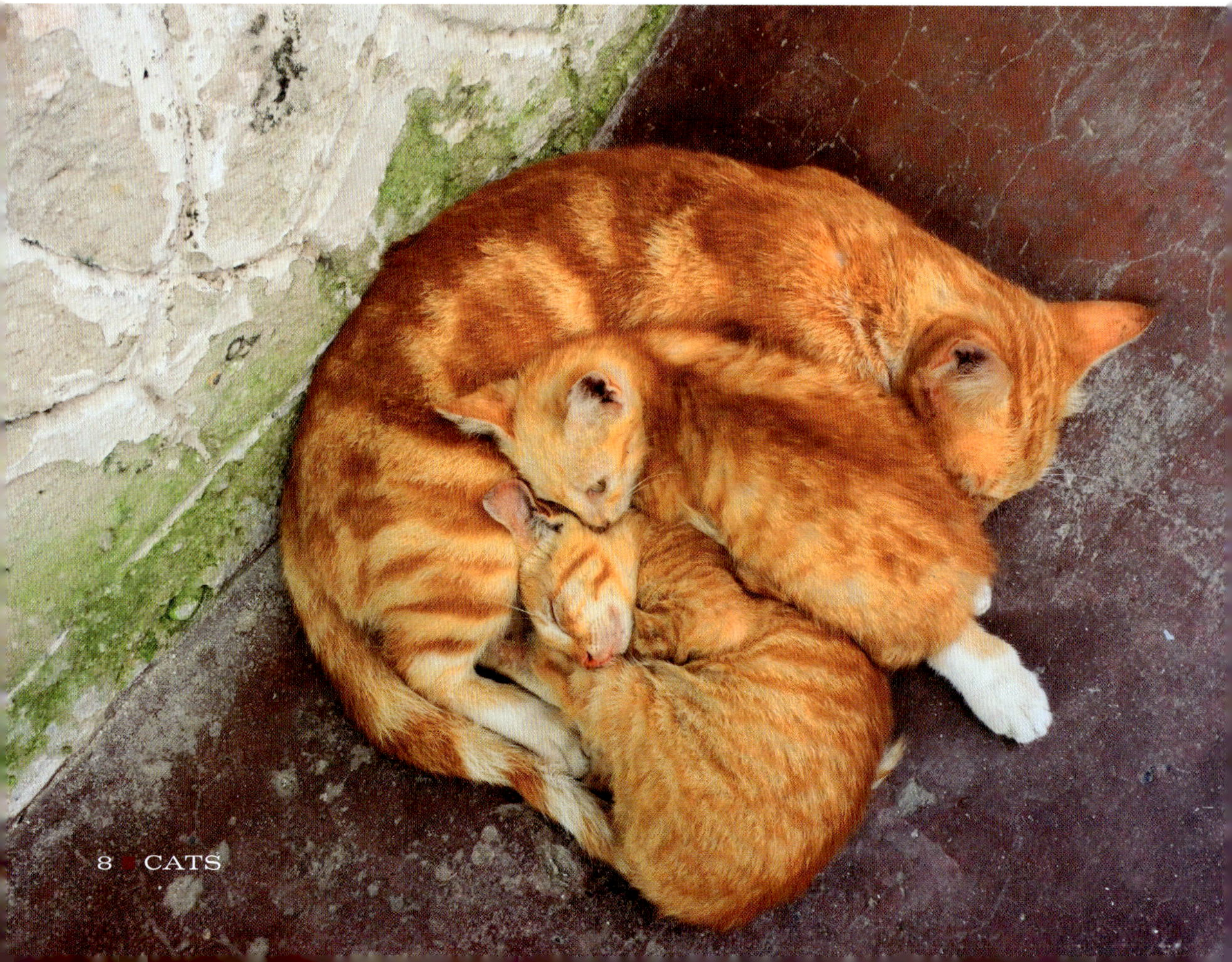

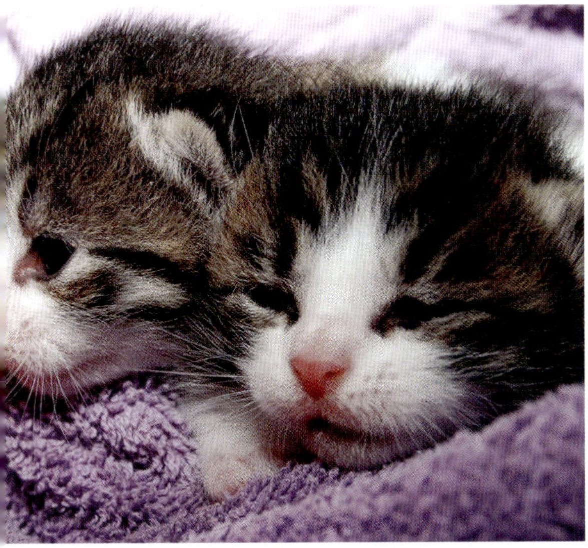
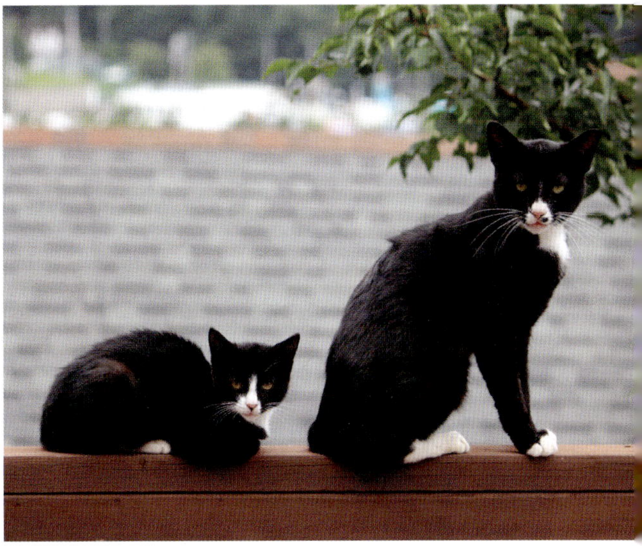
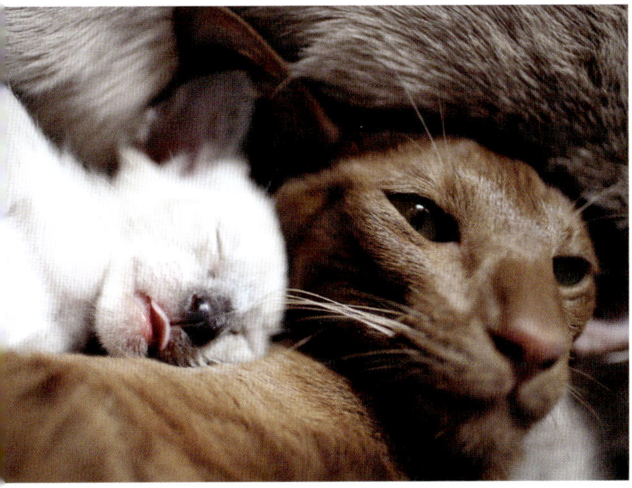
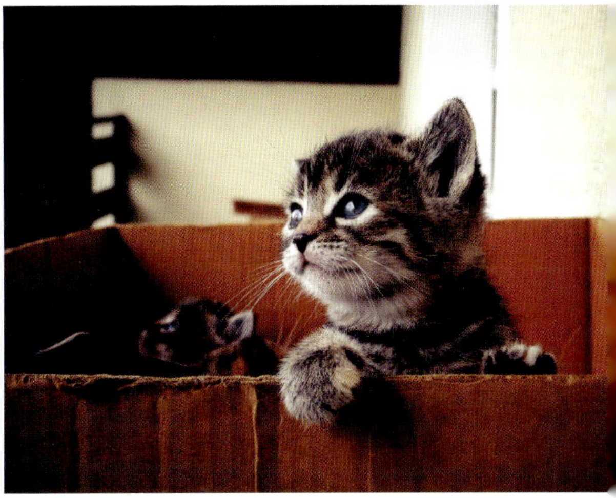
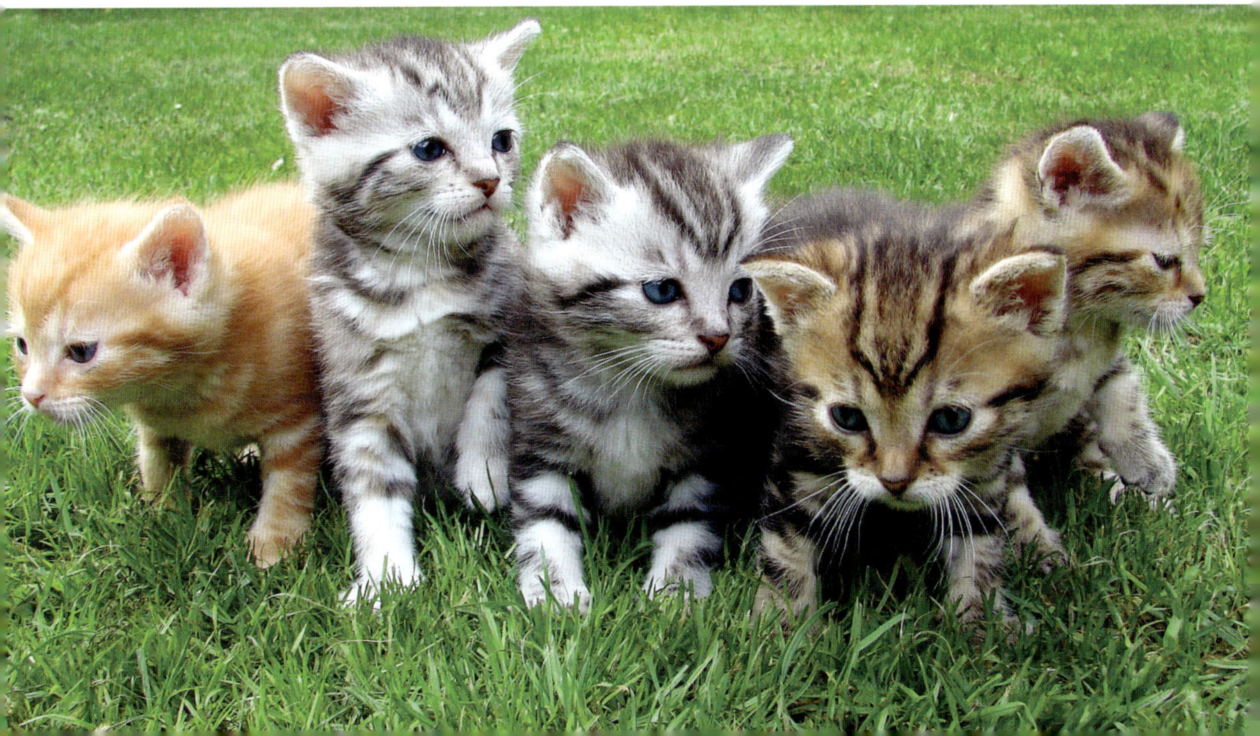

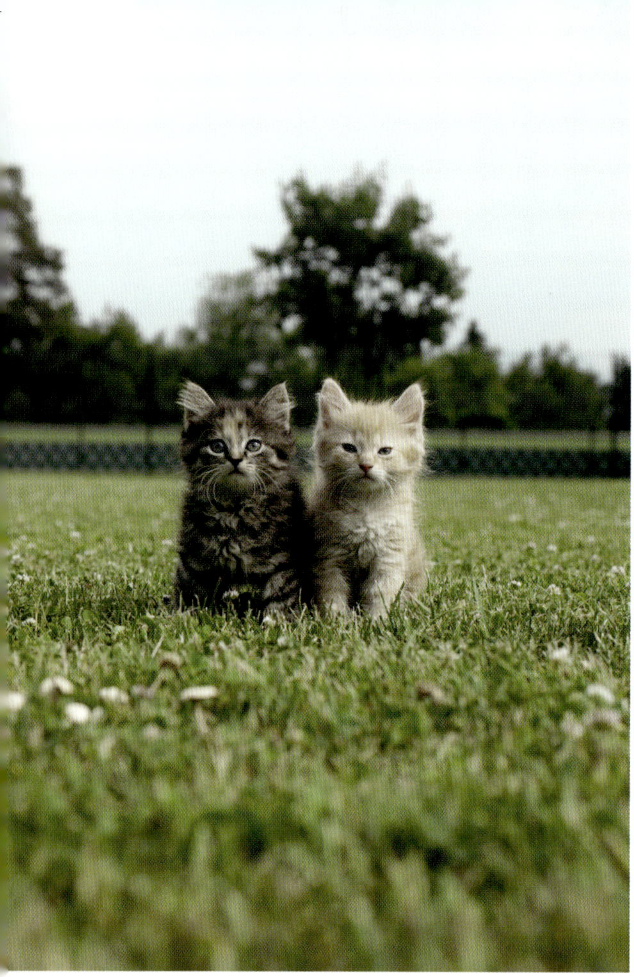
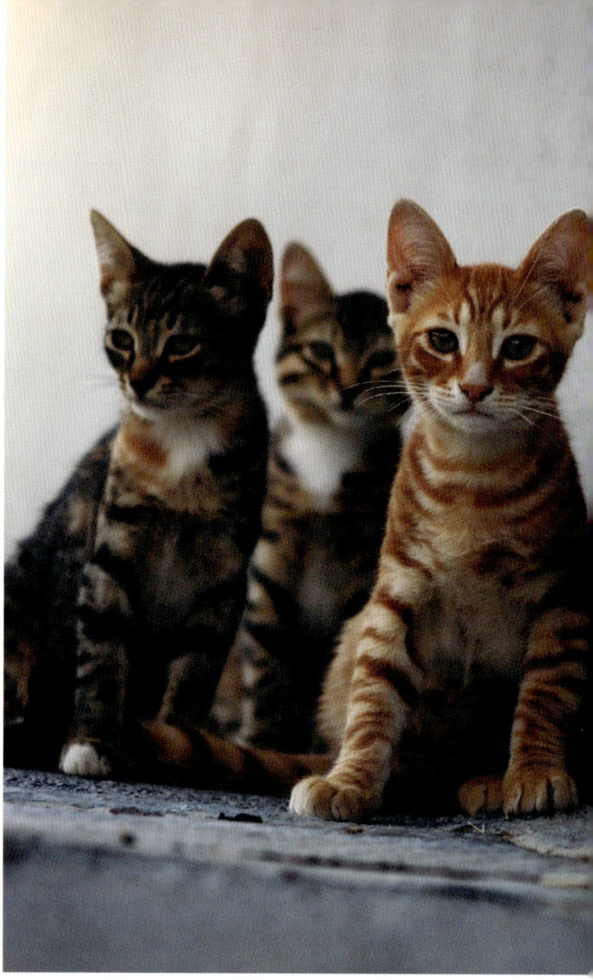
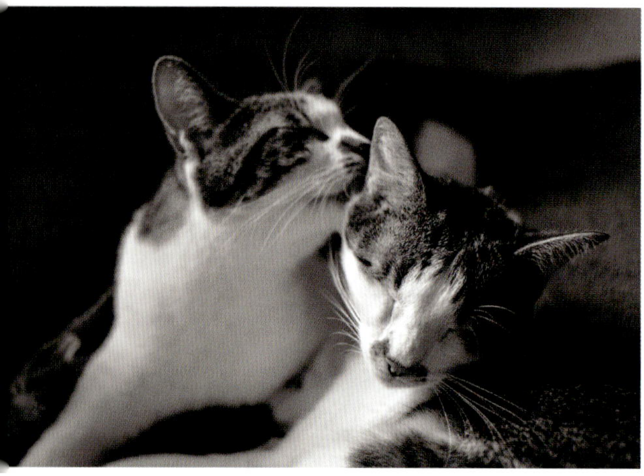
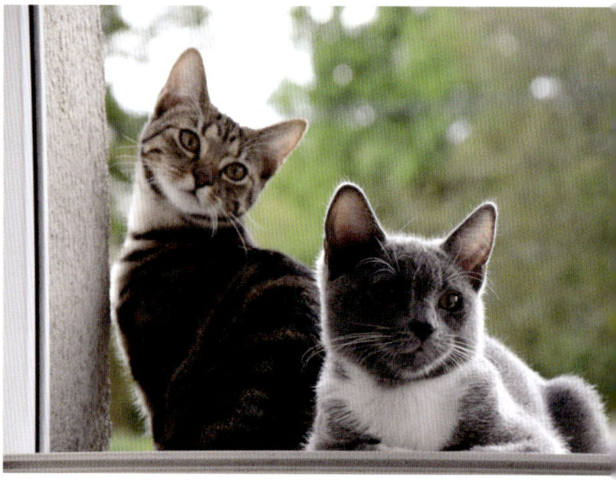
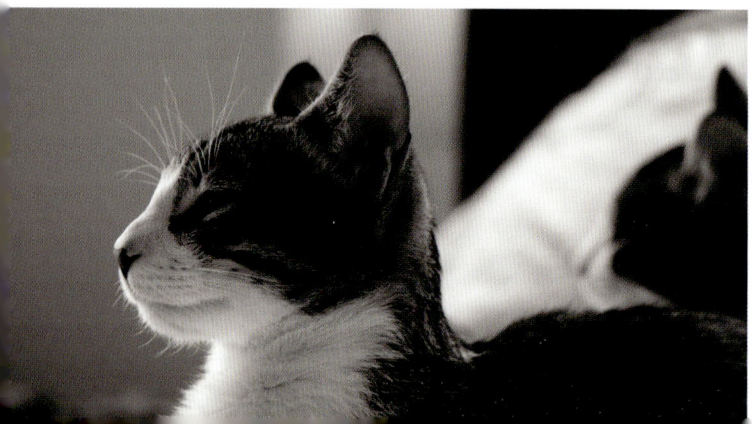
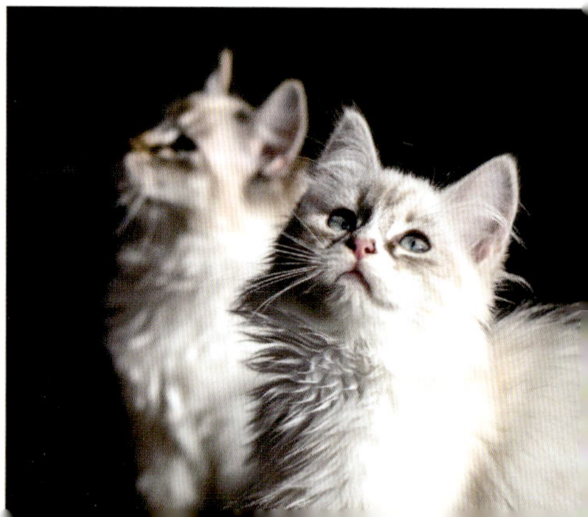

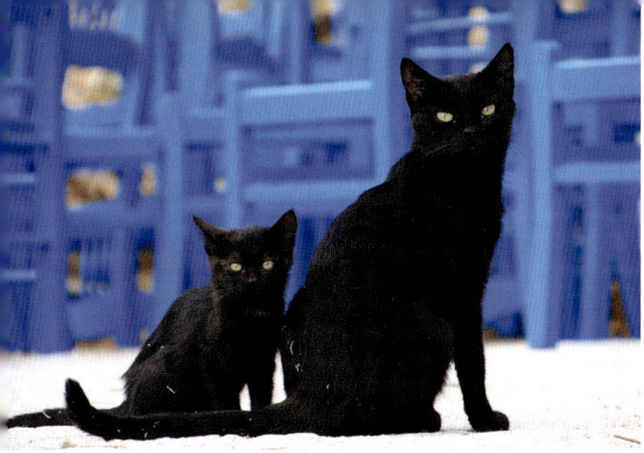

"No matter how much cats fight, there always seem to be plenty of kittens."

—Abraham Lincoln, president

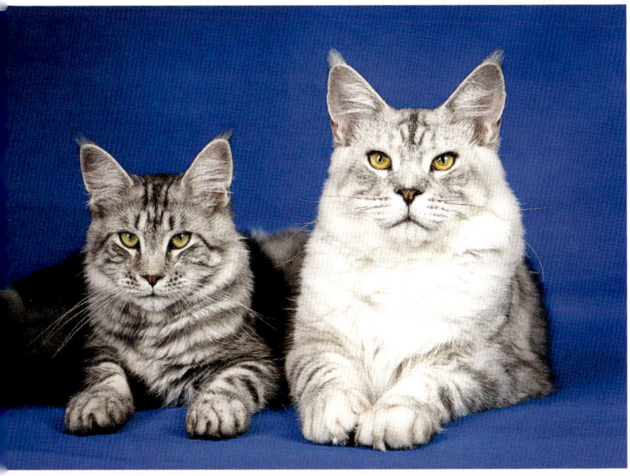

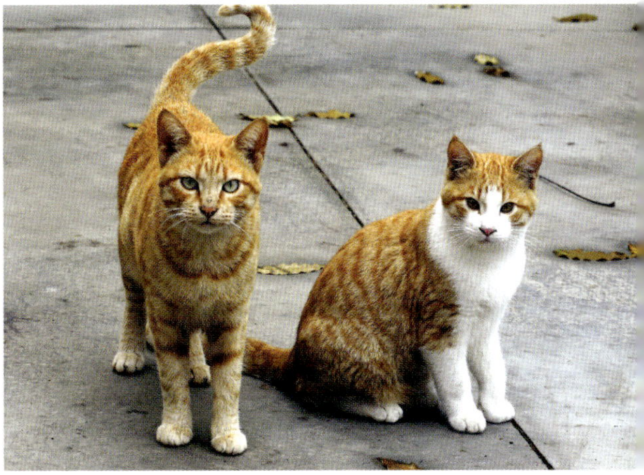

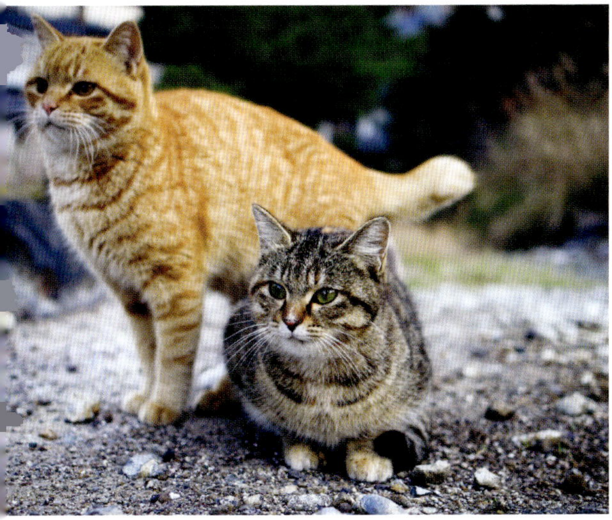

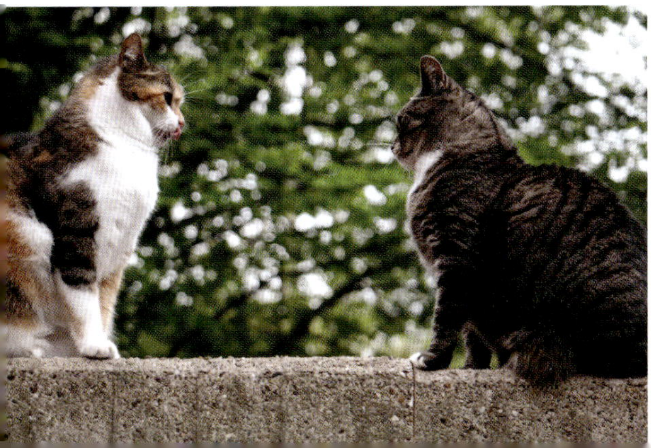

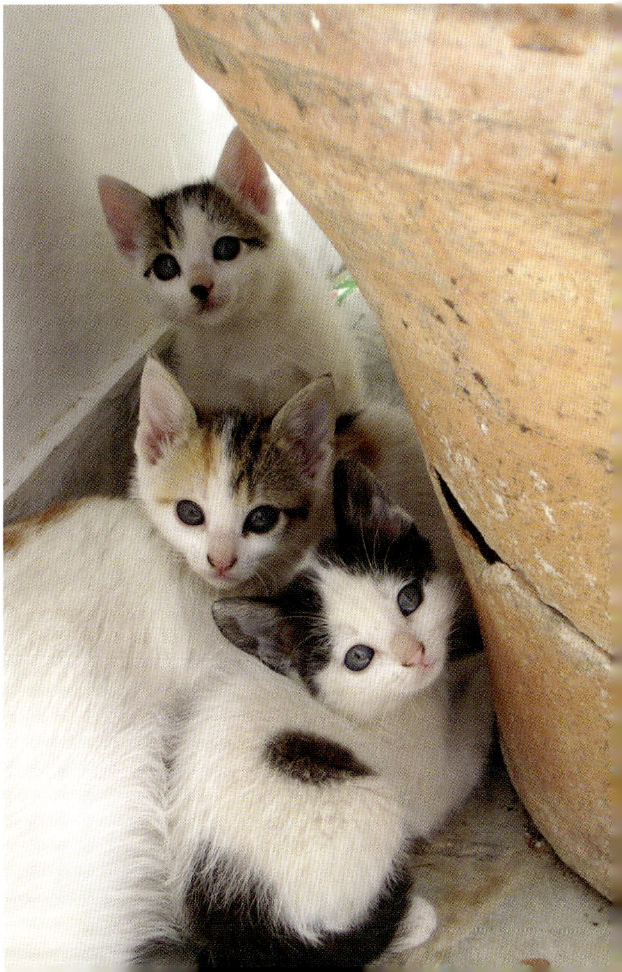

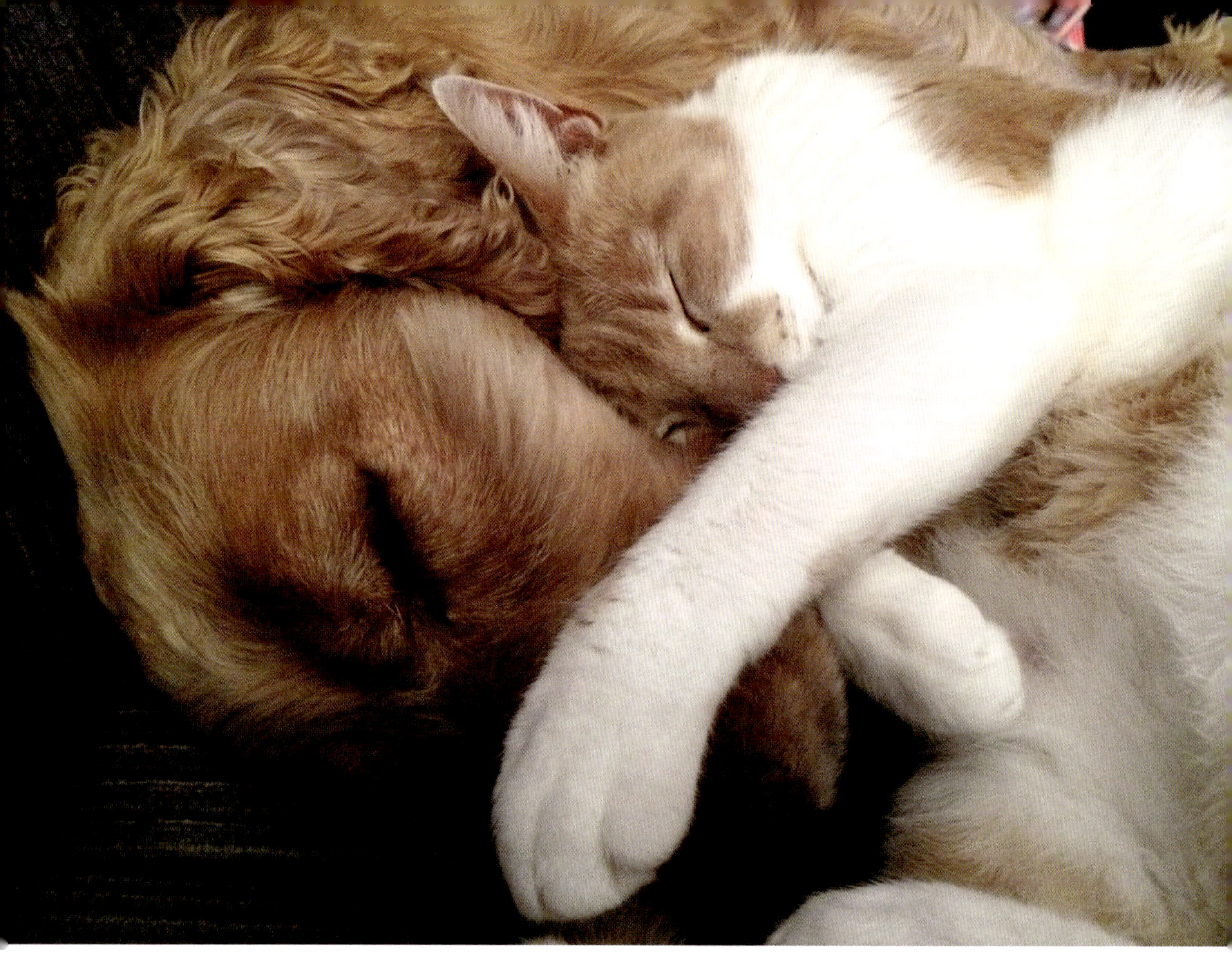

"I had been told that the training procedure with cats was difficult. It's not. Mine had me trained in two days."

–Bill Dana, comedian

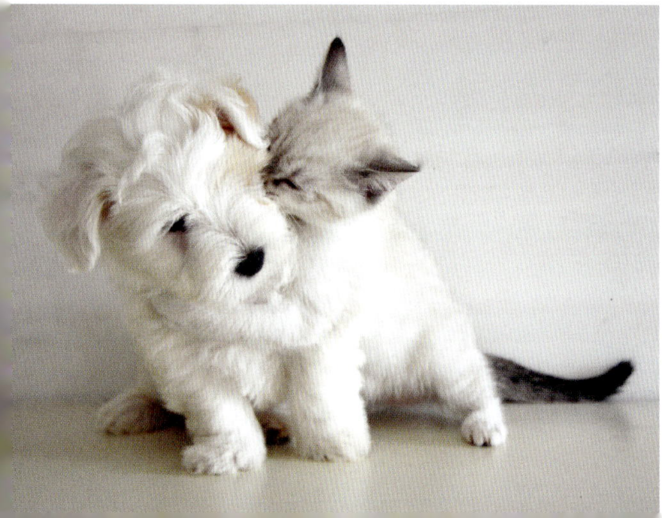

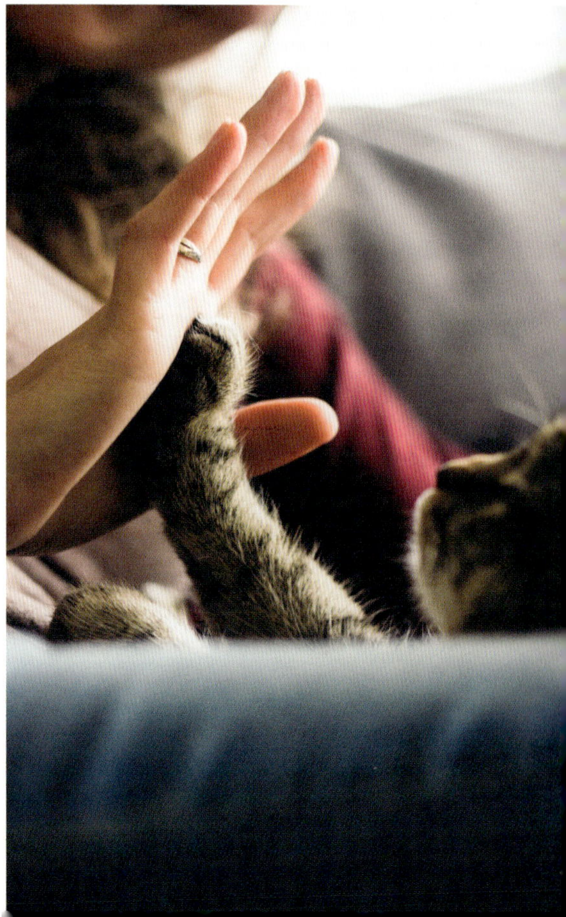

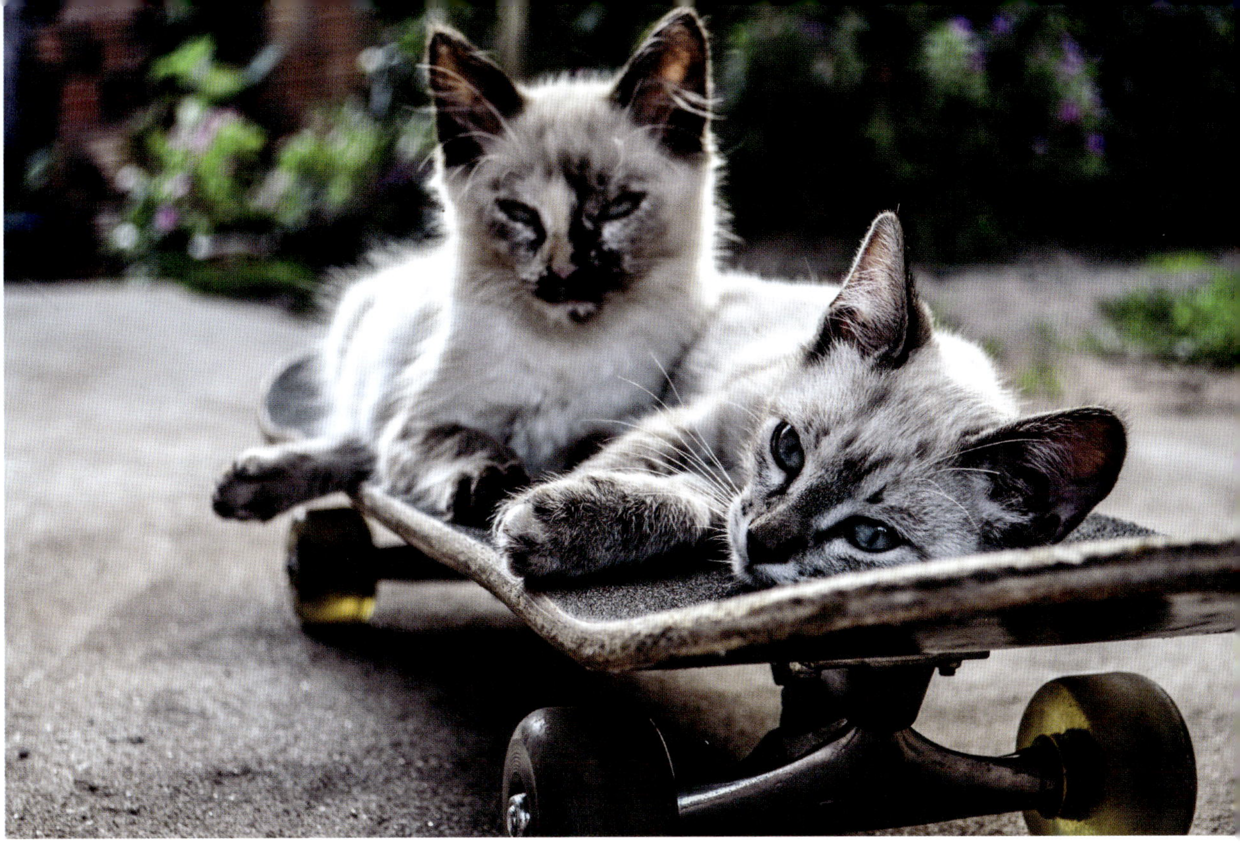

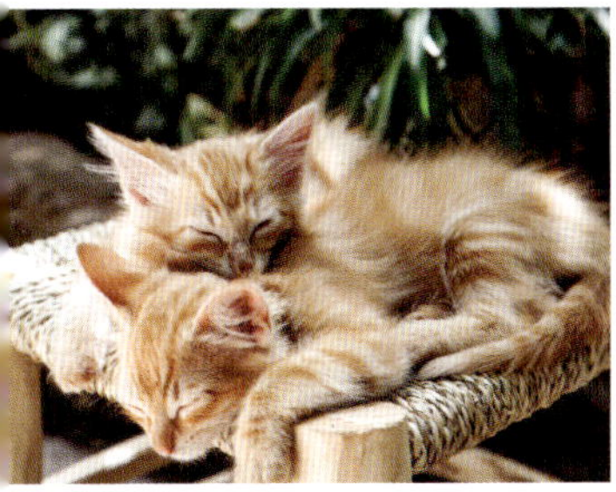

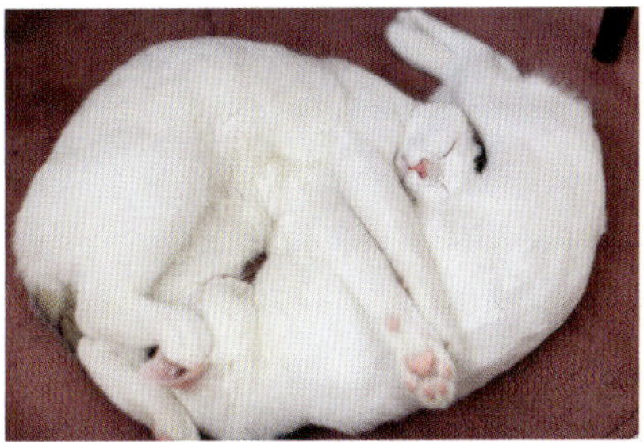

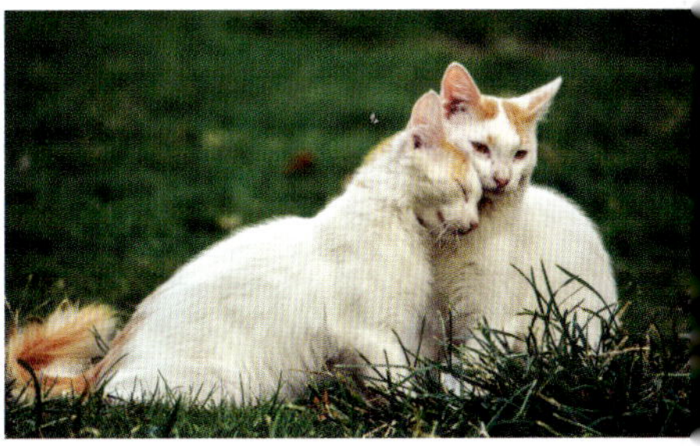

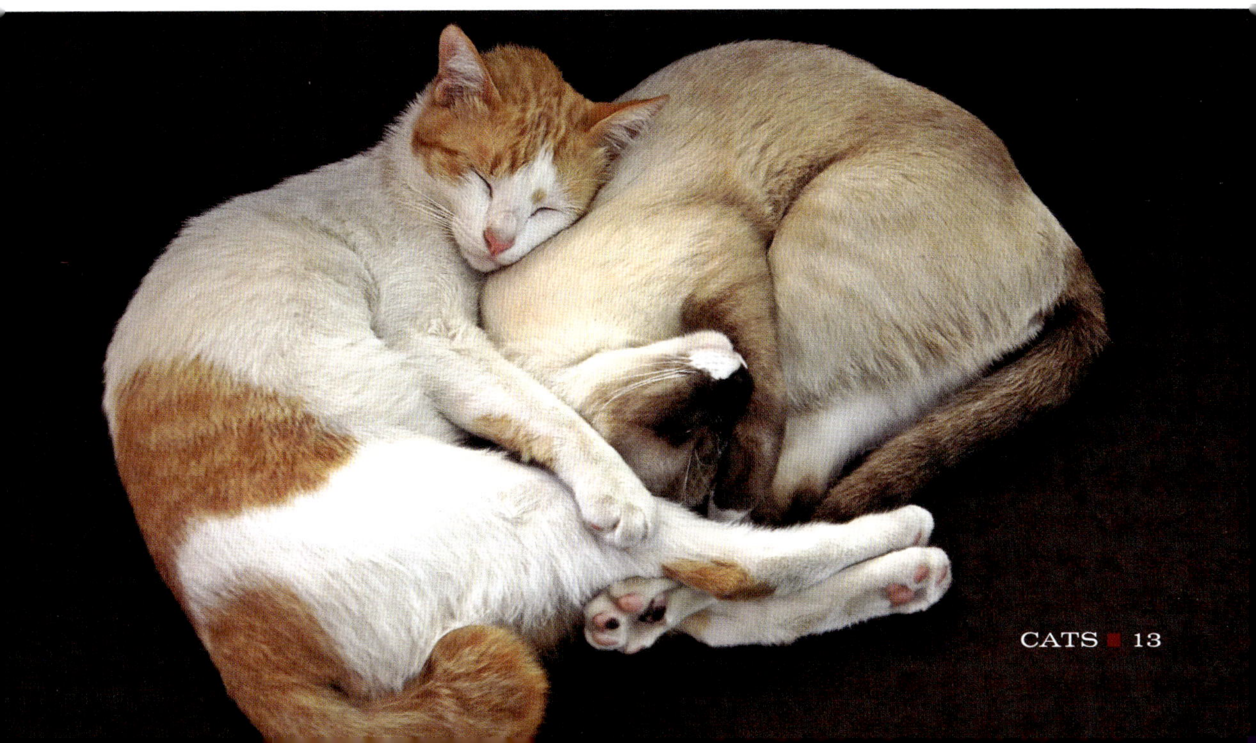

2. Natural Climbers

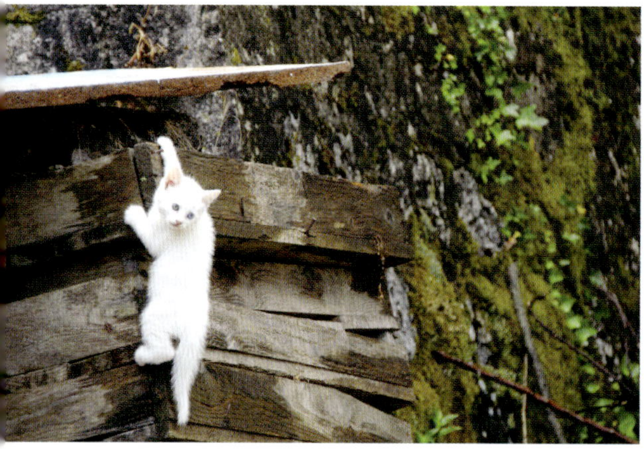

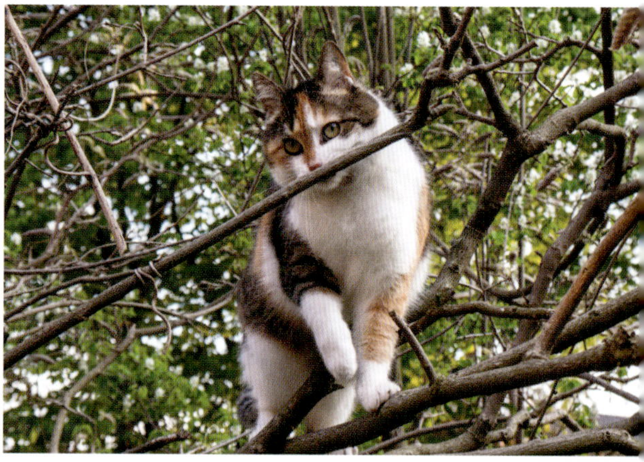

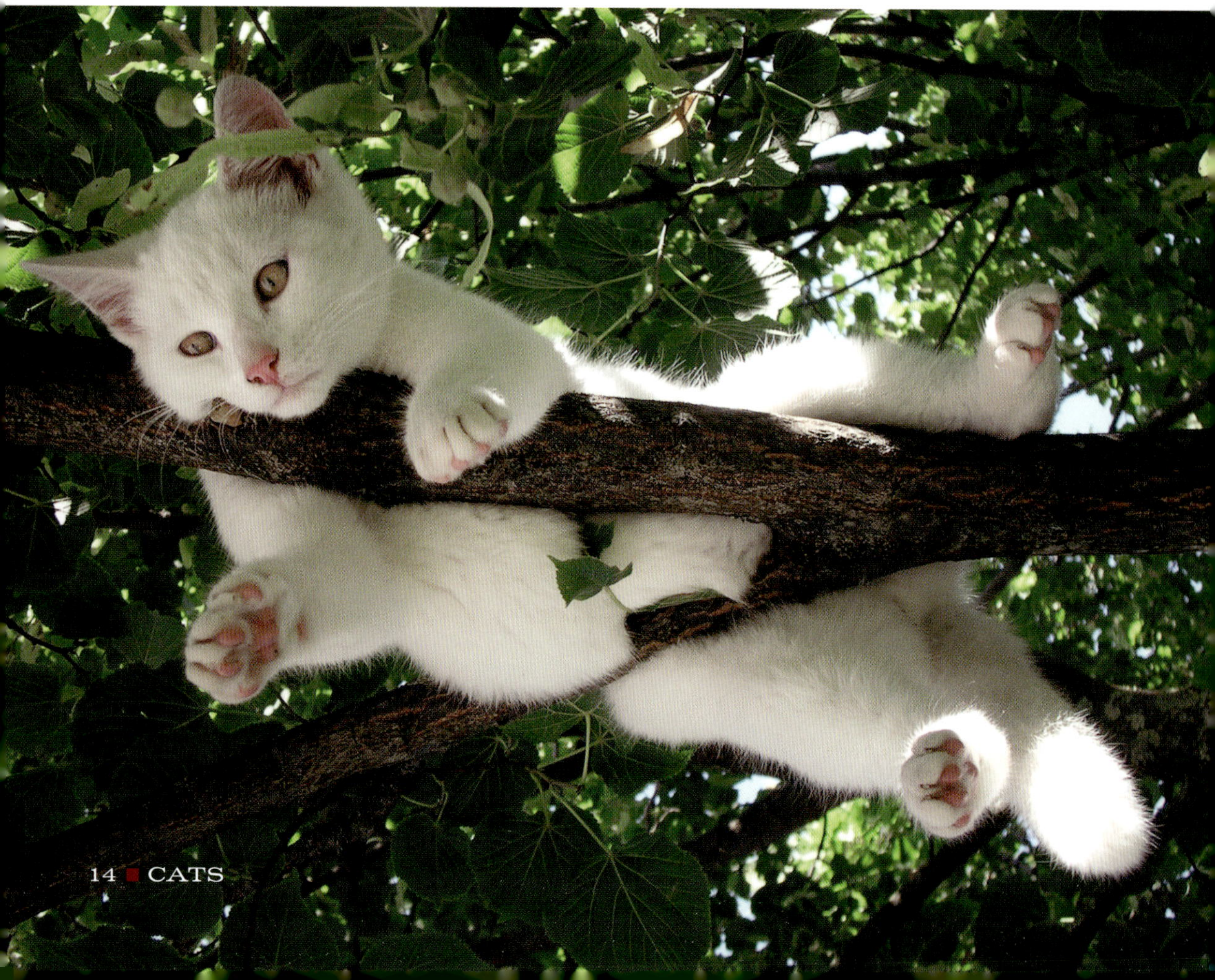

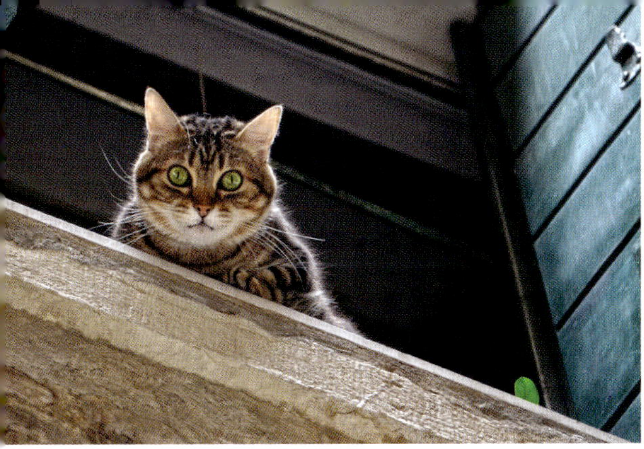
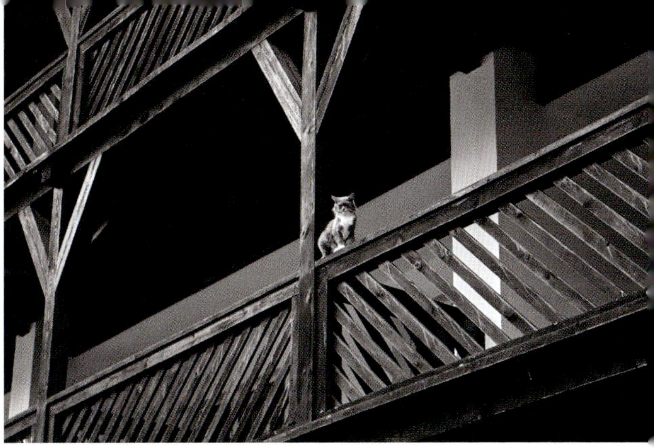
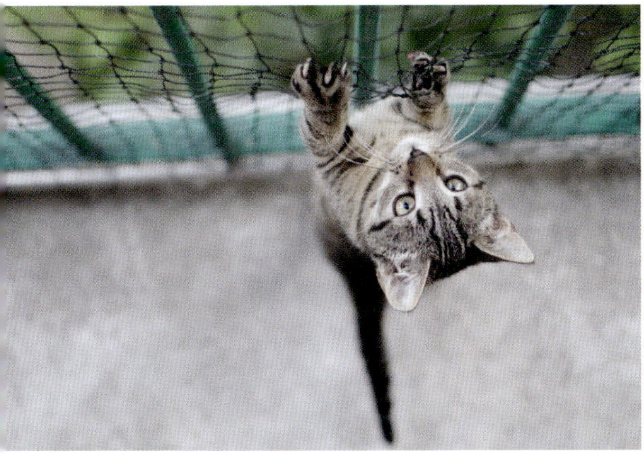
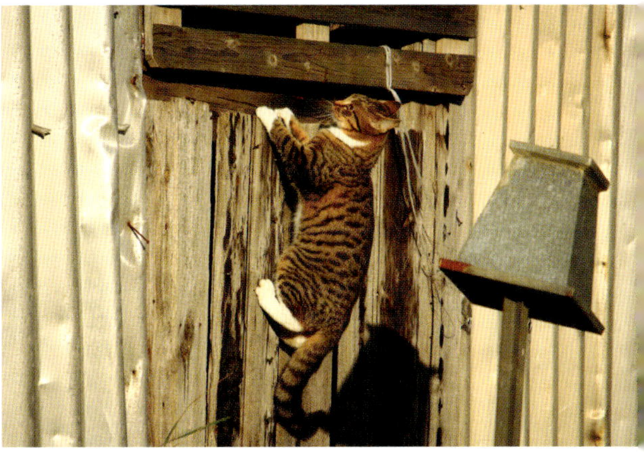
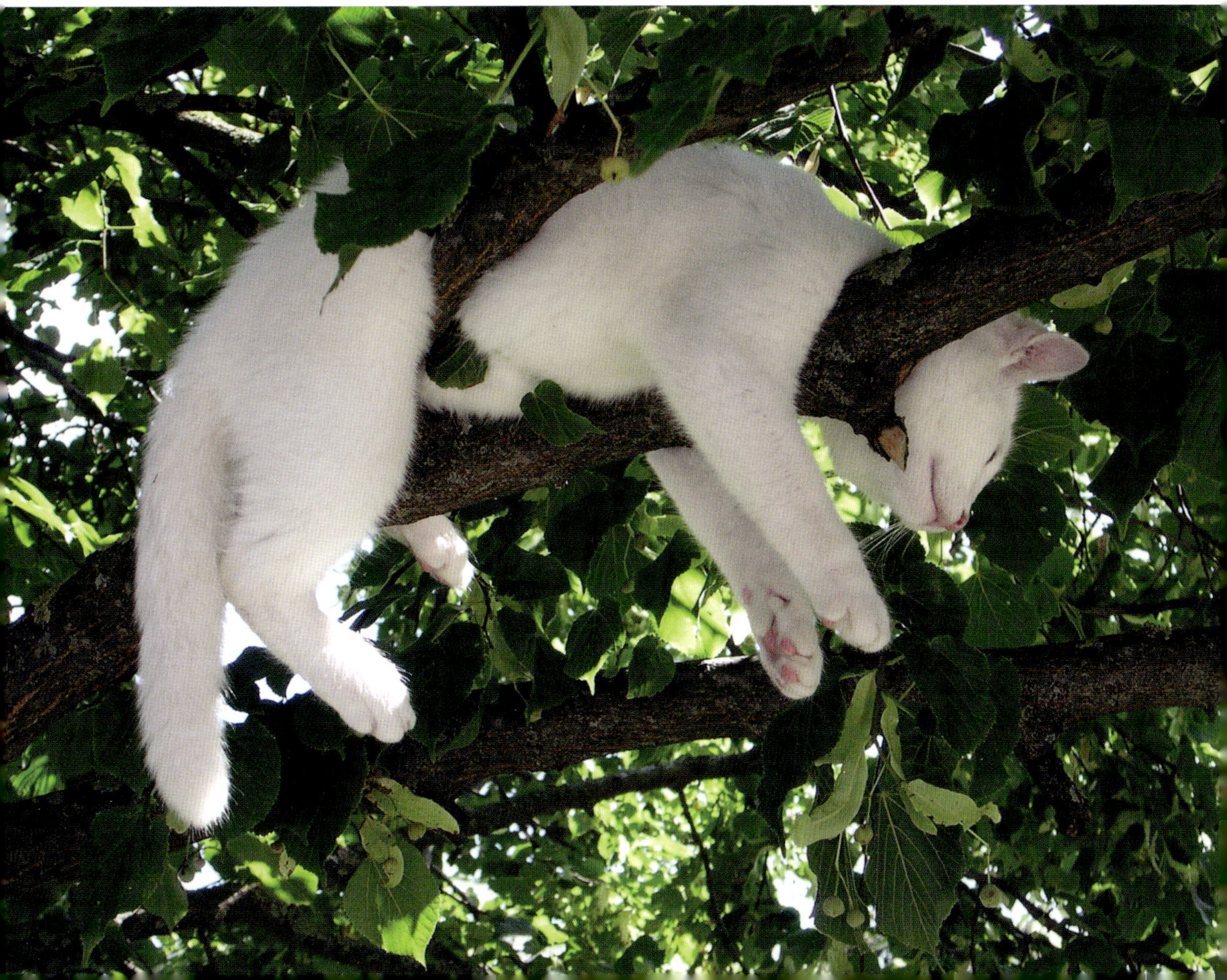

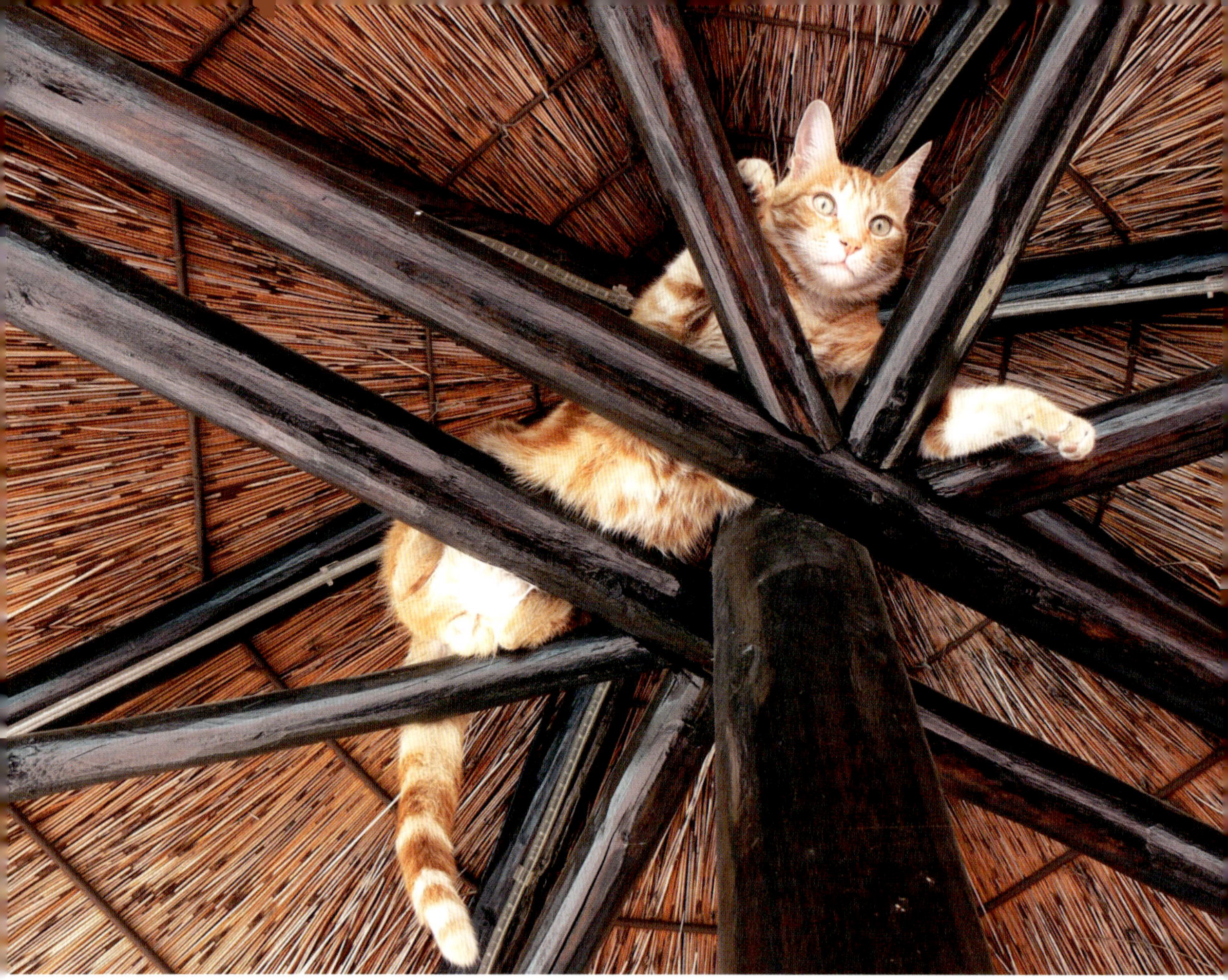

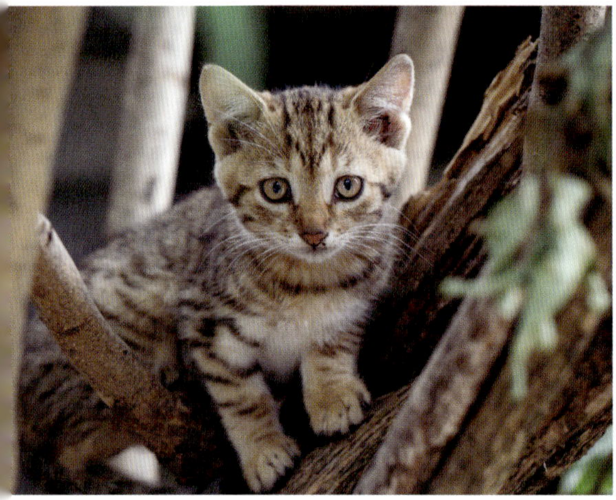

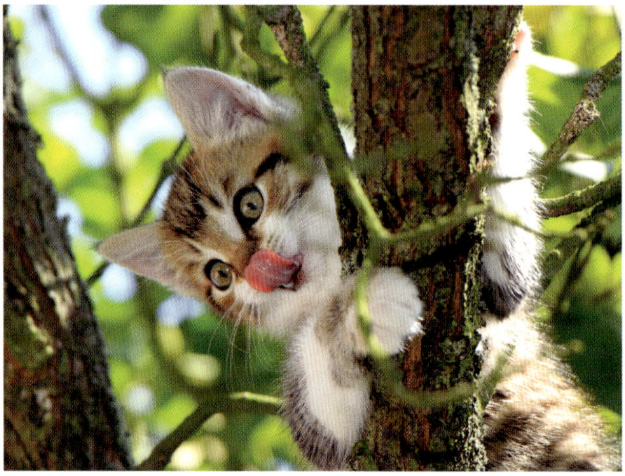

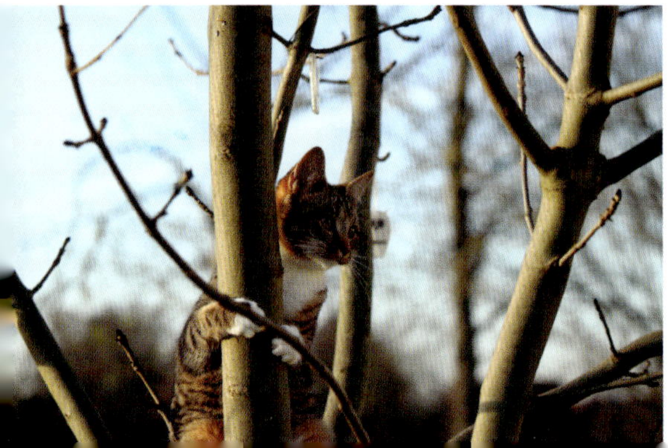

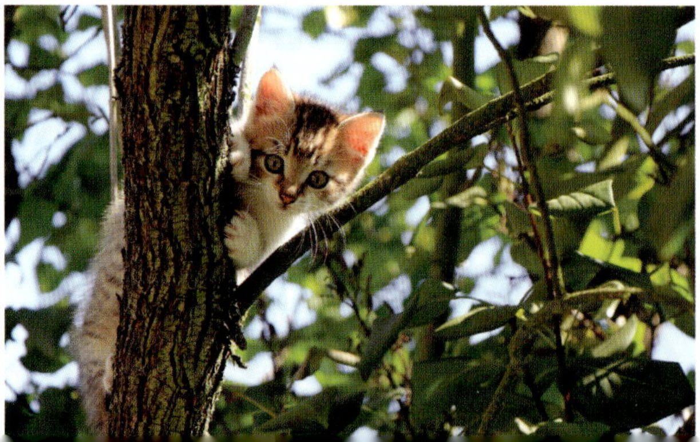

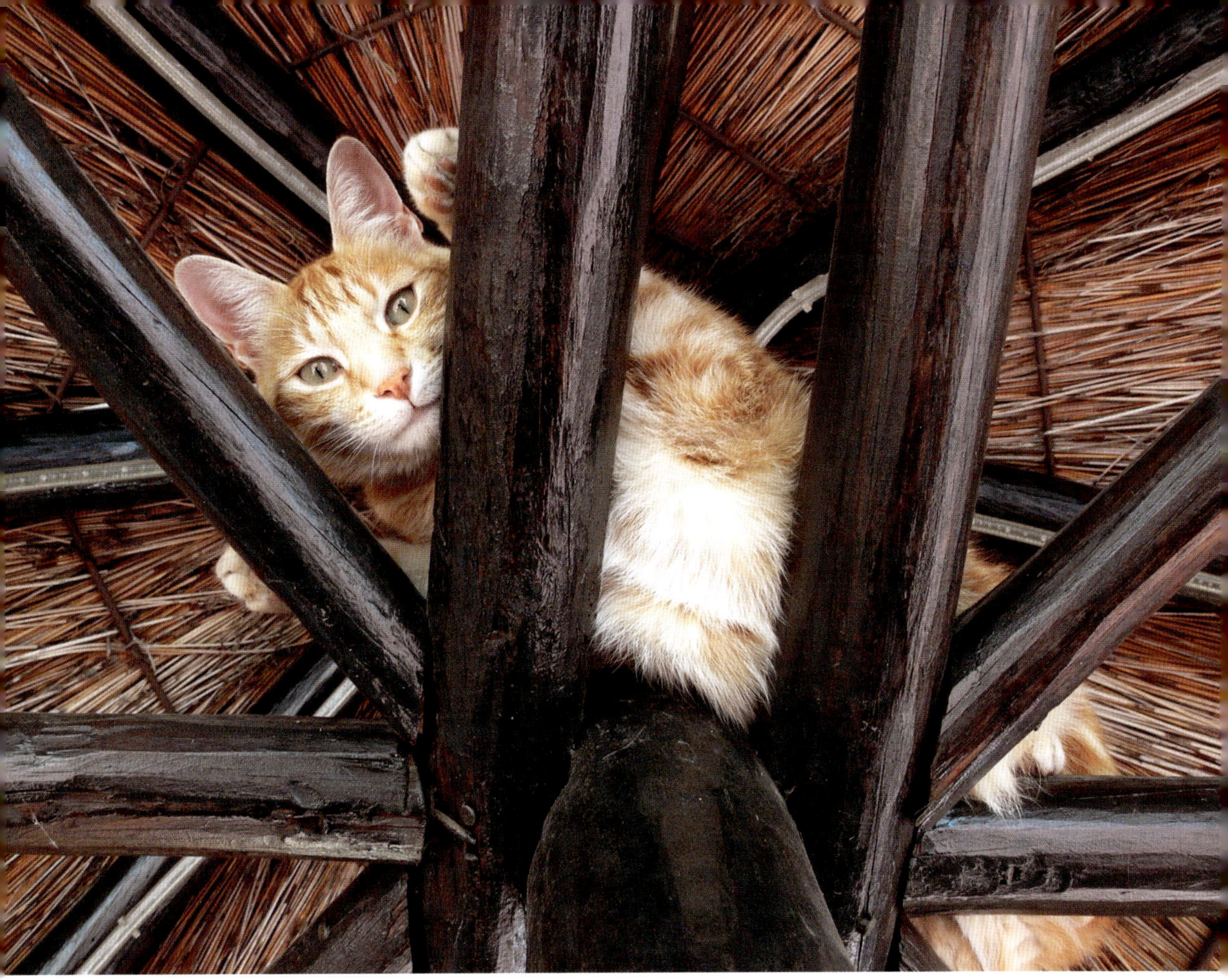

"I believe cats to be spirits come to earth. A cat, I am sure, could walk on a cloud without coming through."

—Jules Verne, author

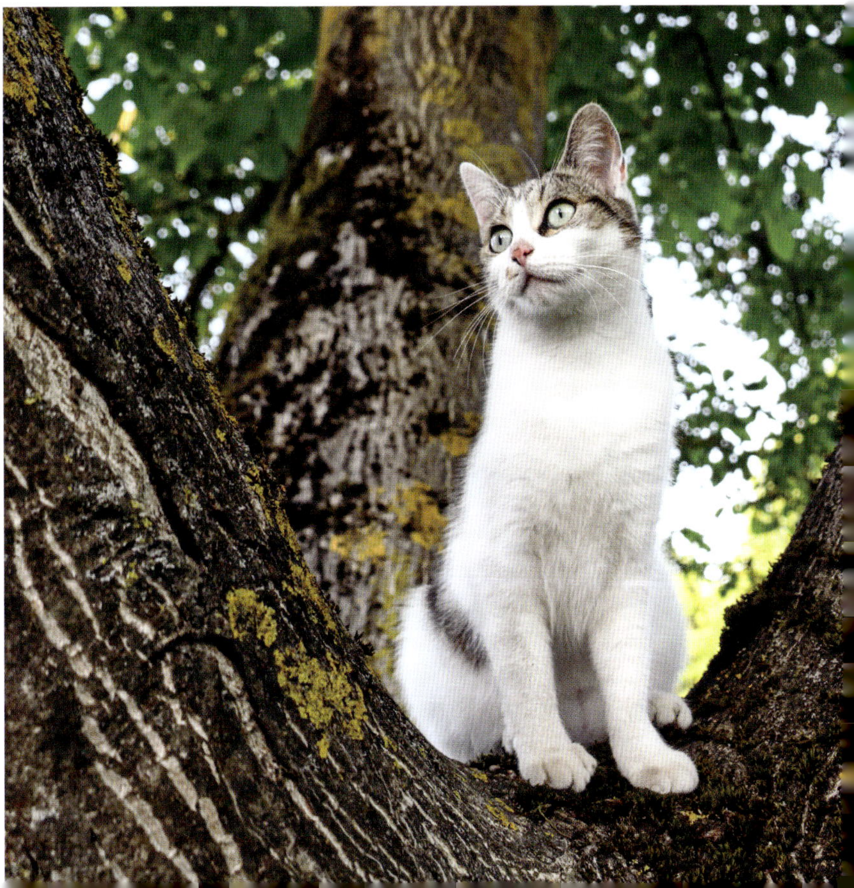

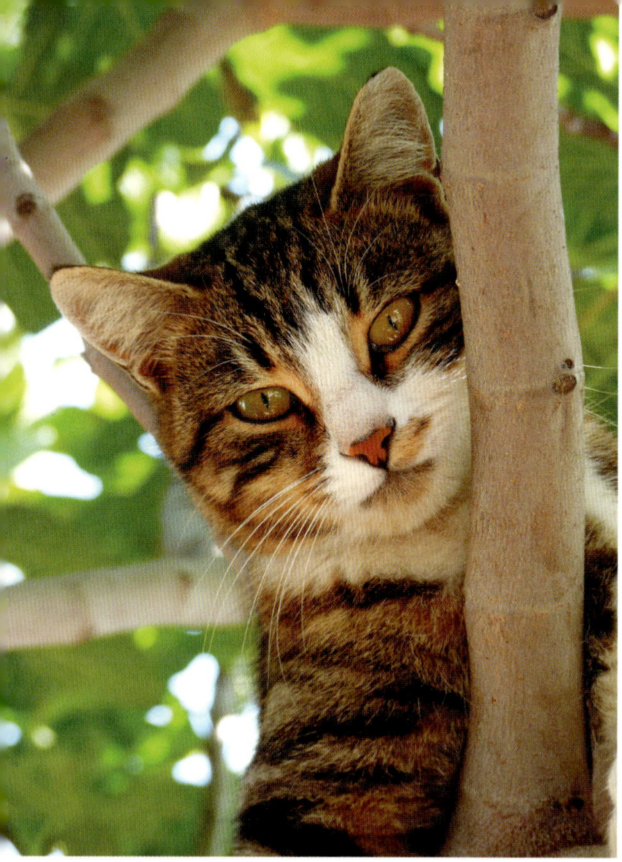

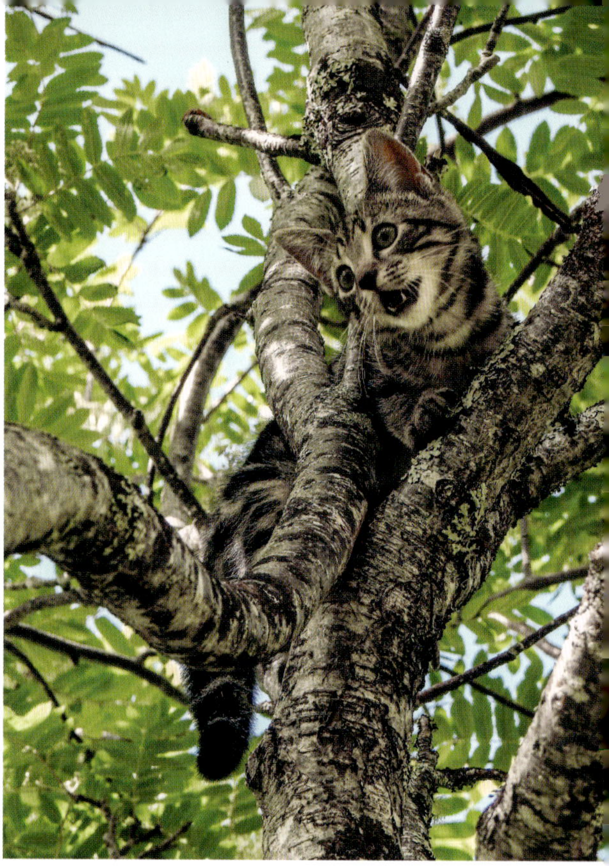

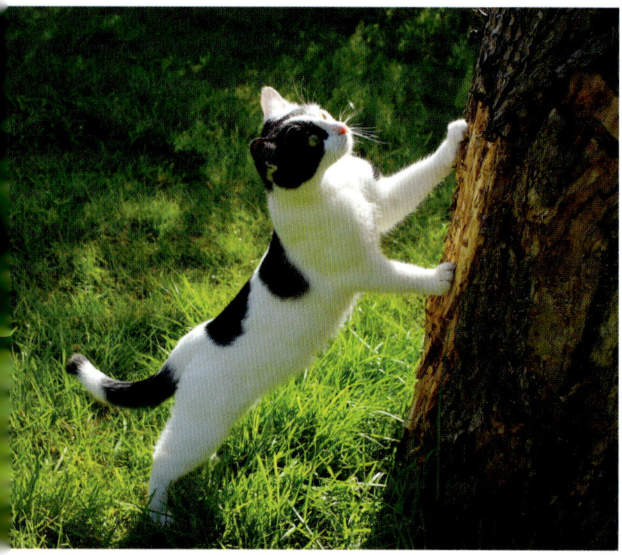

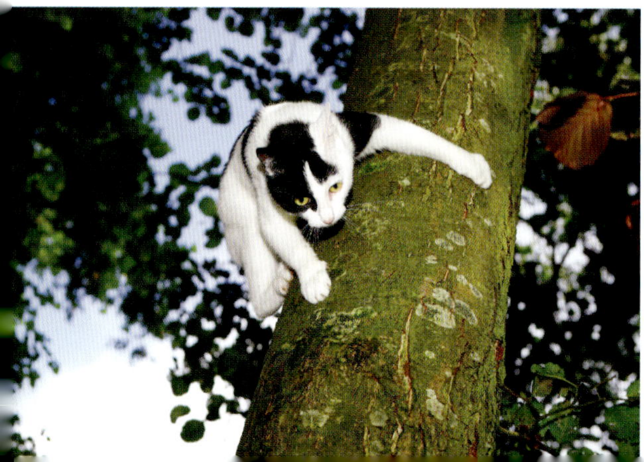

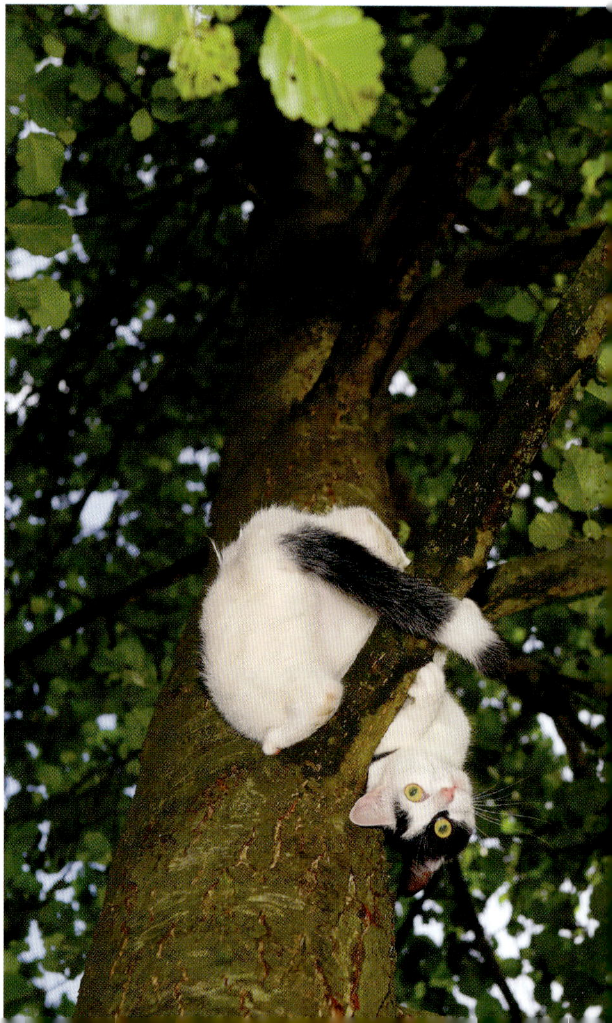

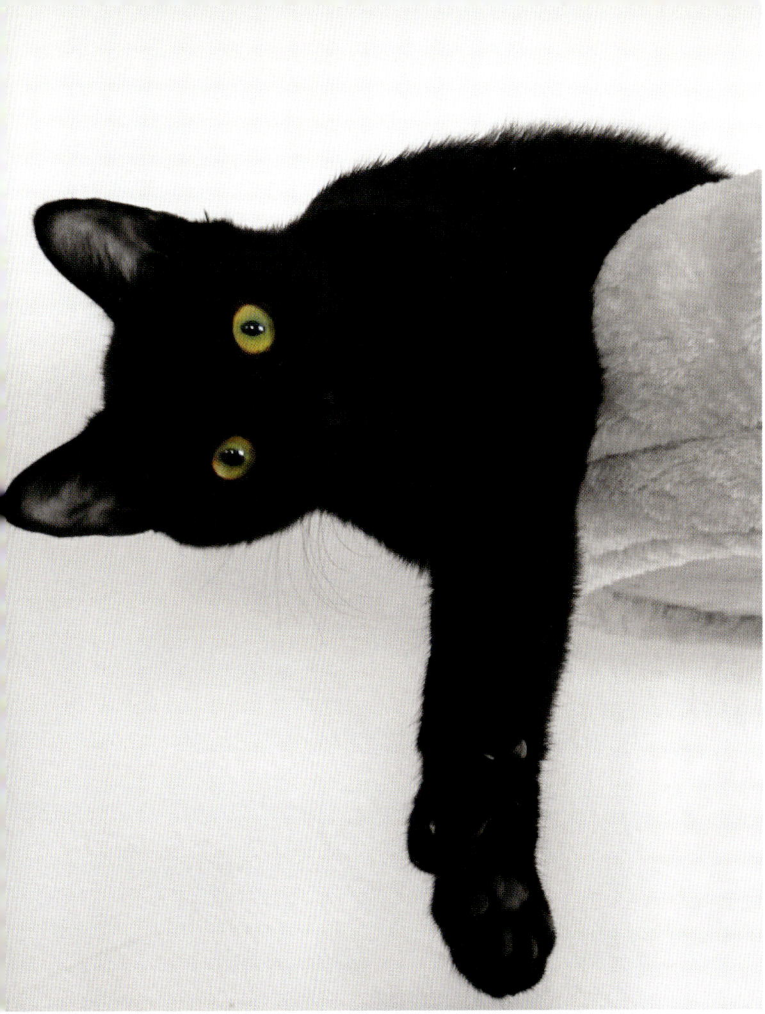
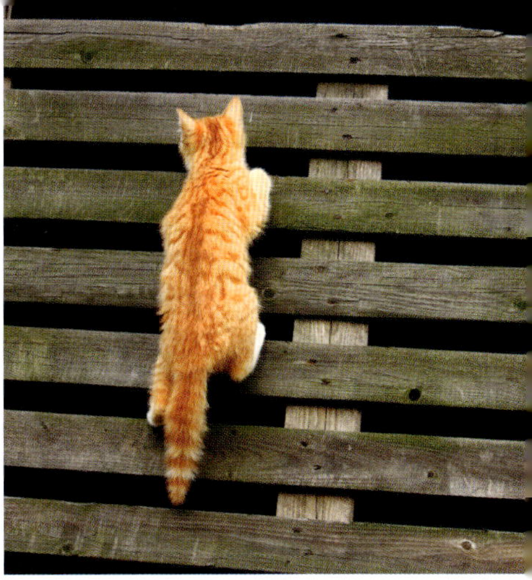
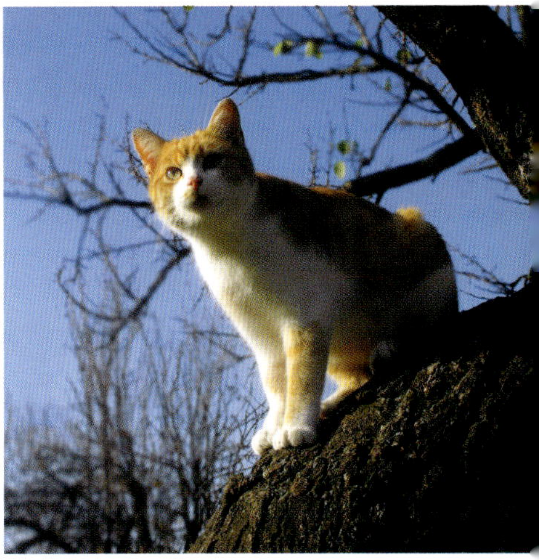
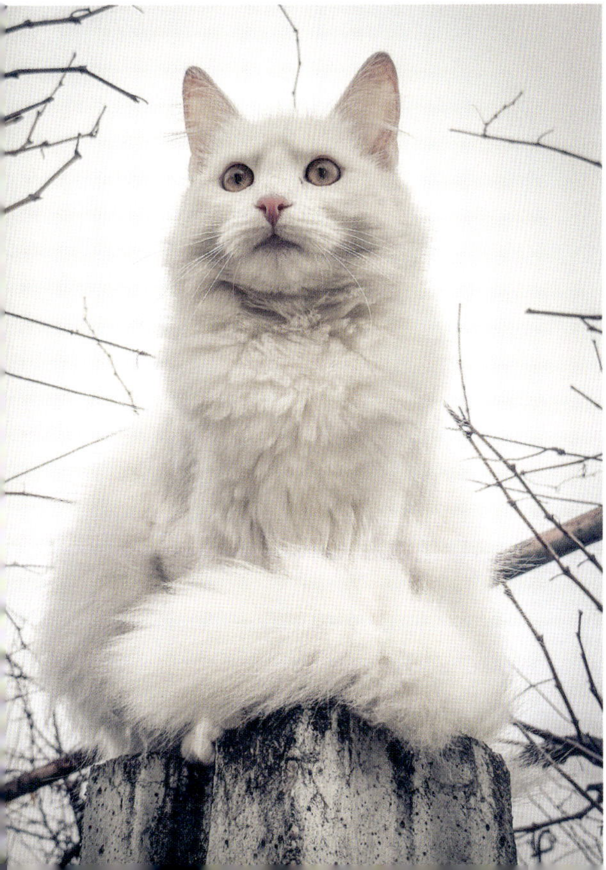
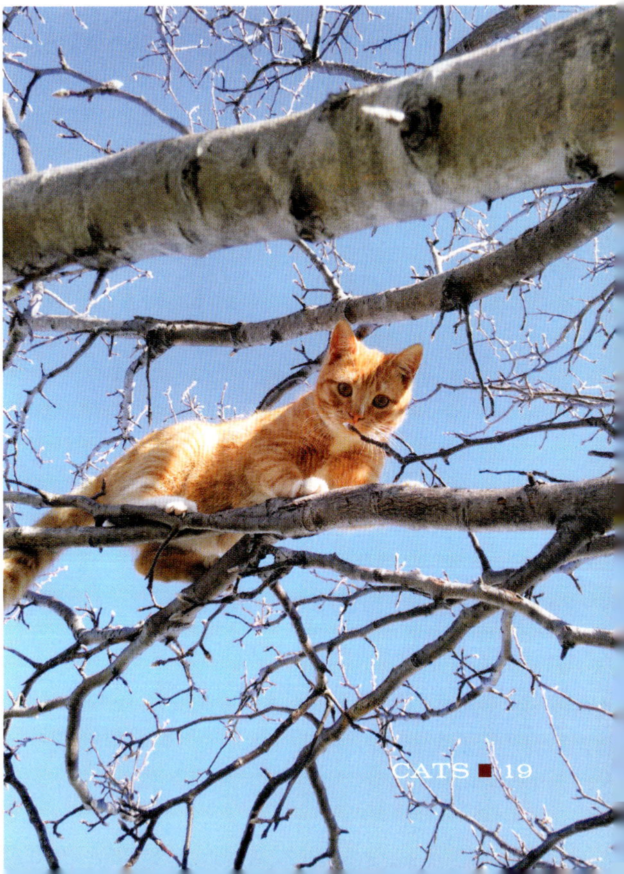

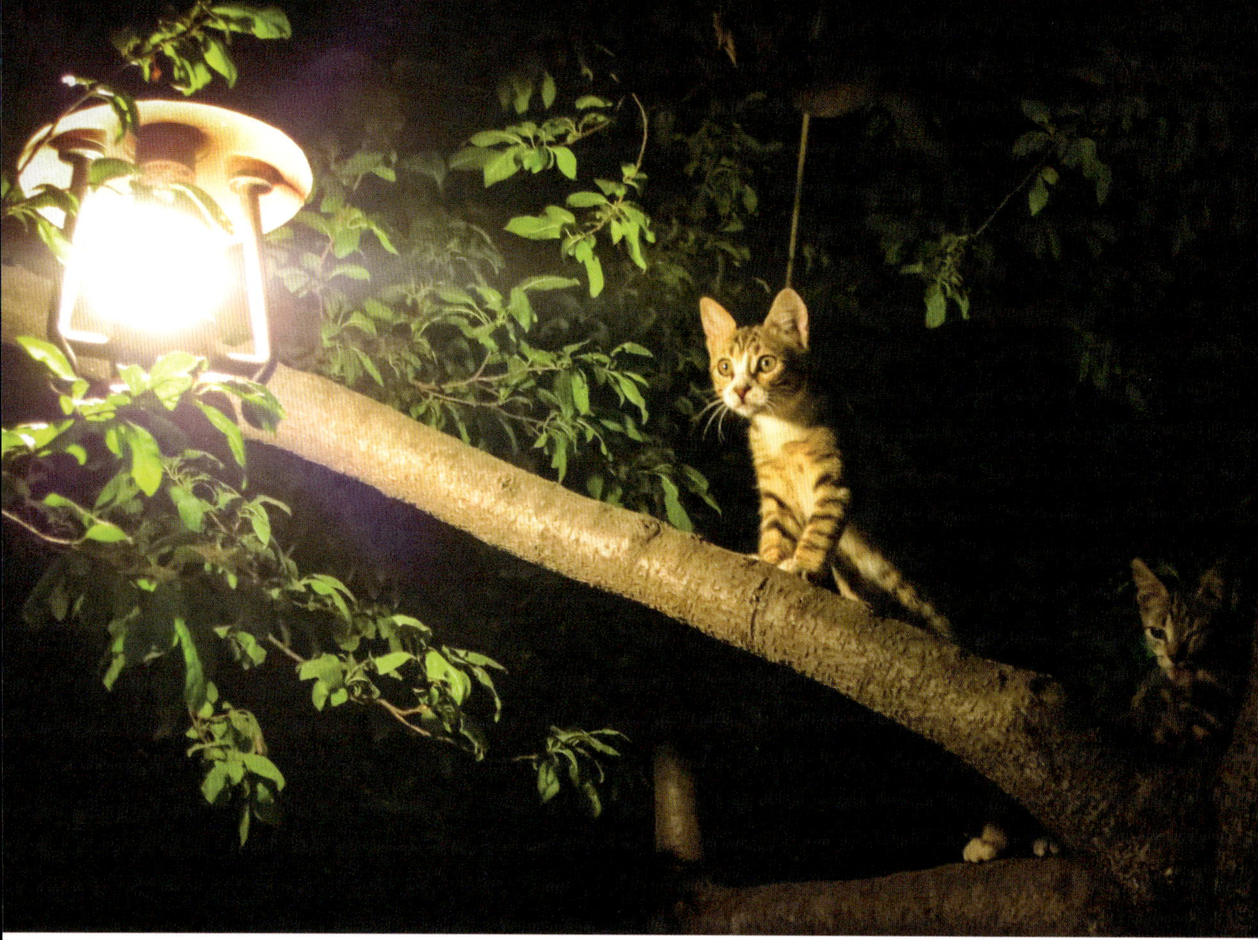

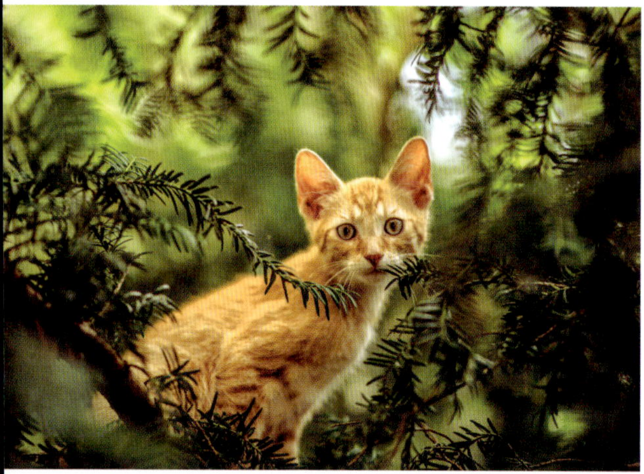

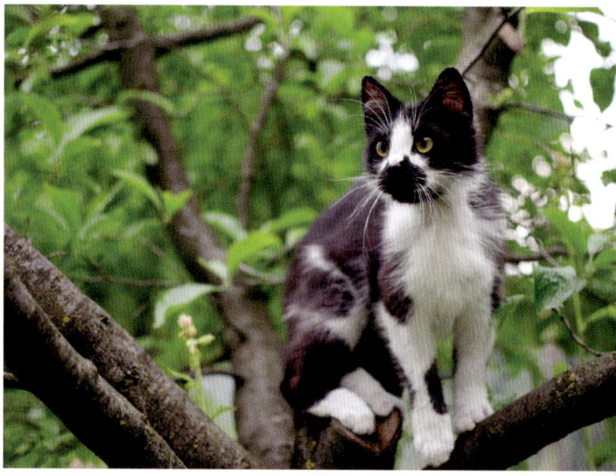

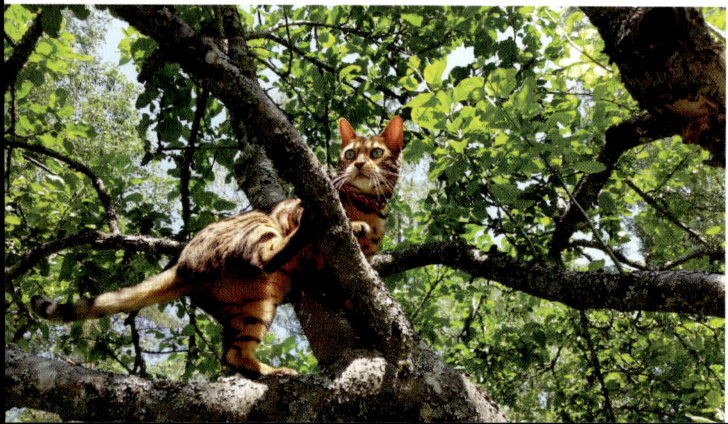

"Never try to outstubborn a cat."

–Robert A. Heinlein, author

3. Favorite Toys

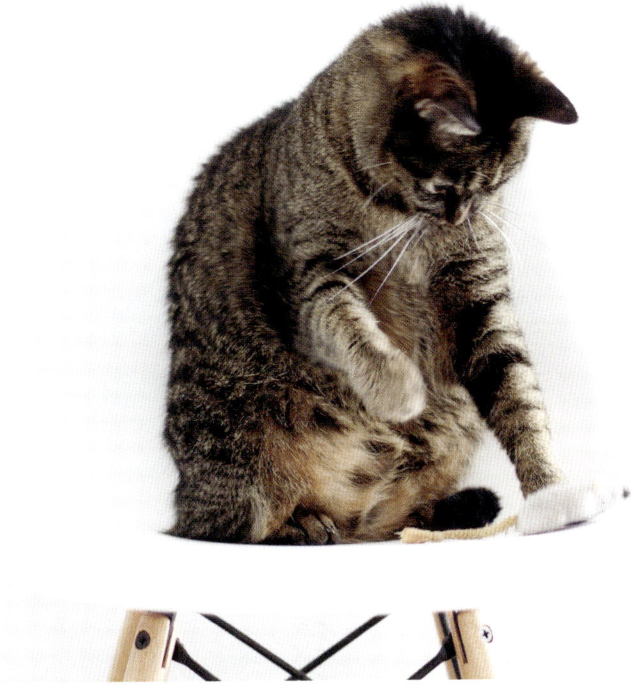

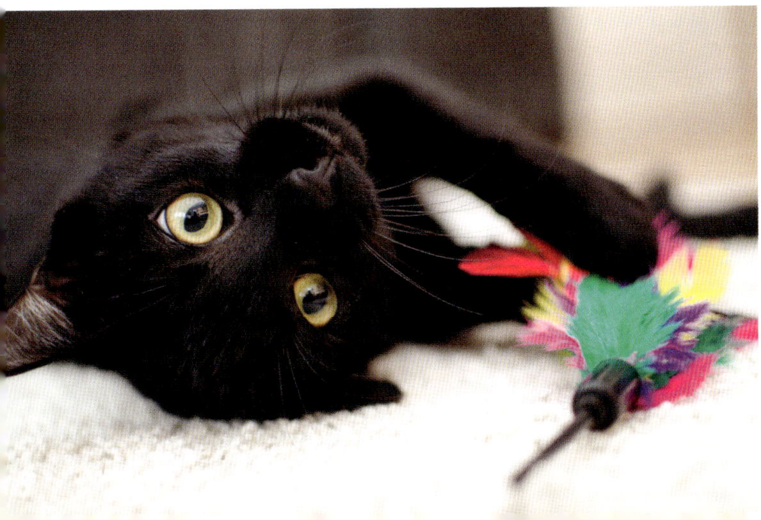

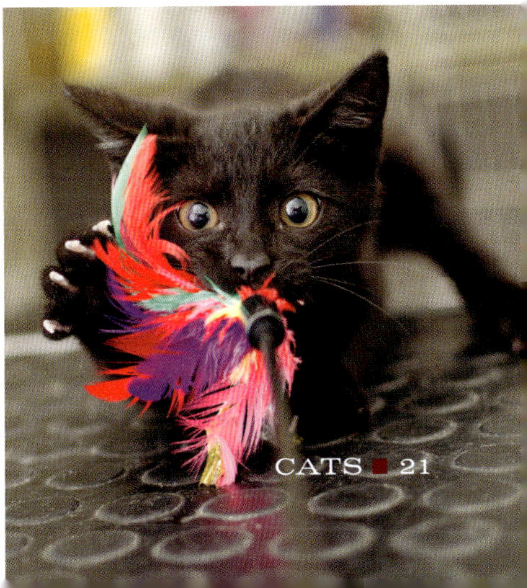

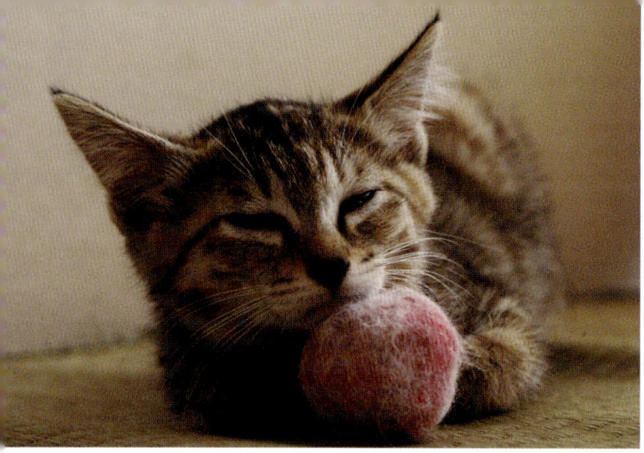
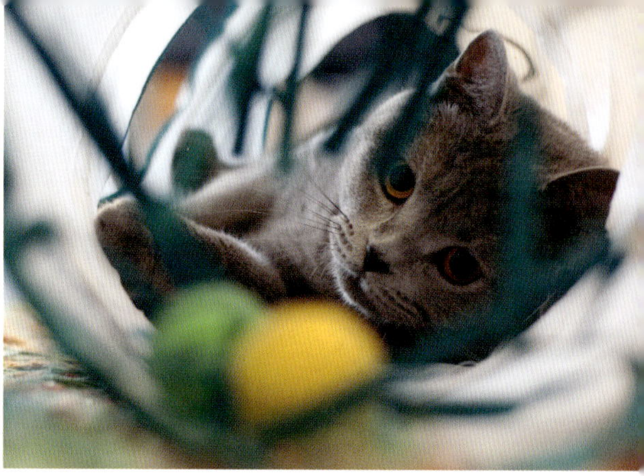
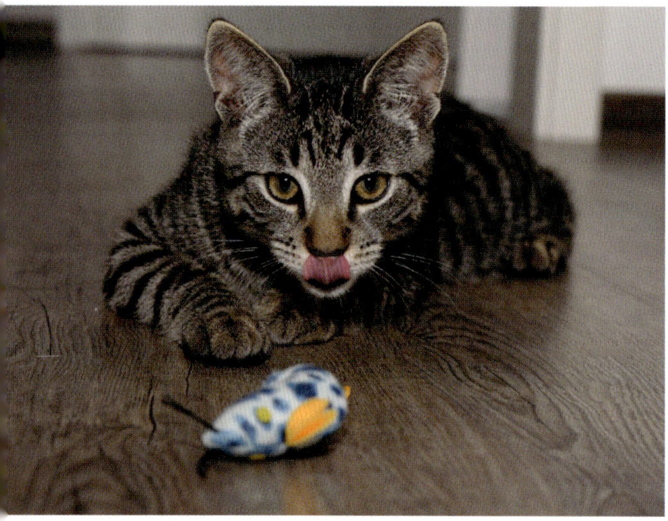
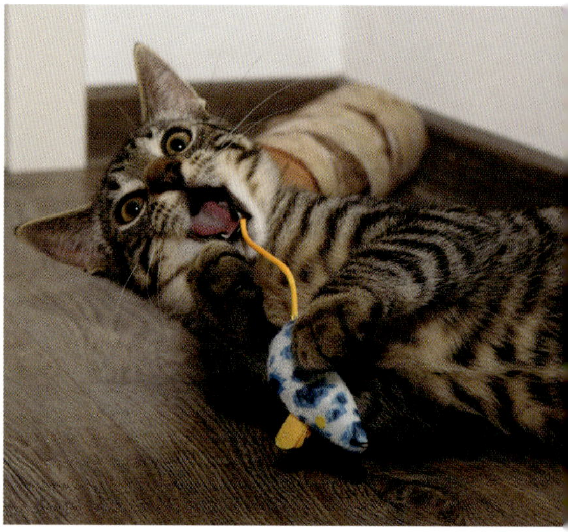
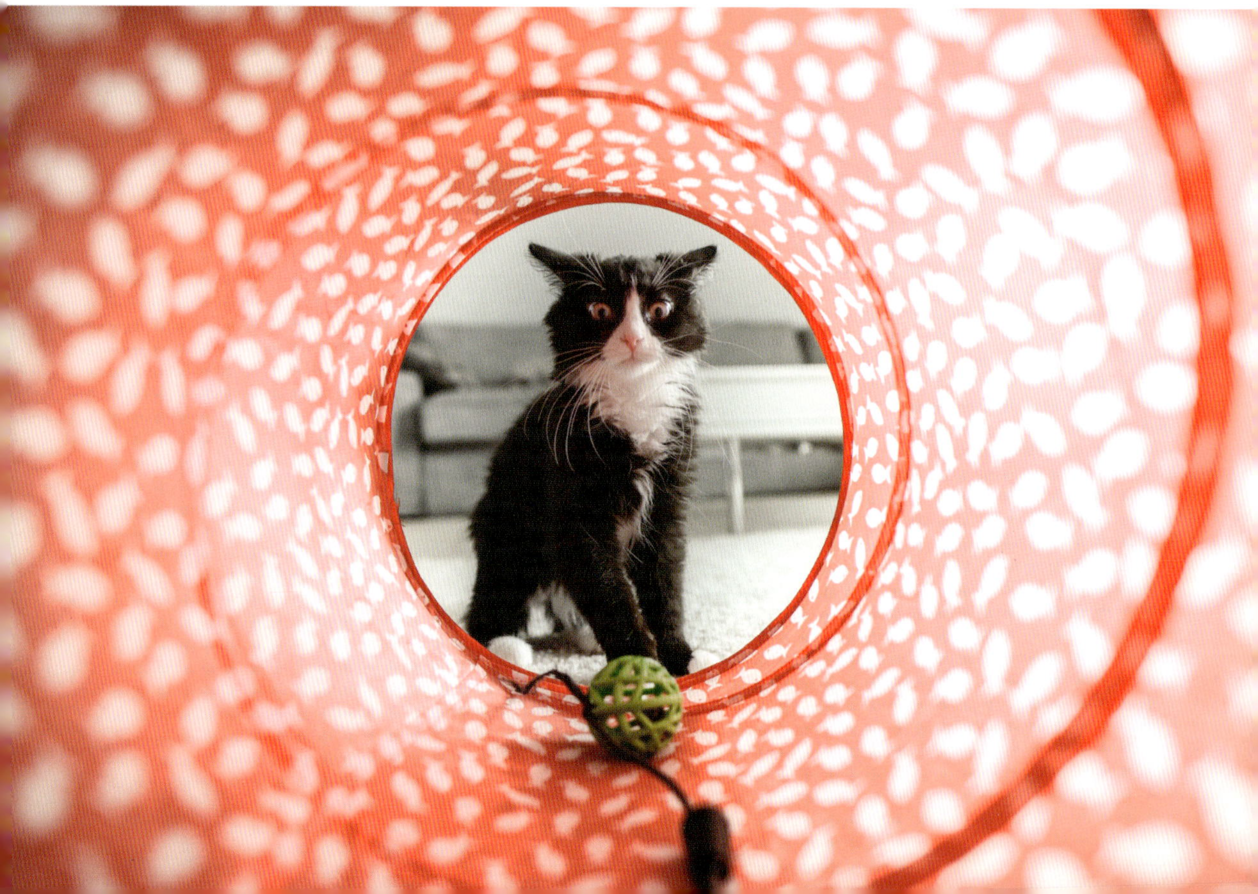

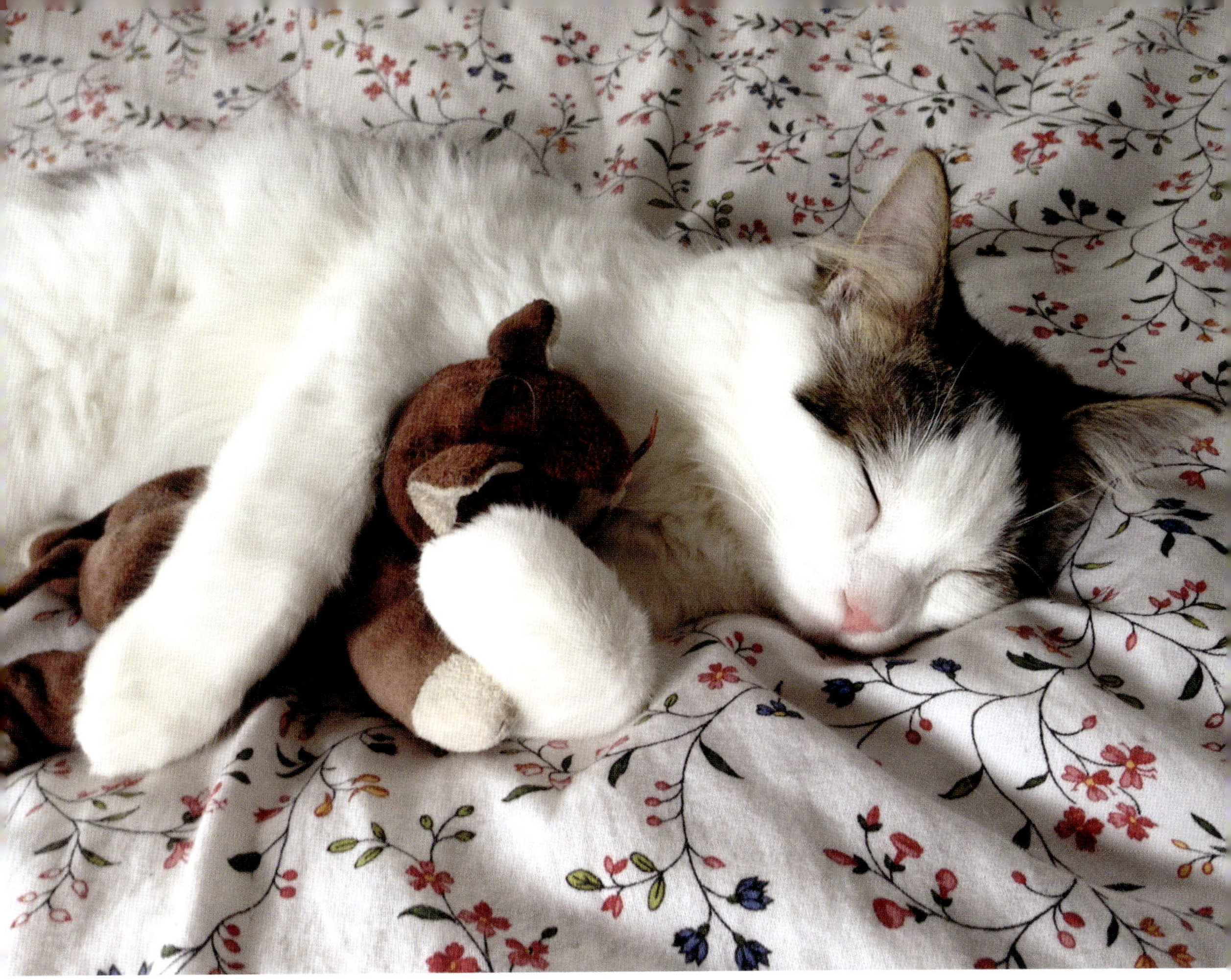
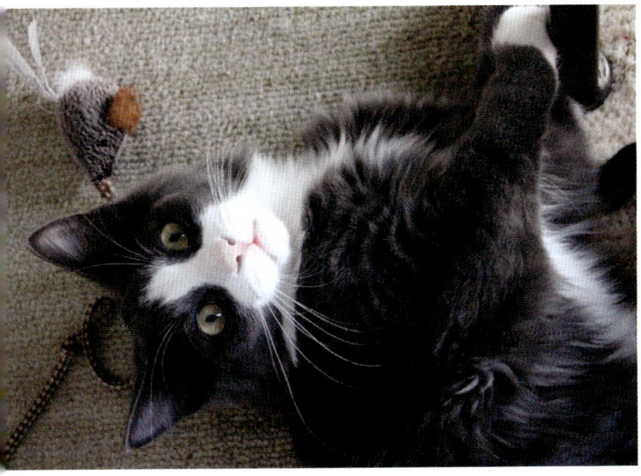
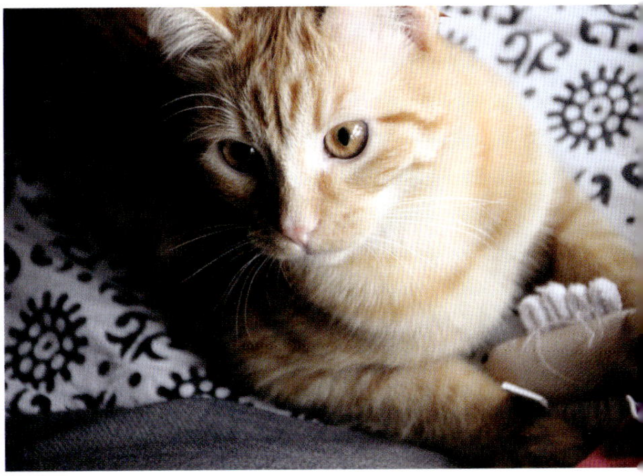
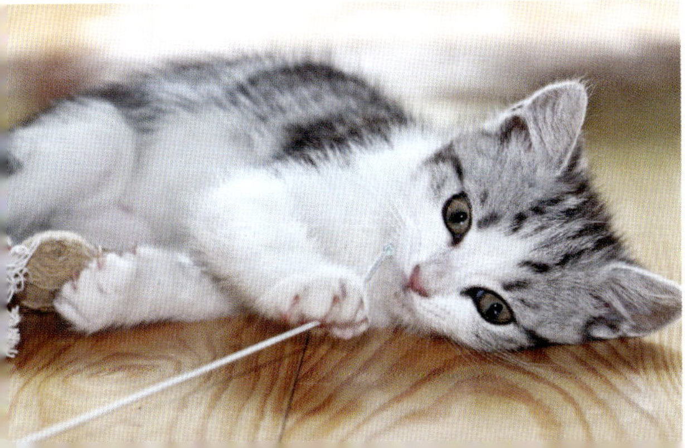
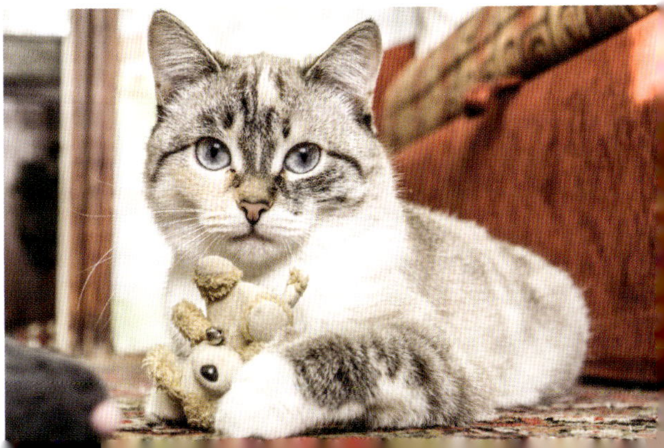

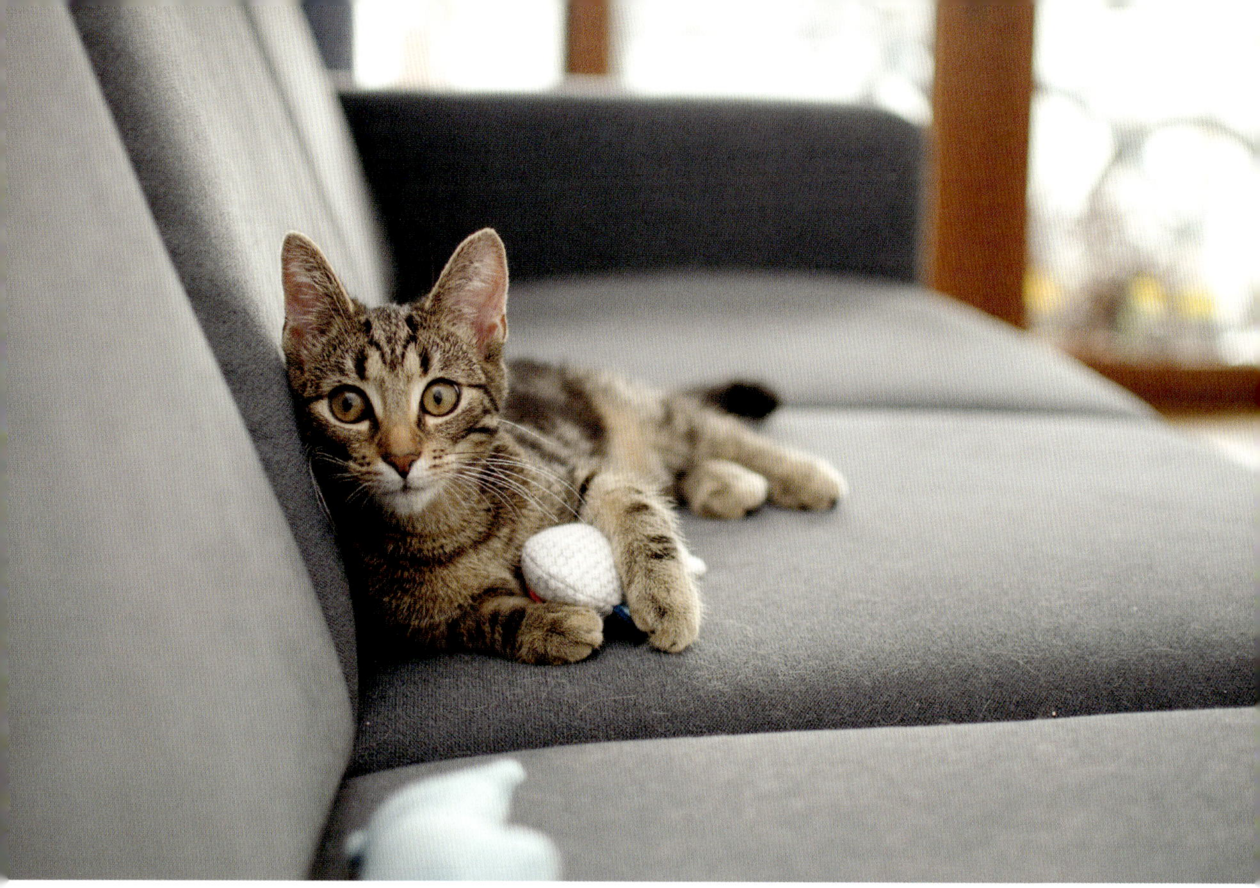

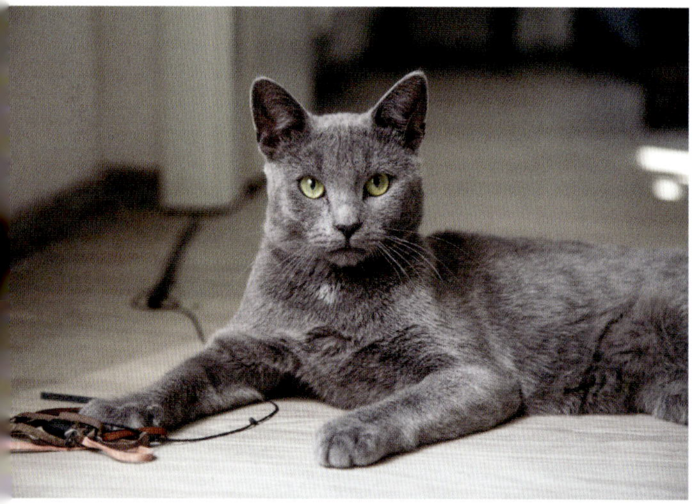

“As anyone who has ever been around a cat for any length of time well knows, cats have enormous patience with the limitations of the human kind.”

–Cleveland Amory, author and animal rights activist

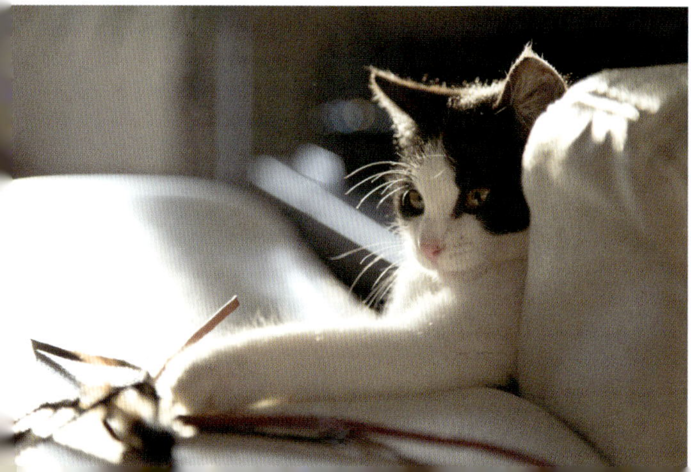

4. Adventure and Curiosity

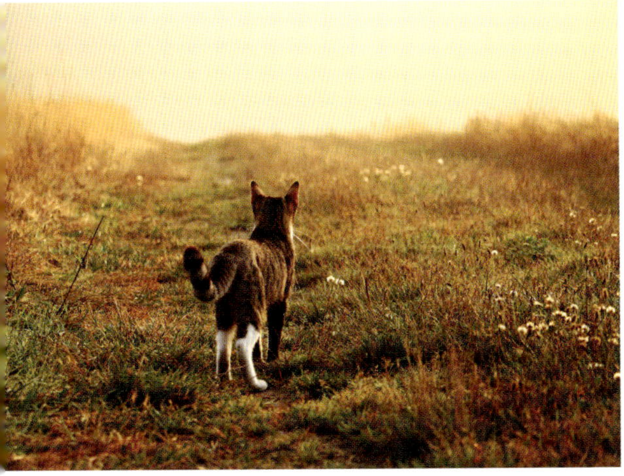

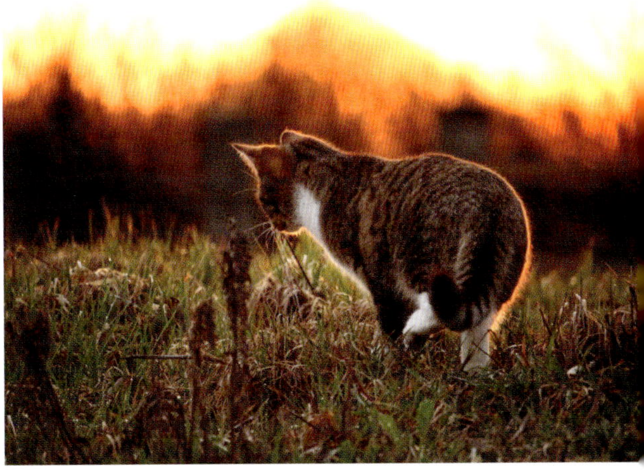

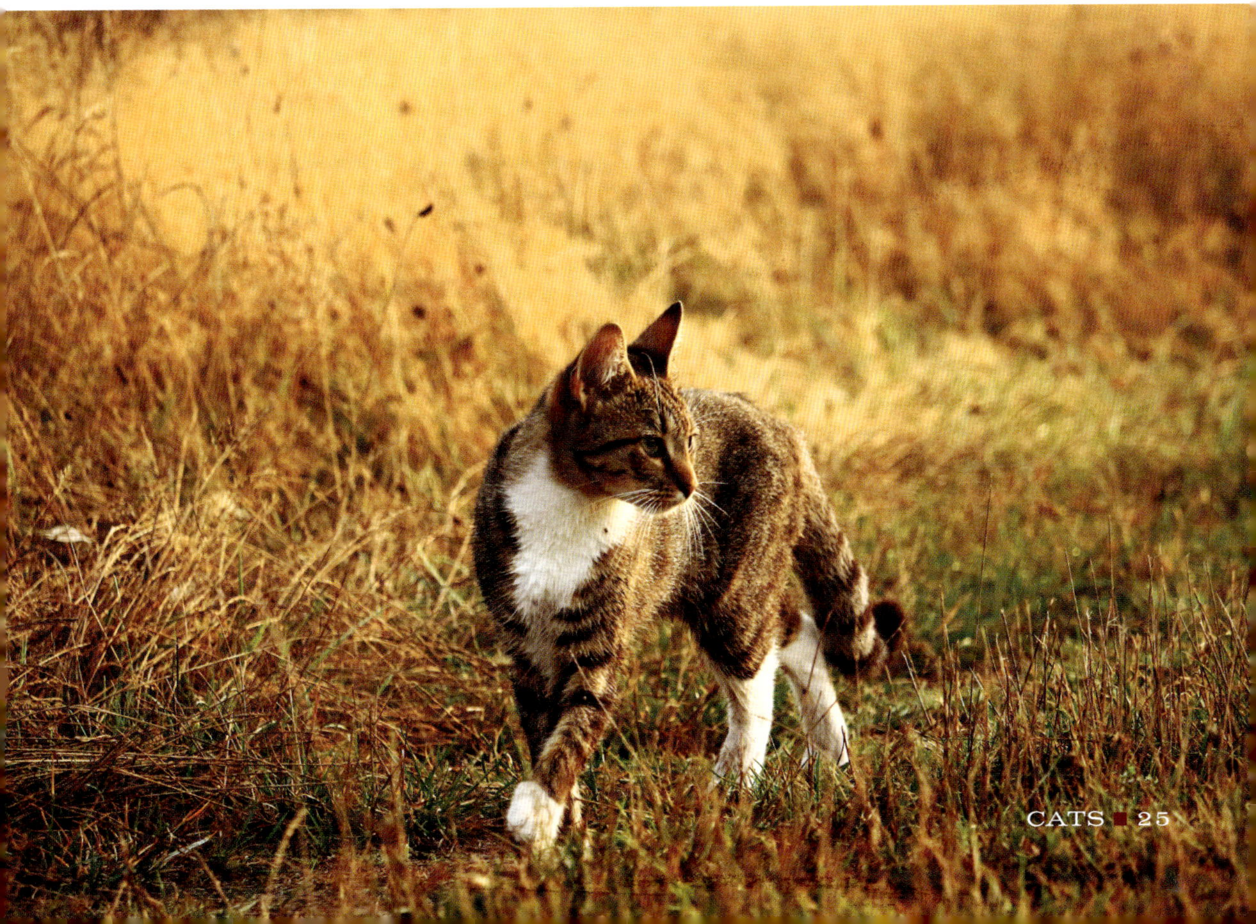

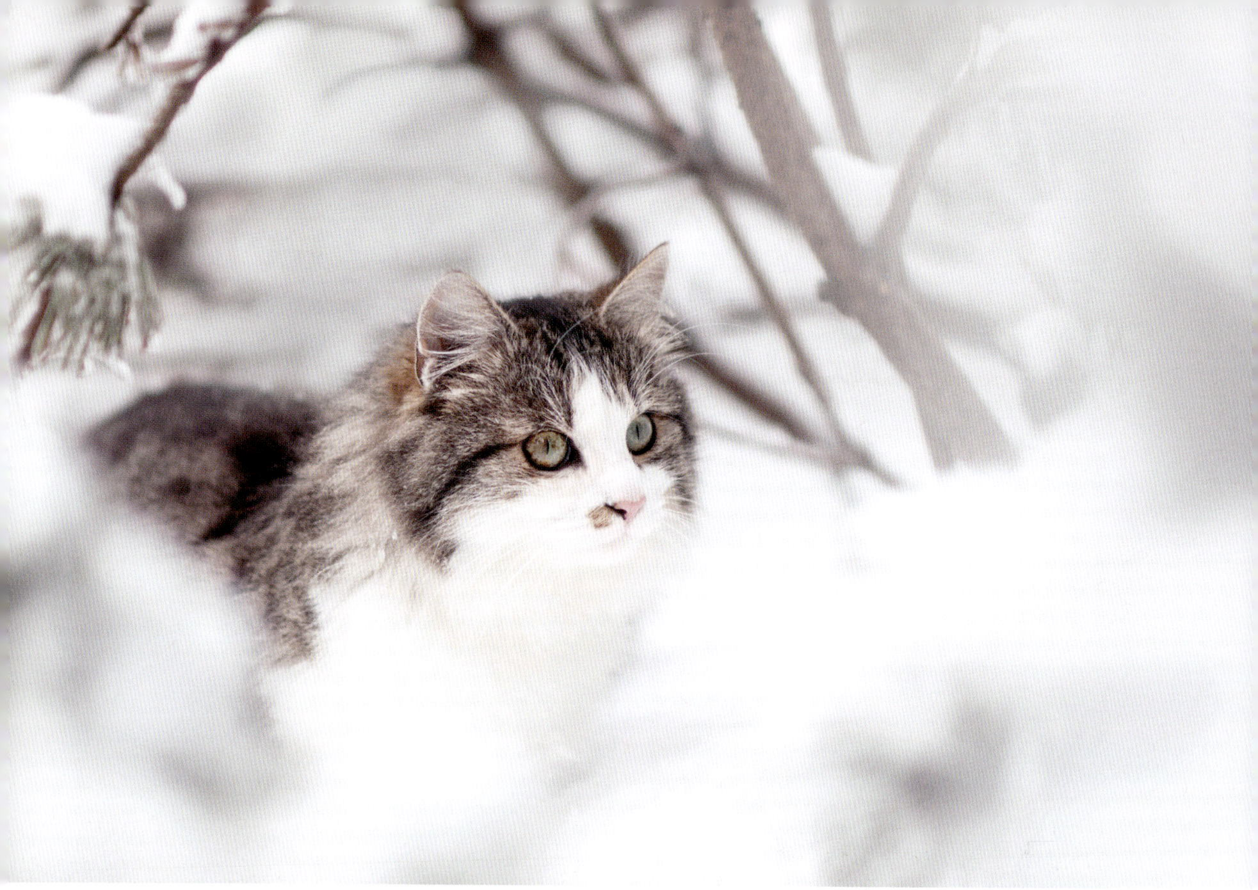
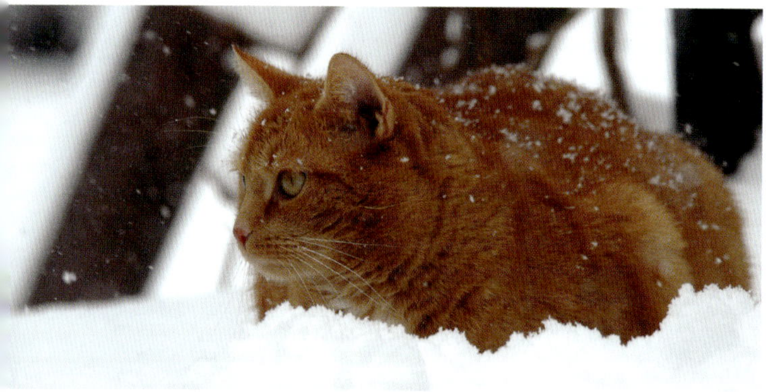
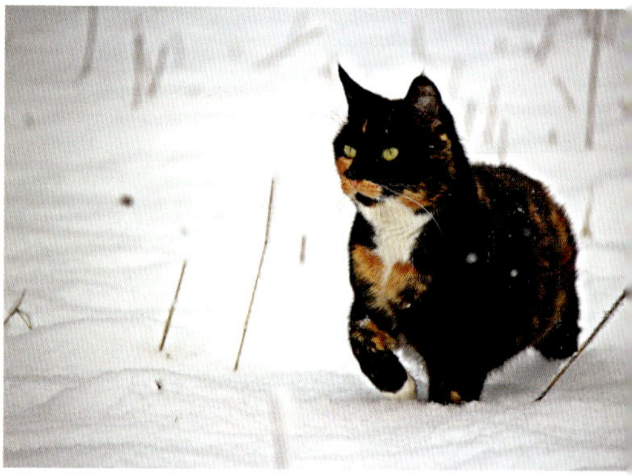
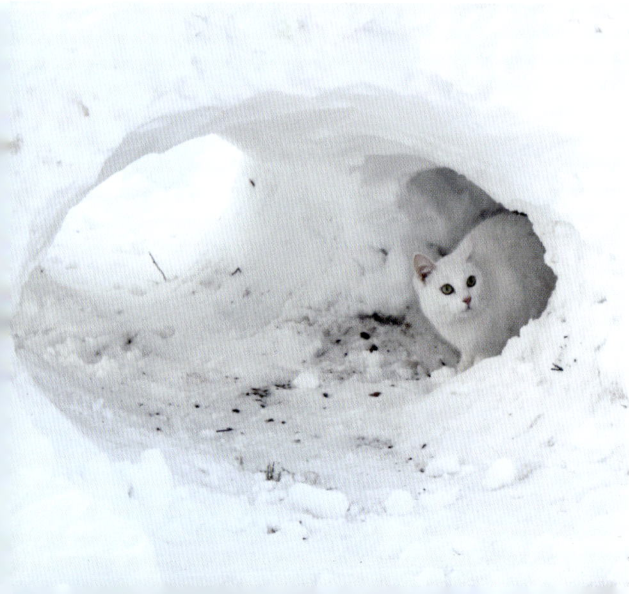
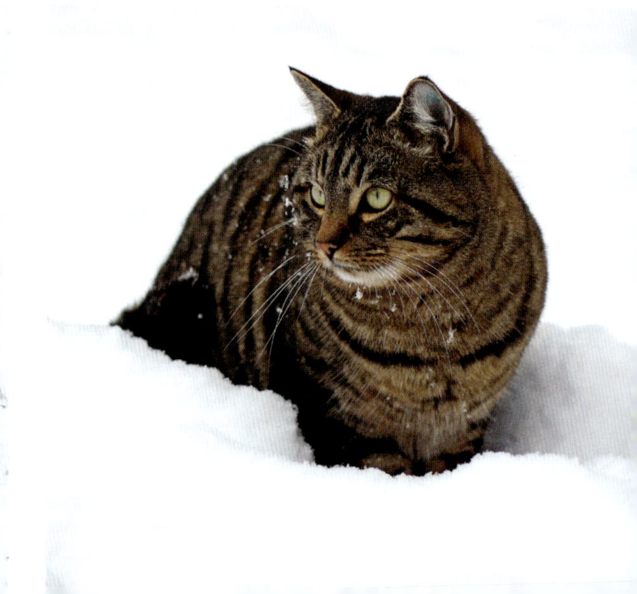

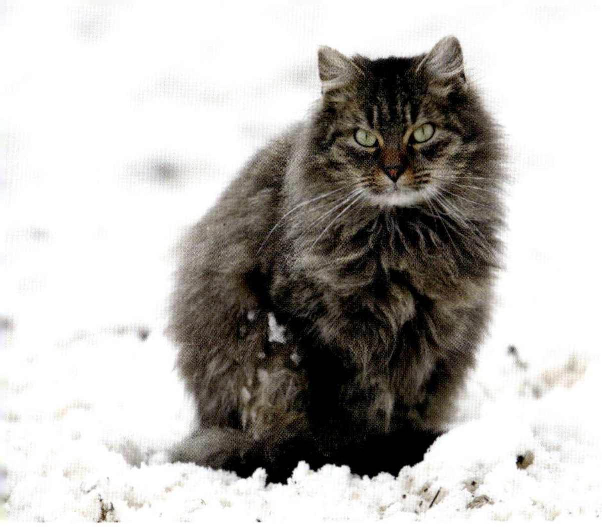
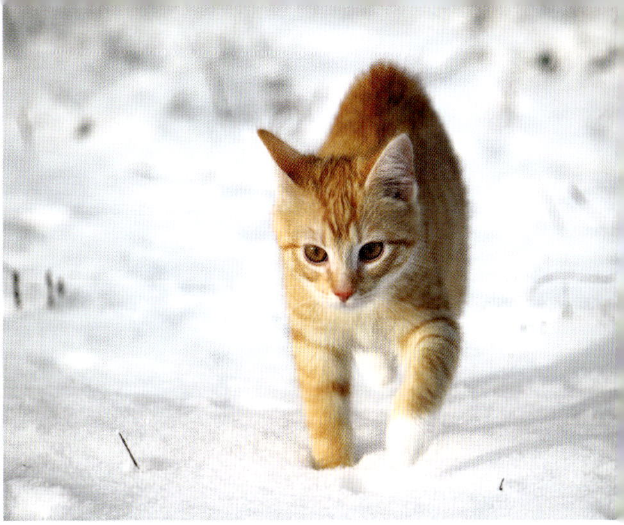
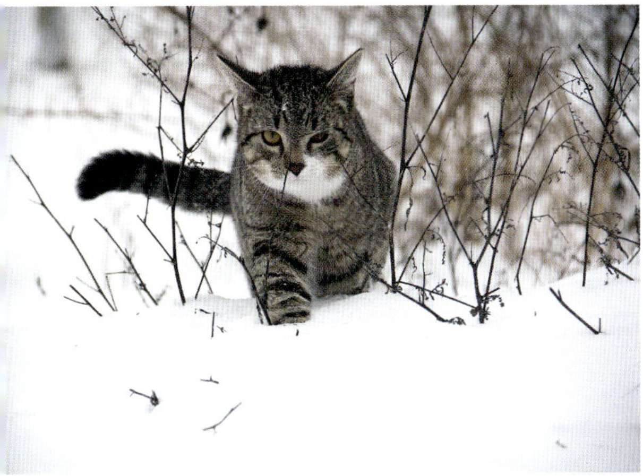
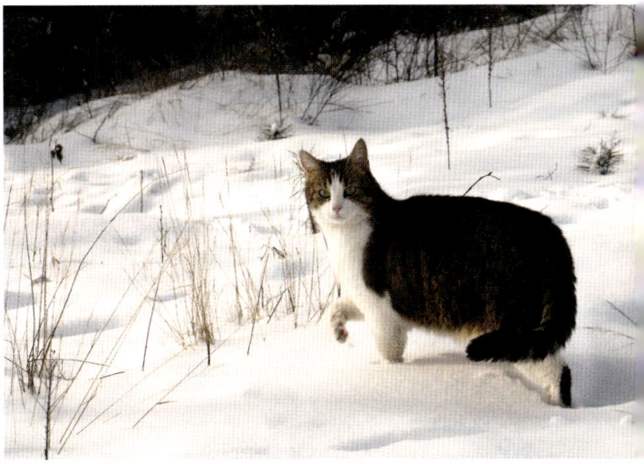
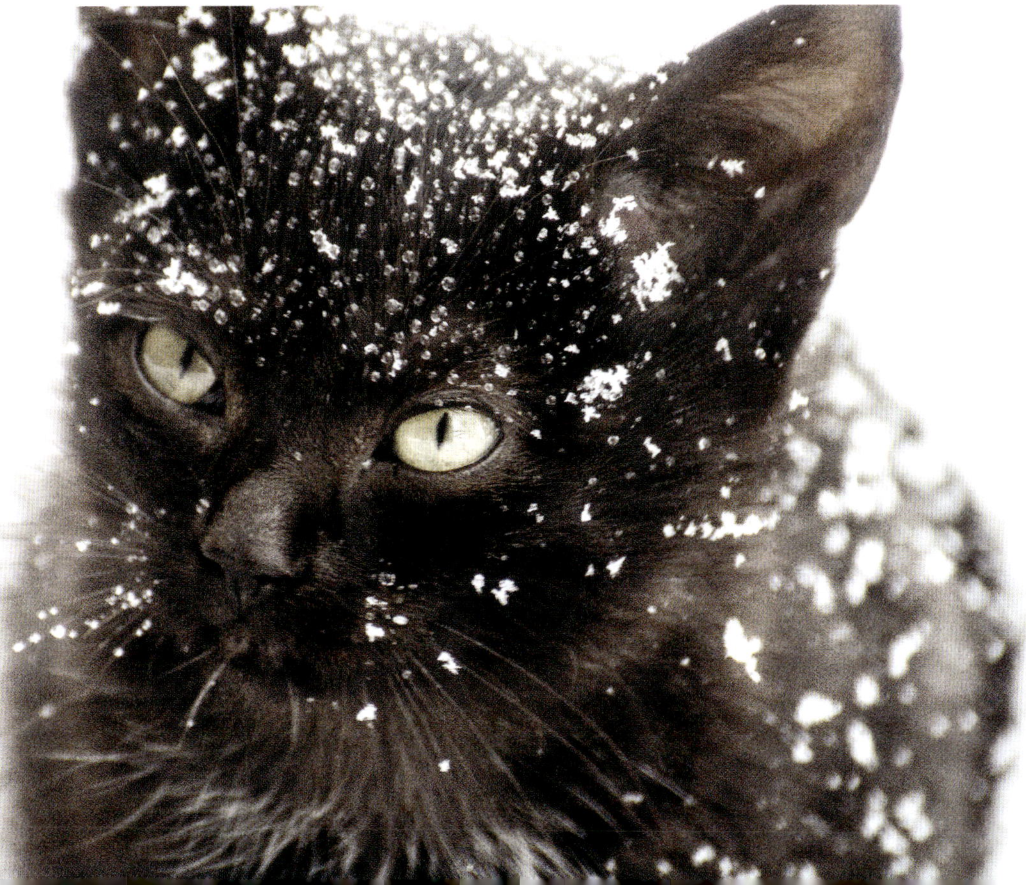

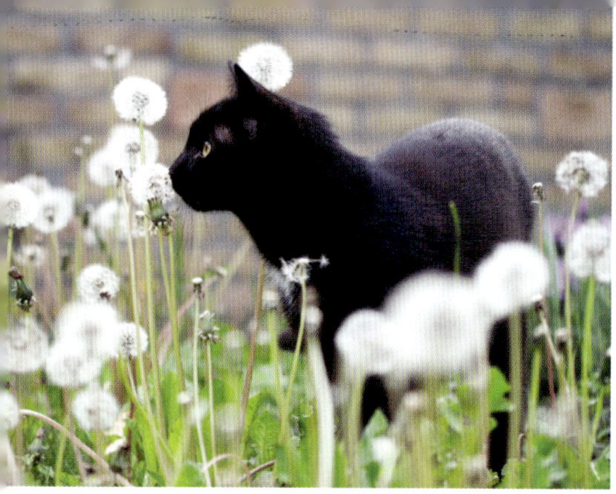
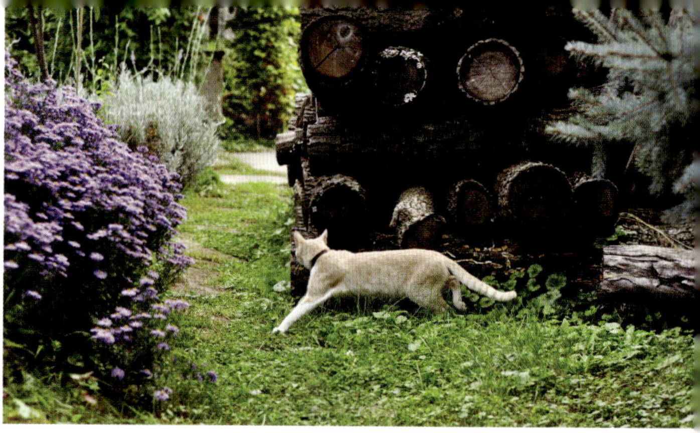
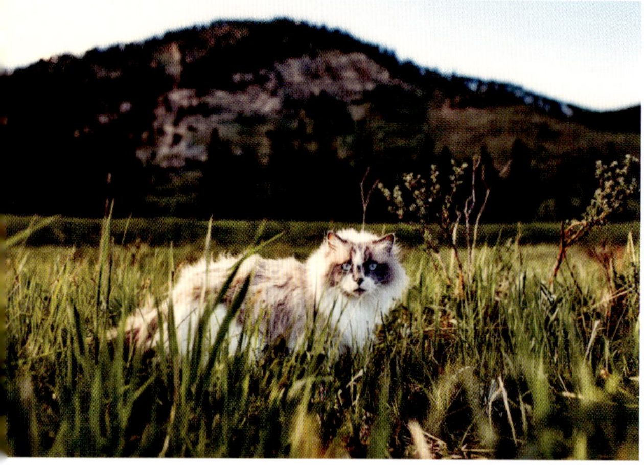
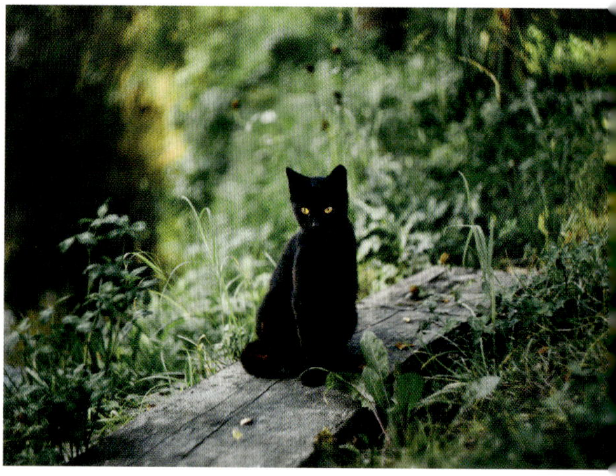
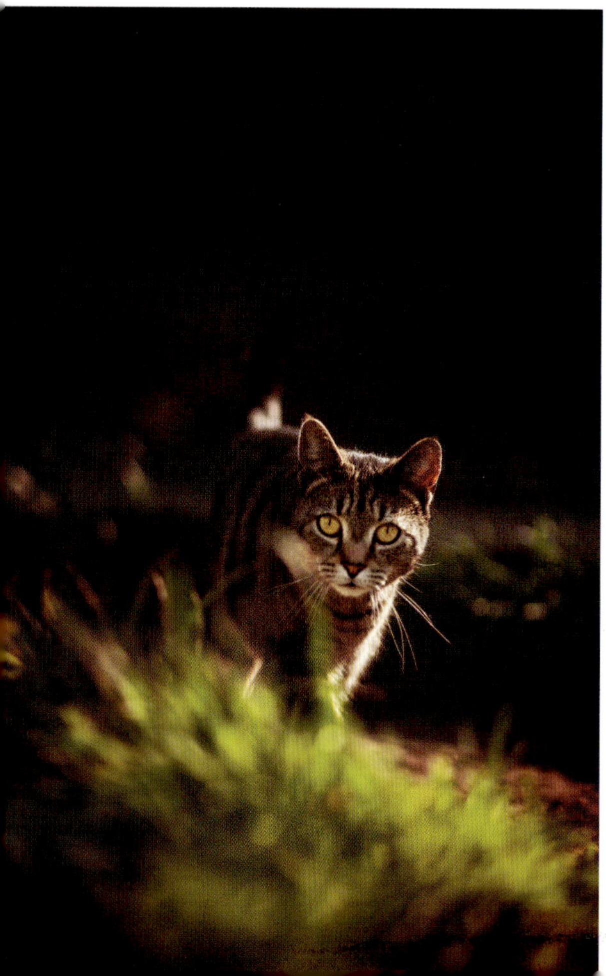
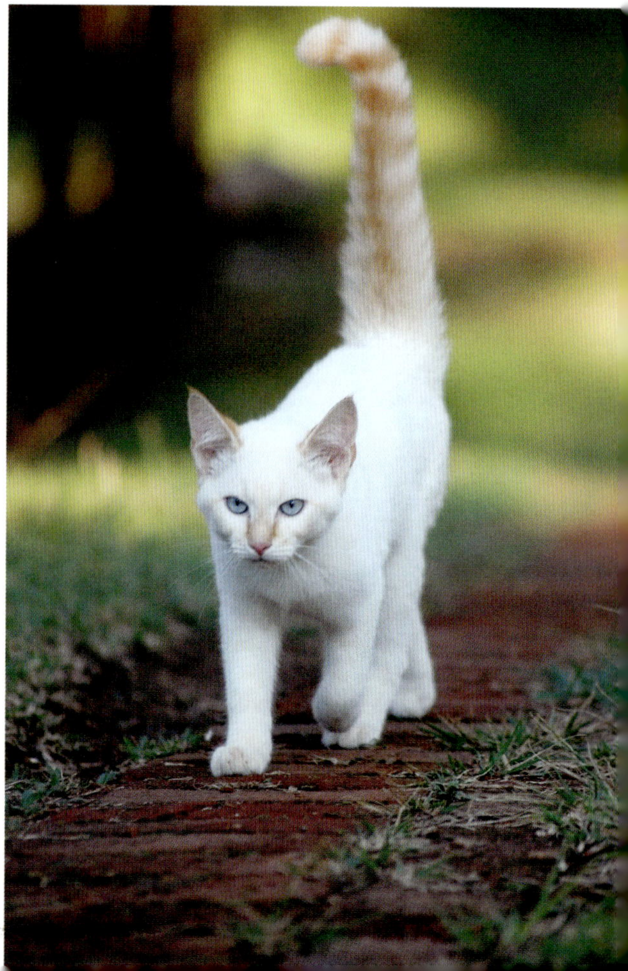

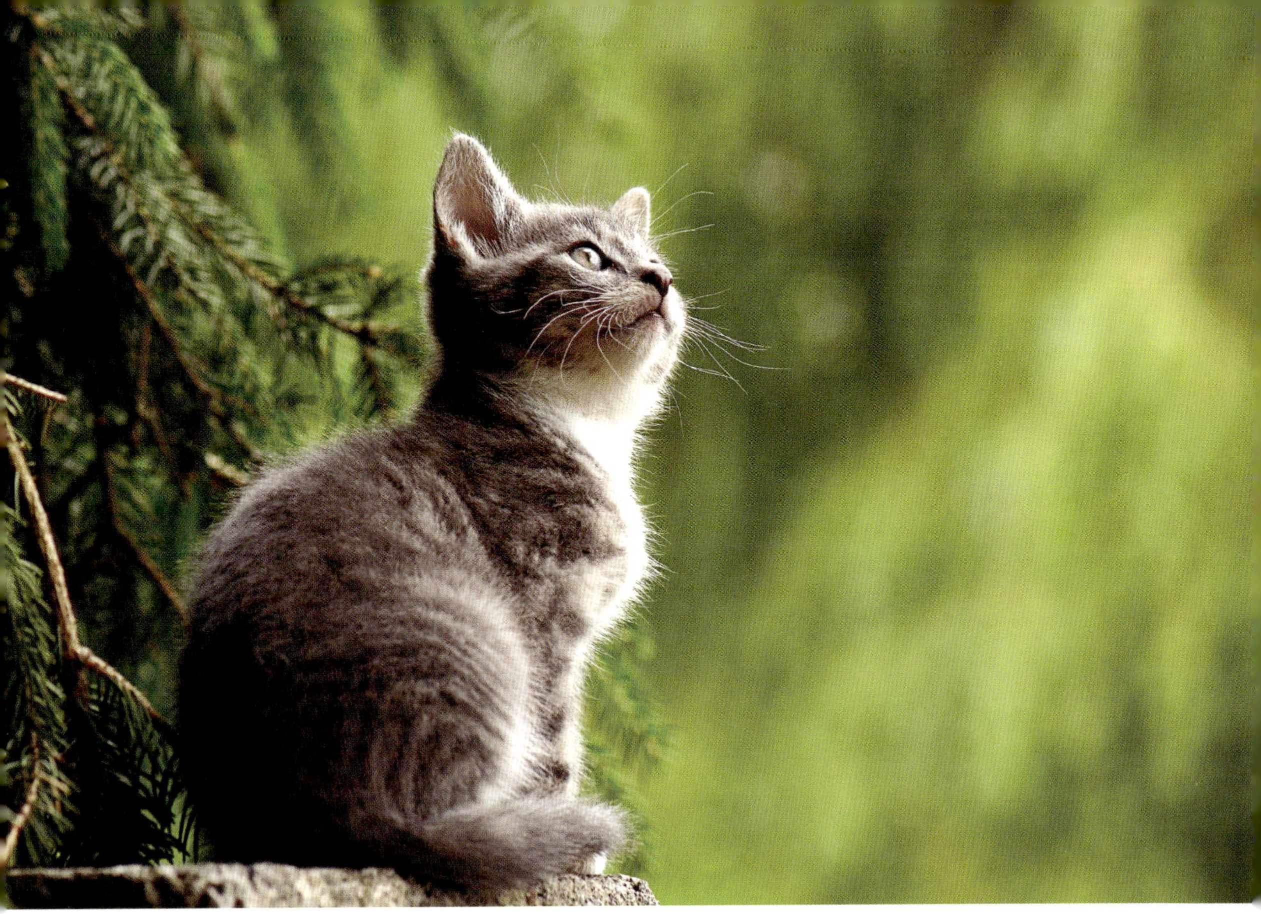

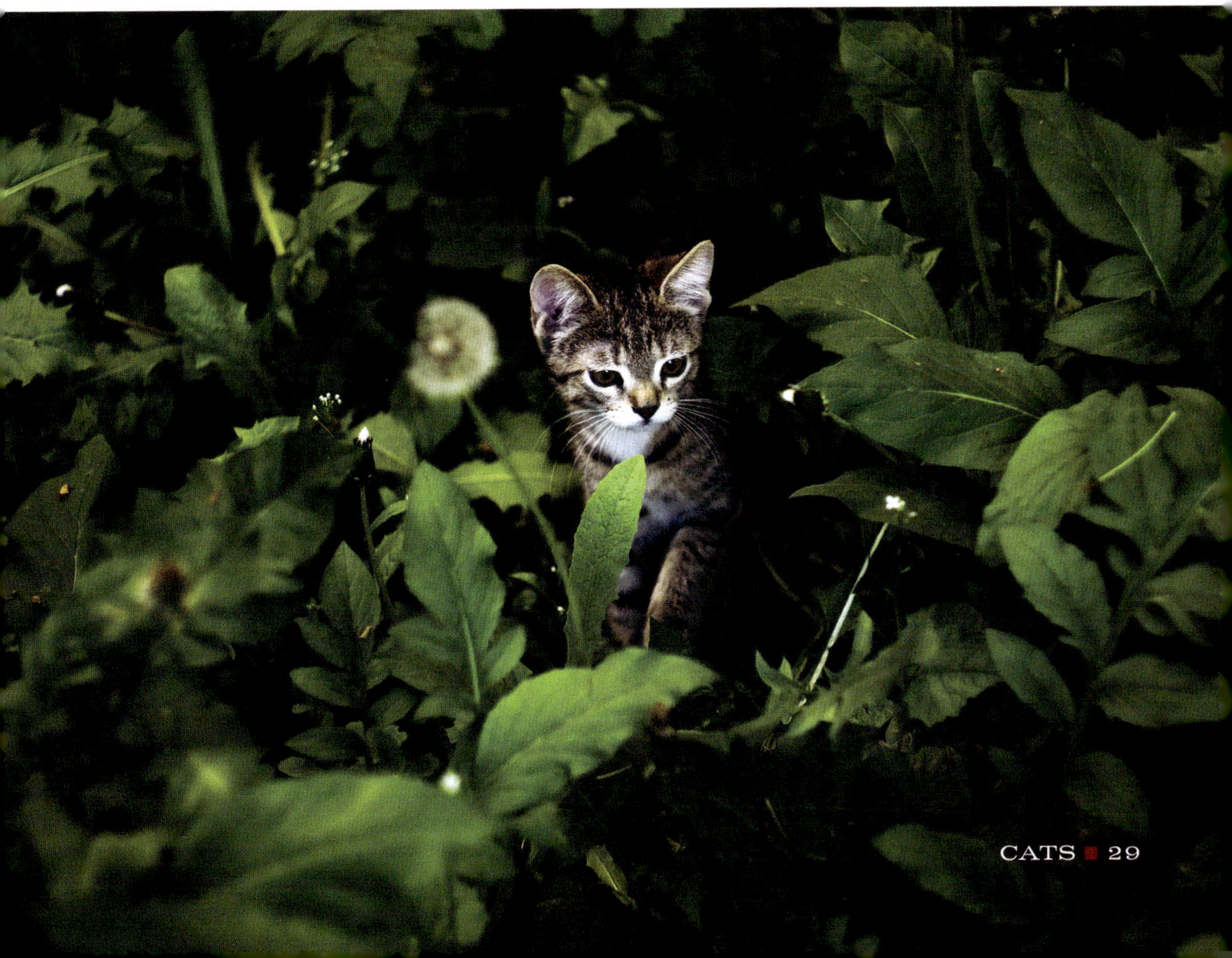

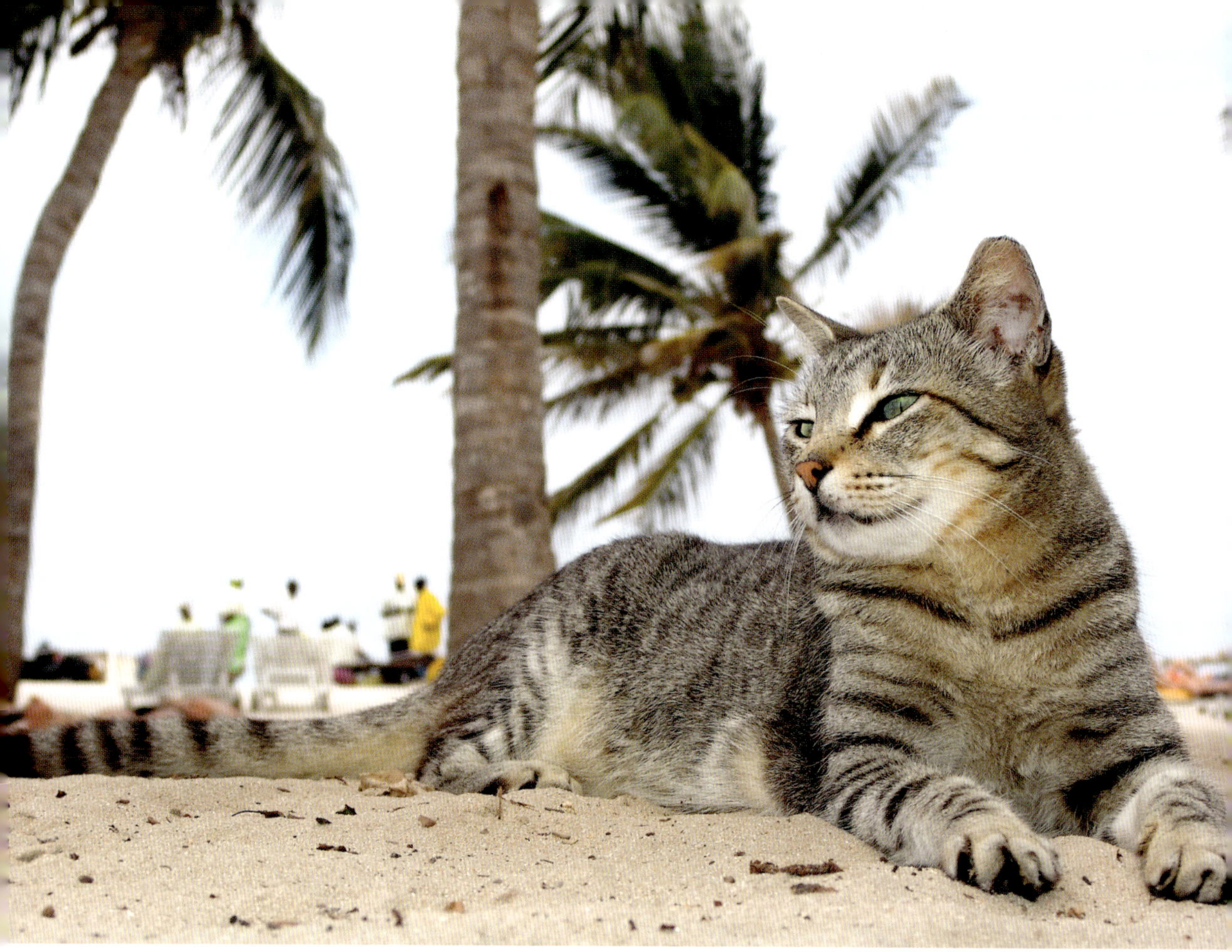
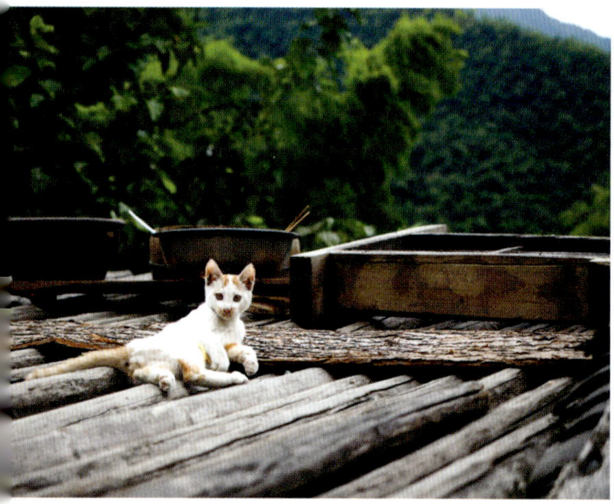
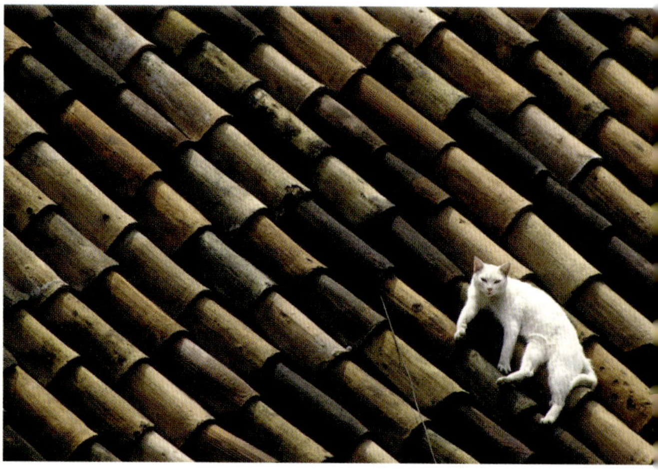
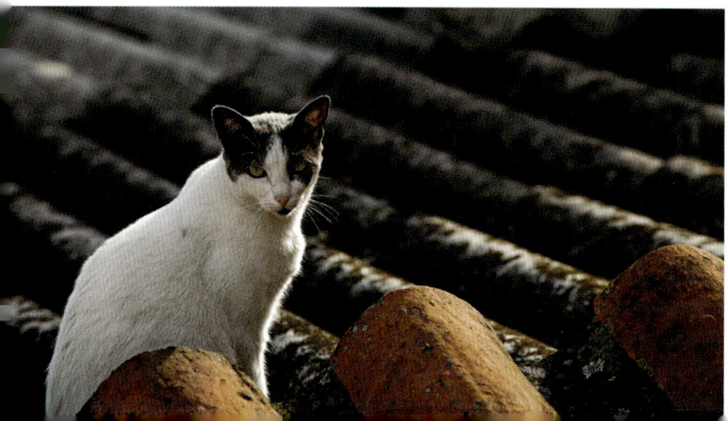
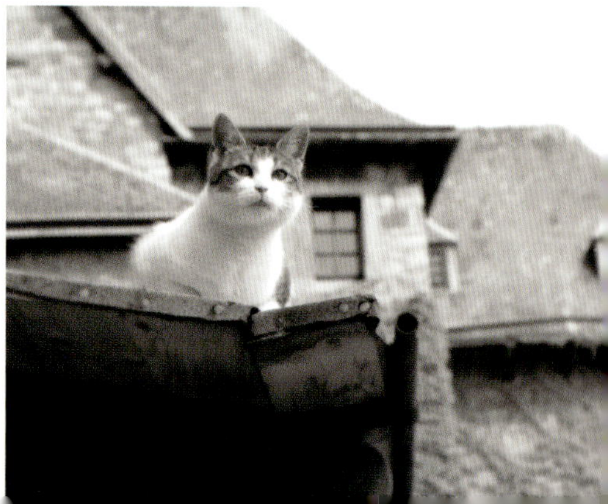

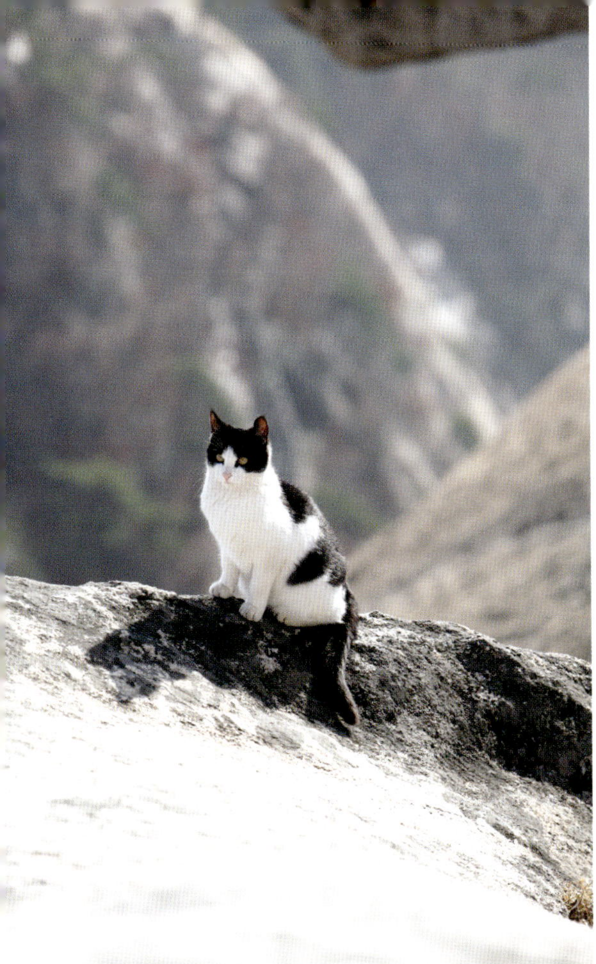
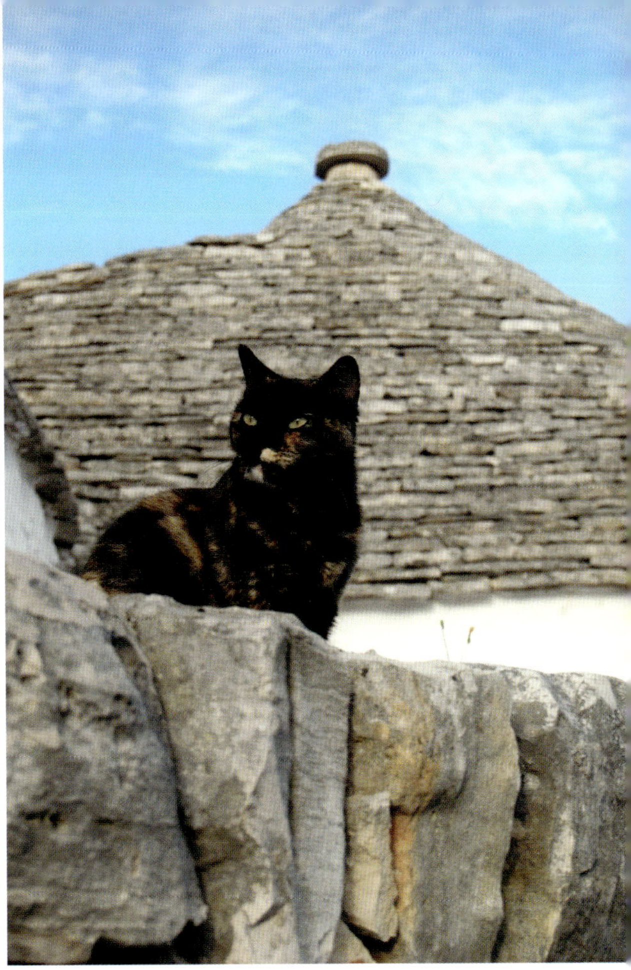
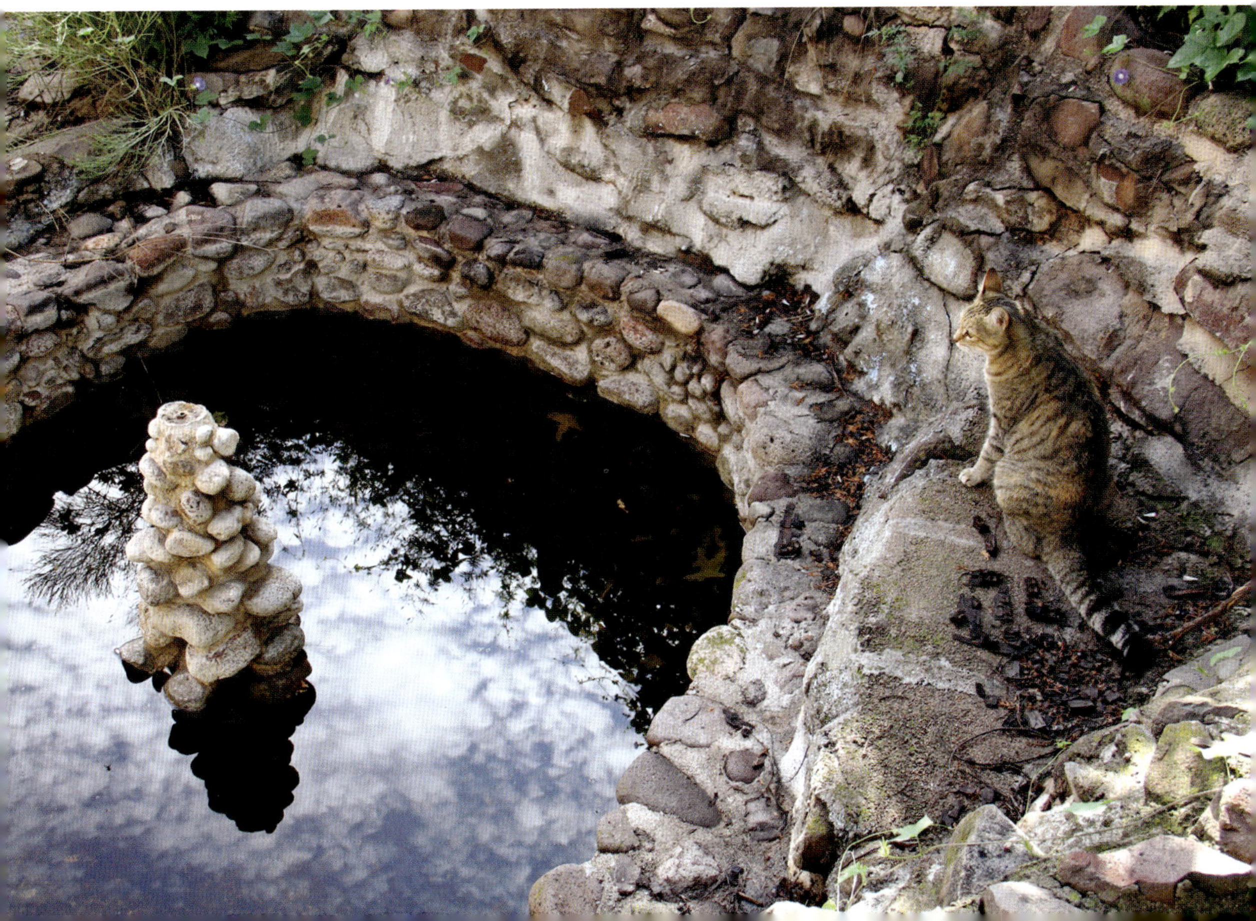

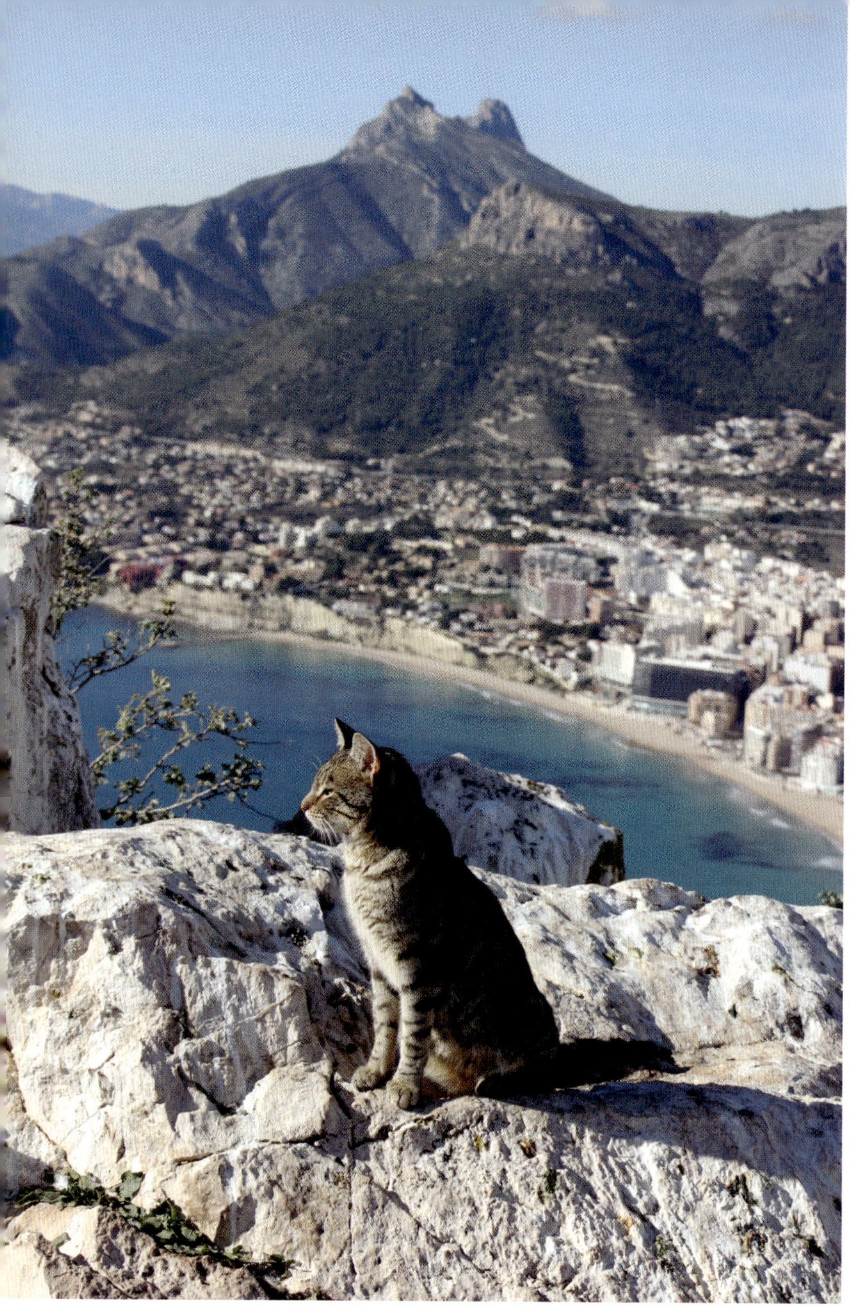

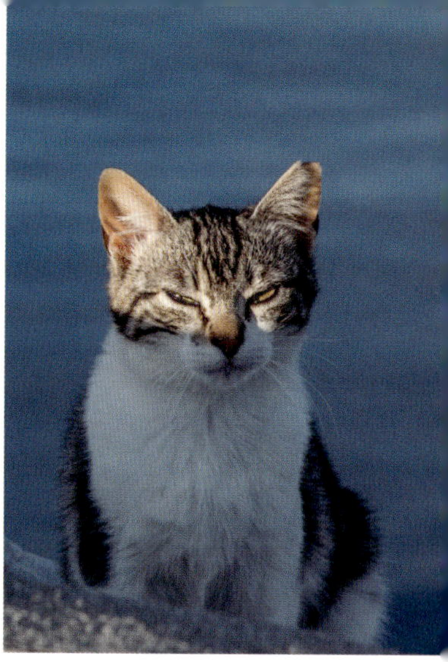

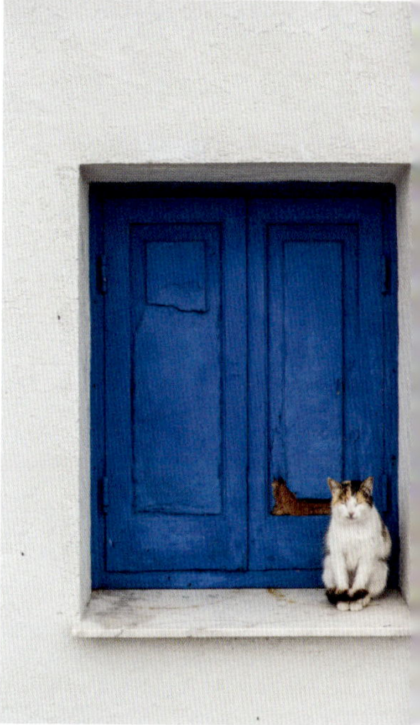

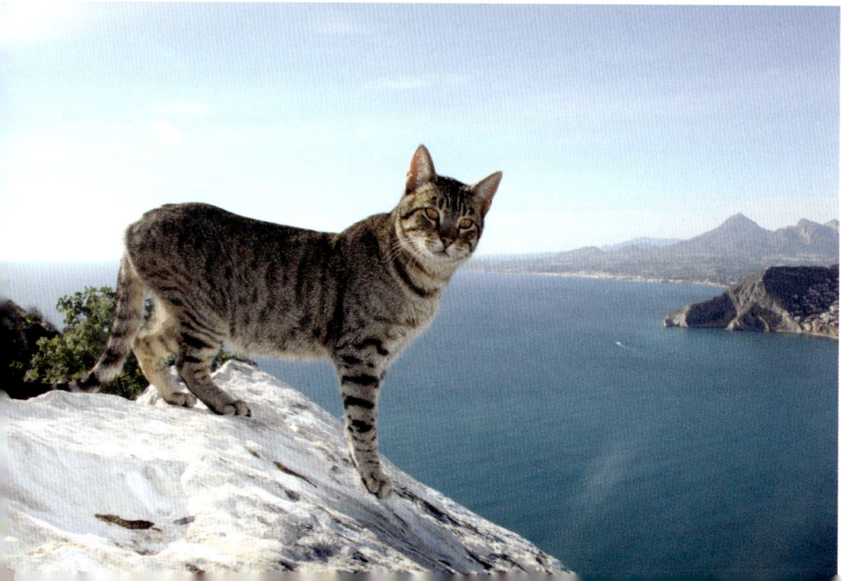

"Cats seem to go on the principle that it never does any harm to ask for what you want."

—Joseph Wood Krutch, writer and naturalist

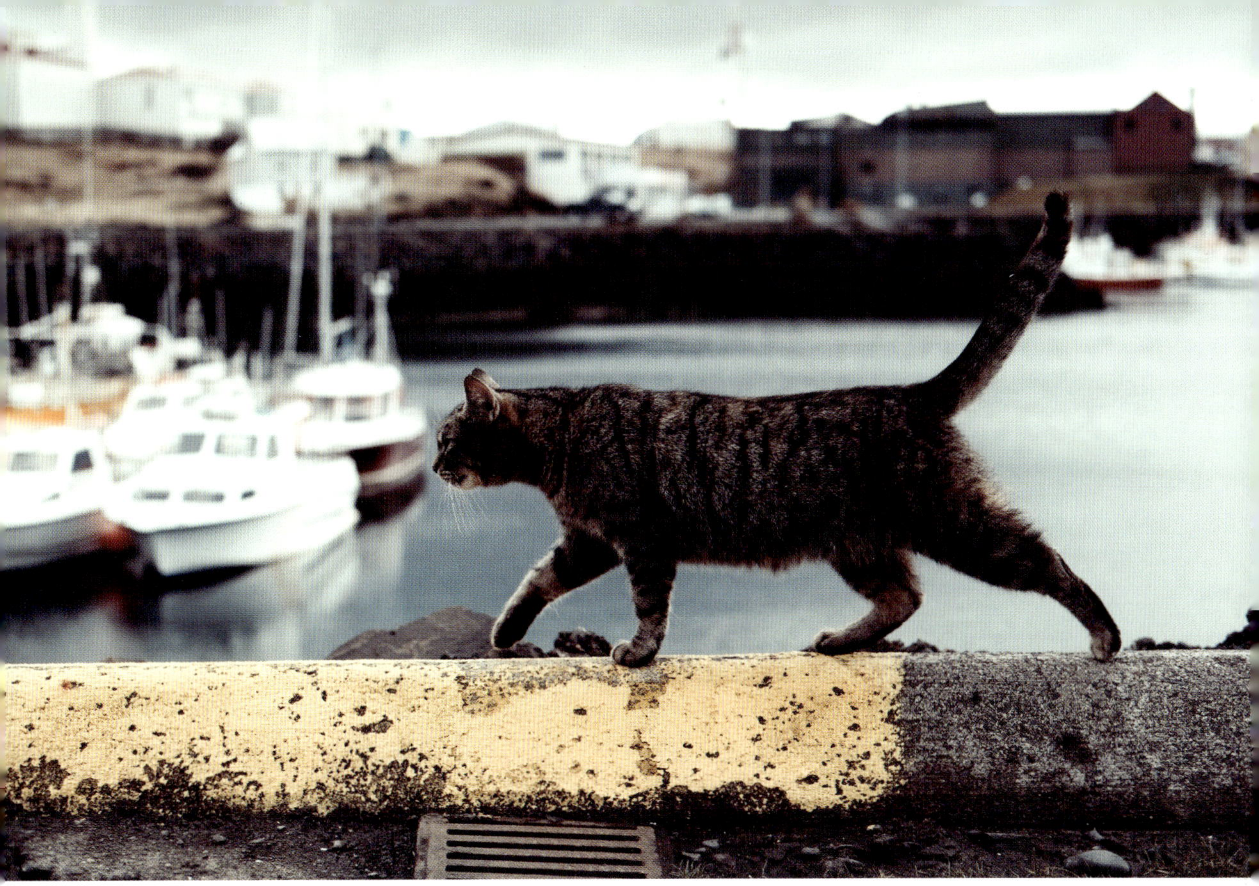
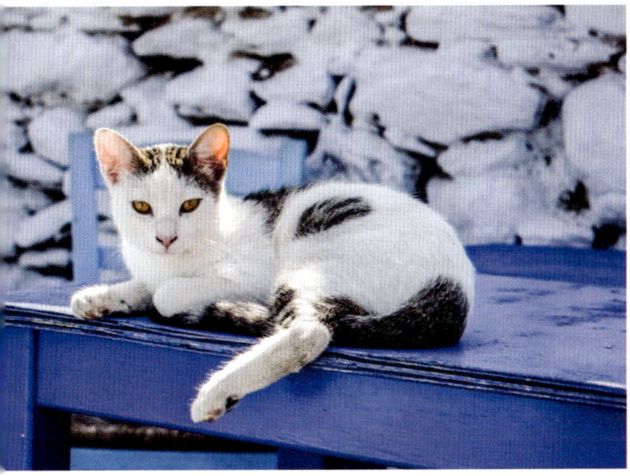
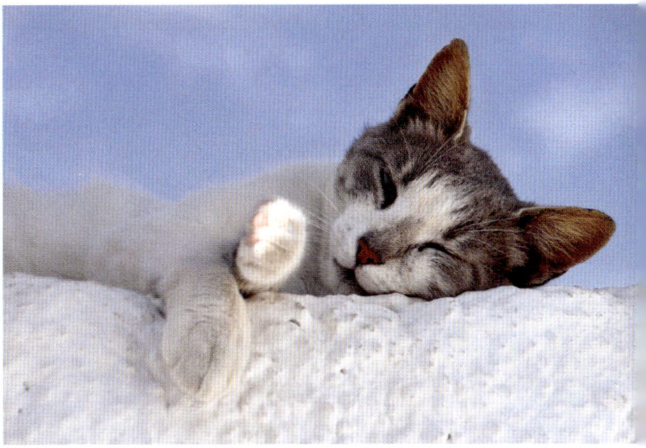
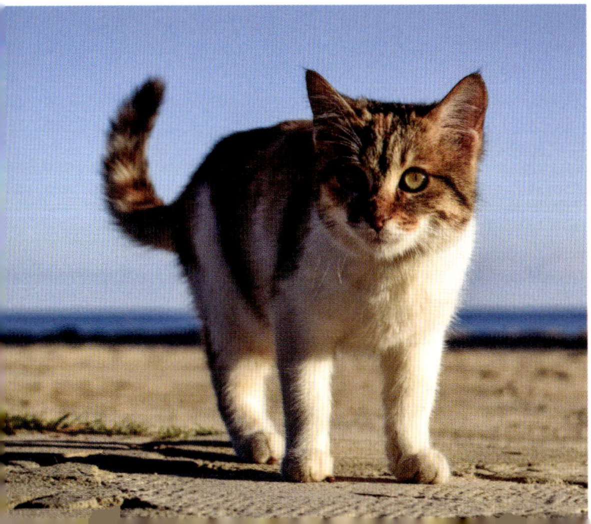
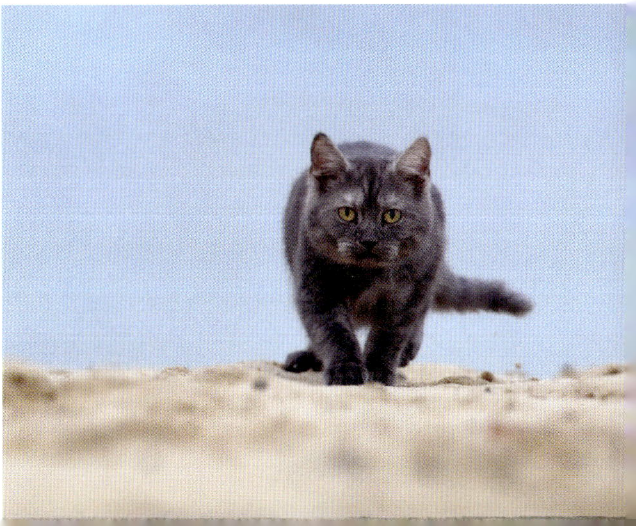

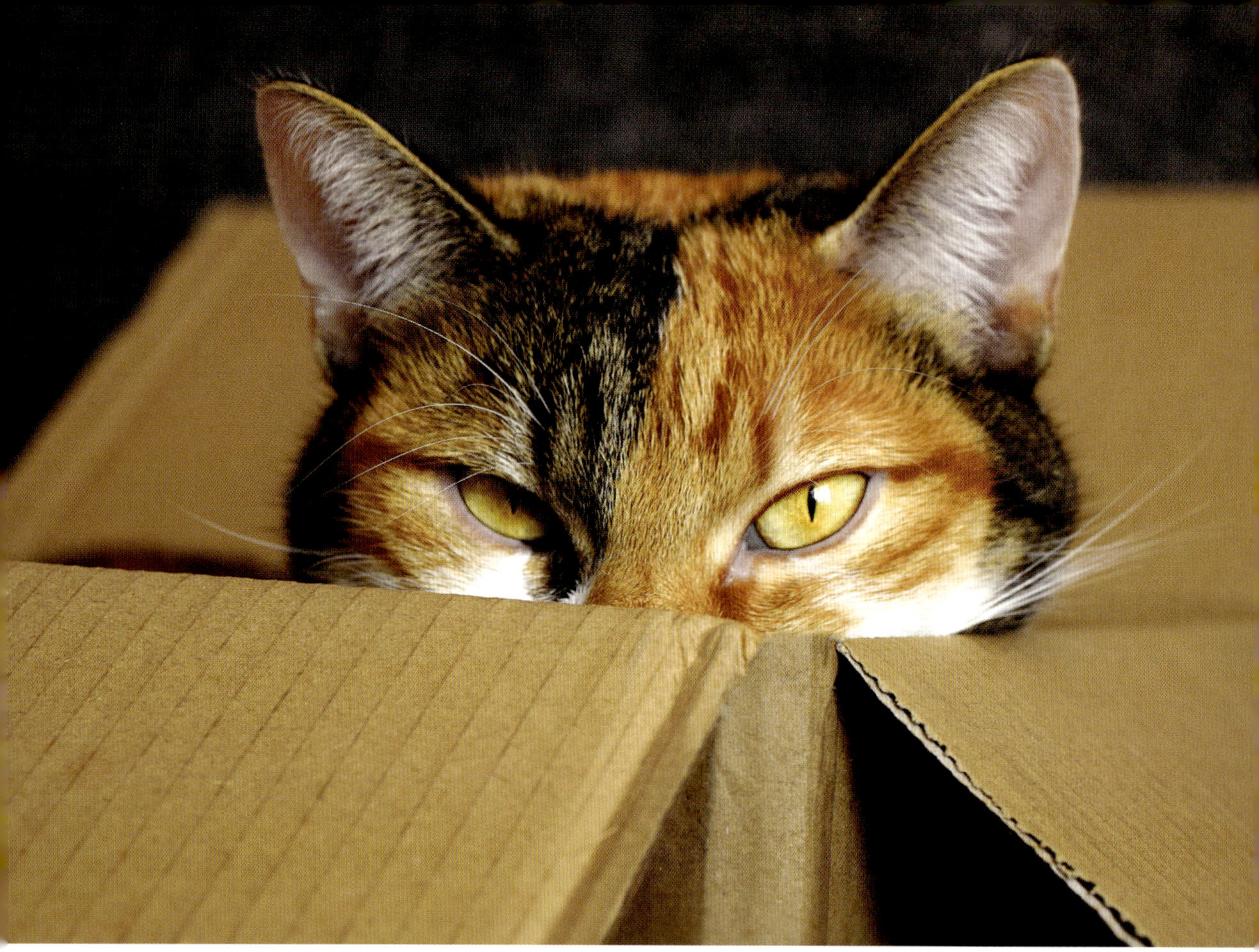
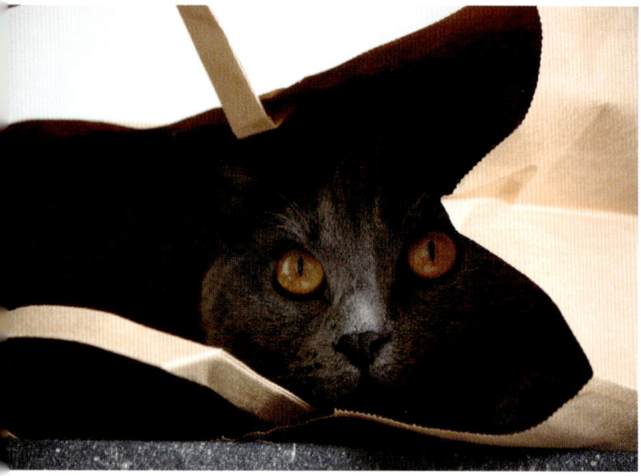
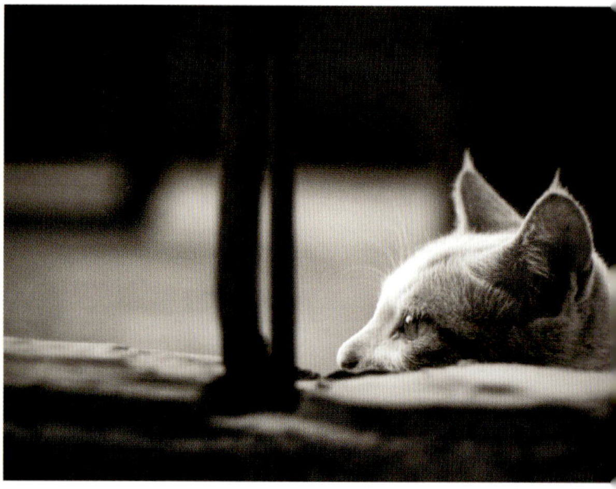
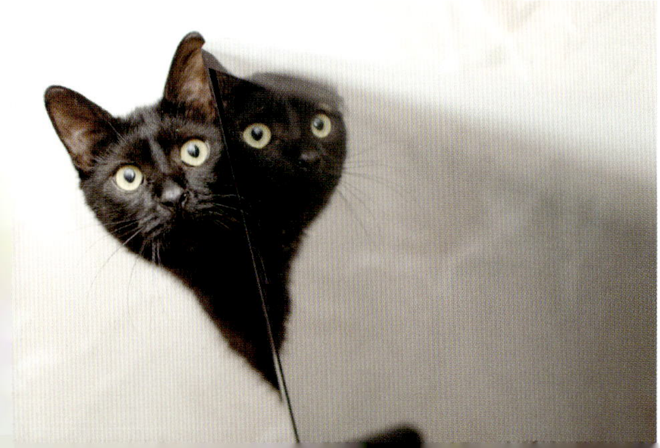
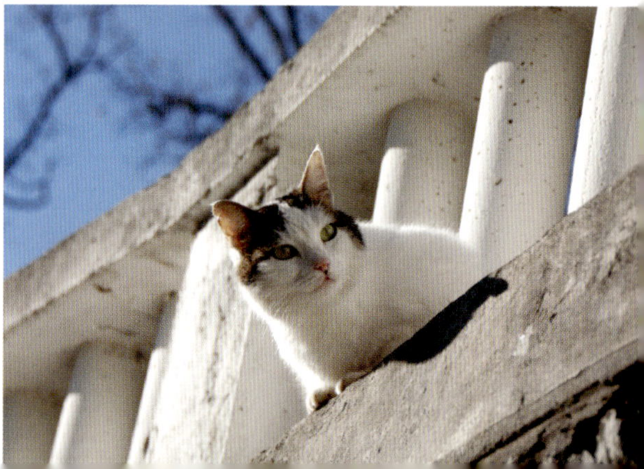

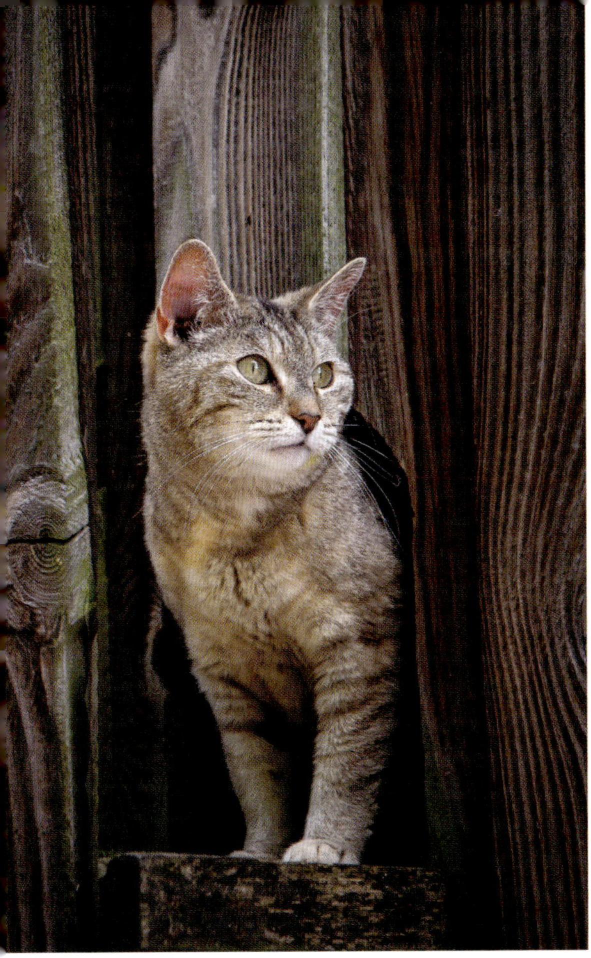
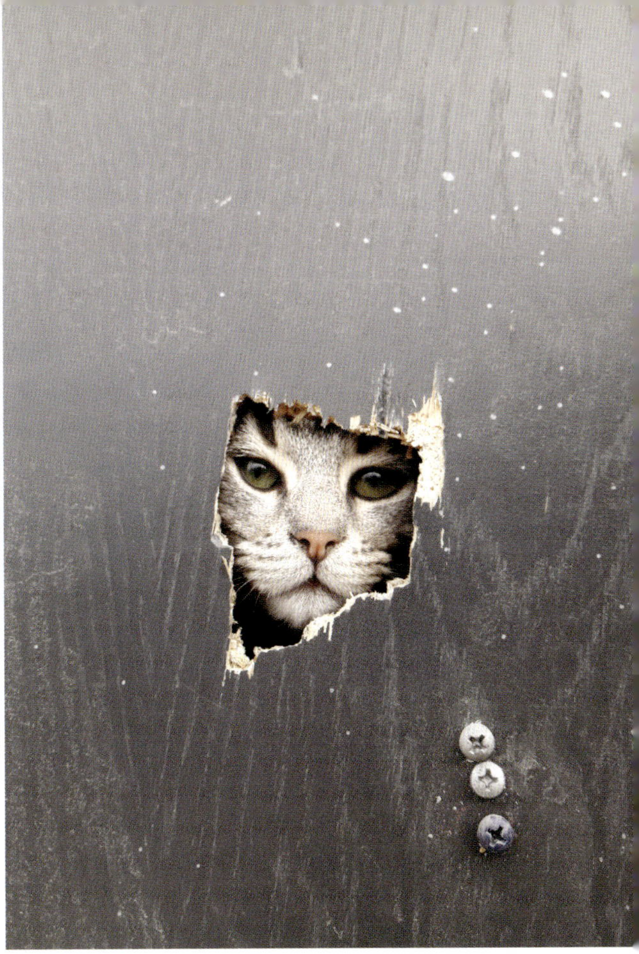
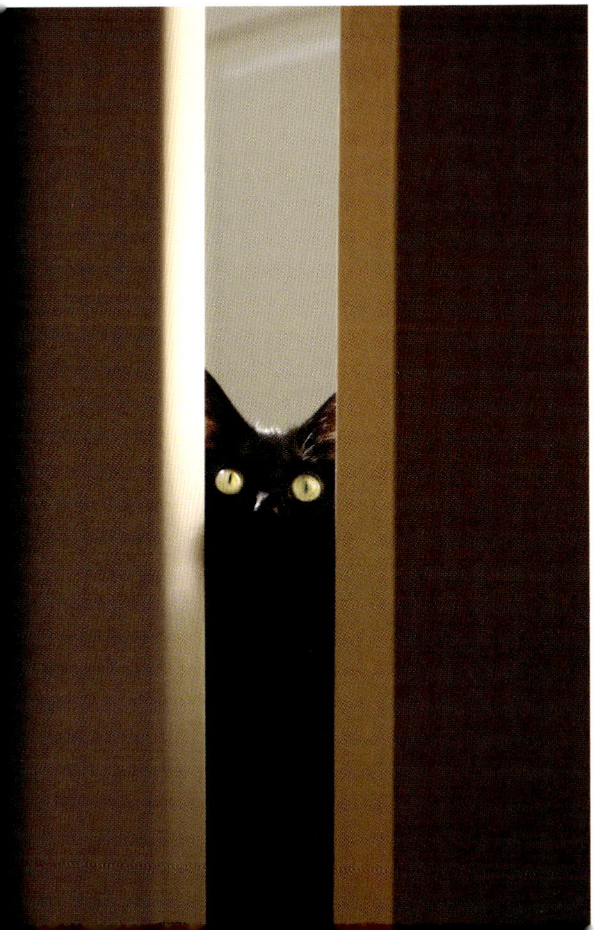
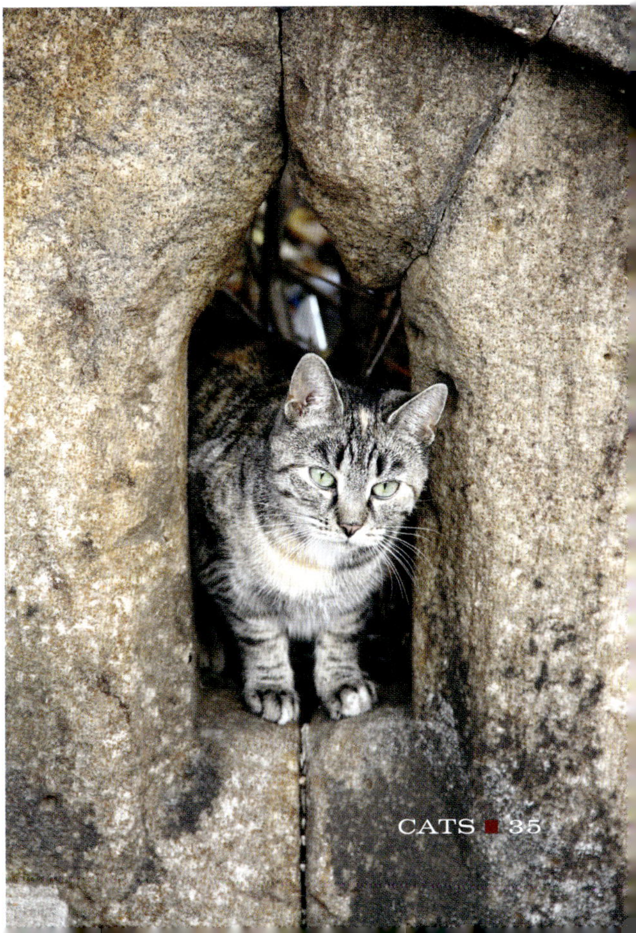

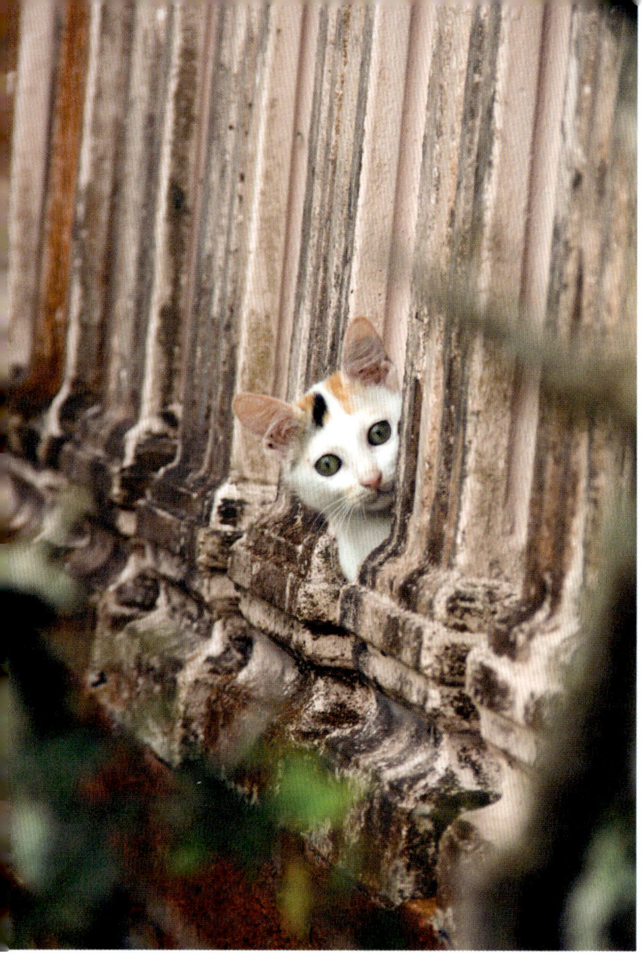
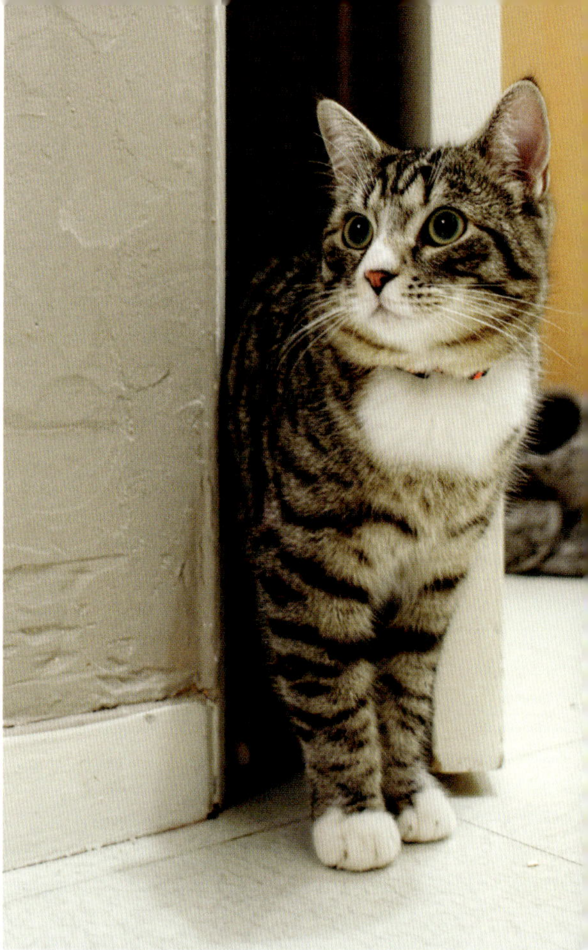
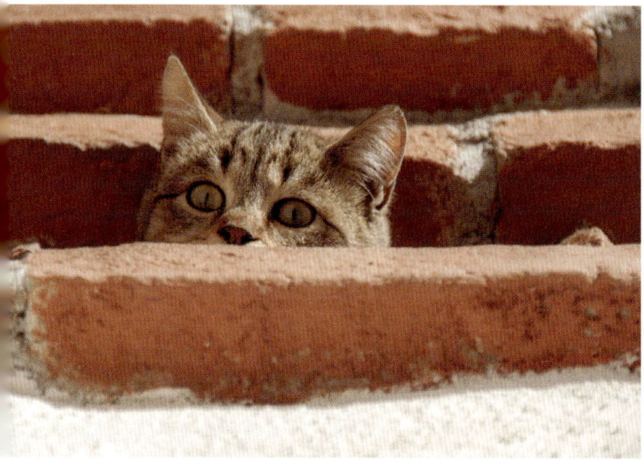
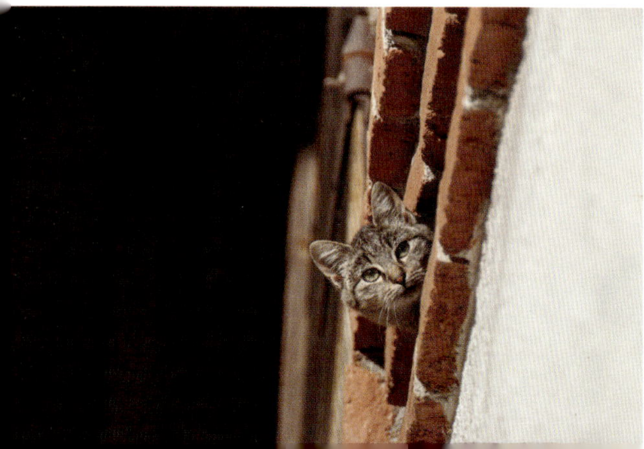
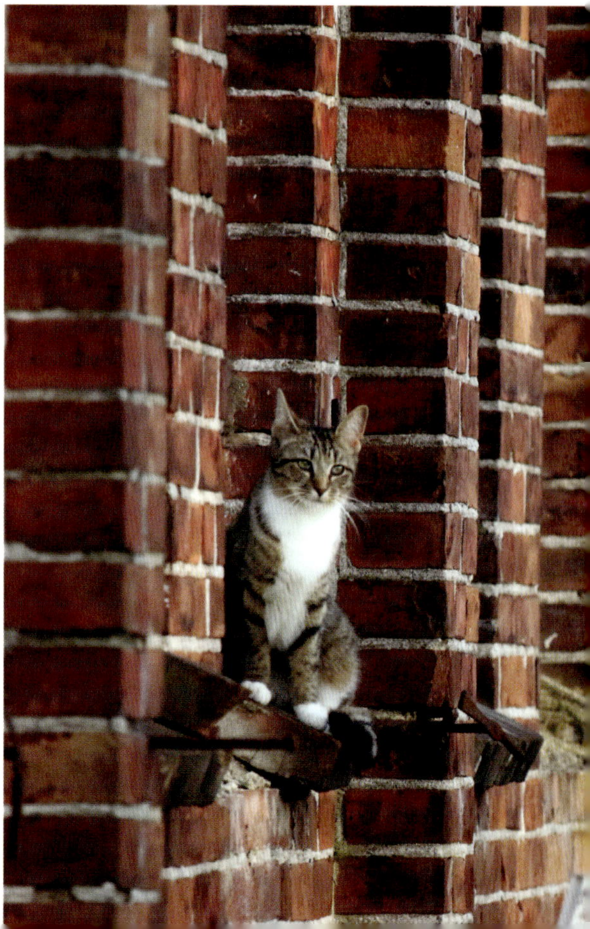

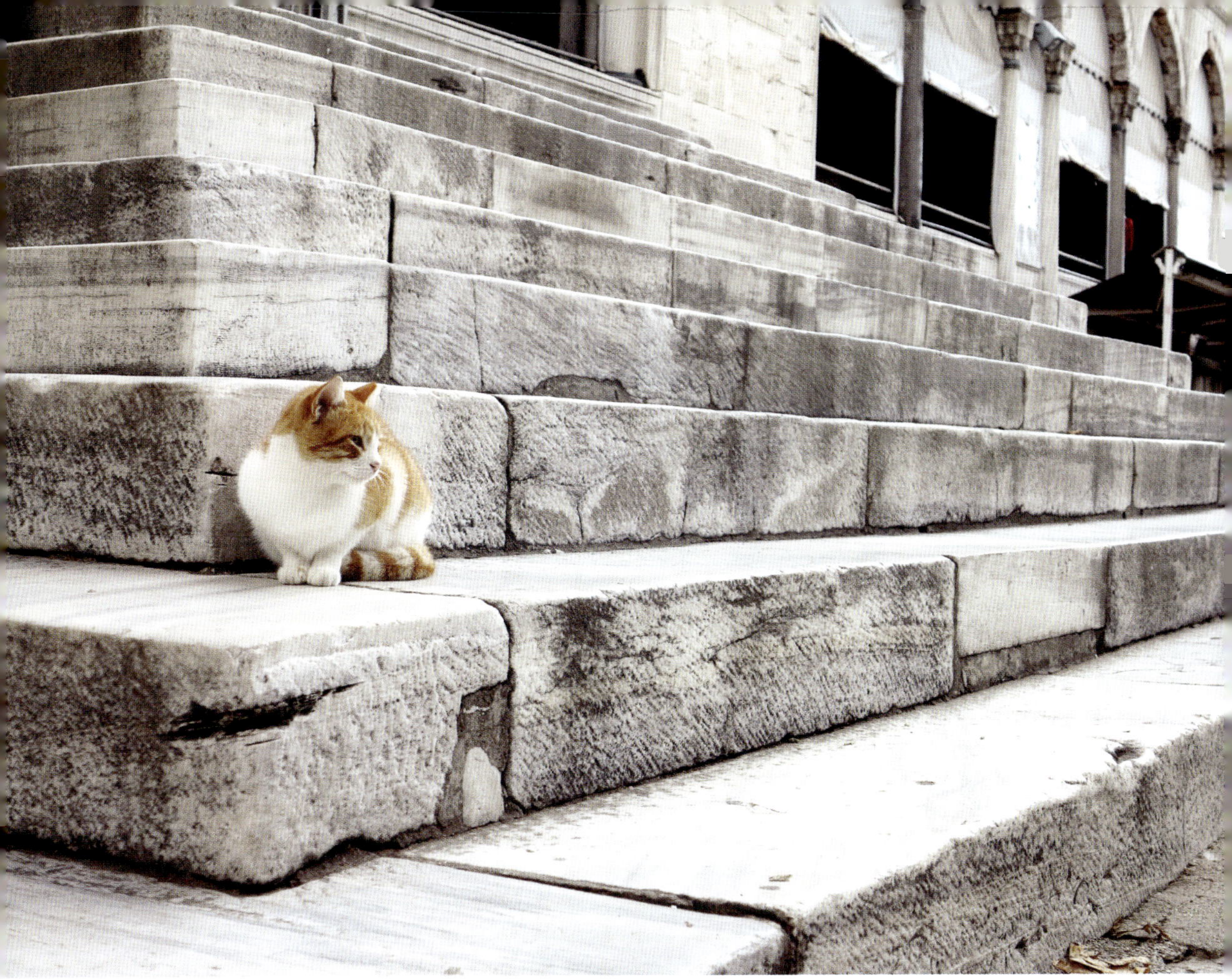

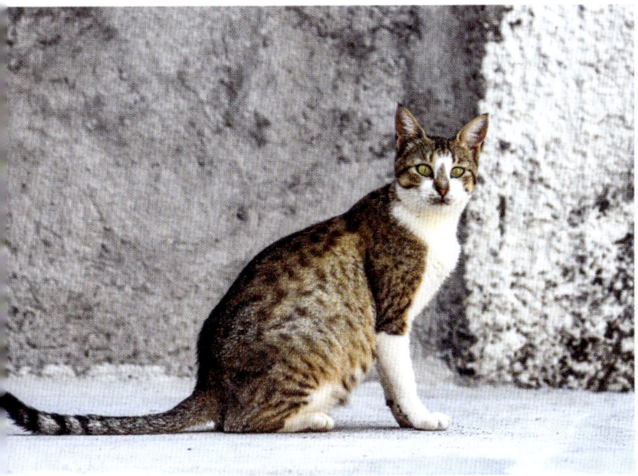

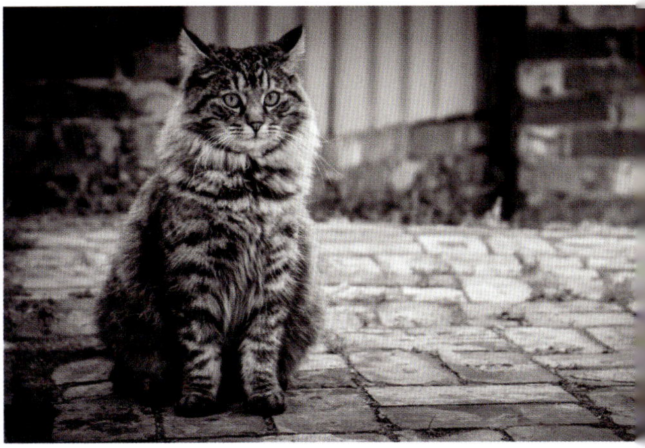

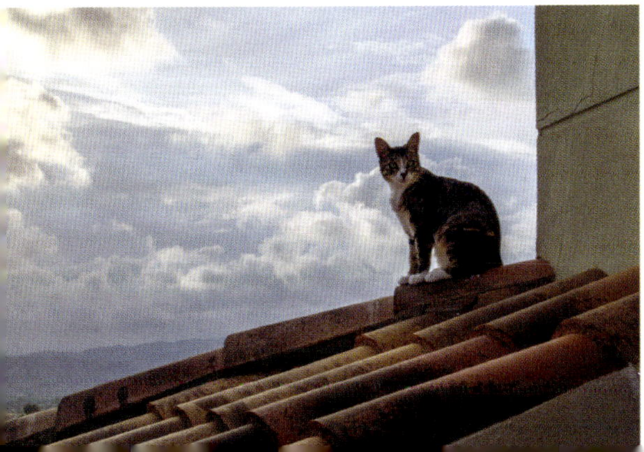

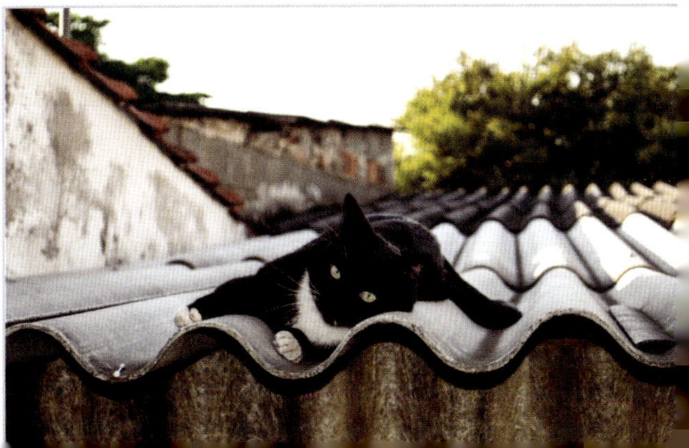

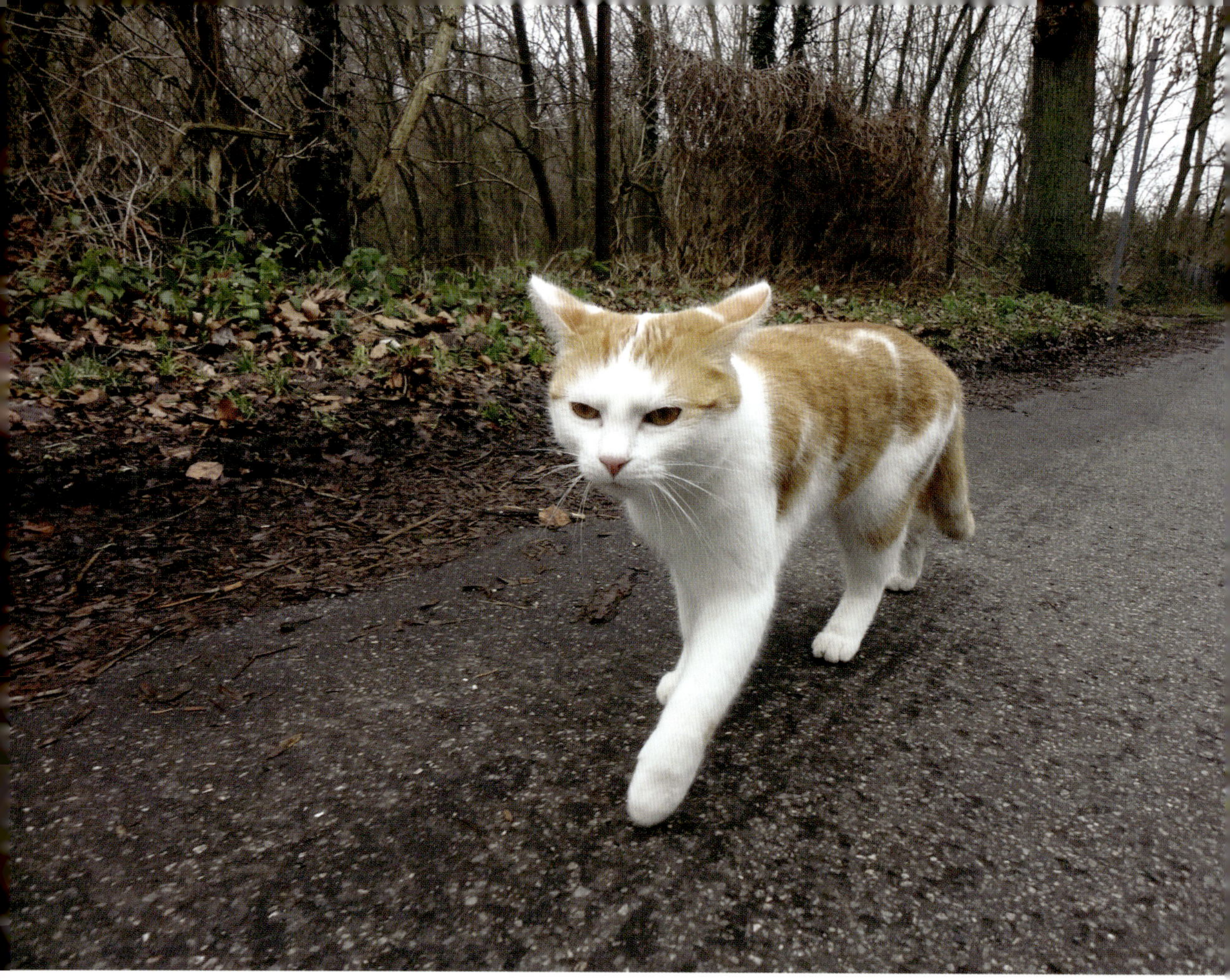
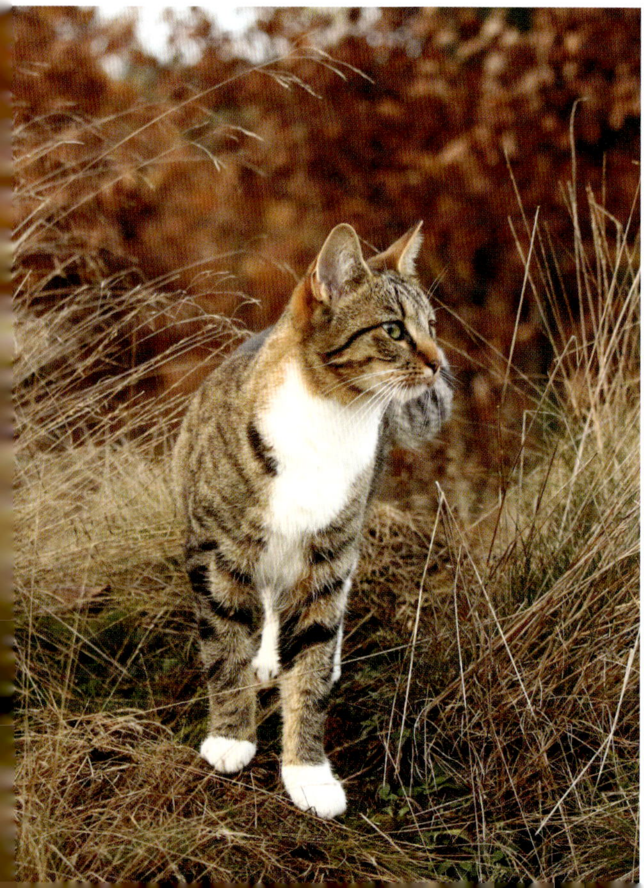
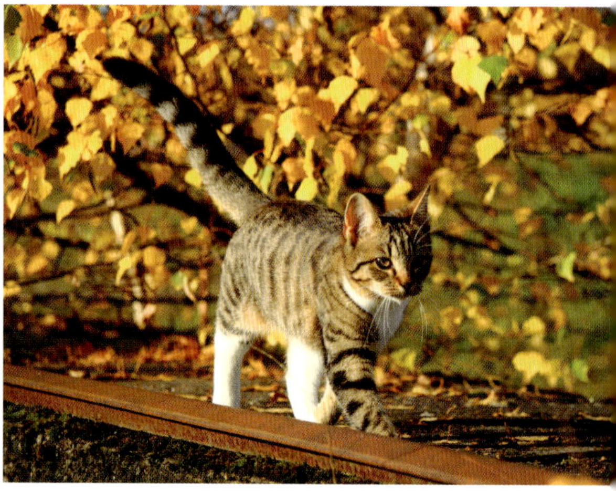
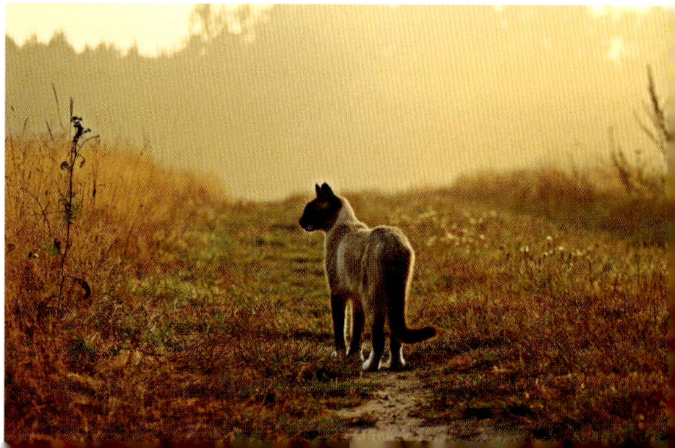

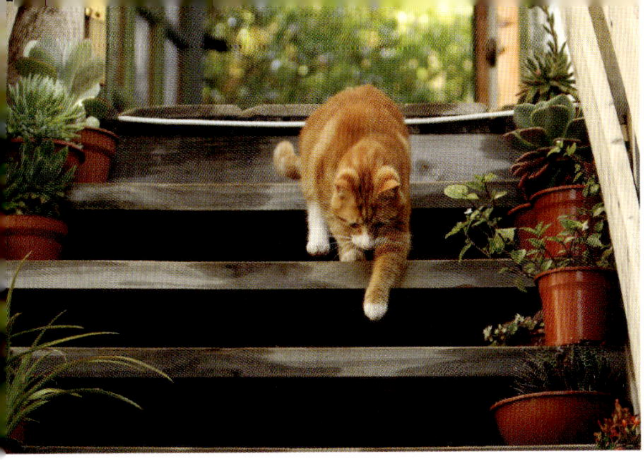
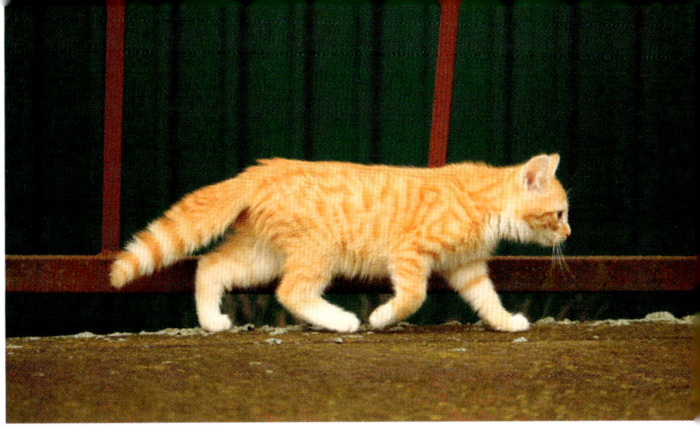
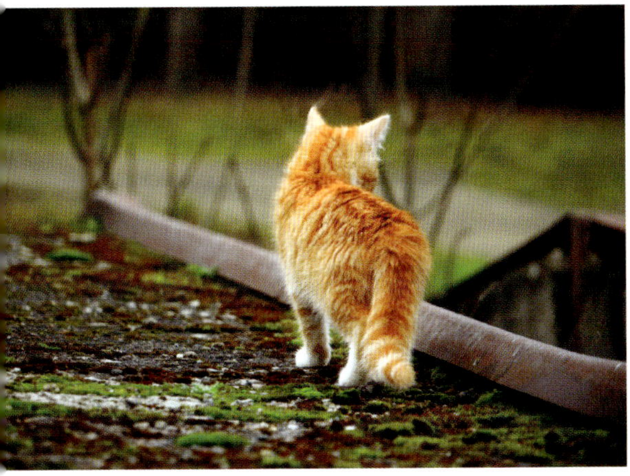
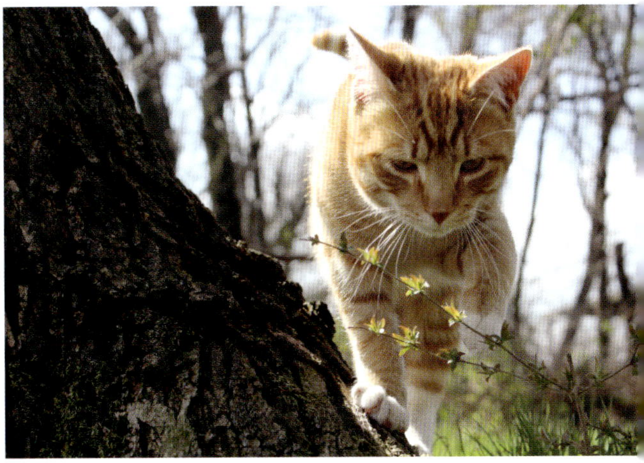
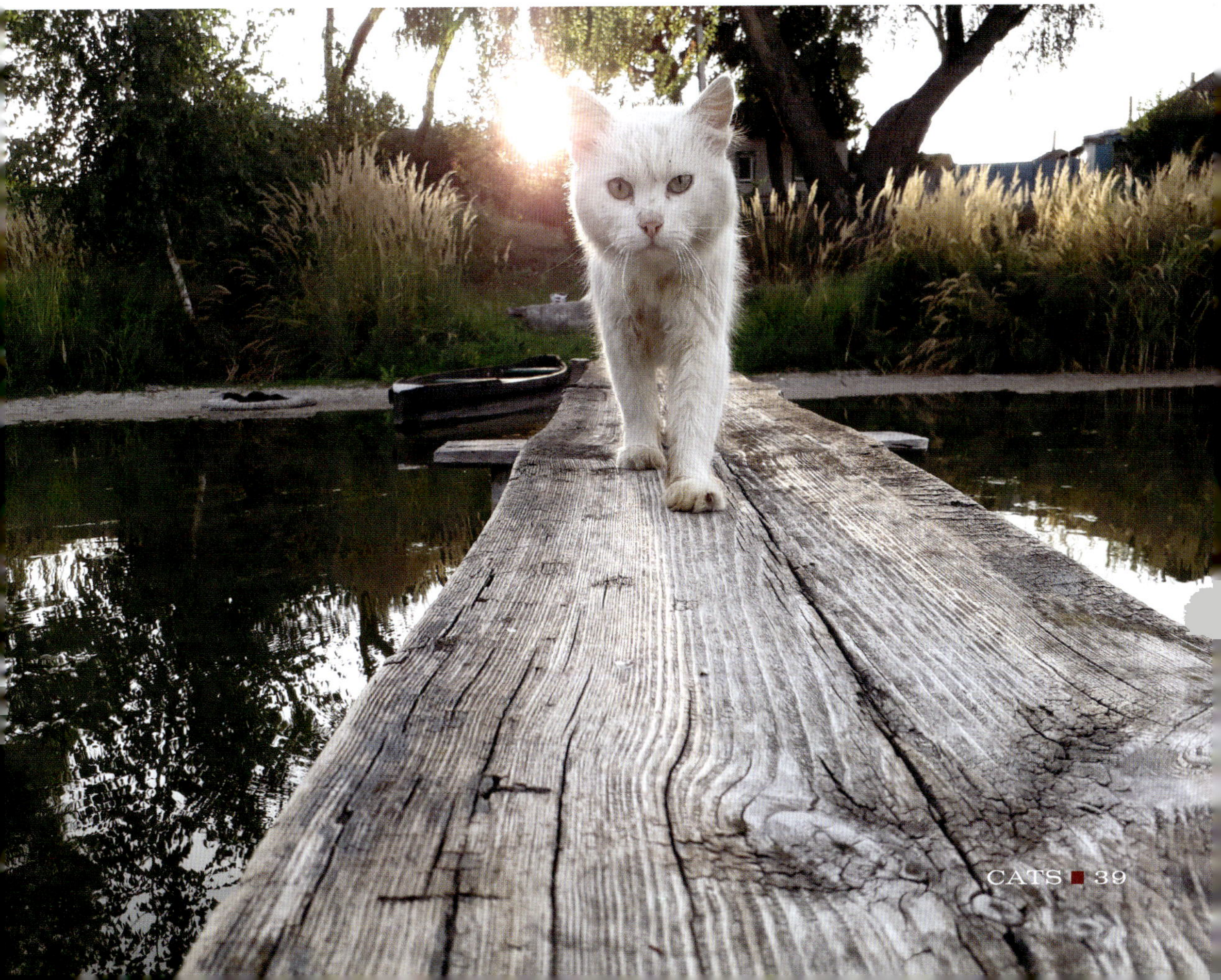

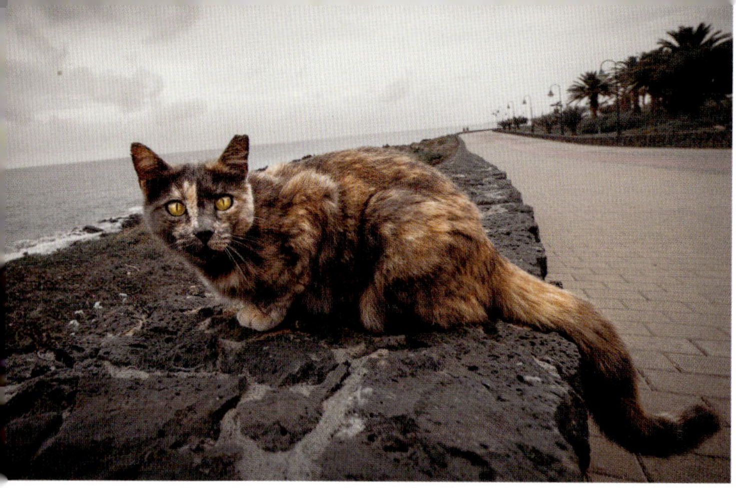
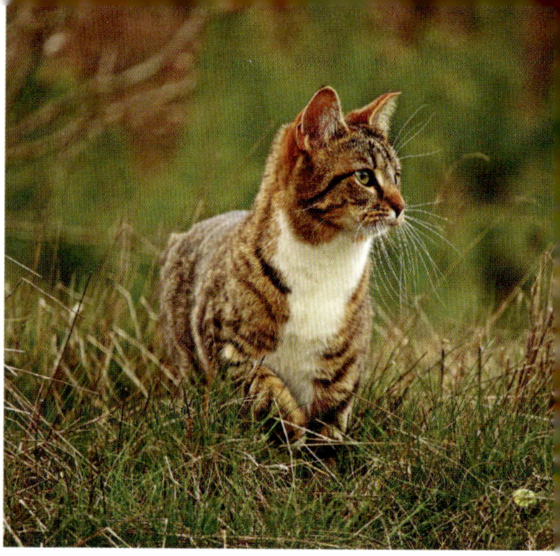
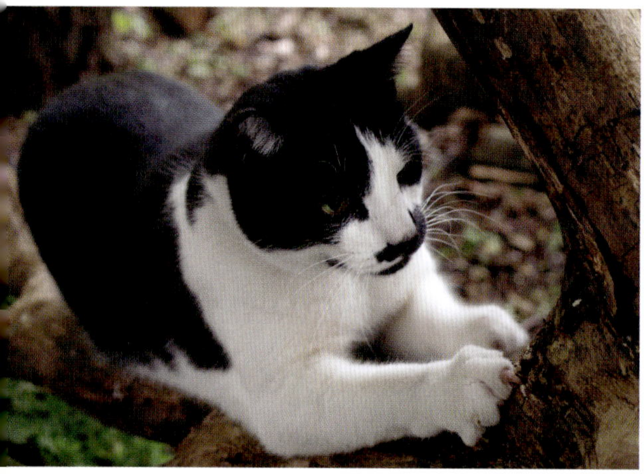
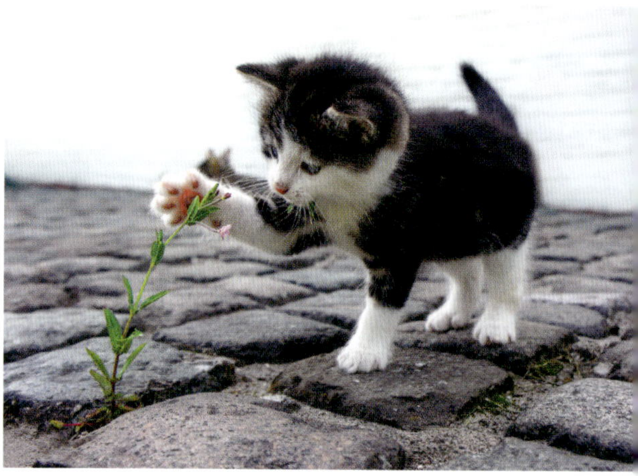
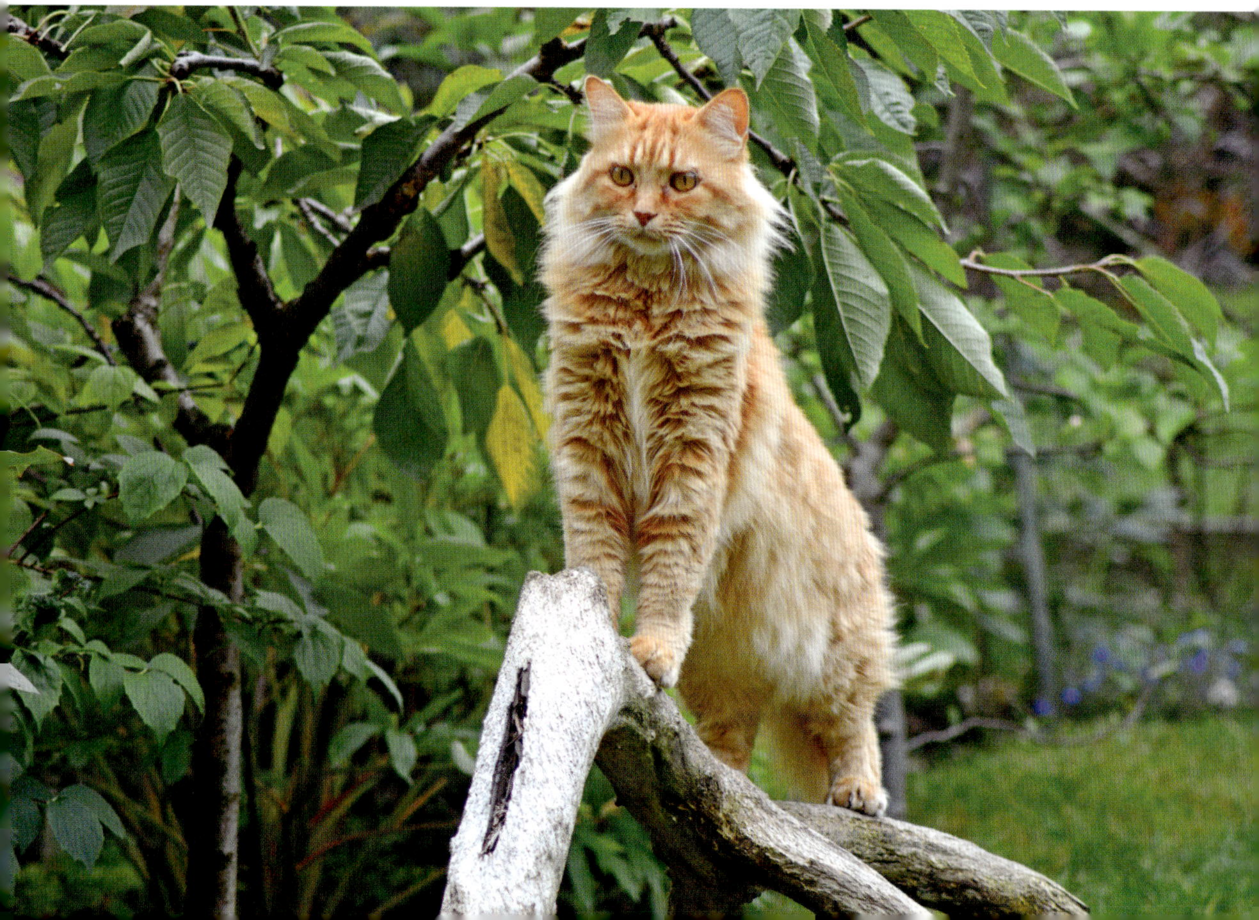

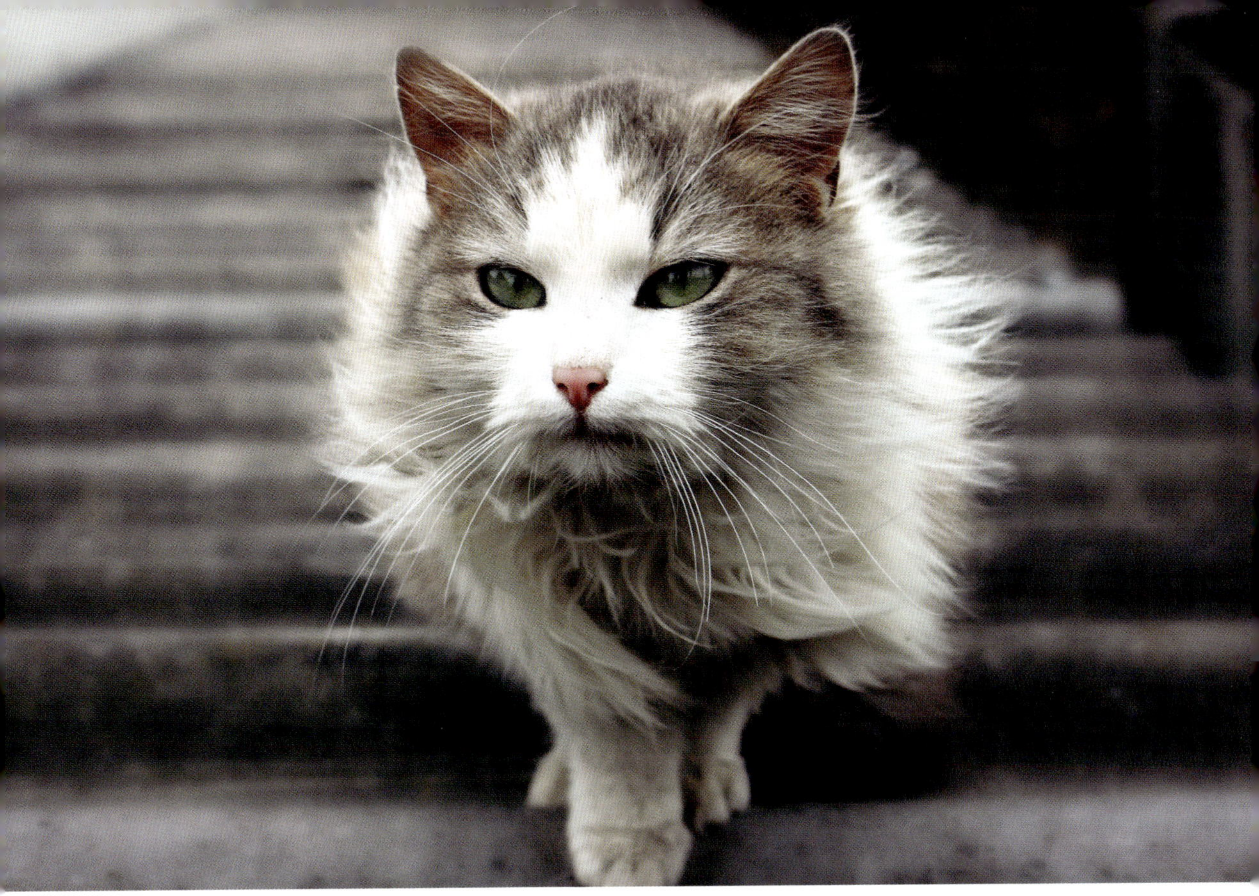

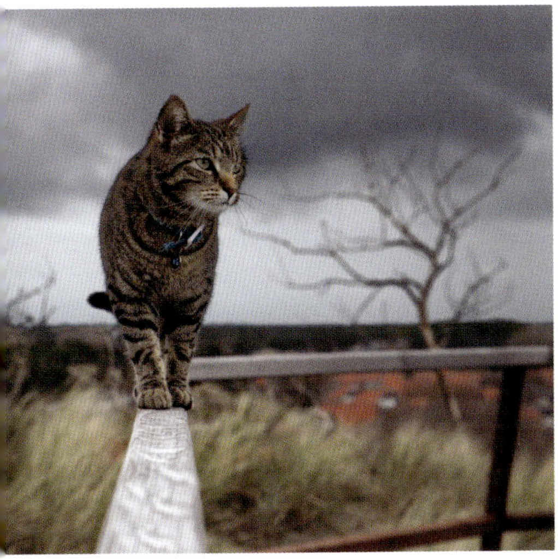

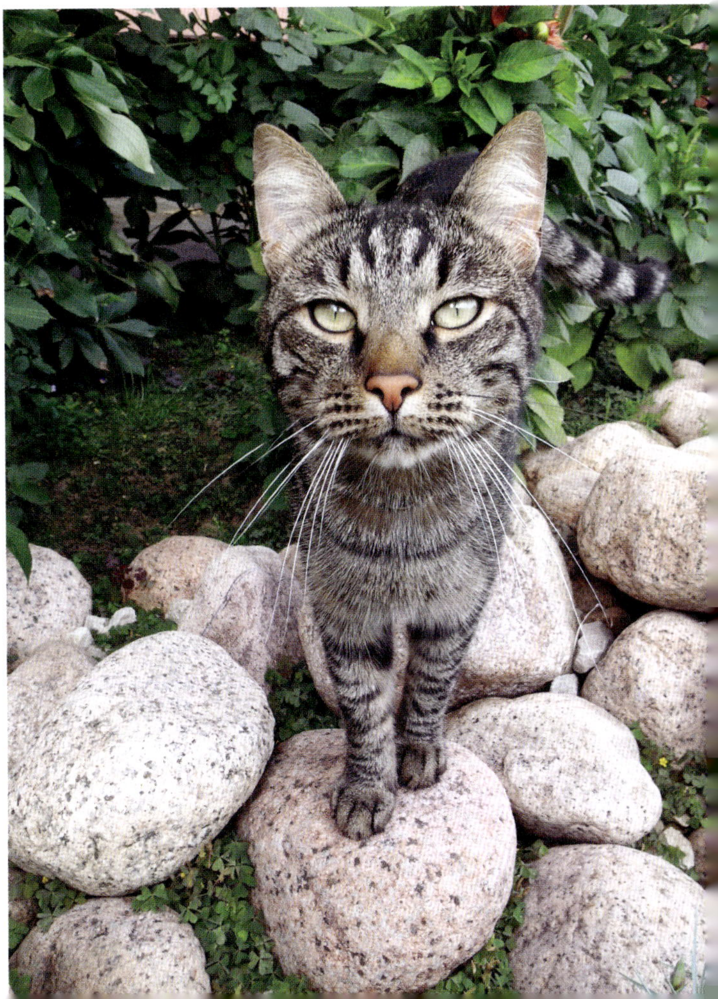

“There are two means of refuge from the miseries of life: music and cats.”

—Albert Schweitzer, theologian and humanitarian

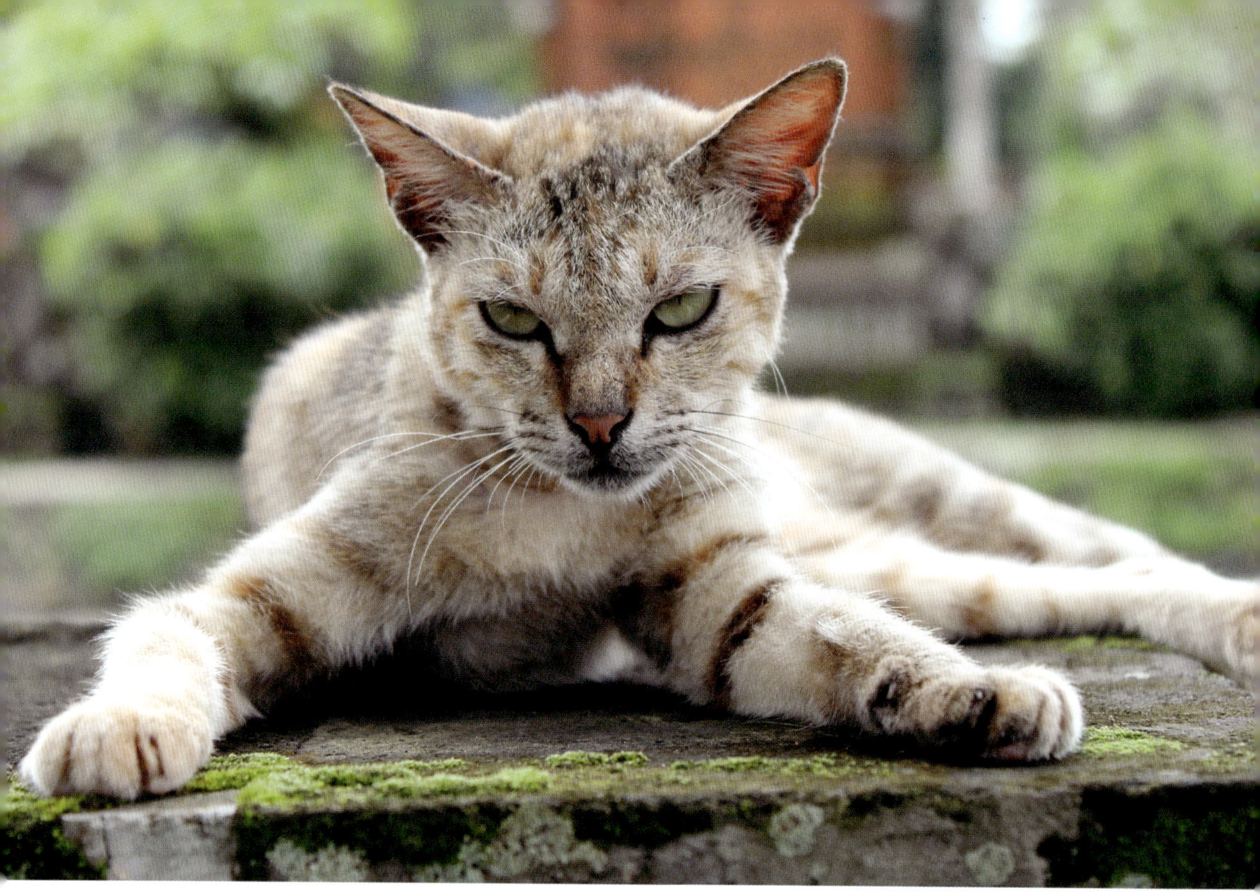

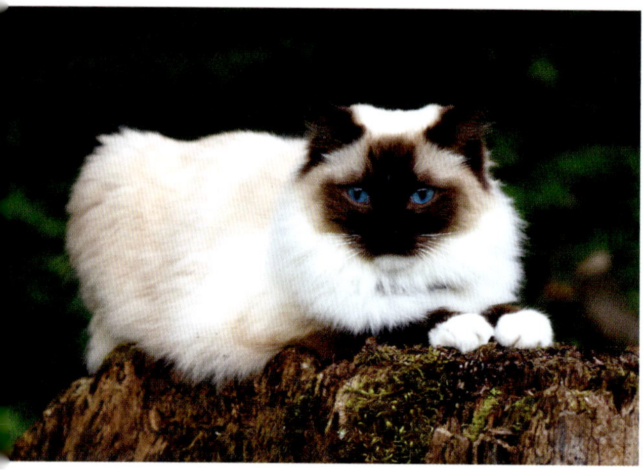

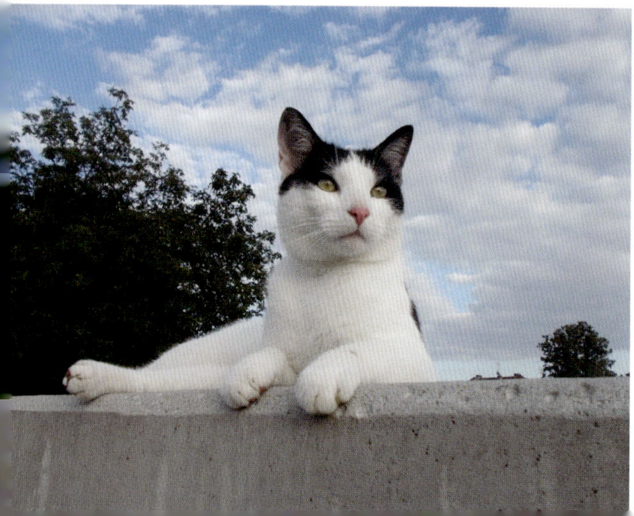

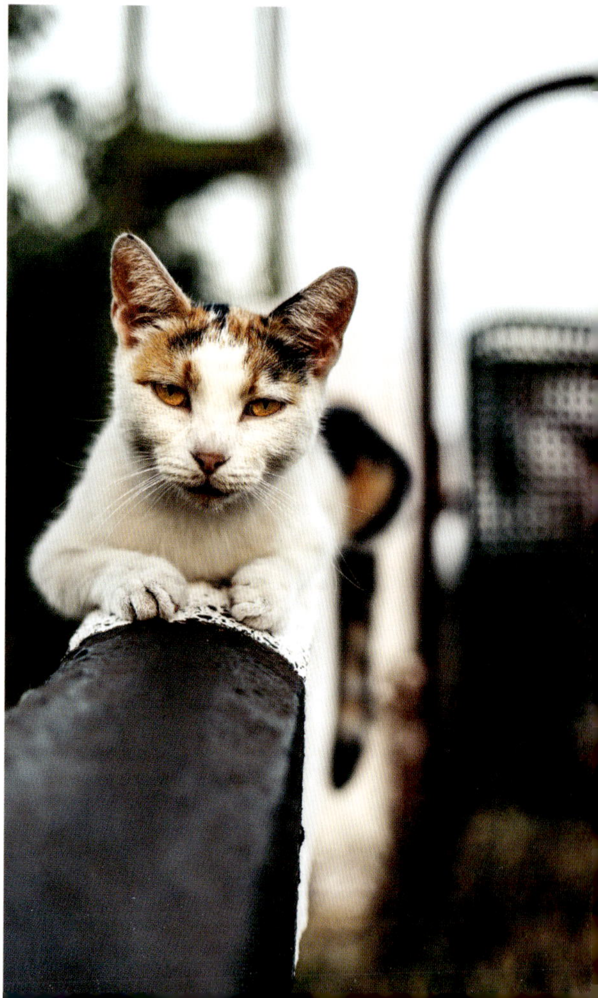

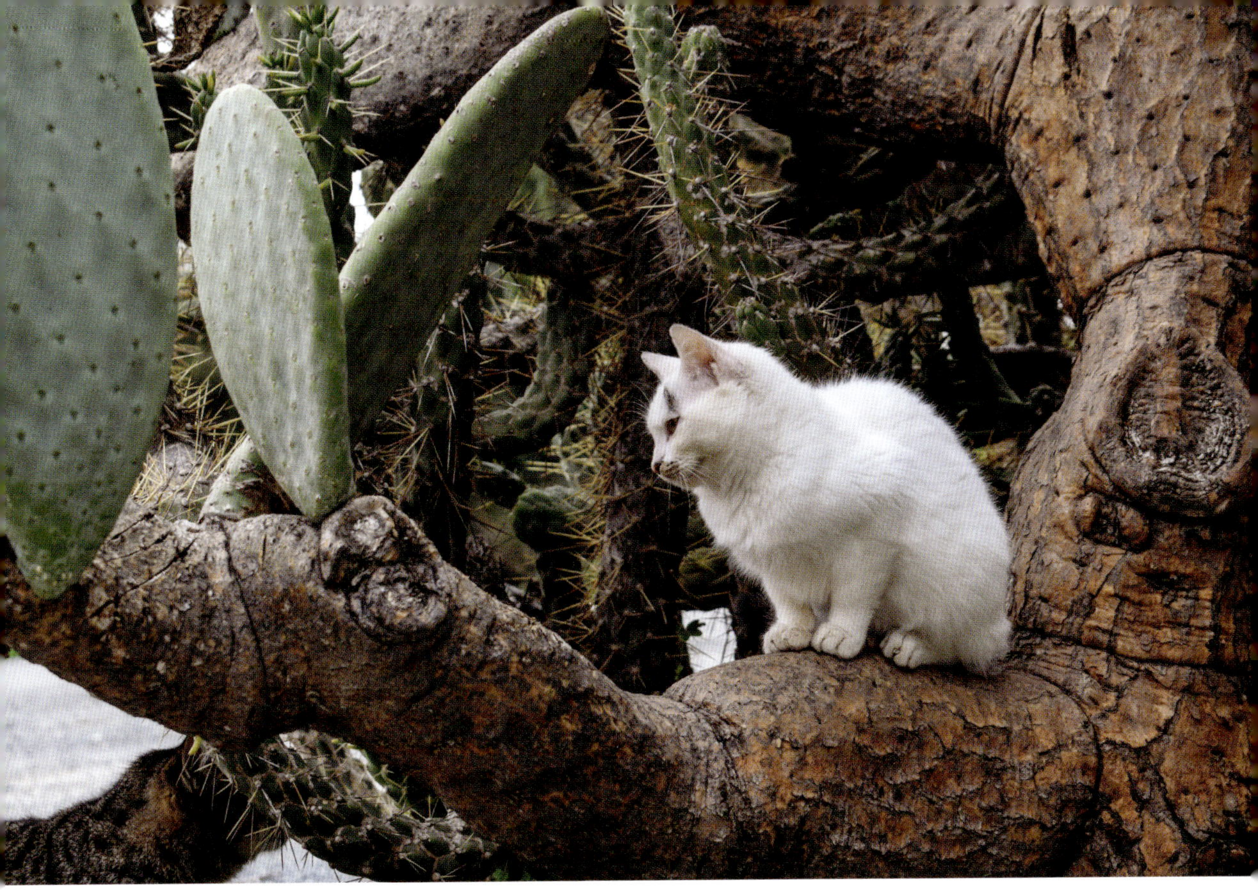
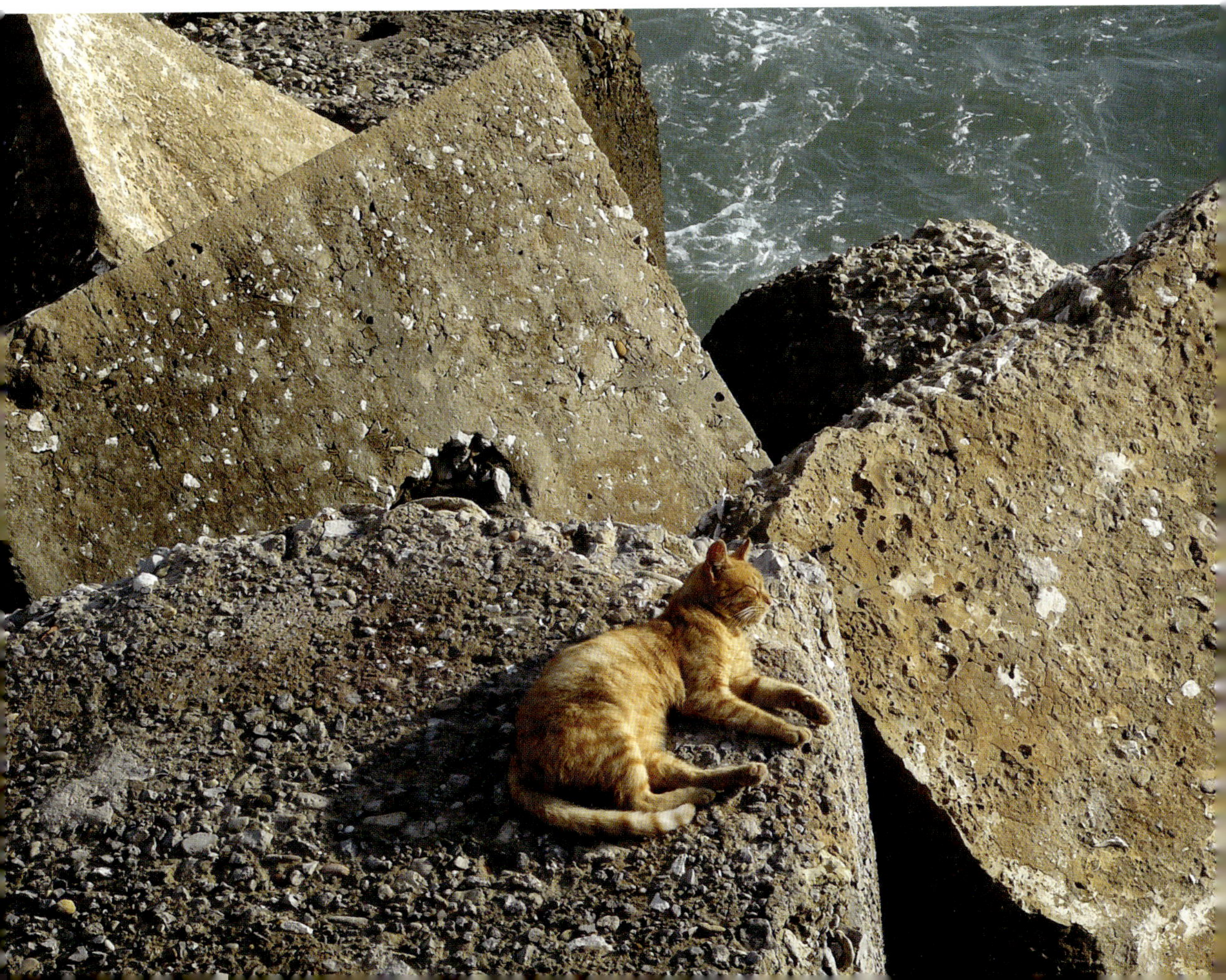

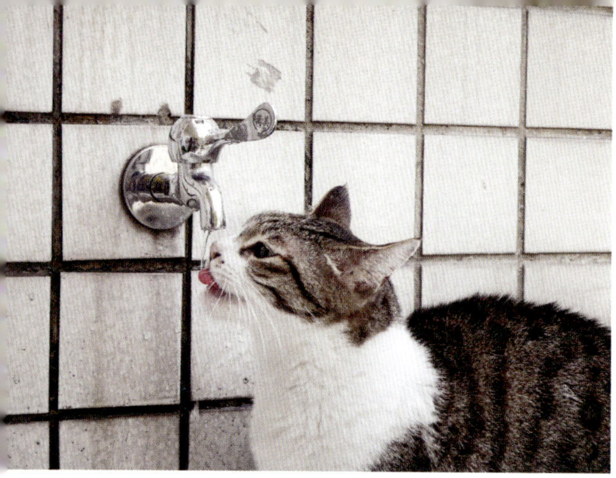
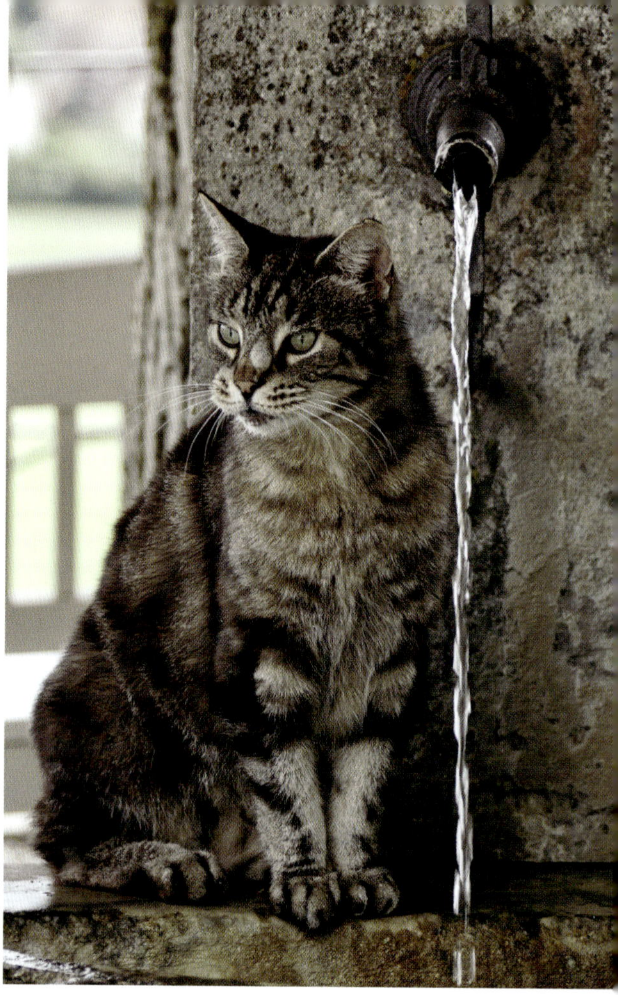
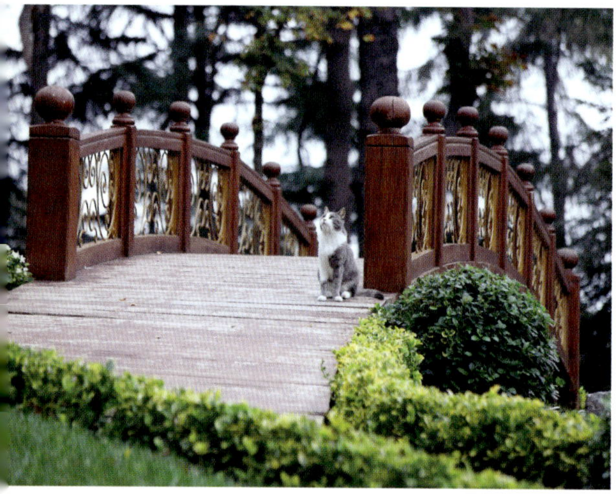
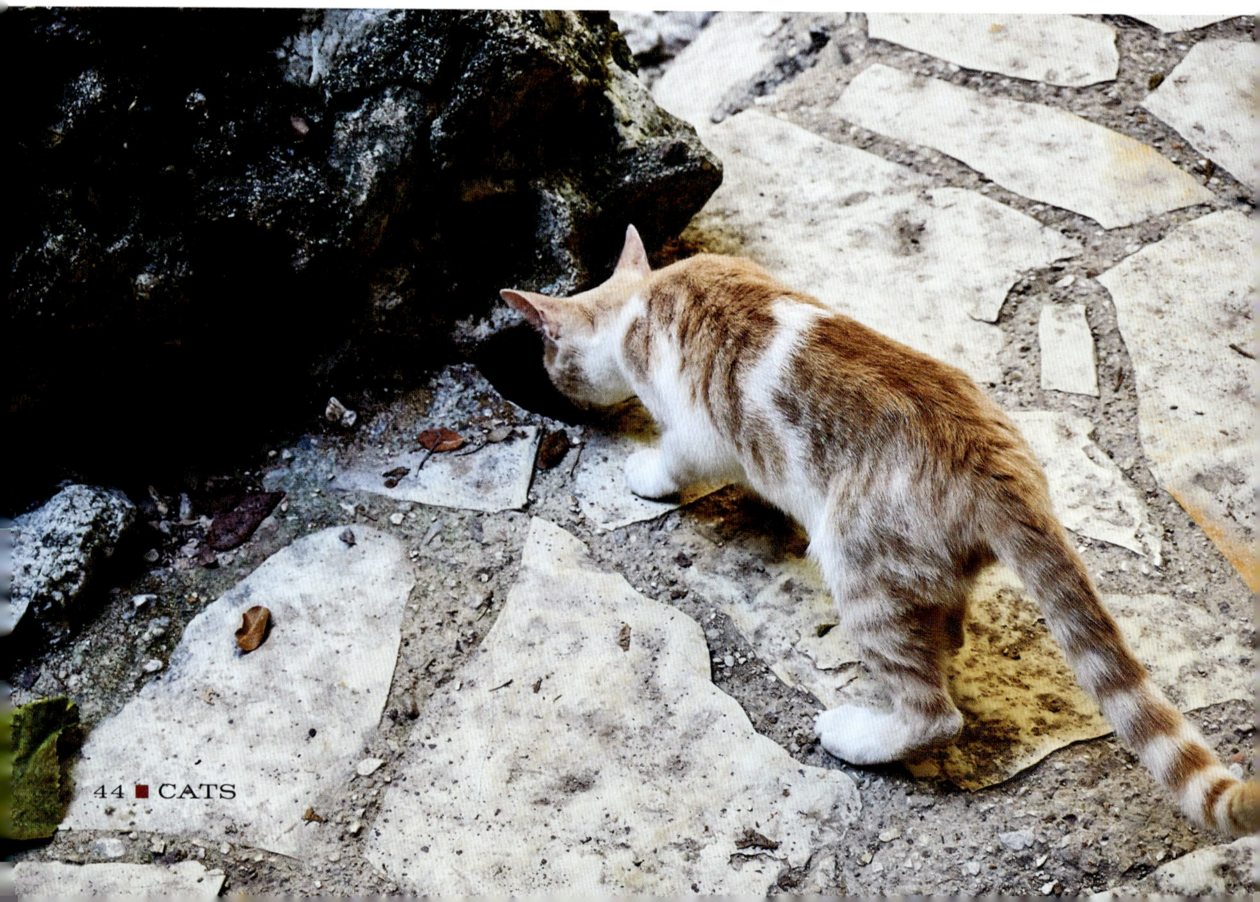

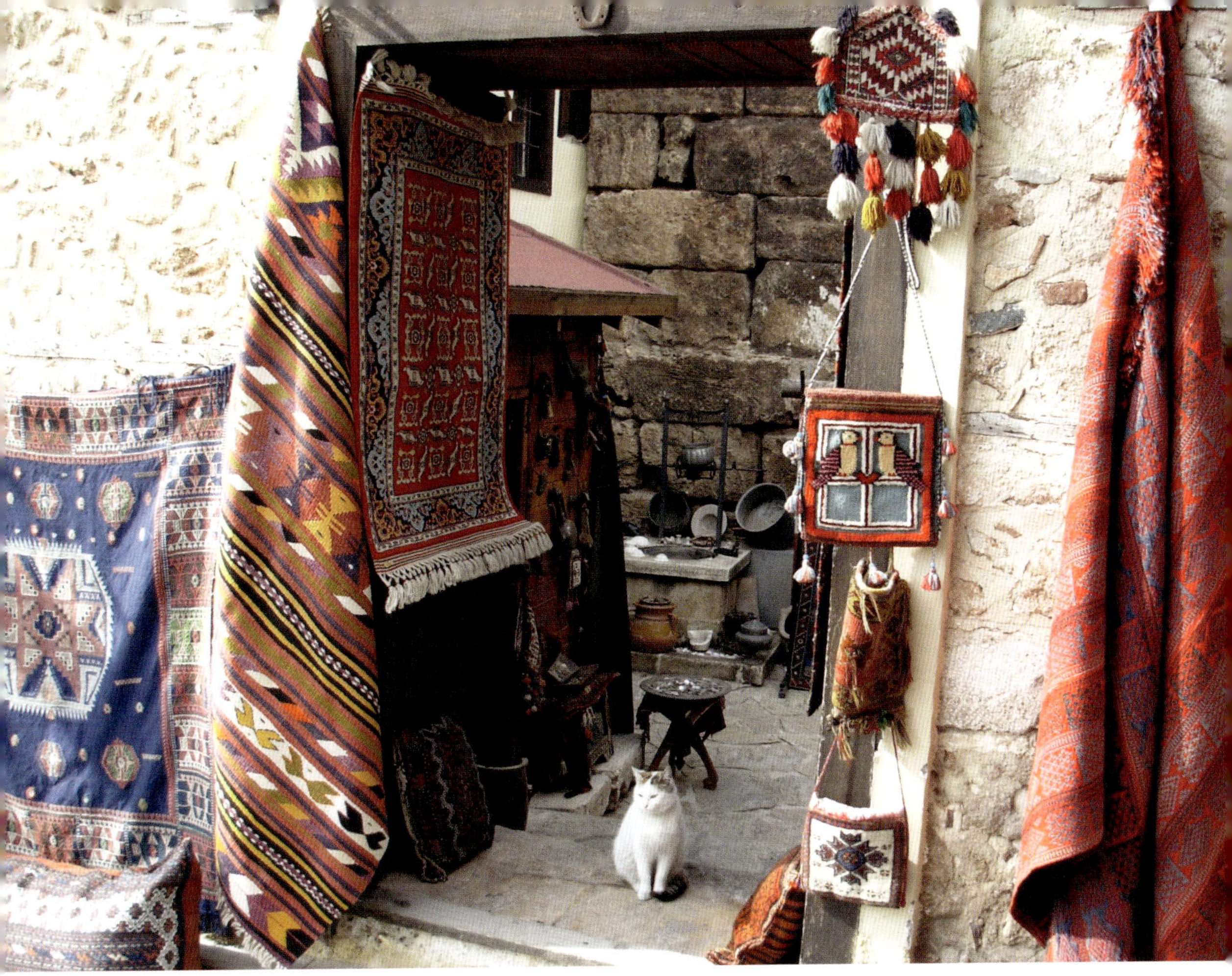

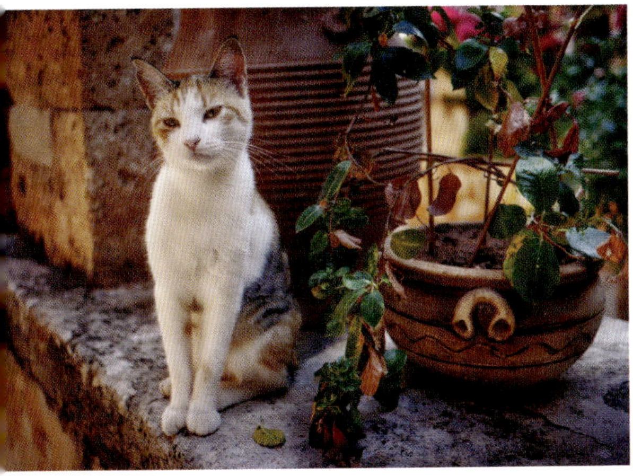

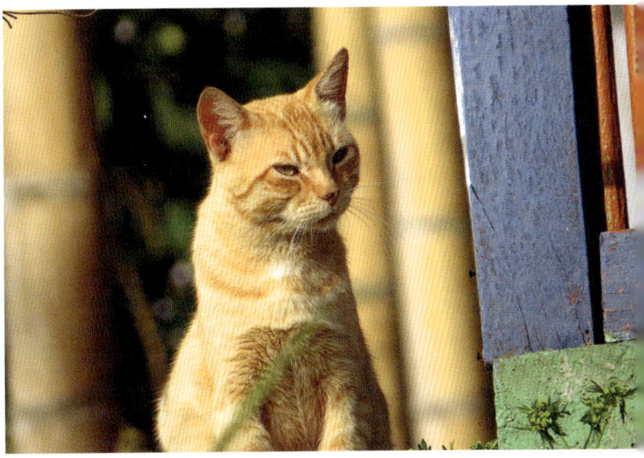

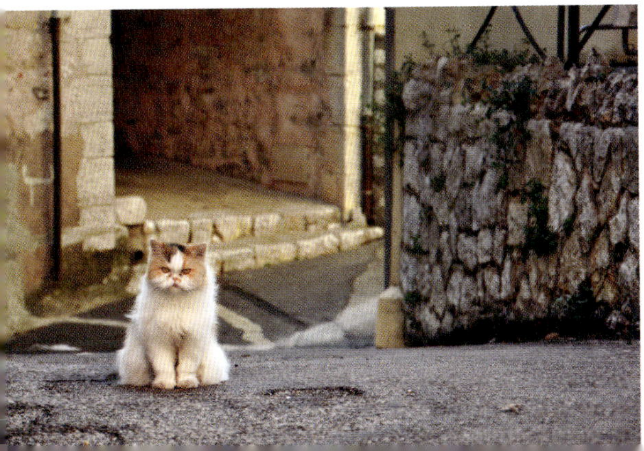

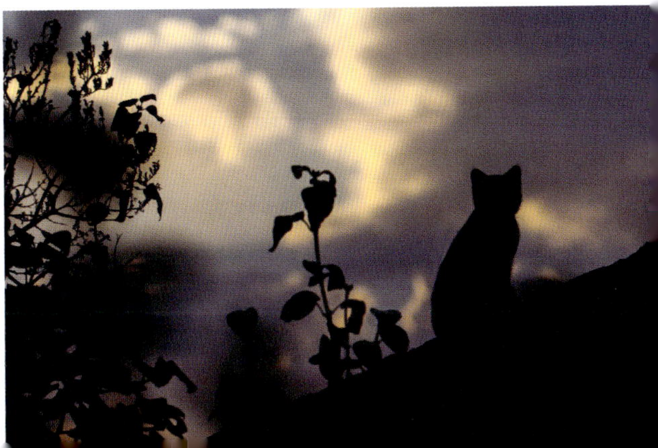

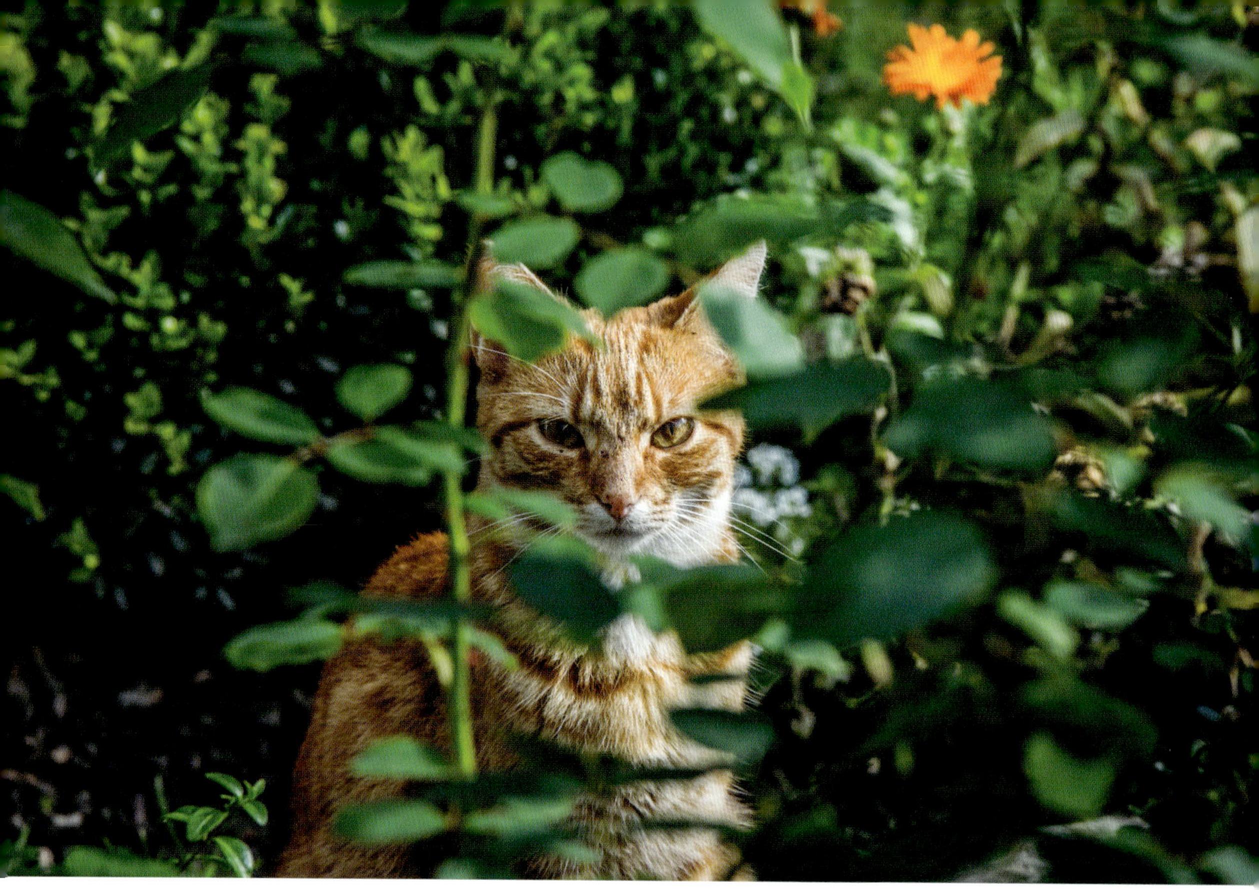
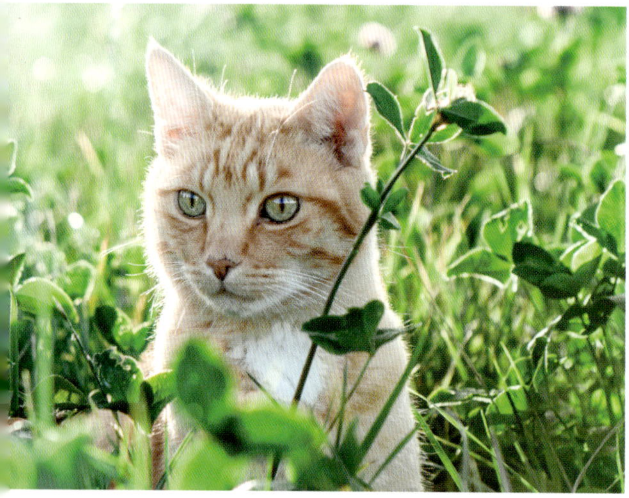
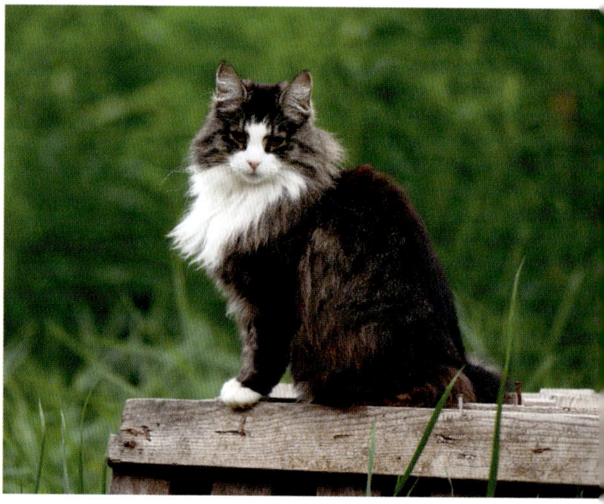
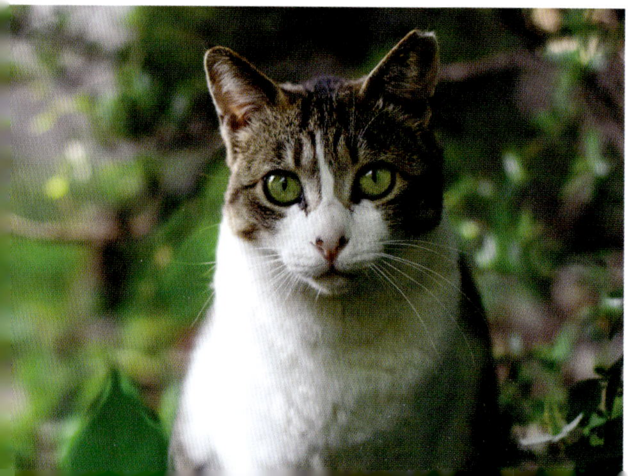
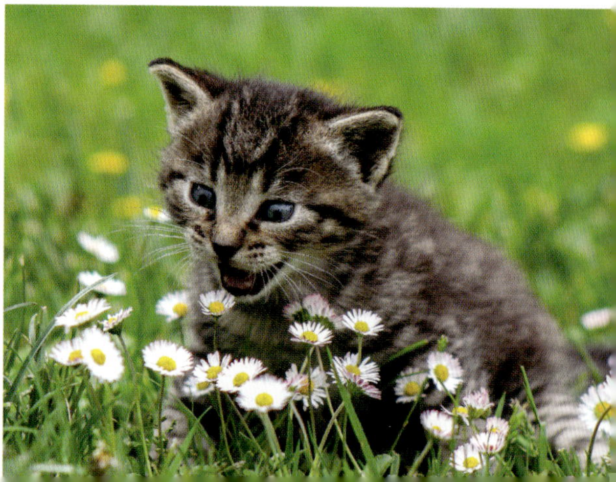

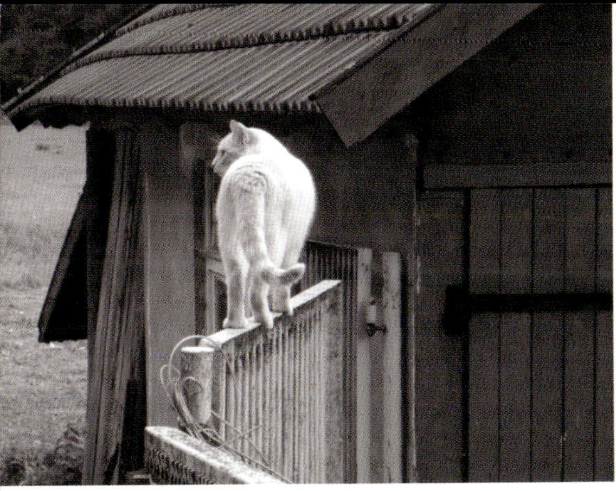
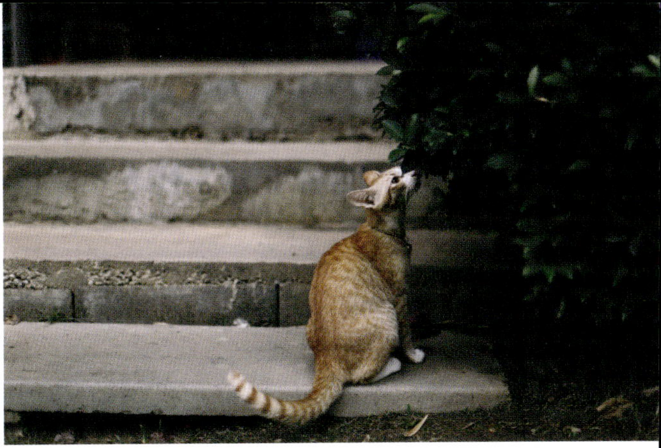
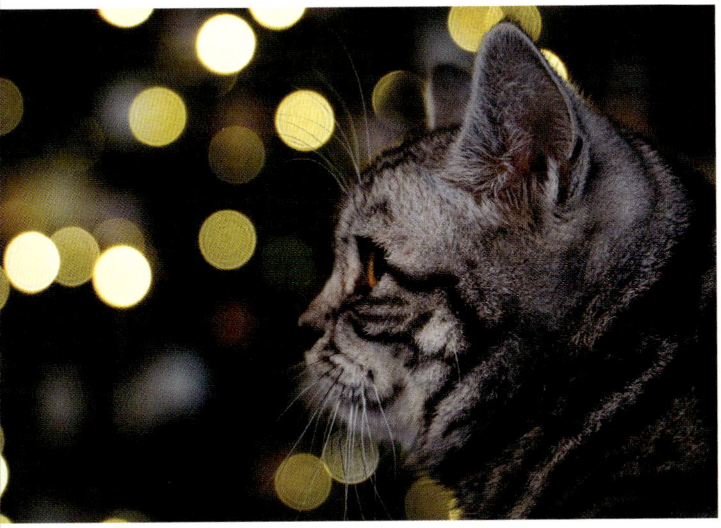
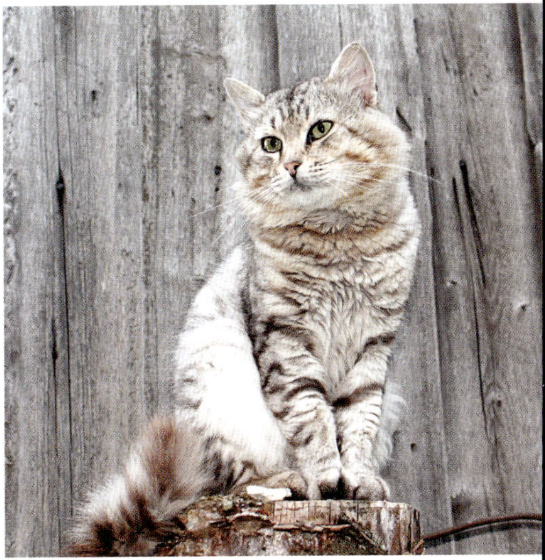
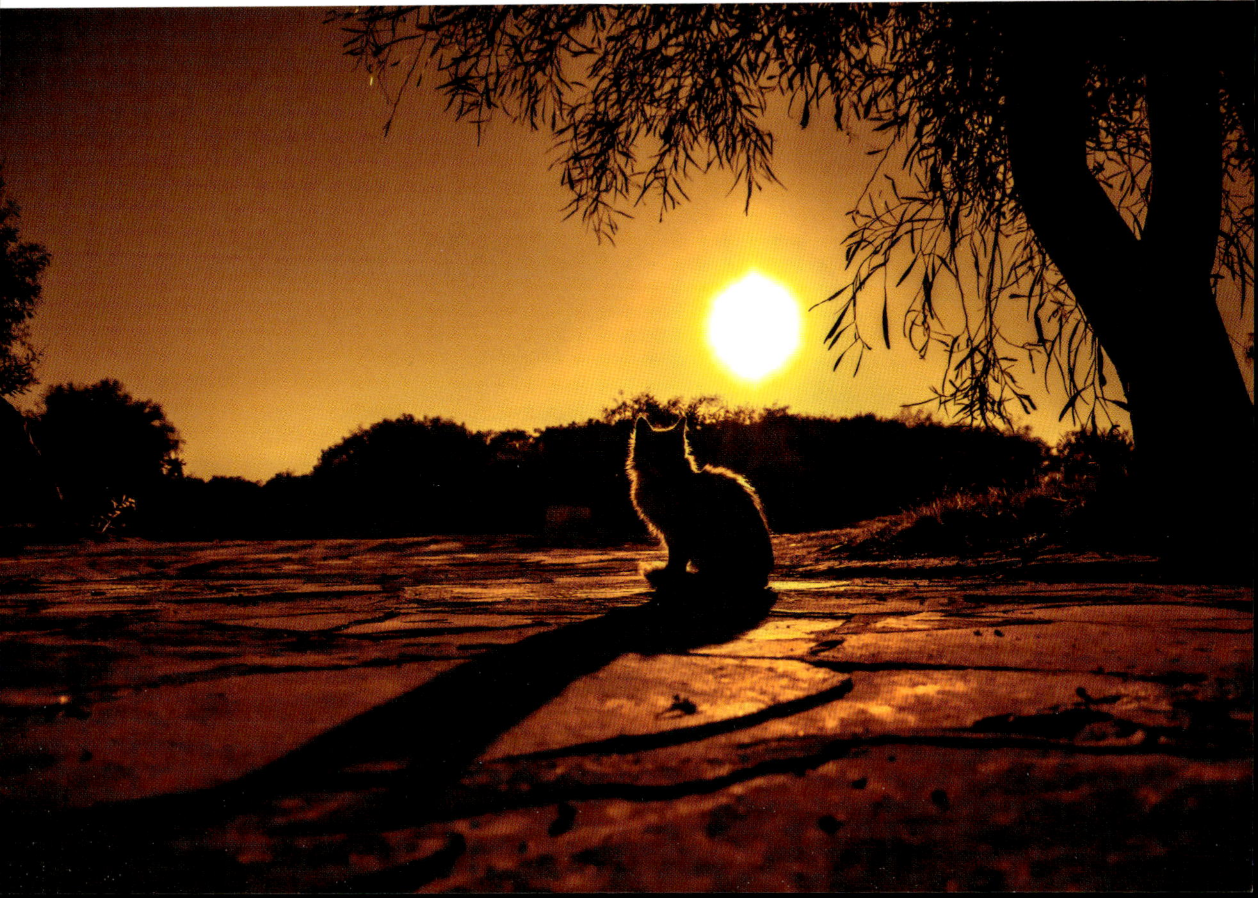

5. Action!

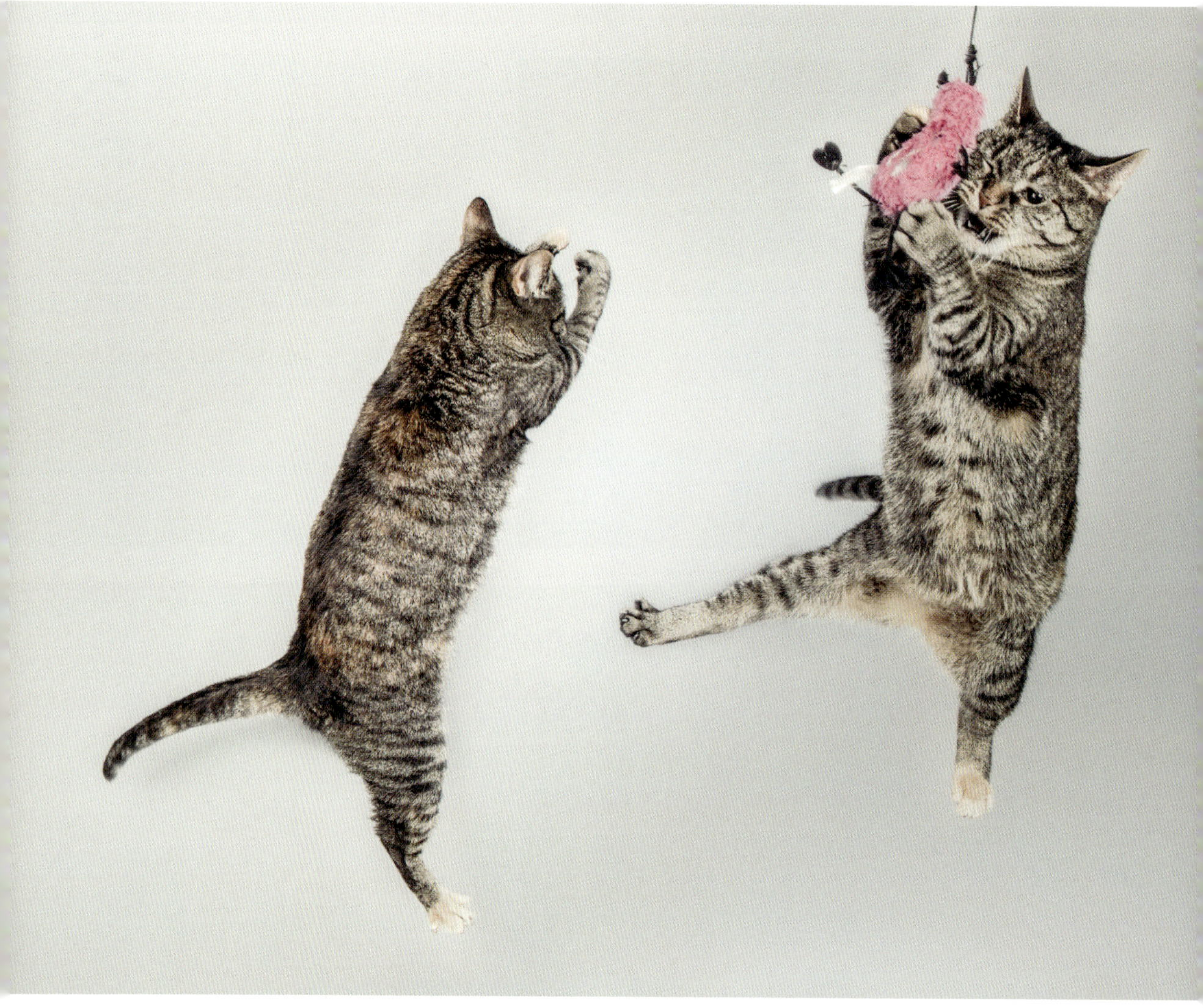

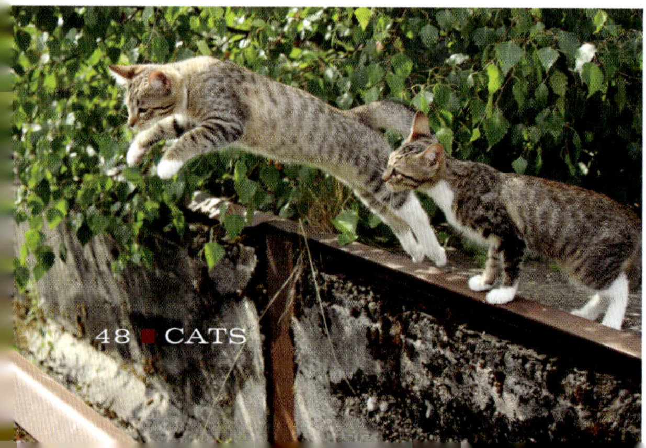

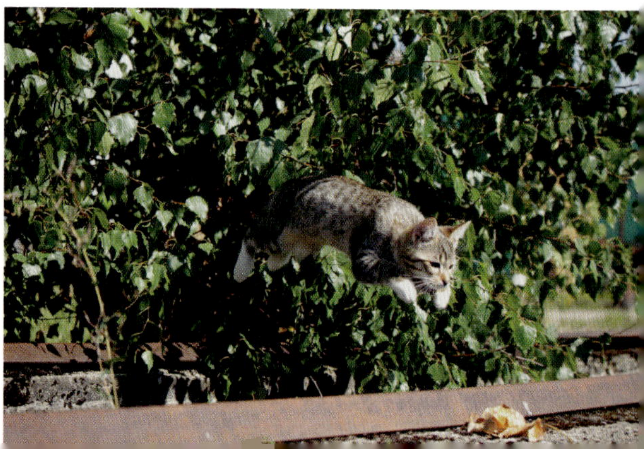

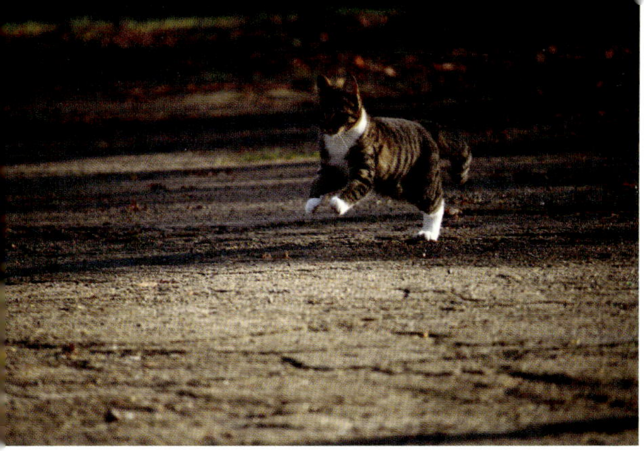
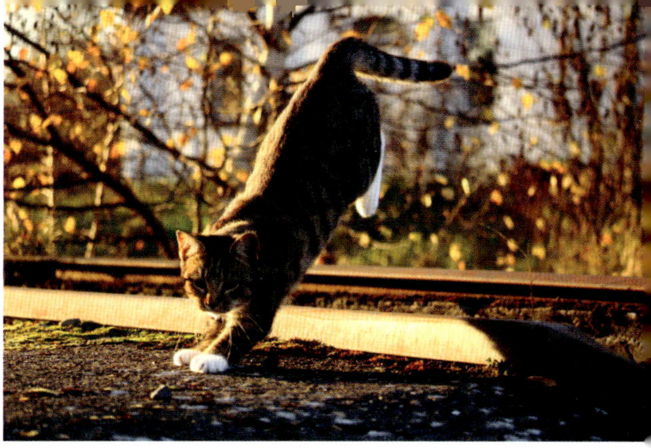
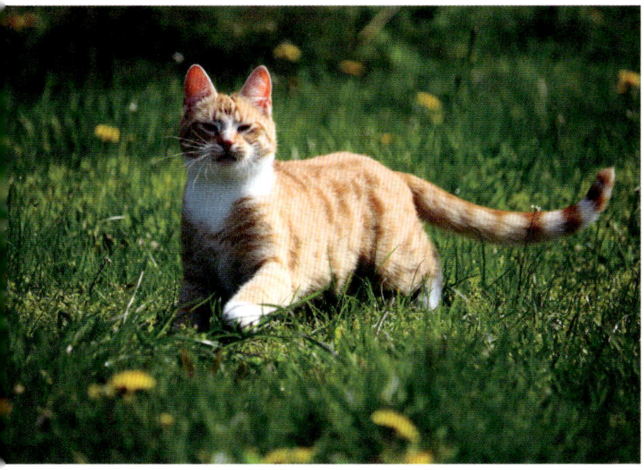
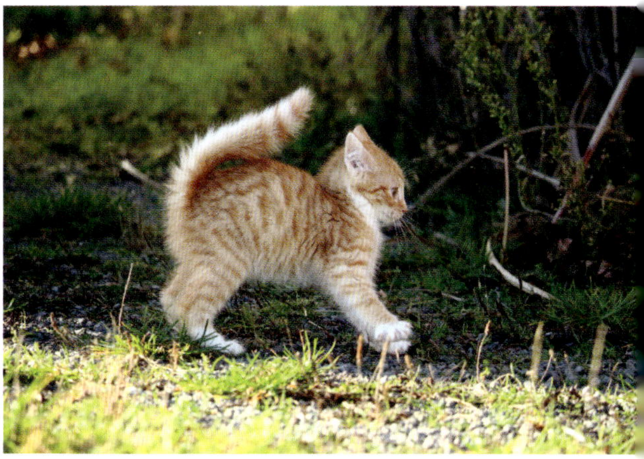
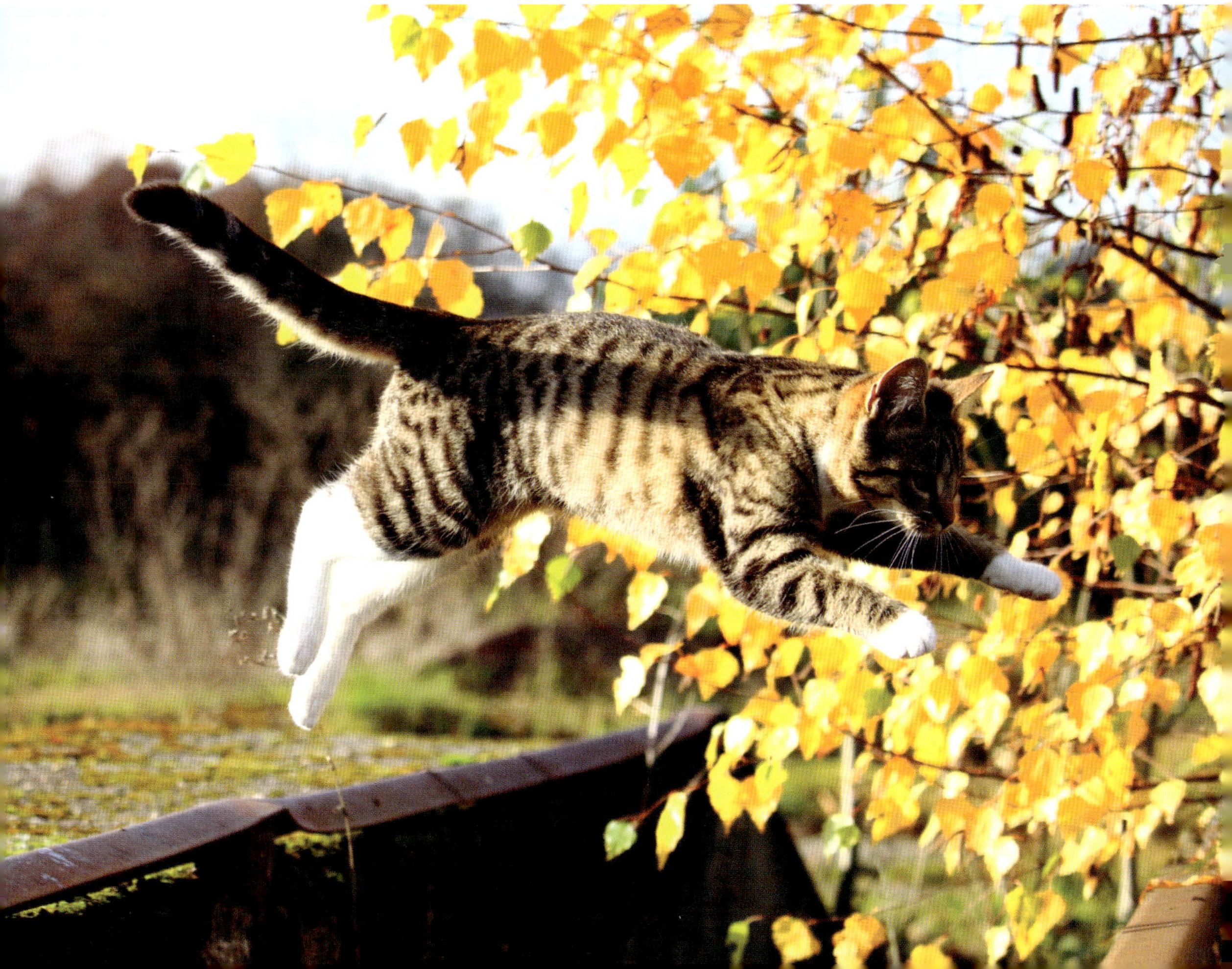

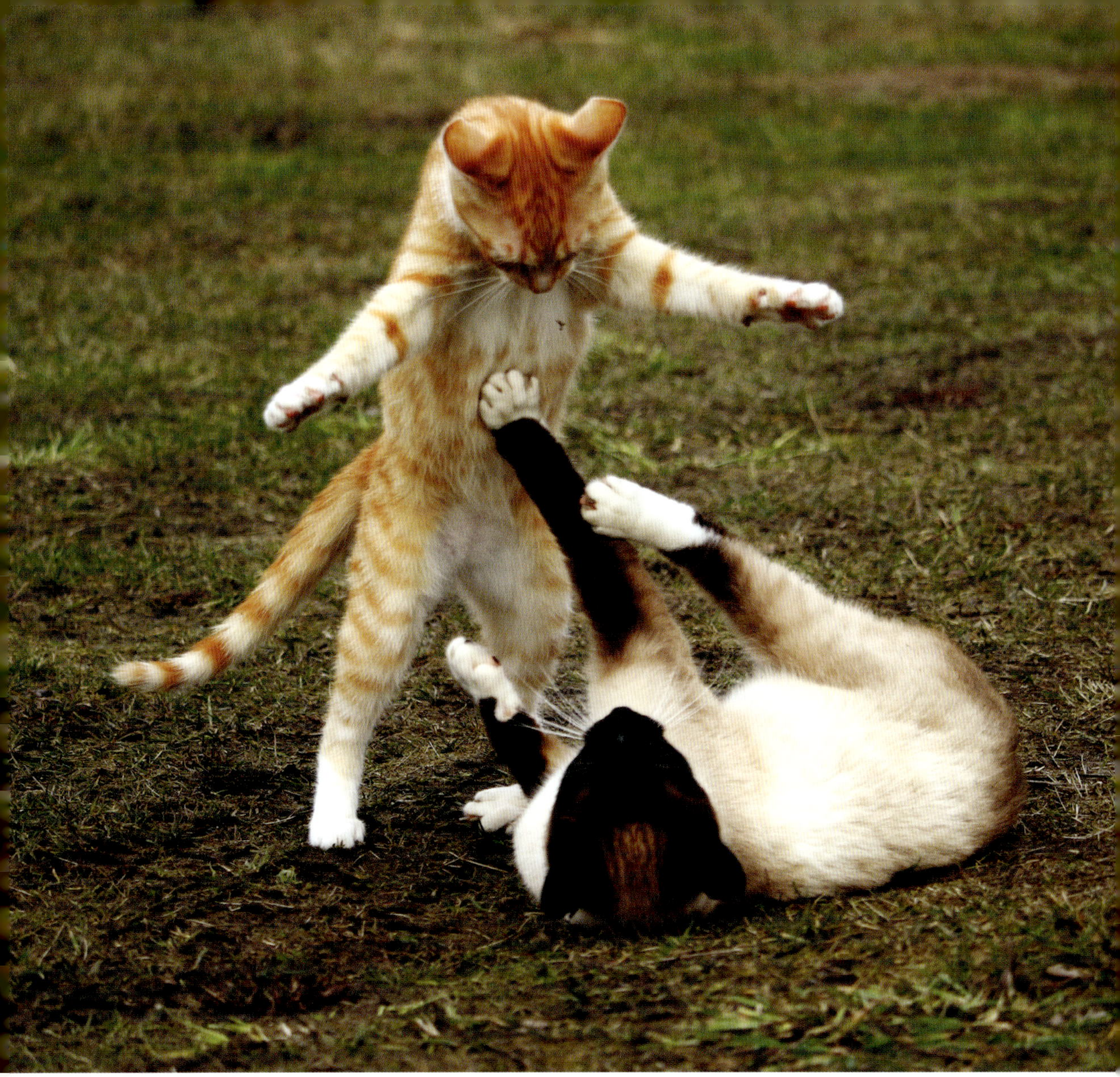
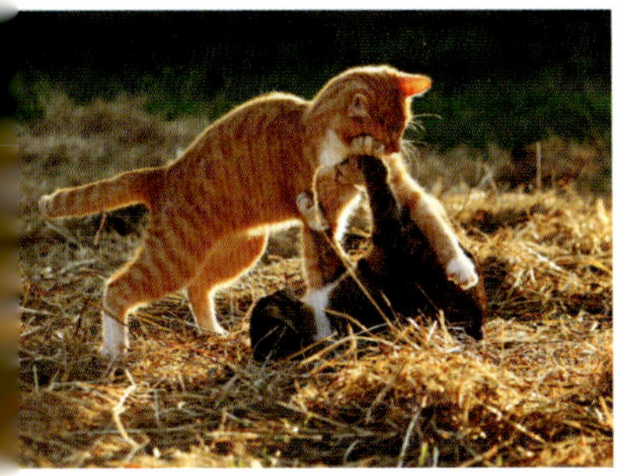
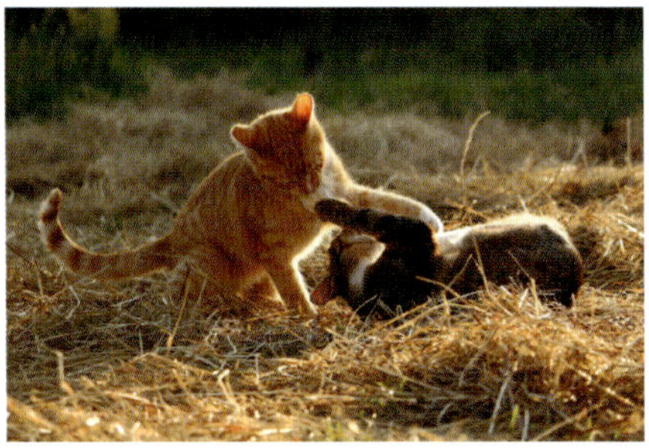
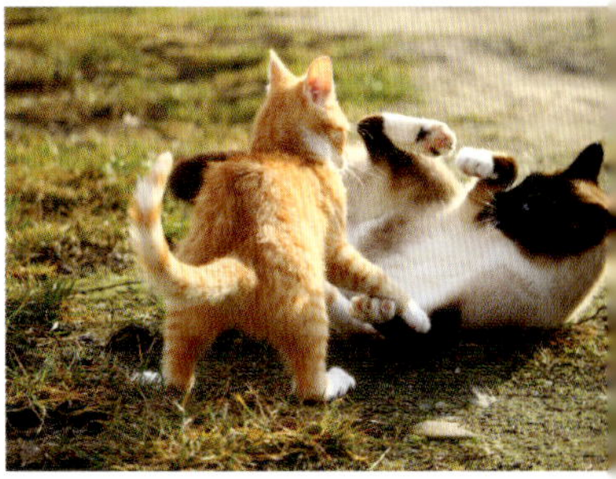
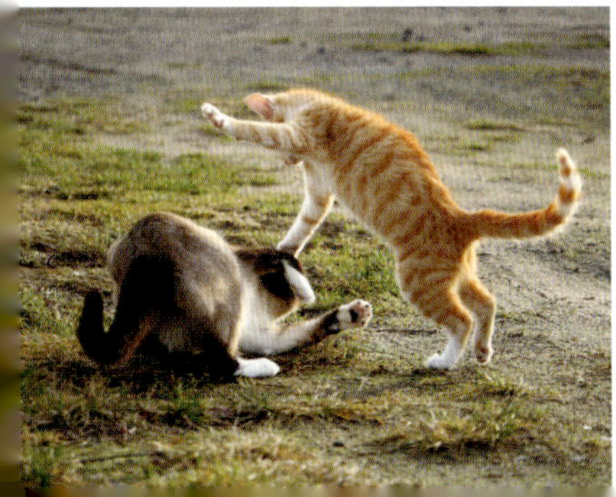
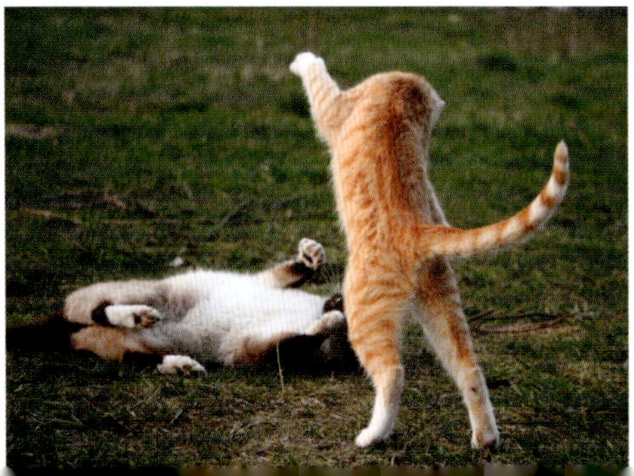
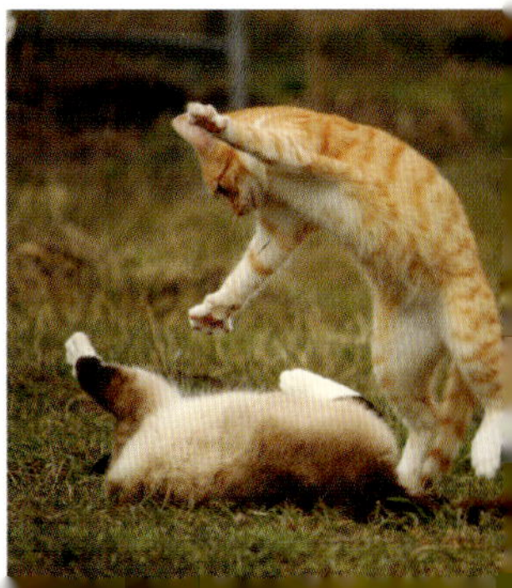

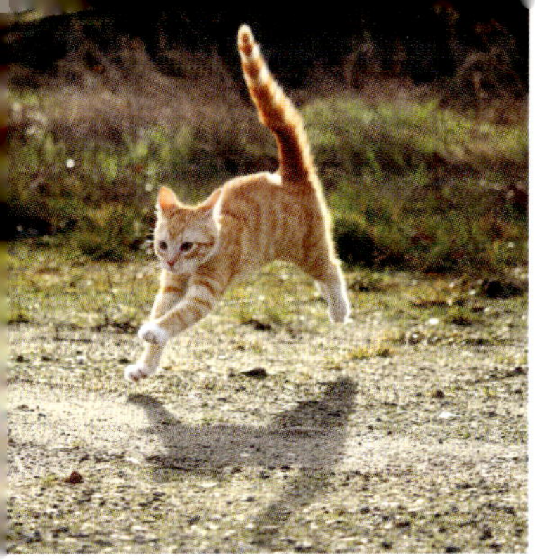
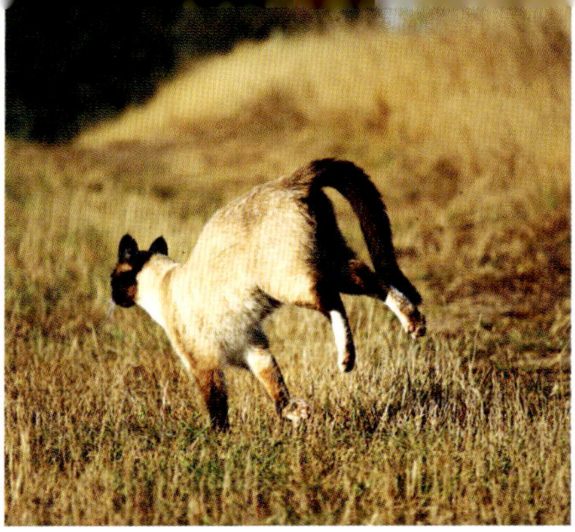
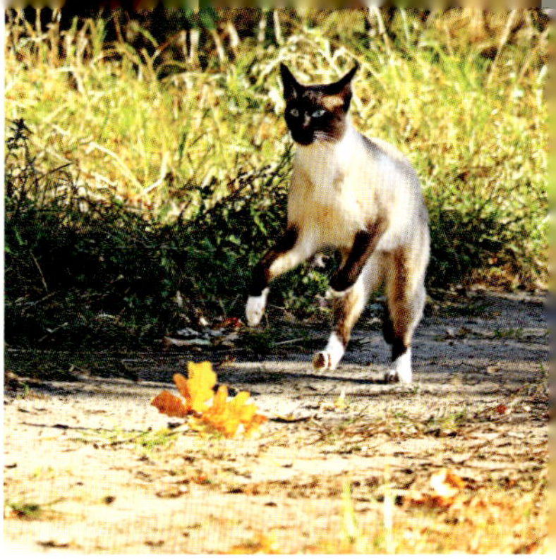
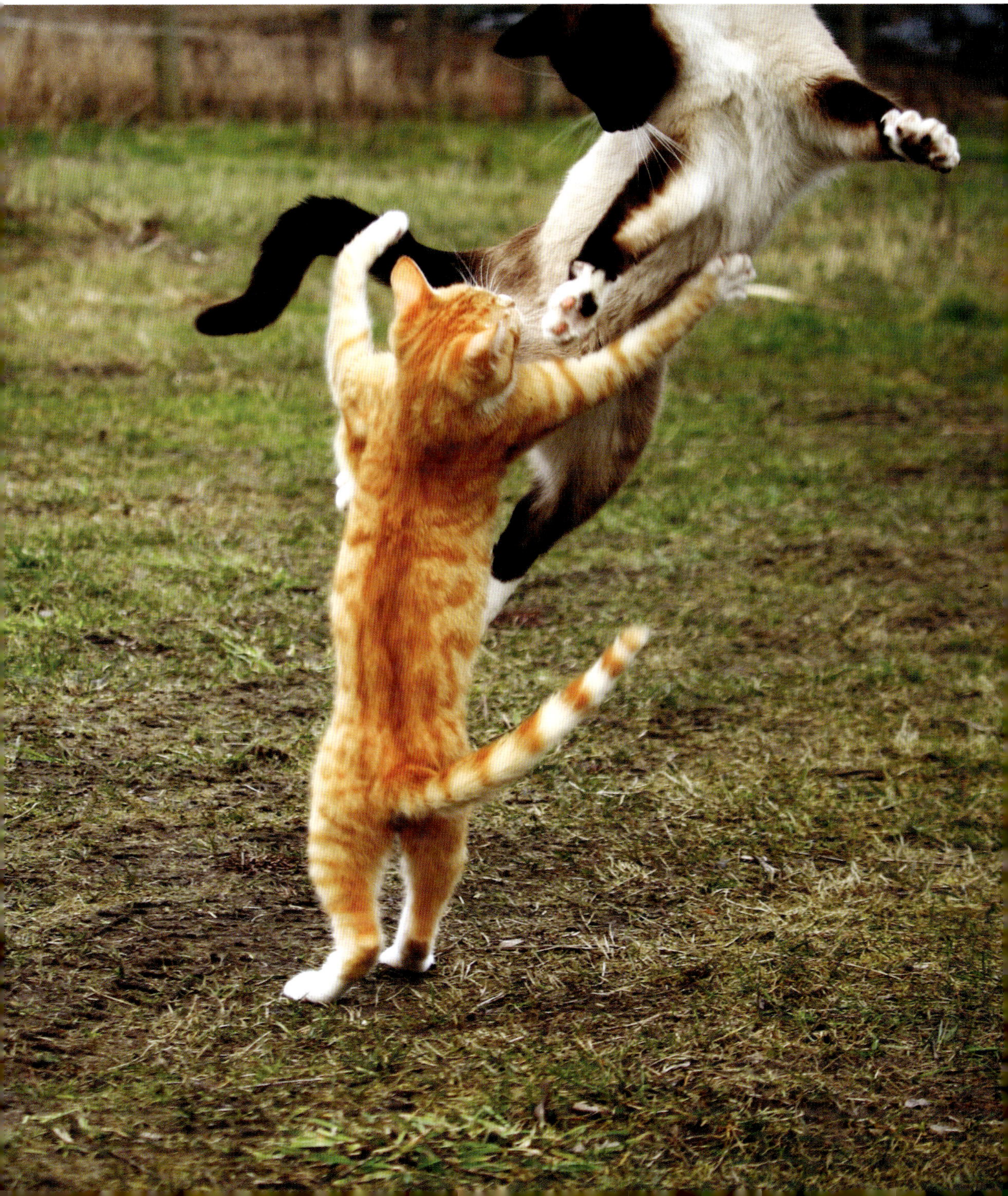

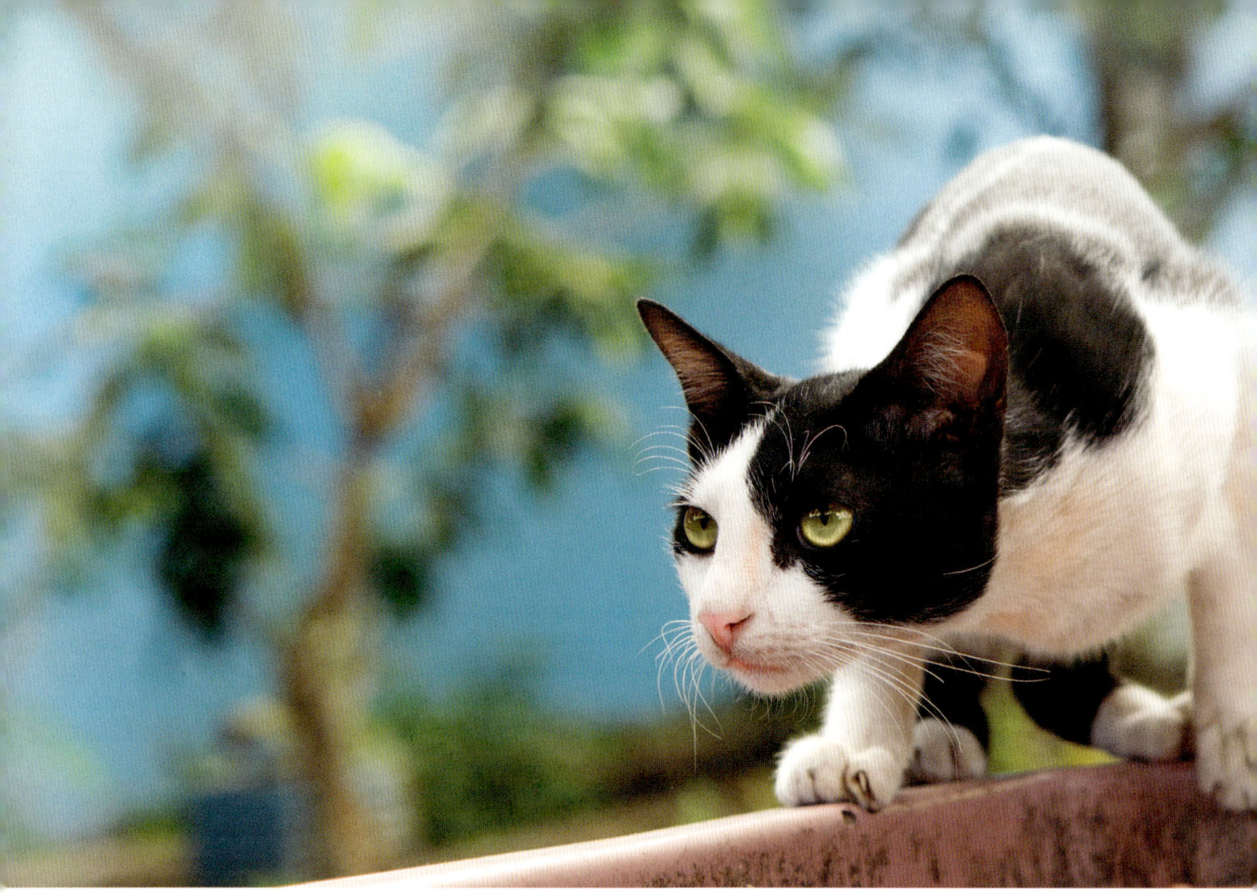

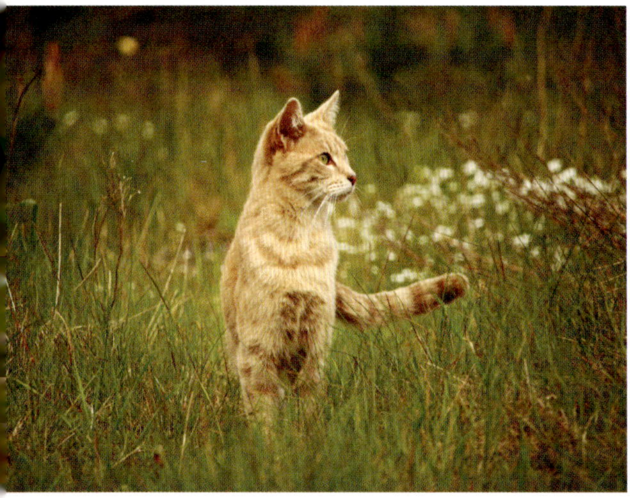

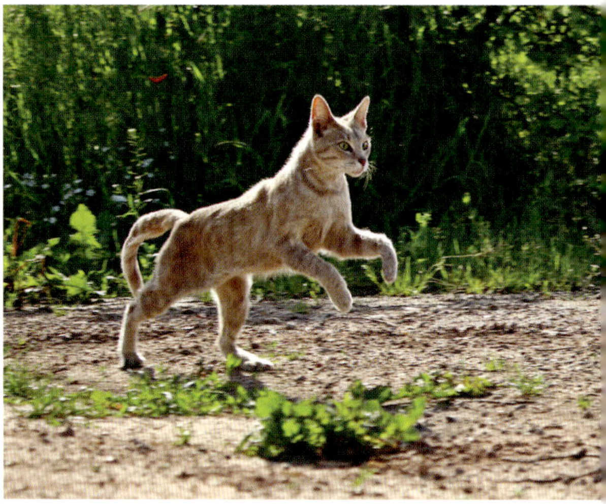

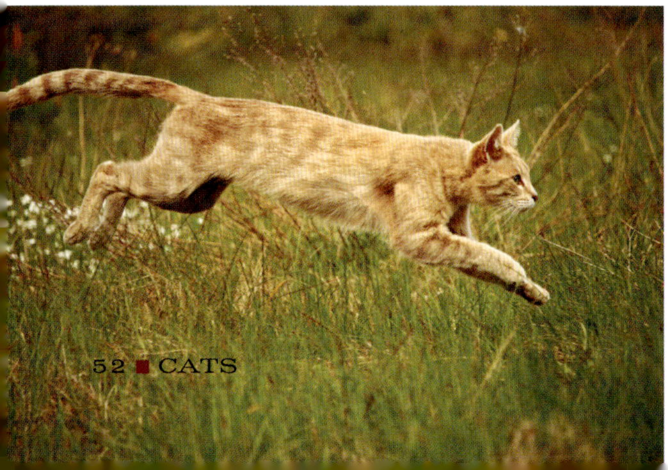

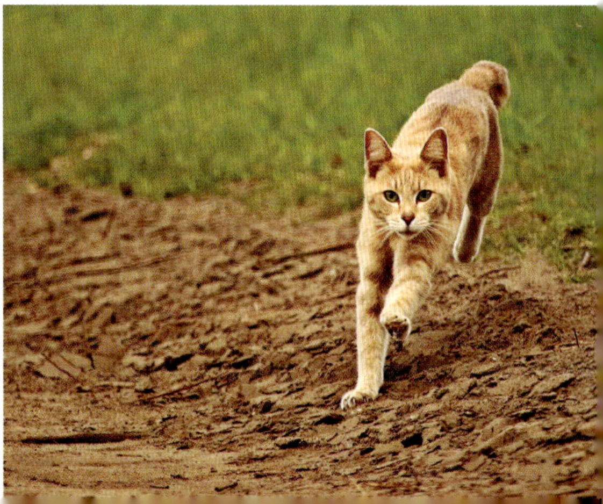

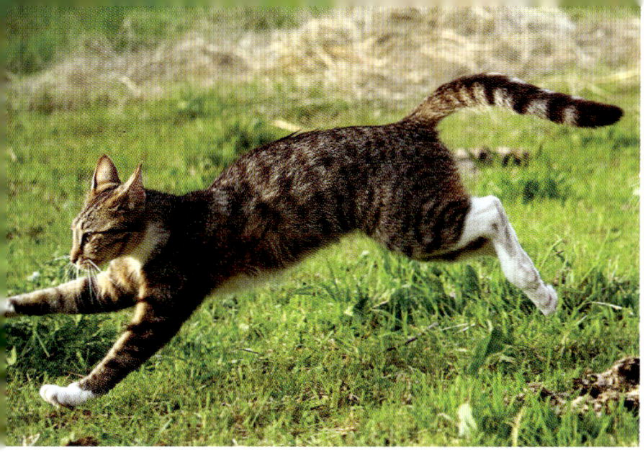
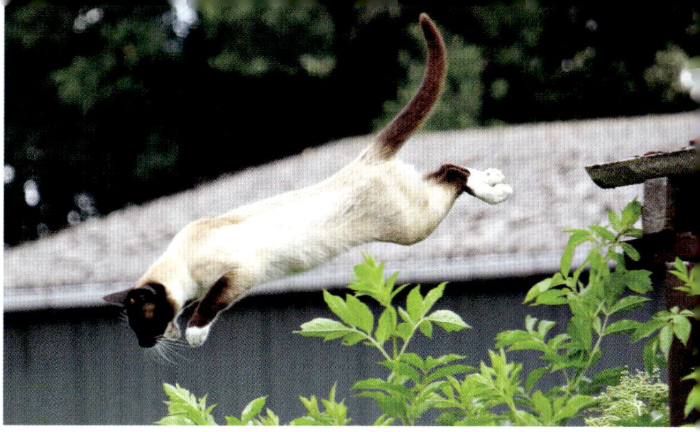
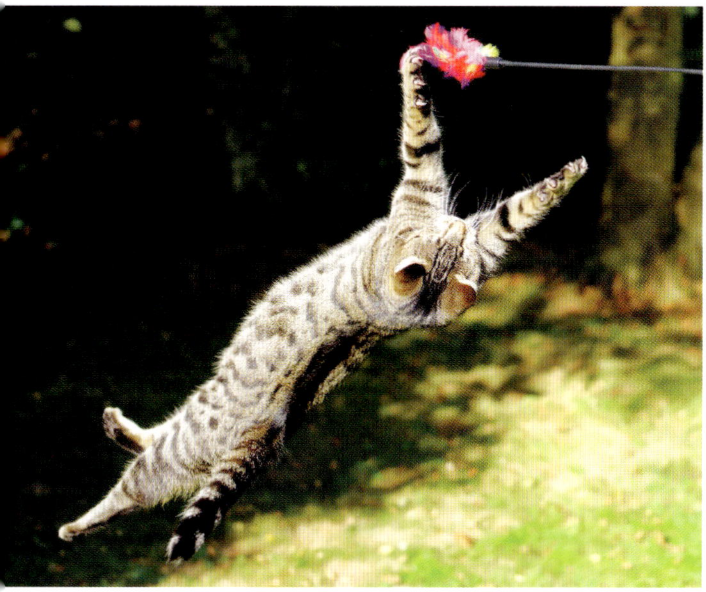
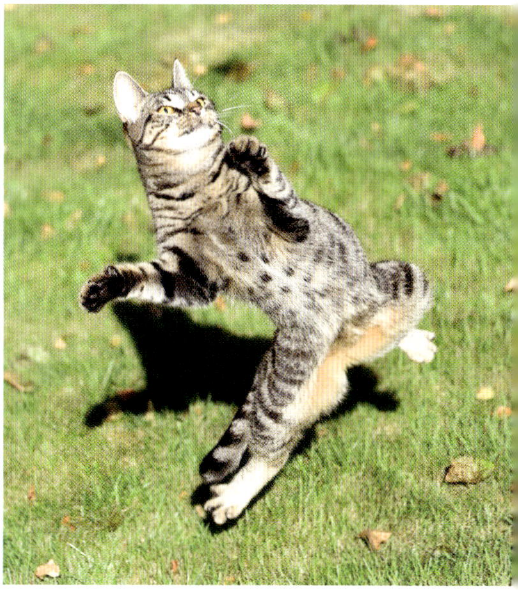
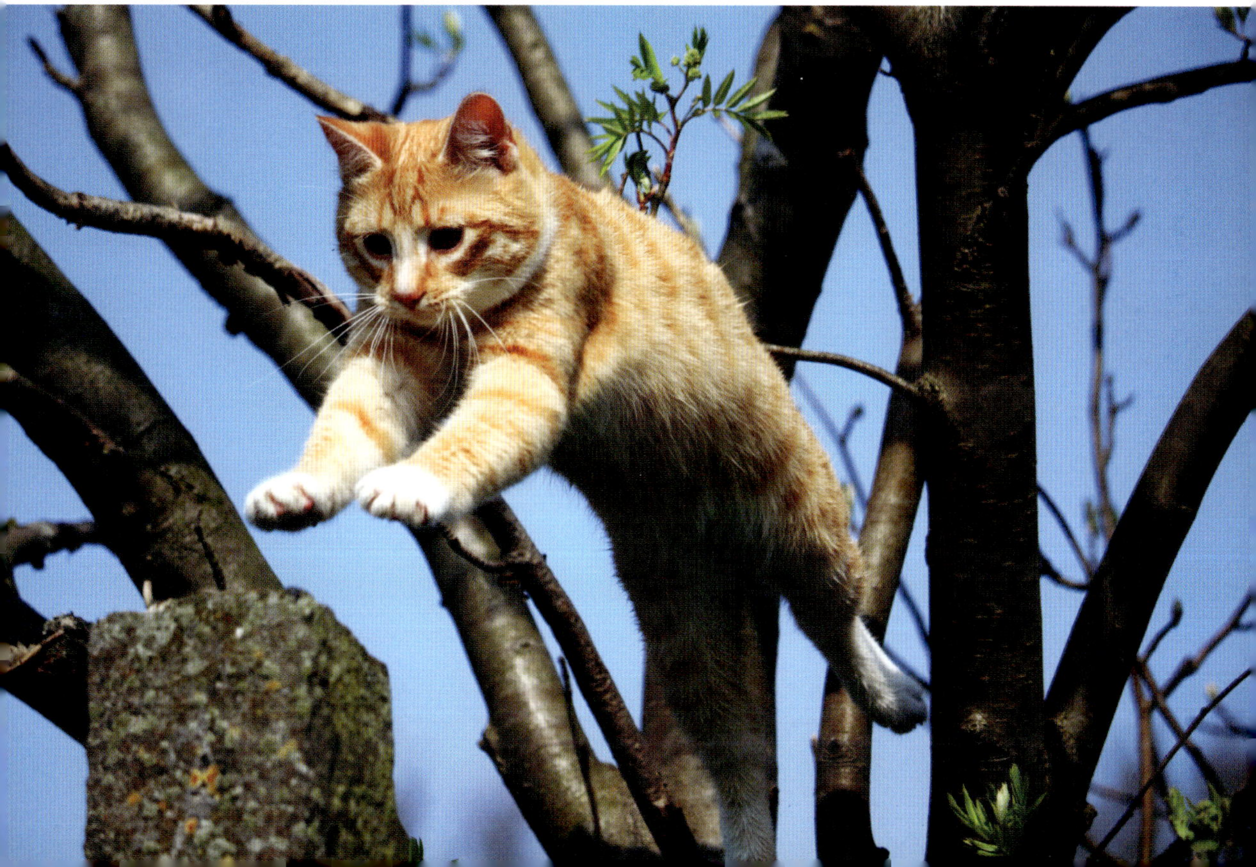

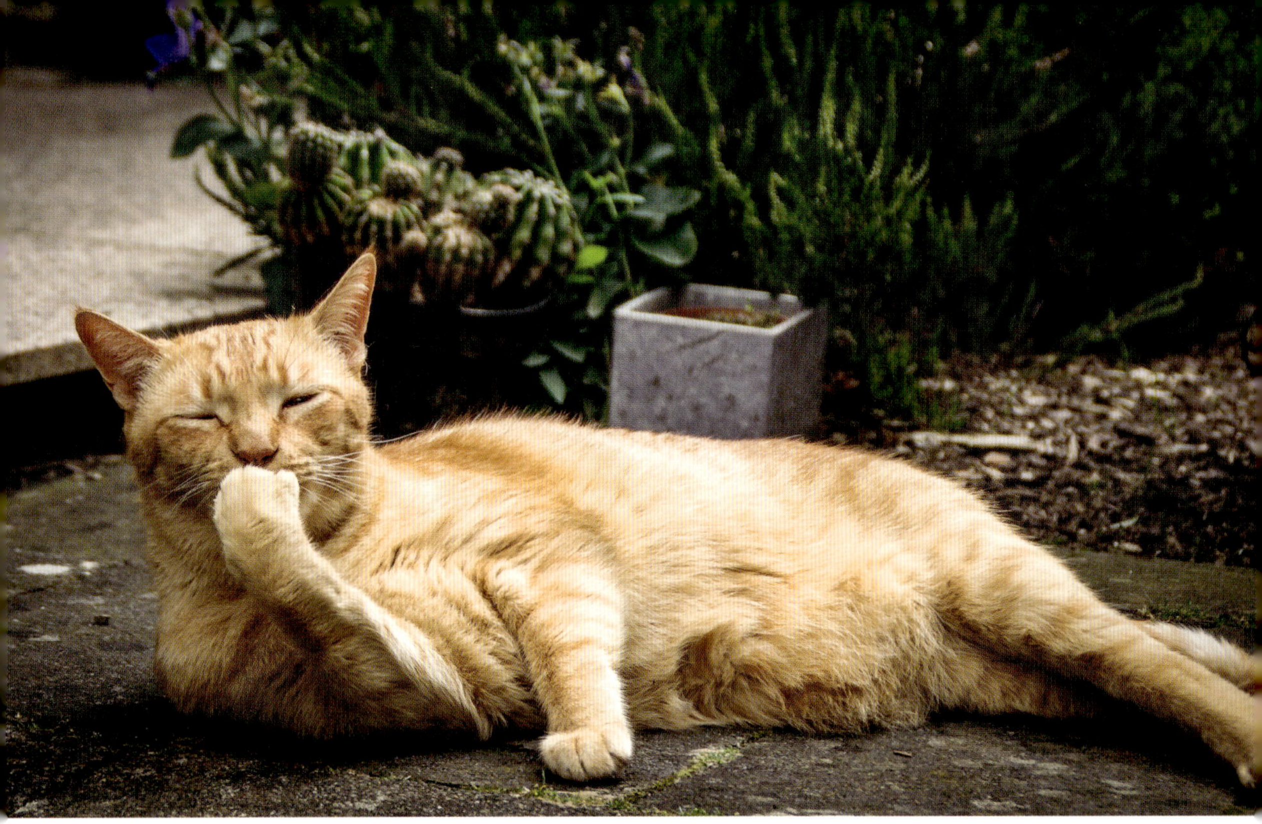
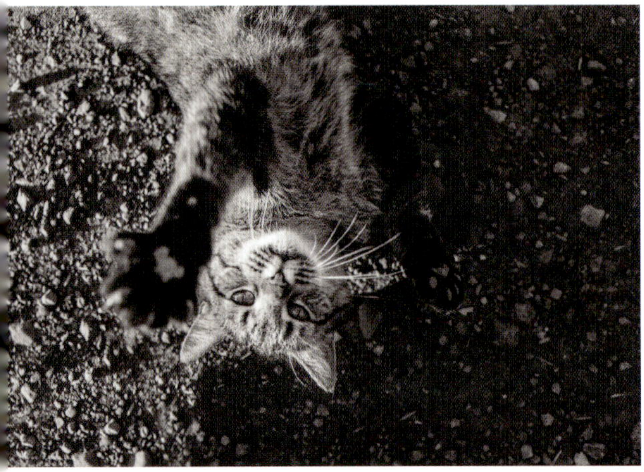
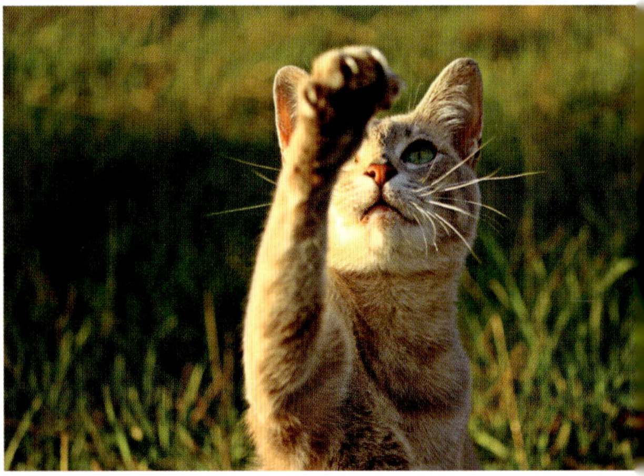
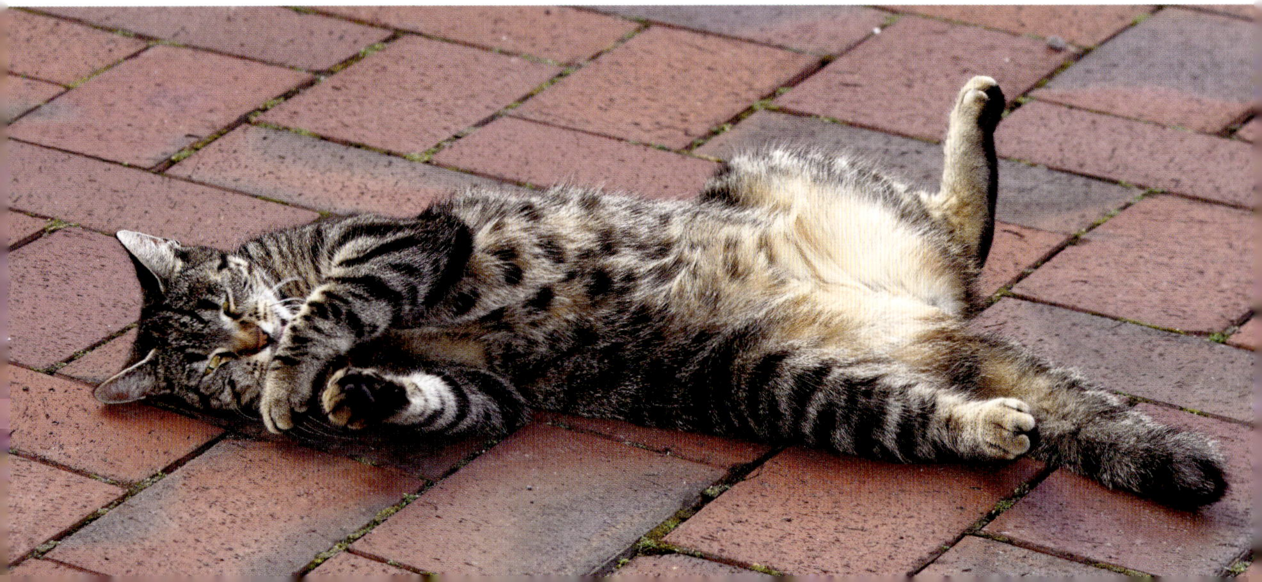

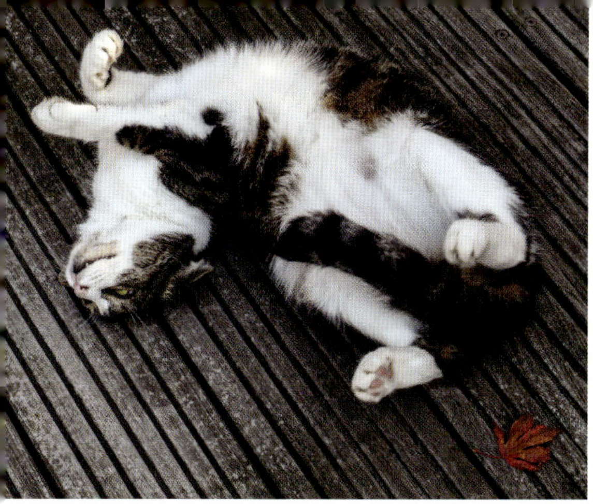
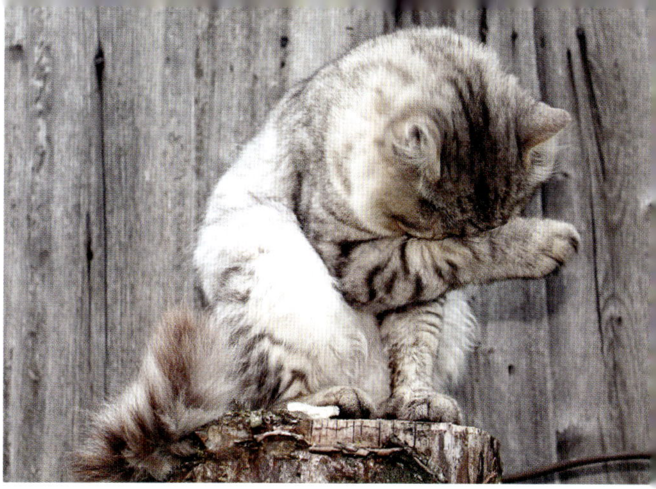
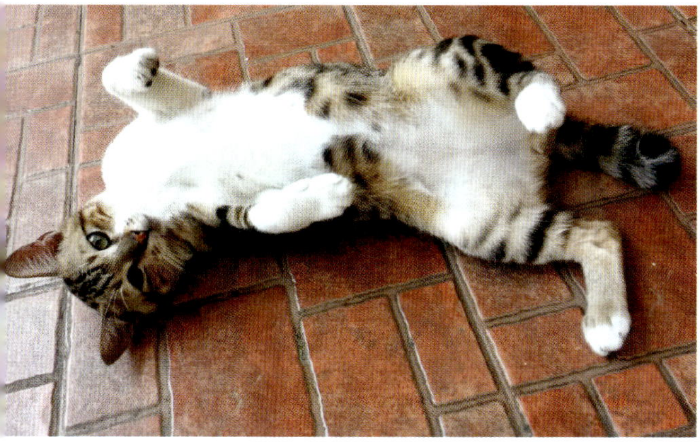
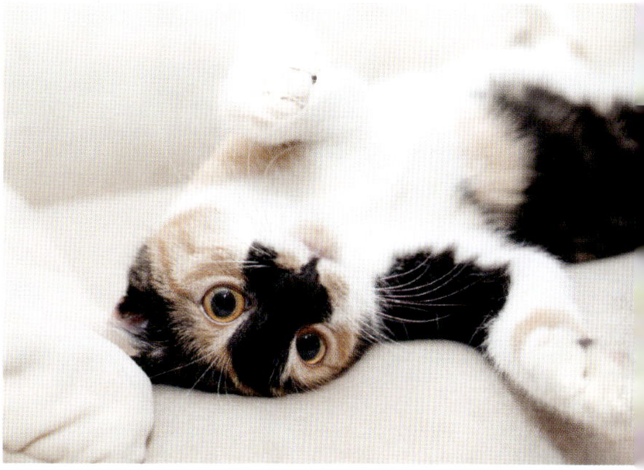
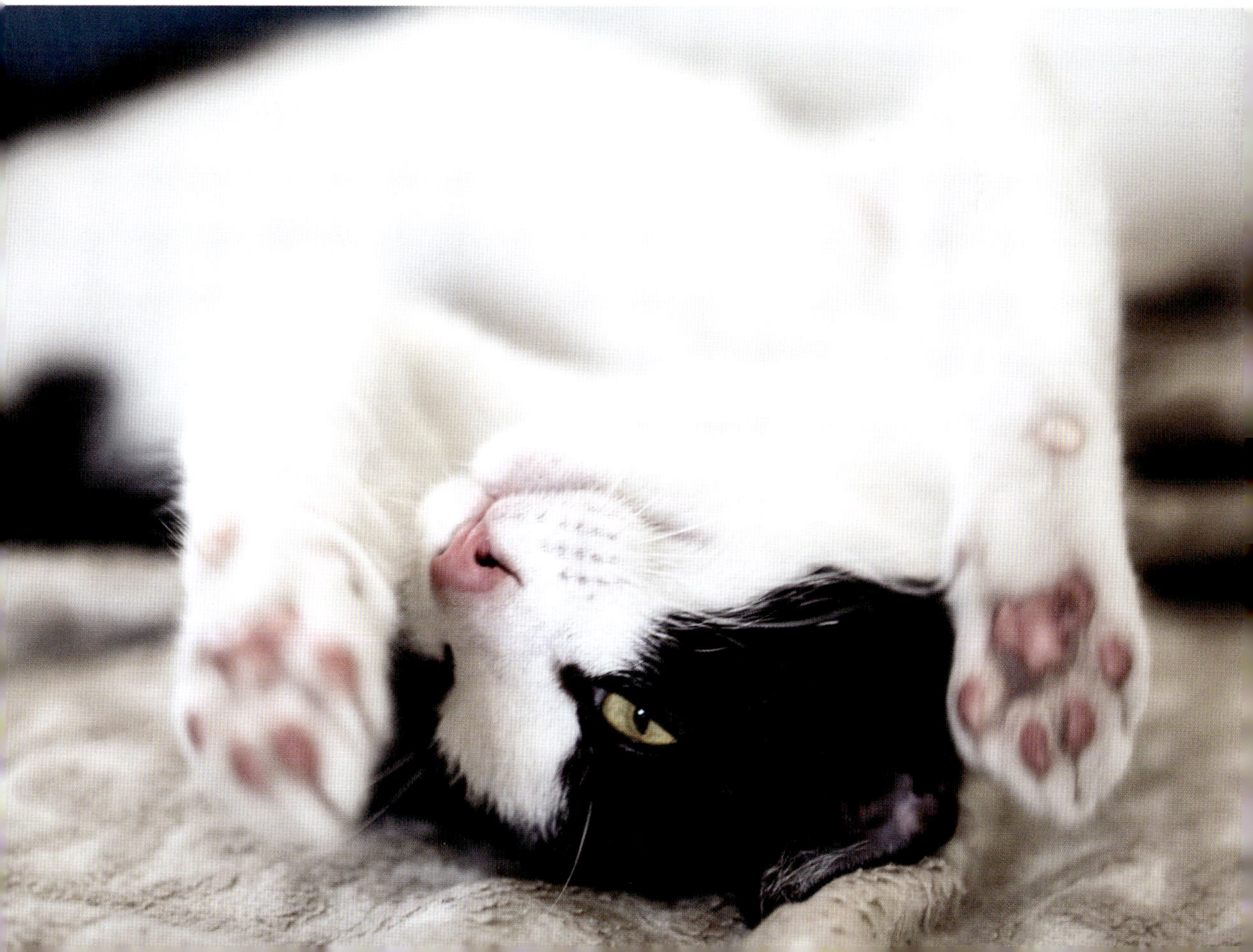

6. Silly and Sweet

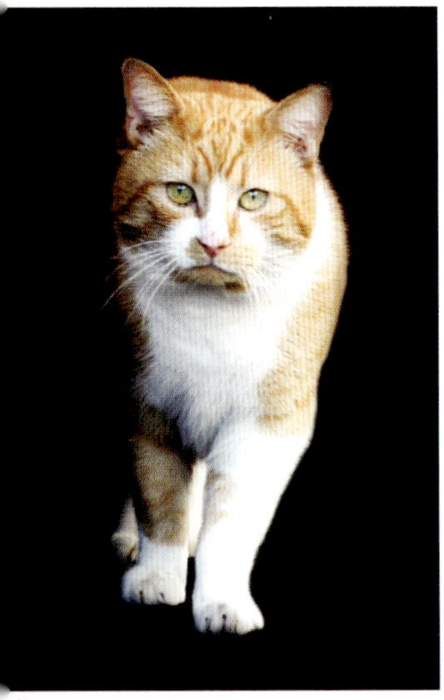

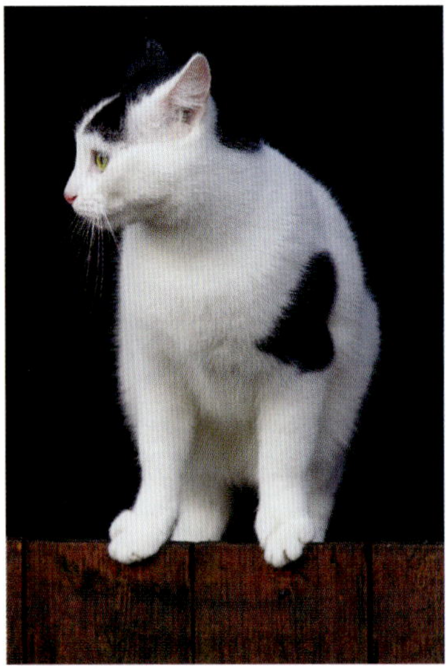

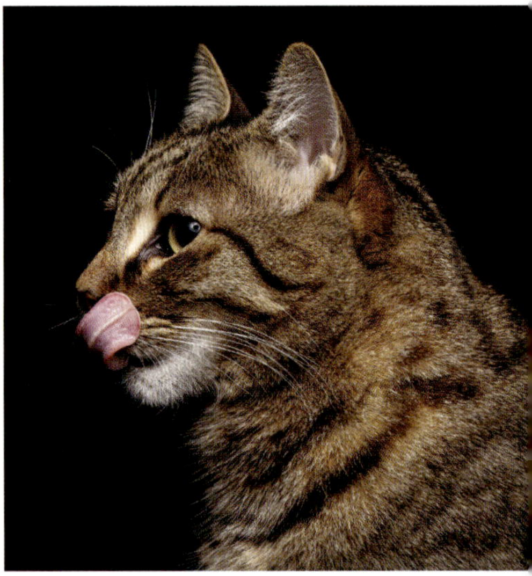

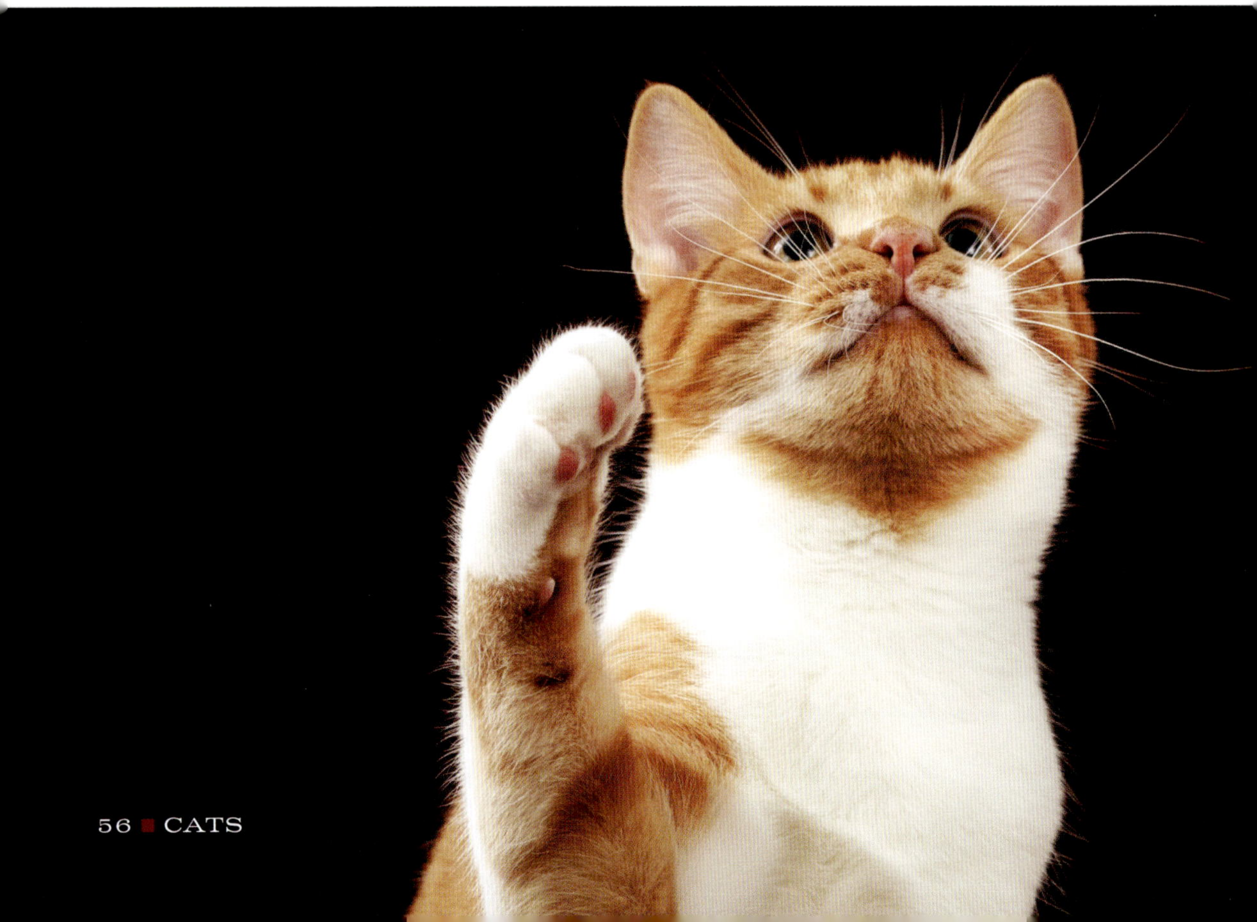

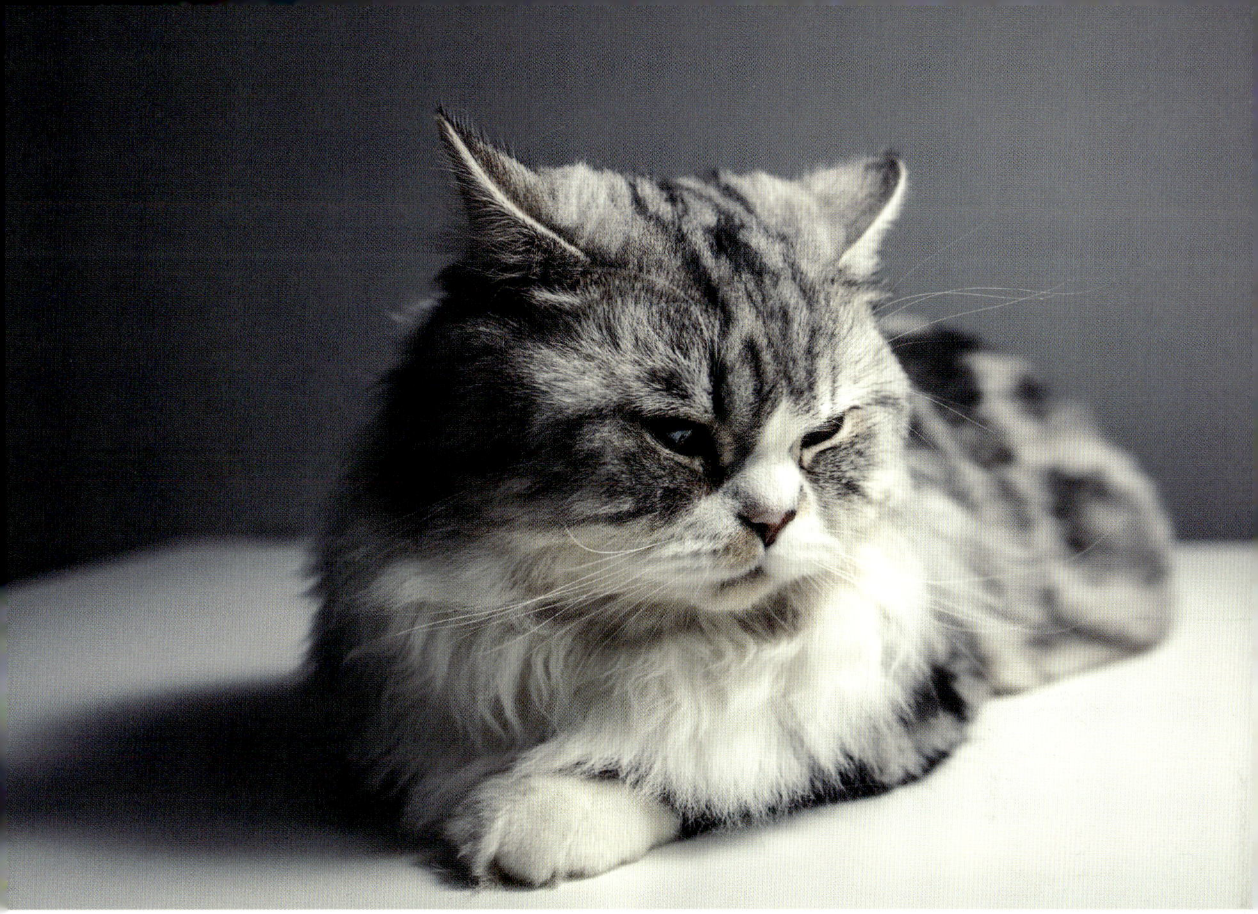
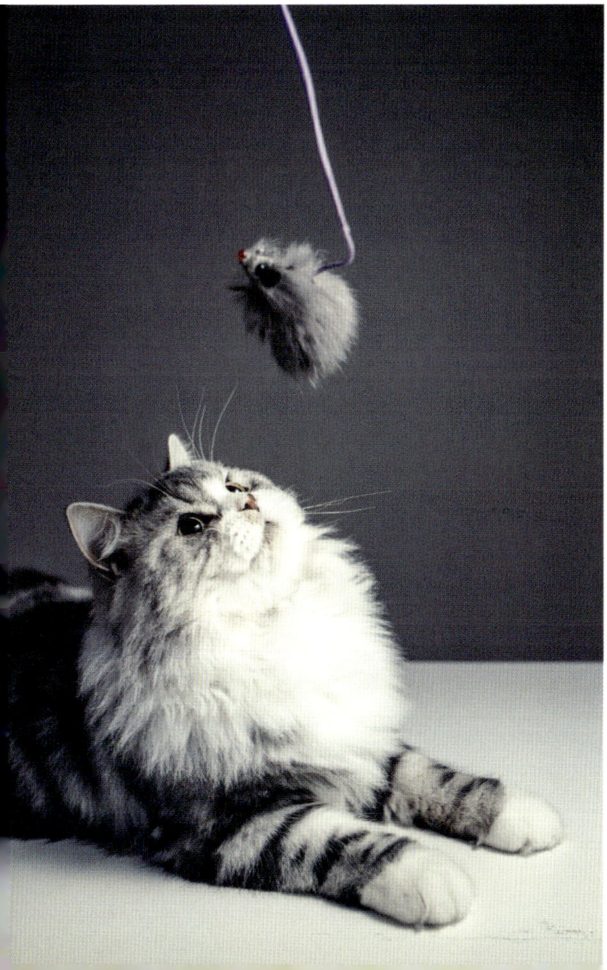
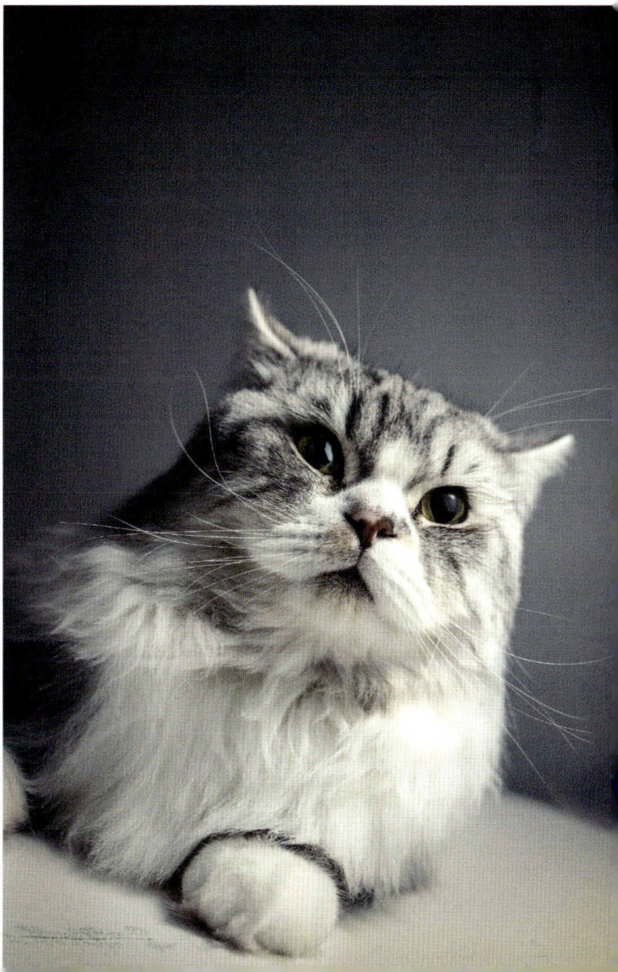

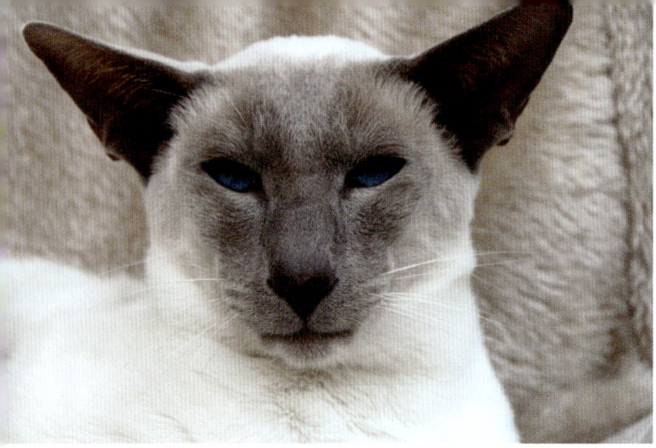
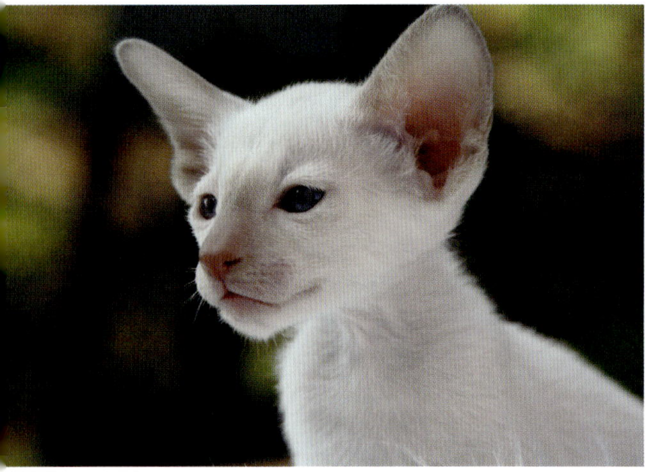
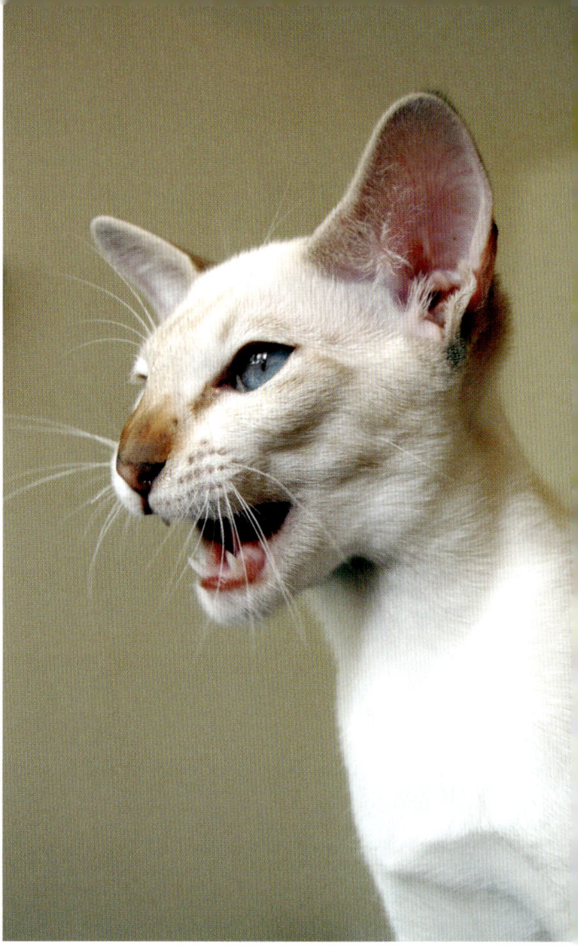
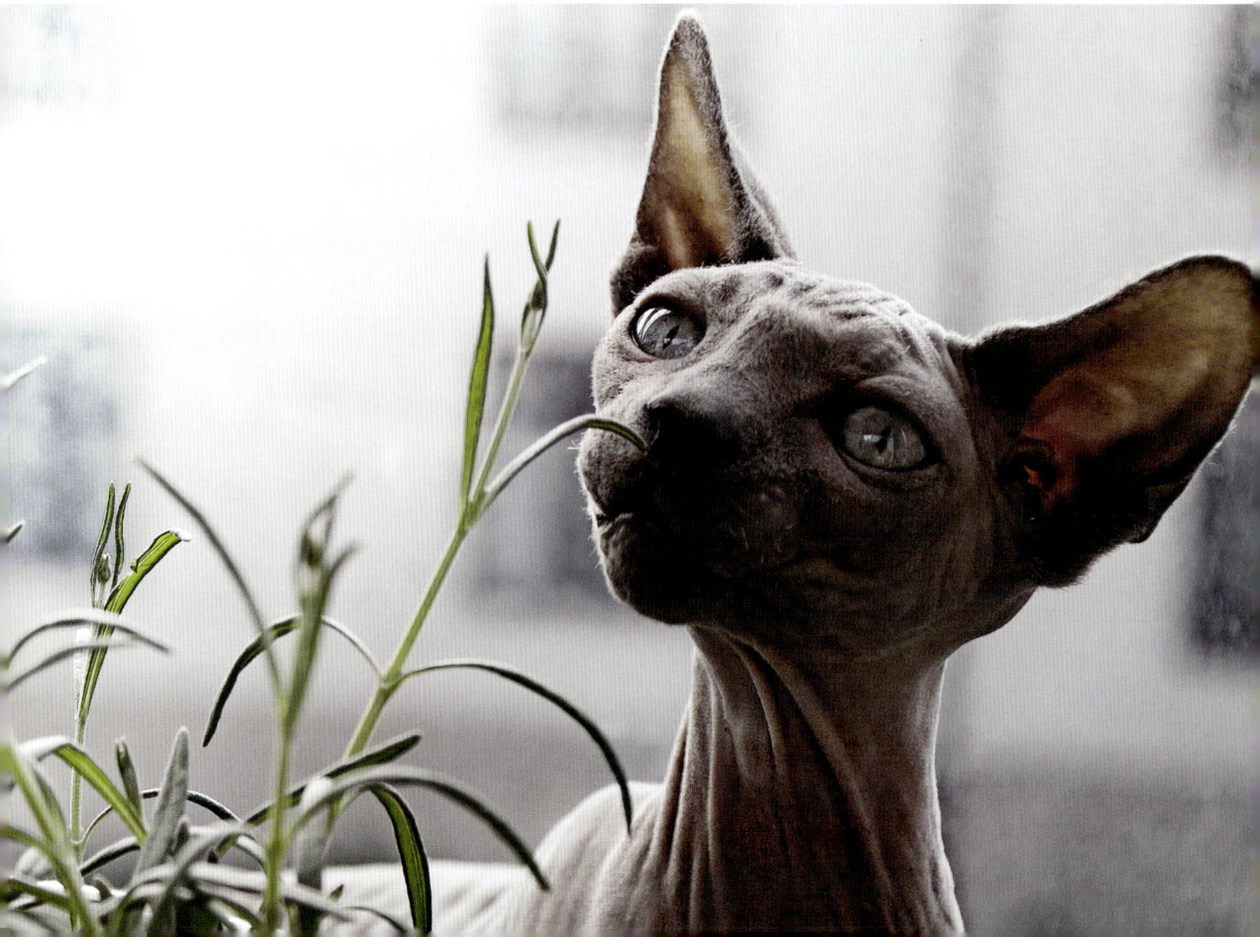

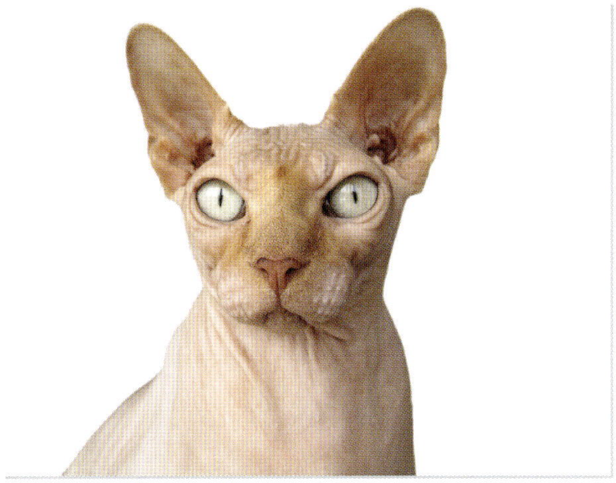
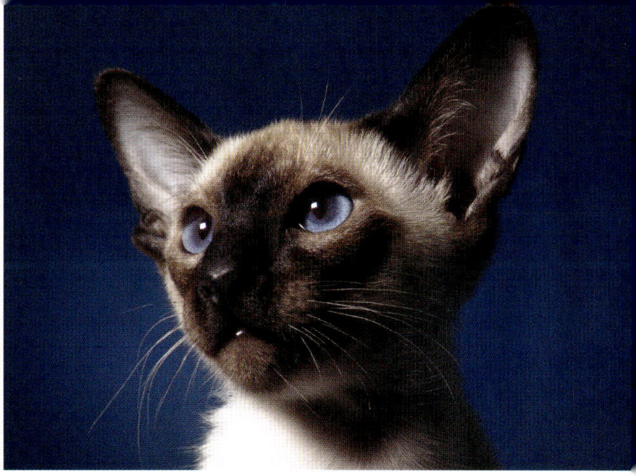
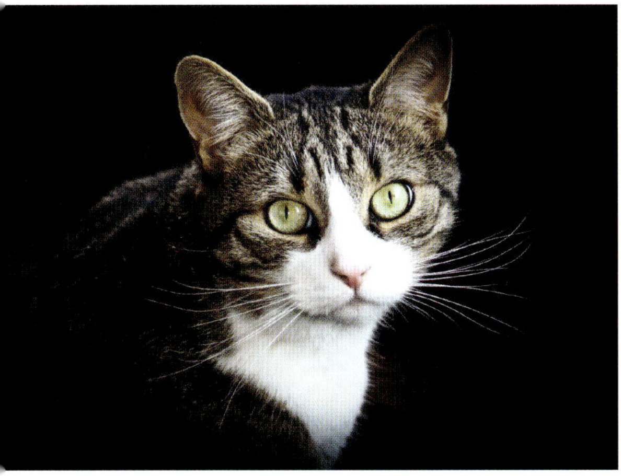
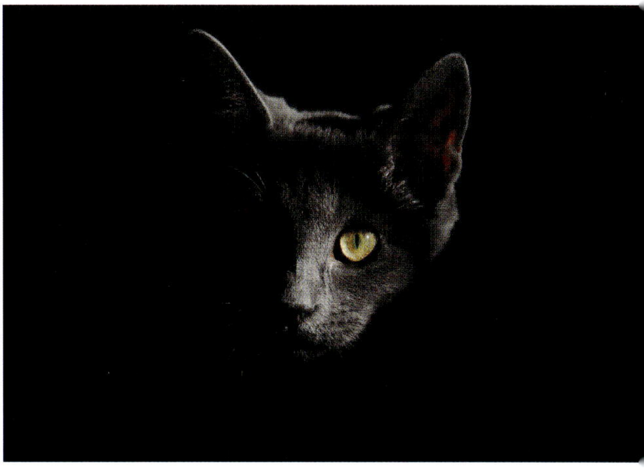
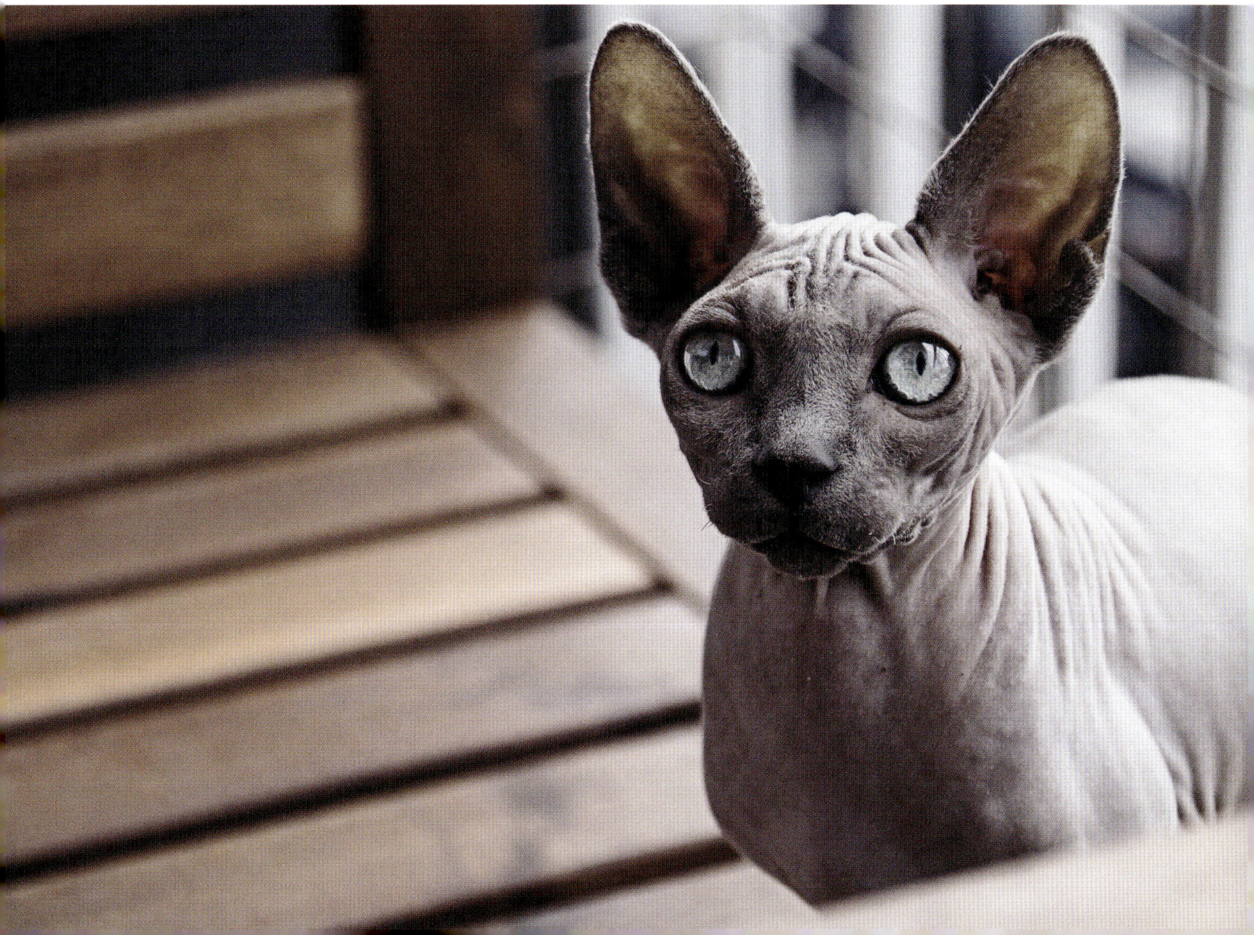

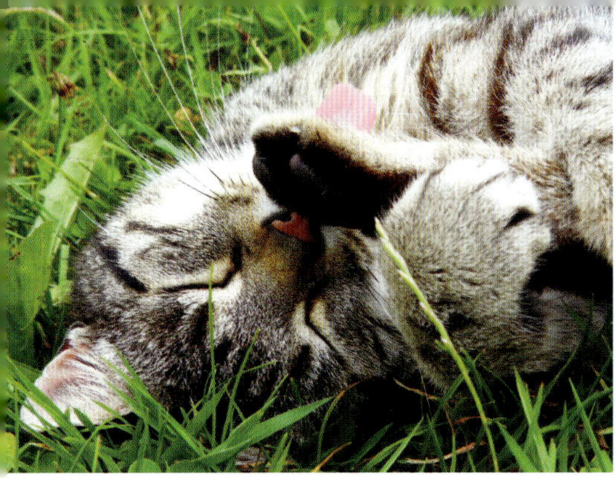

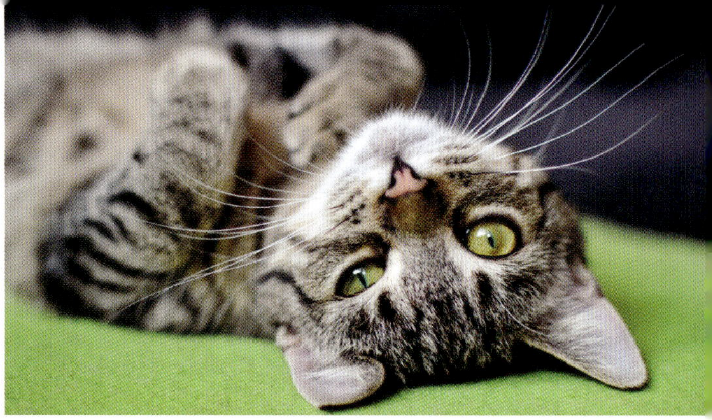

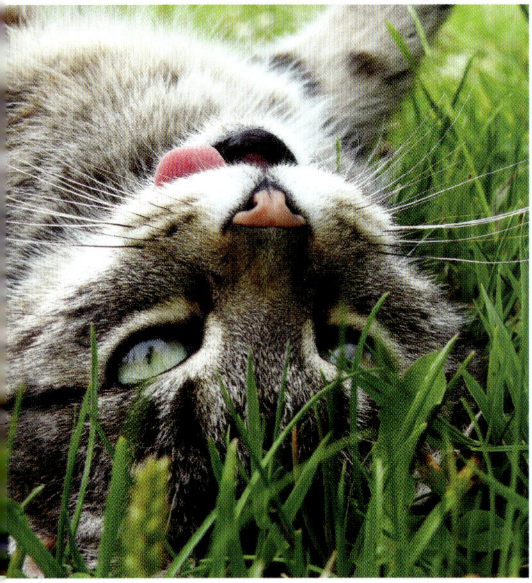

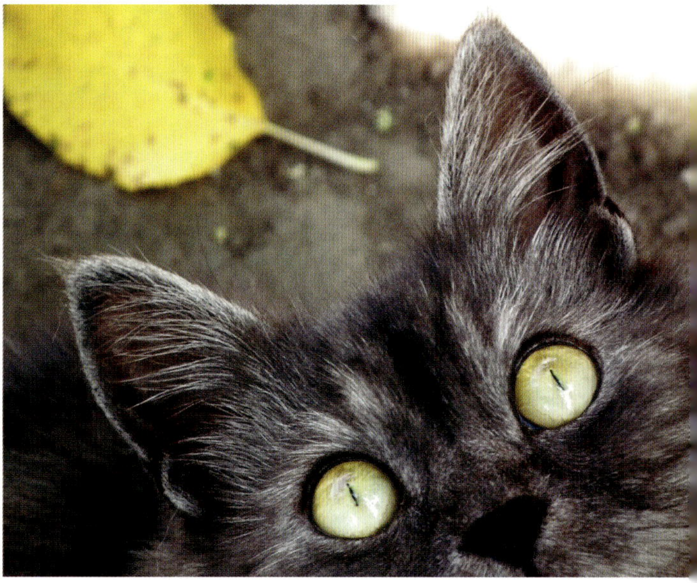

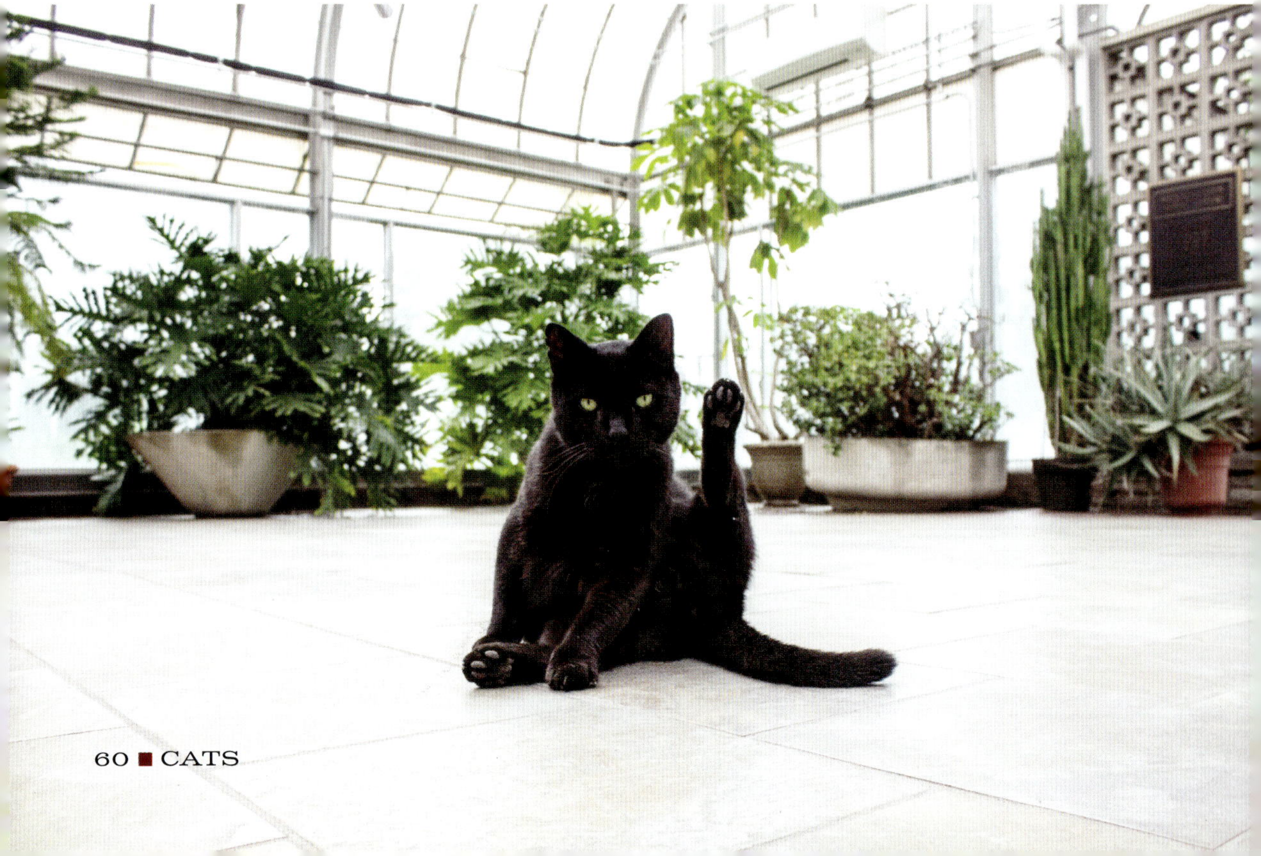

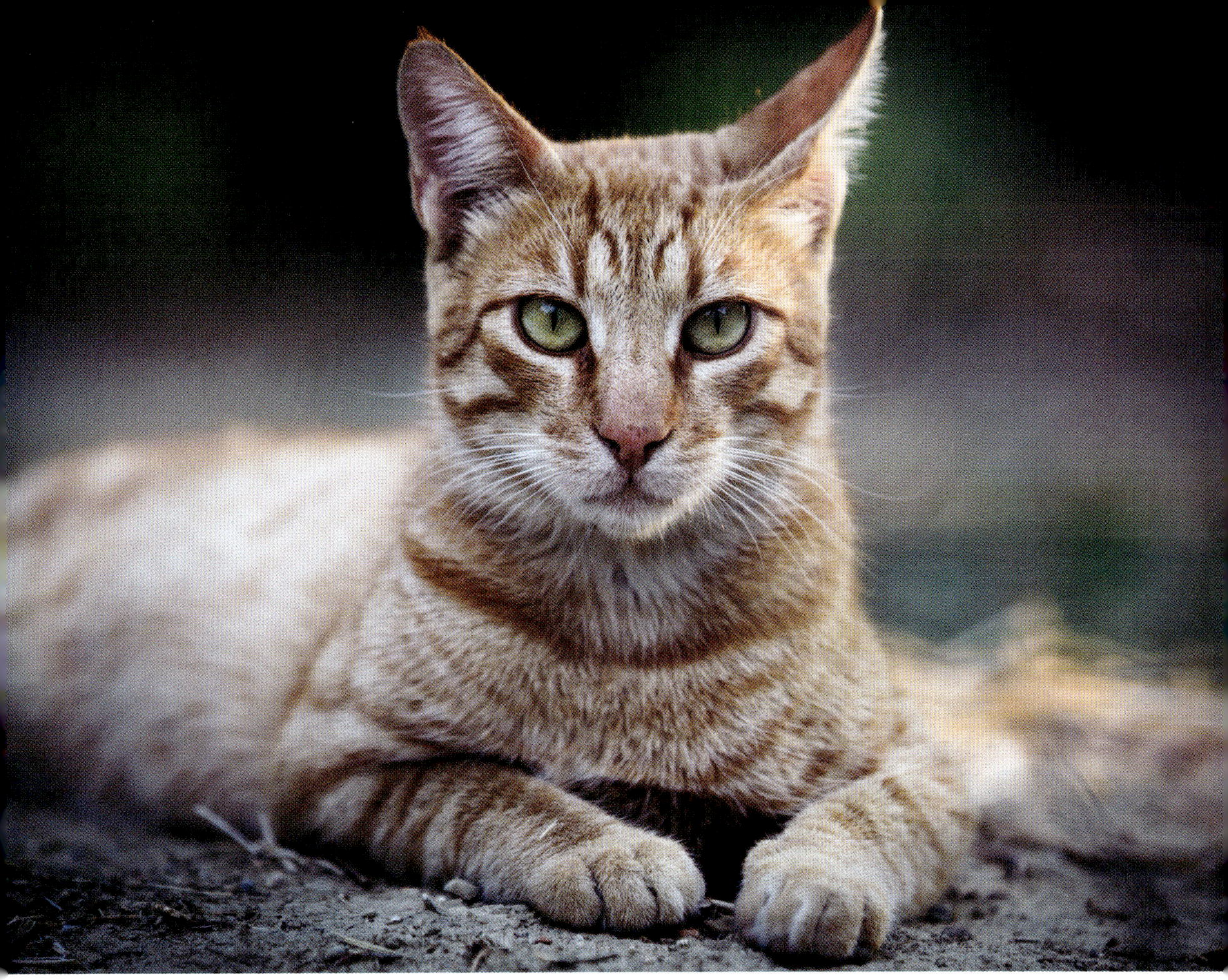
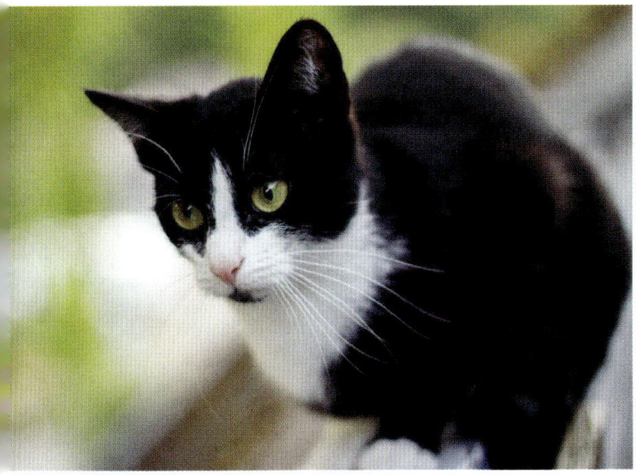
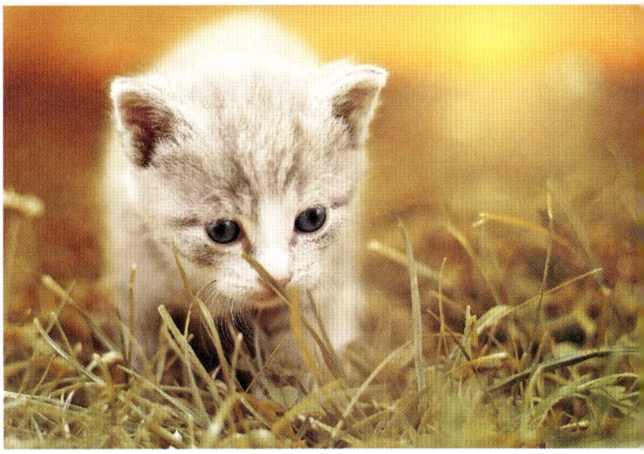
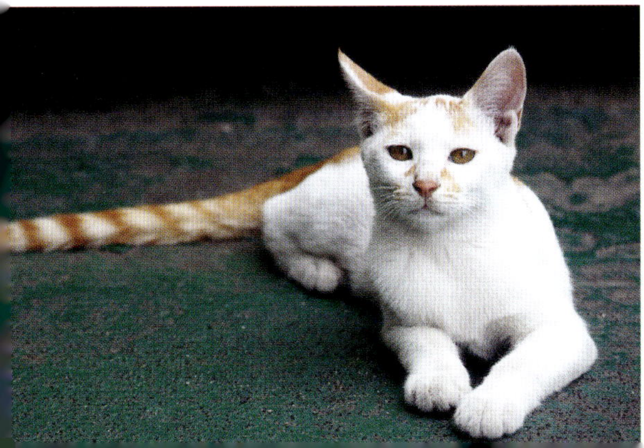
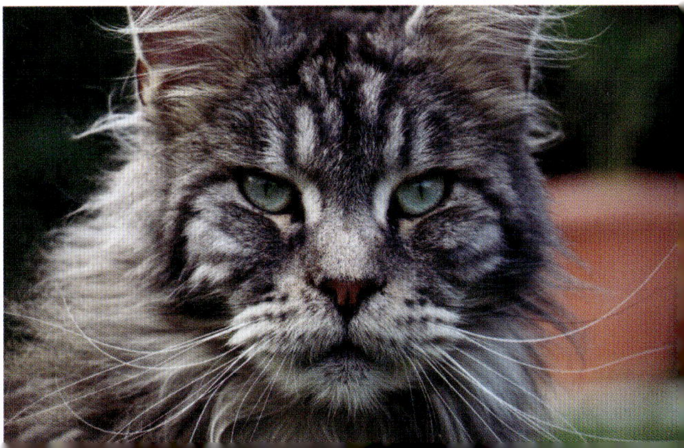

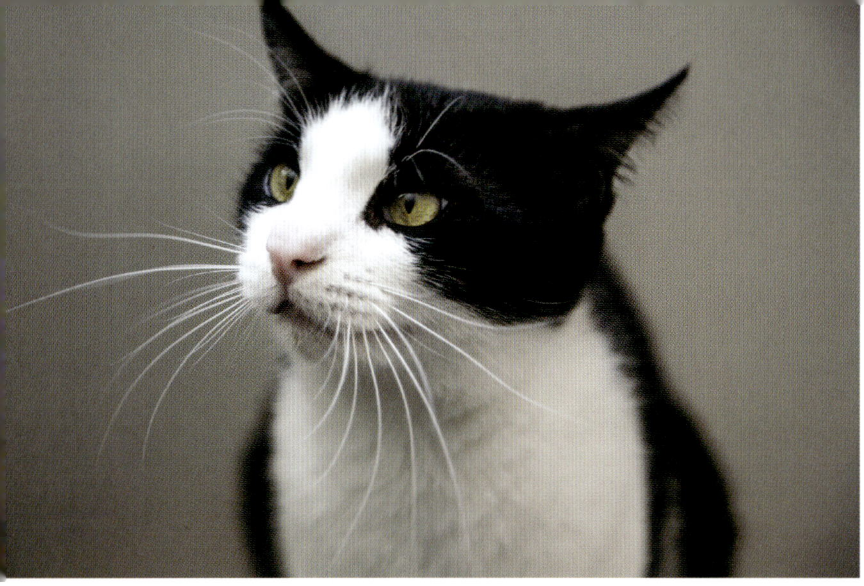
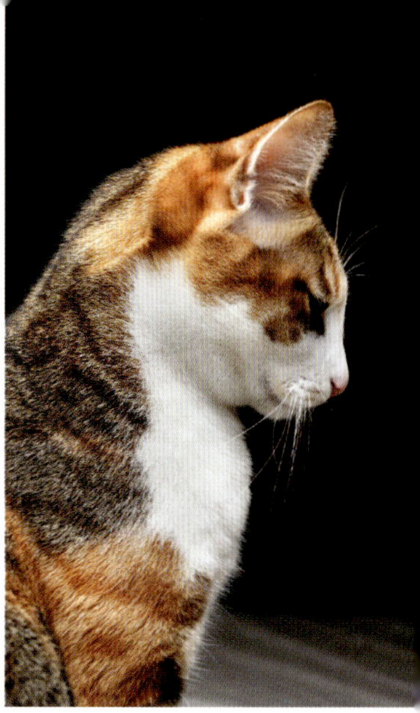
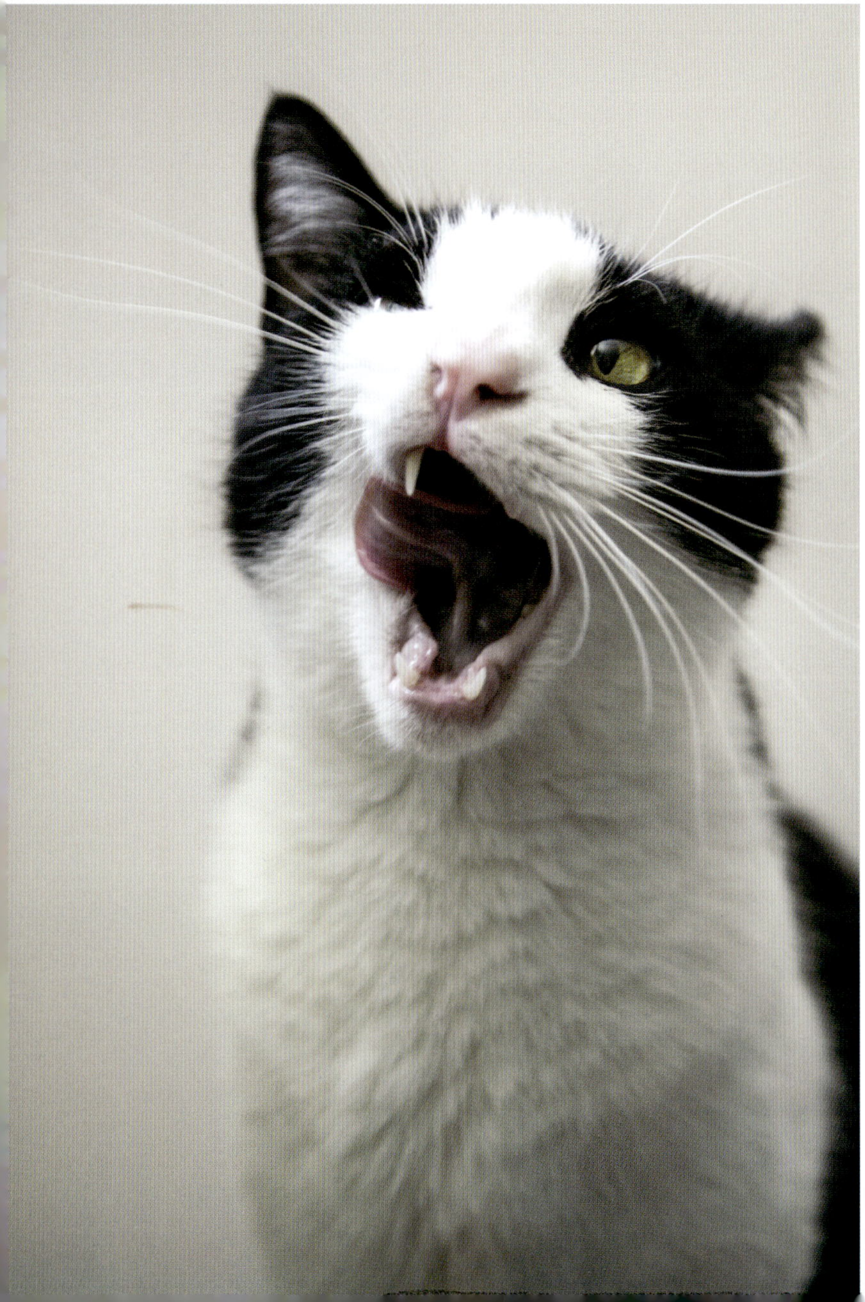
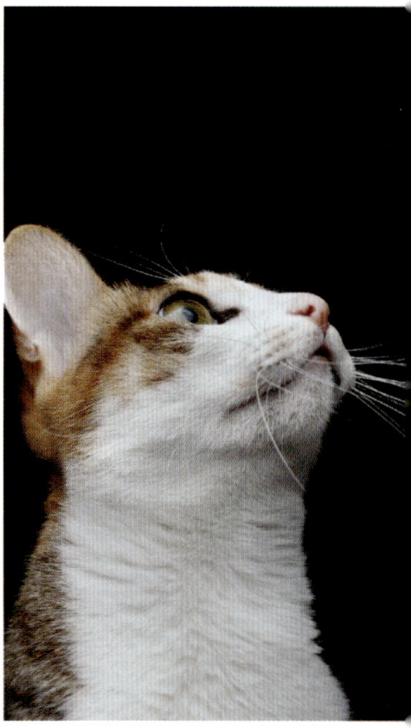
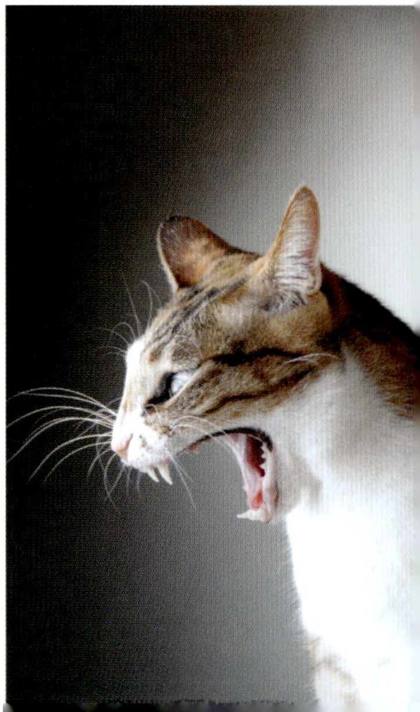

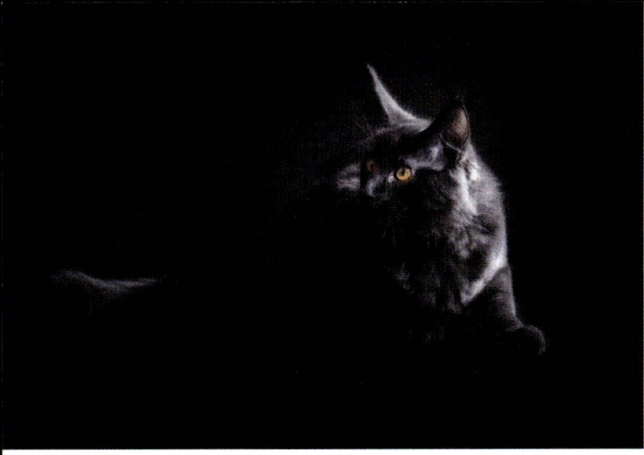
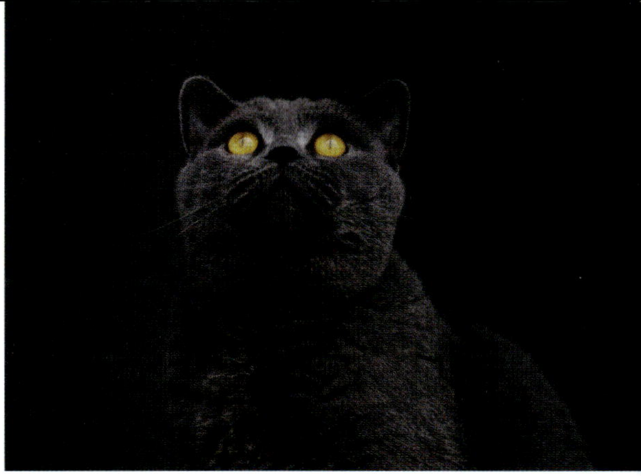
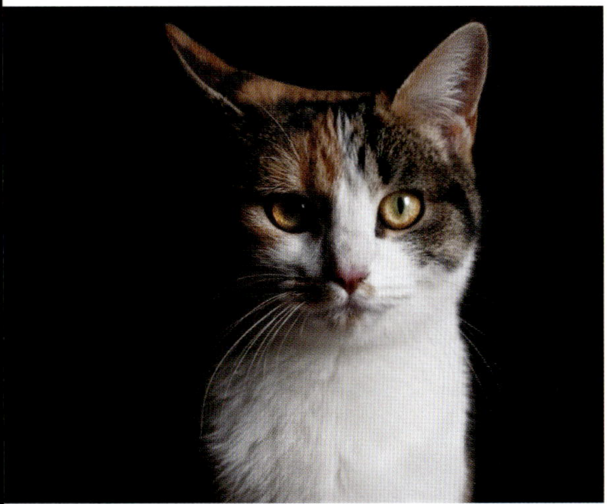
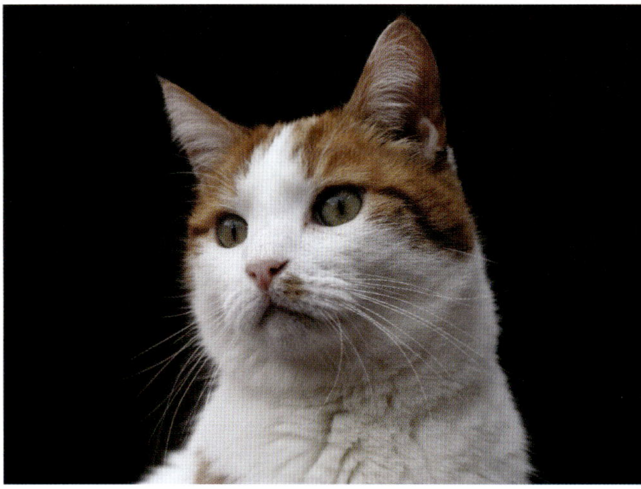
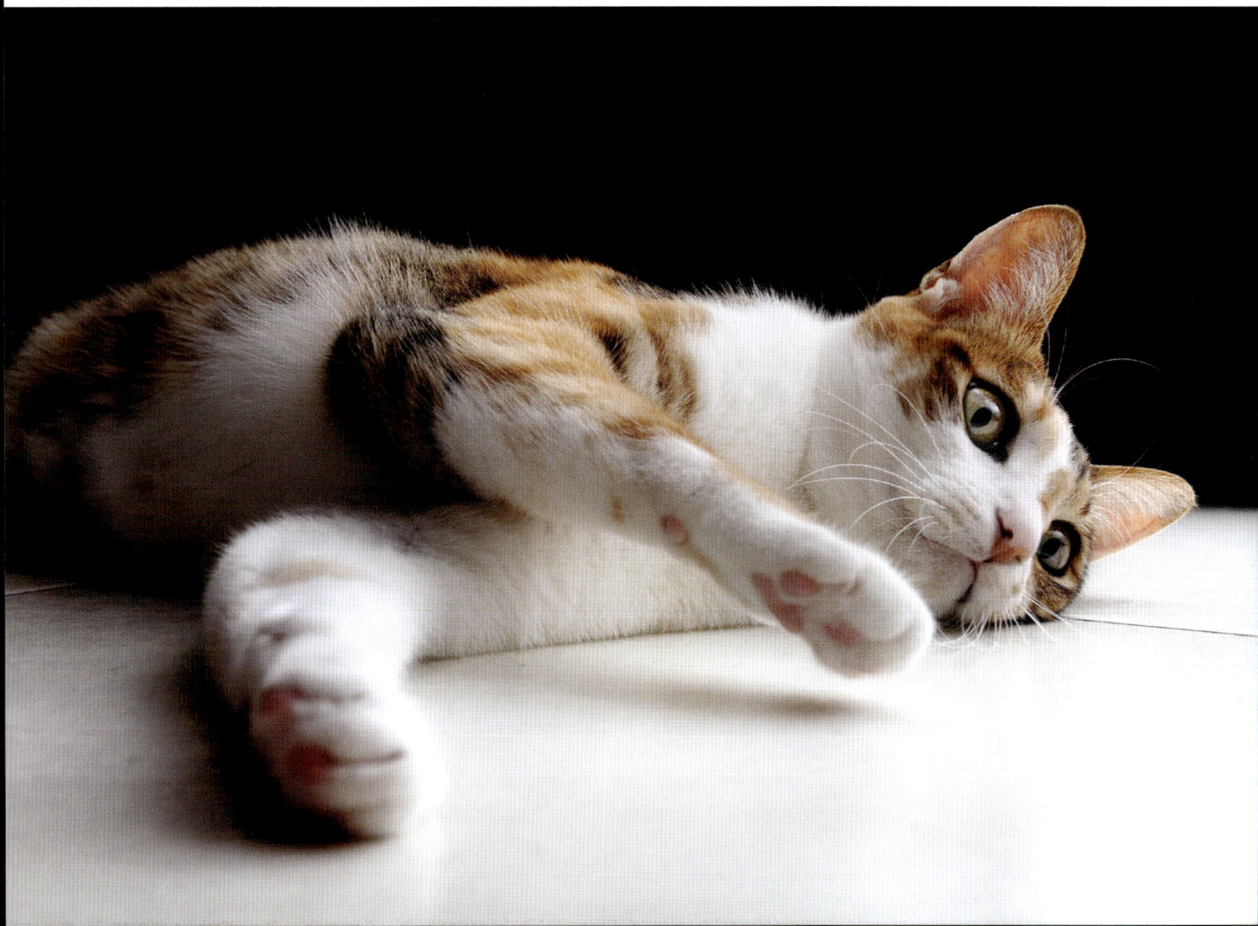

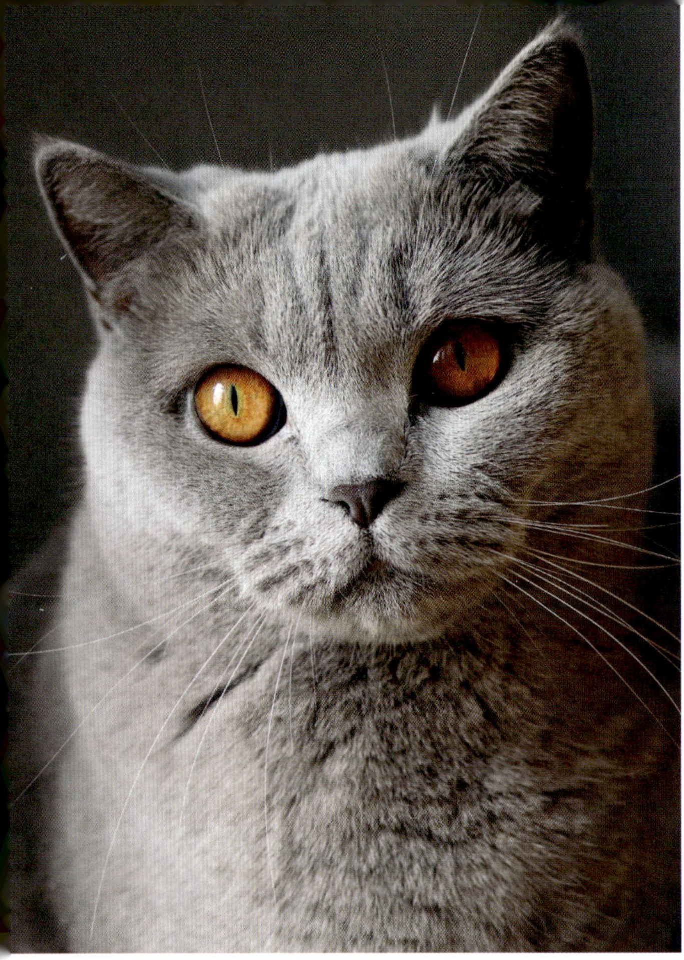
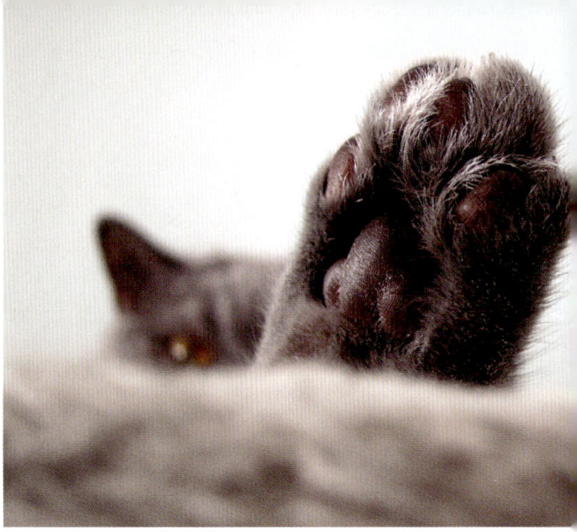
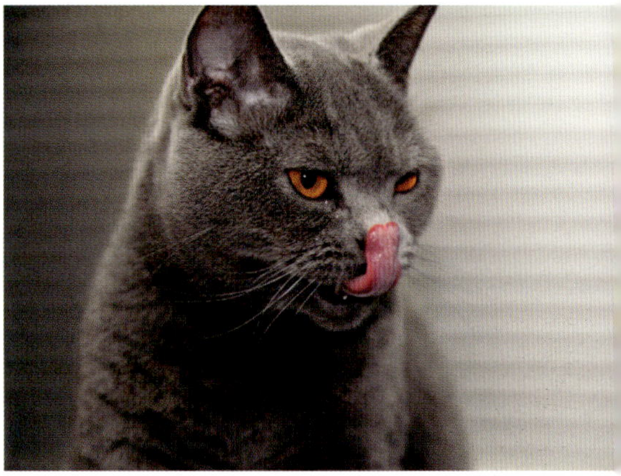
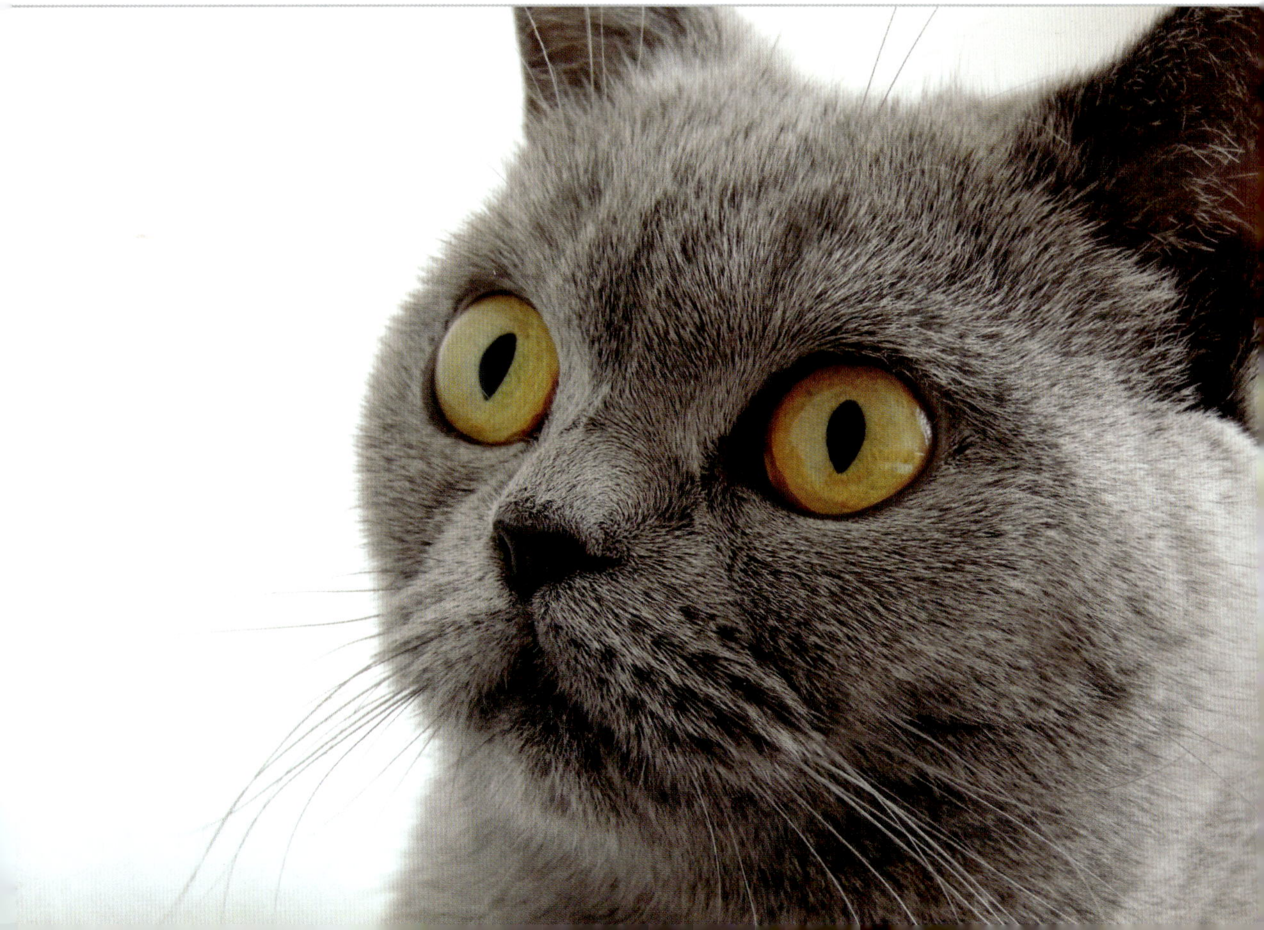

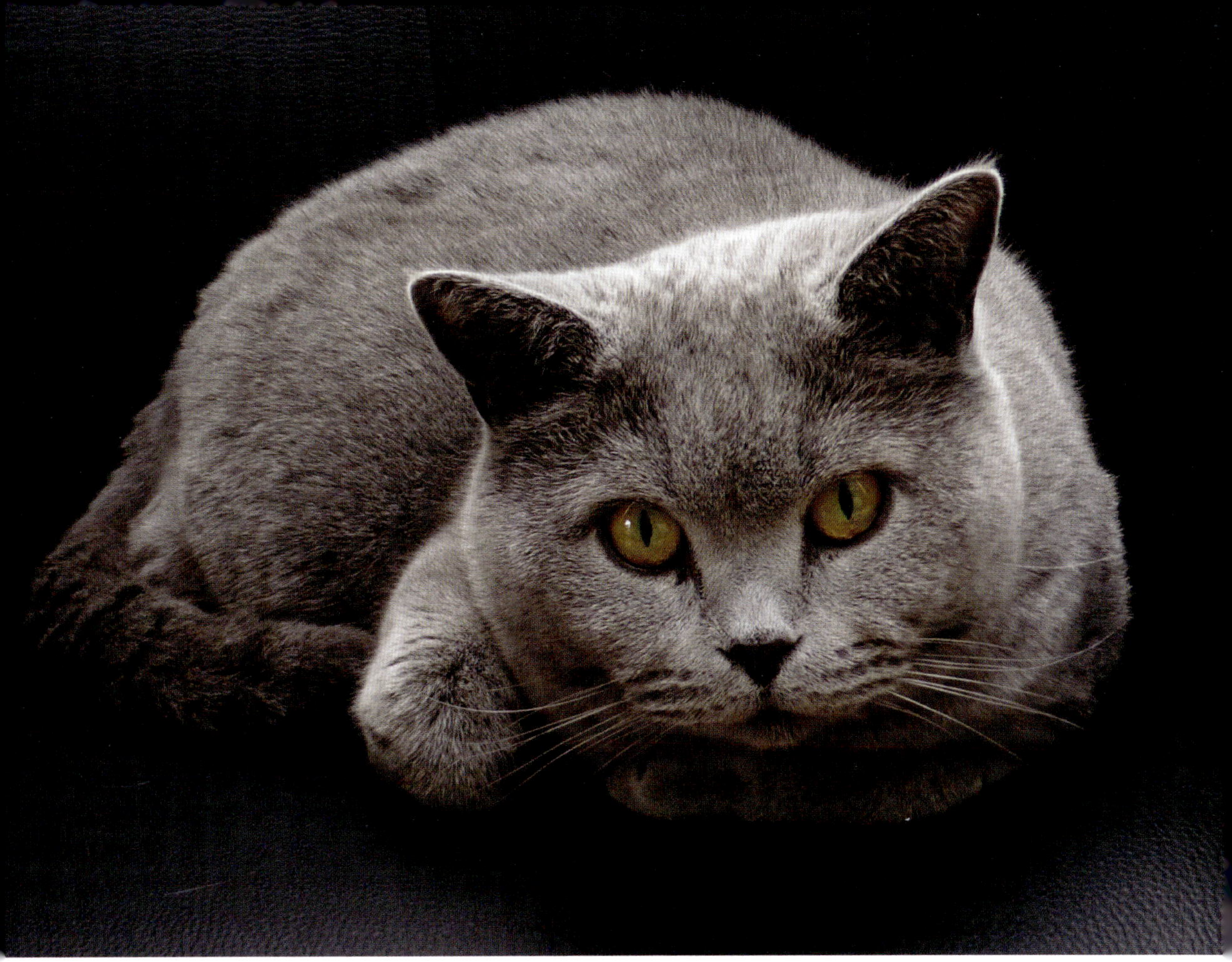

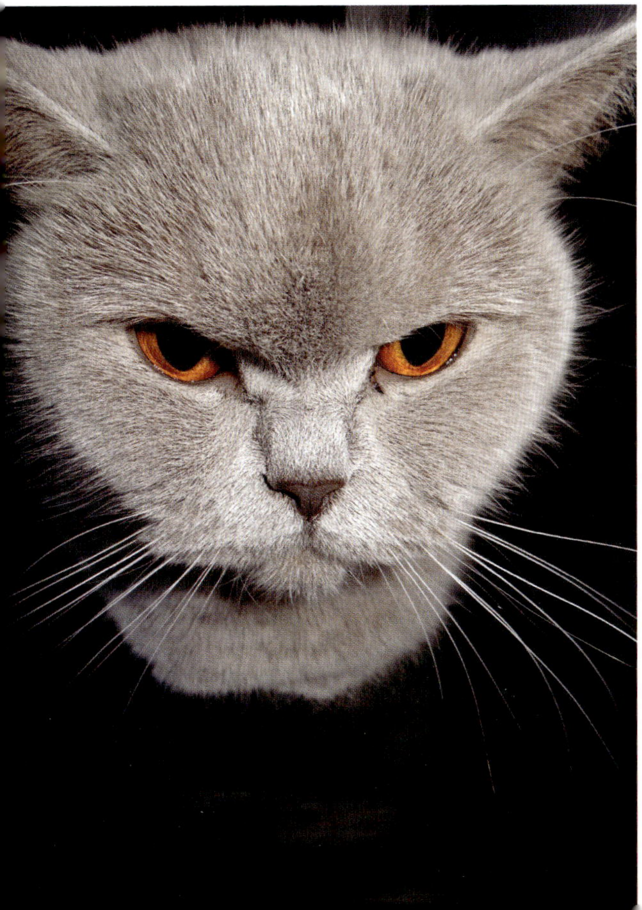

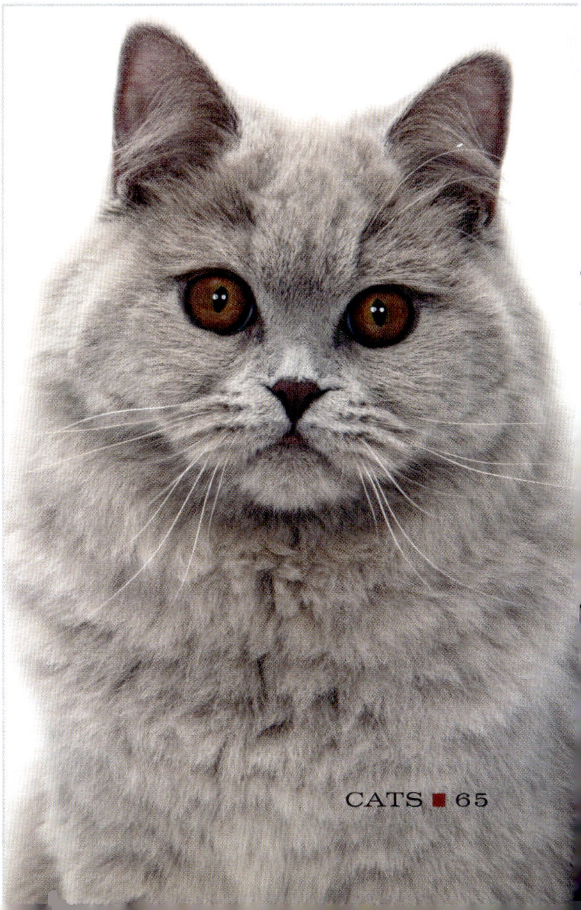

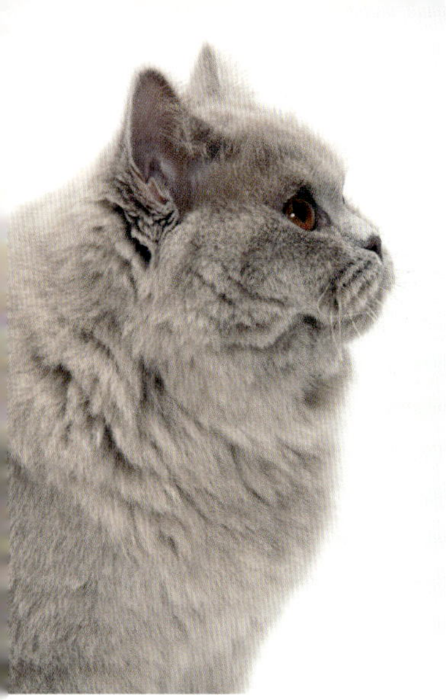
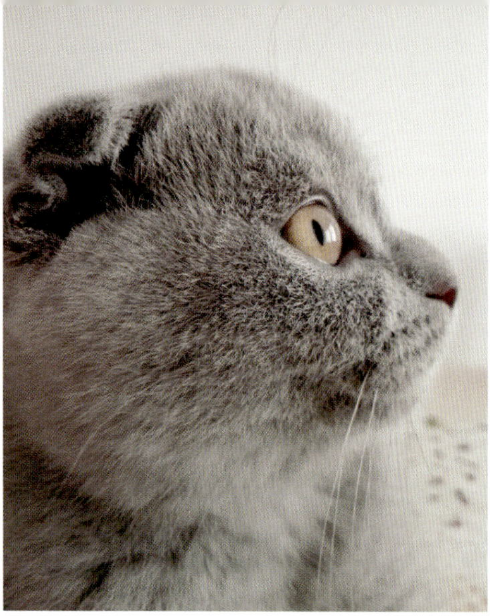
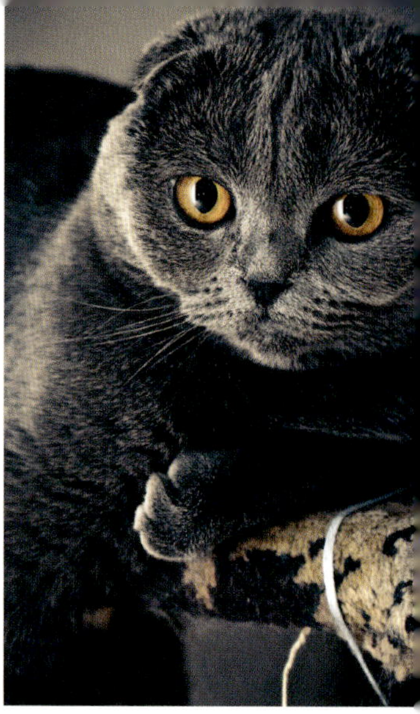
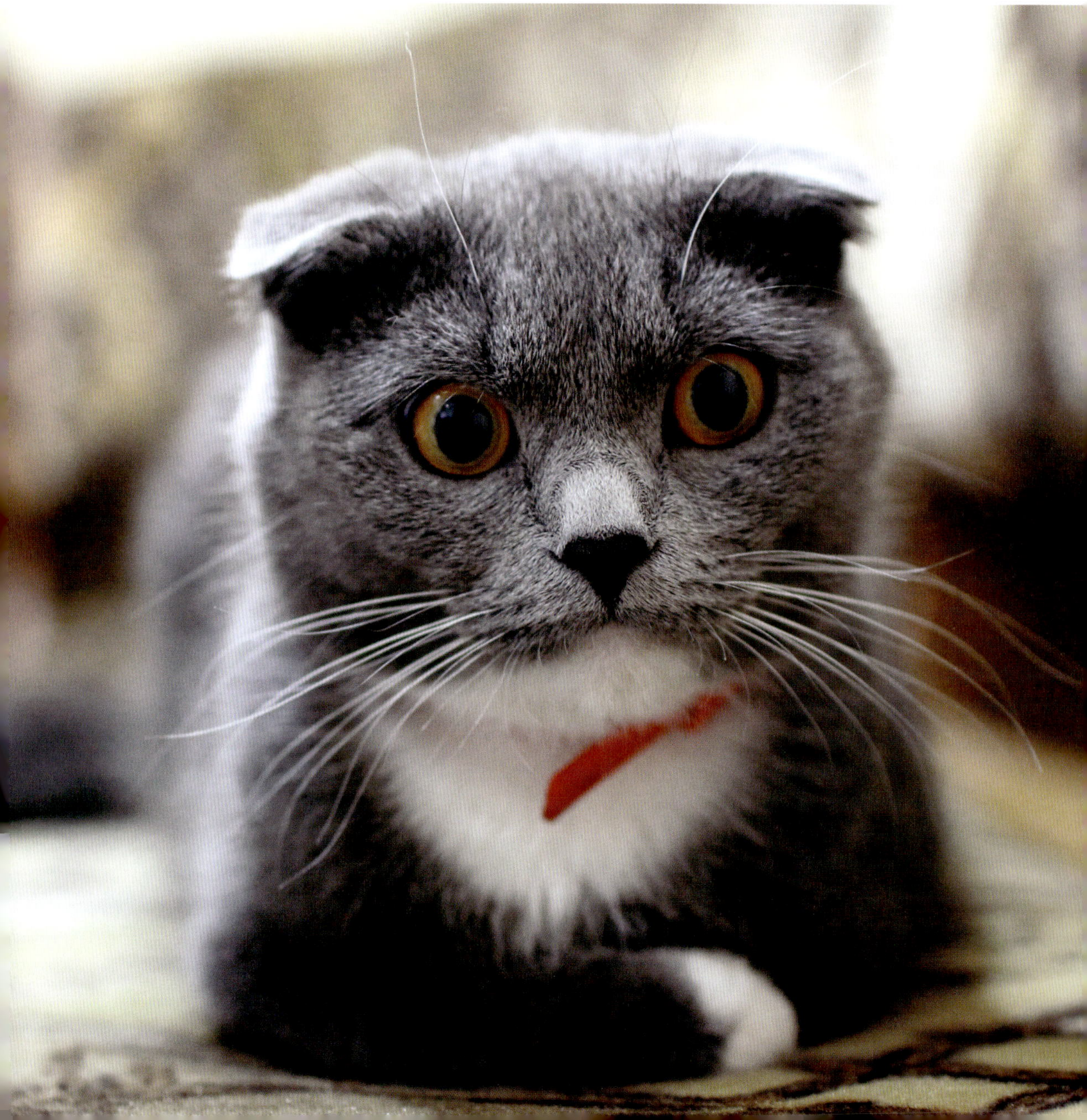

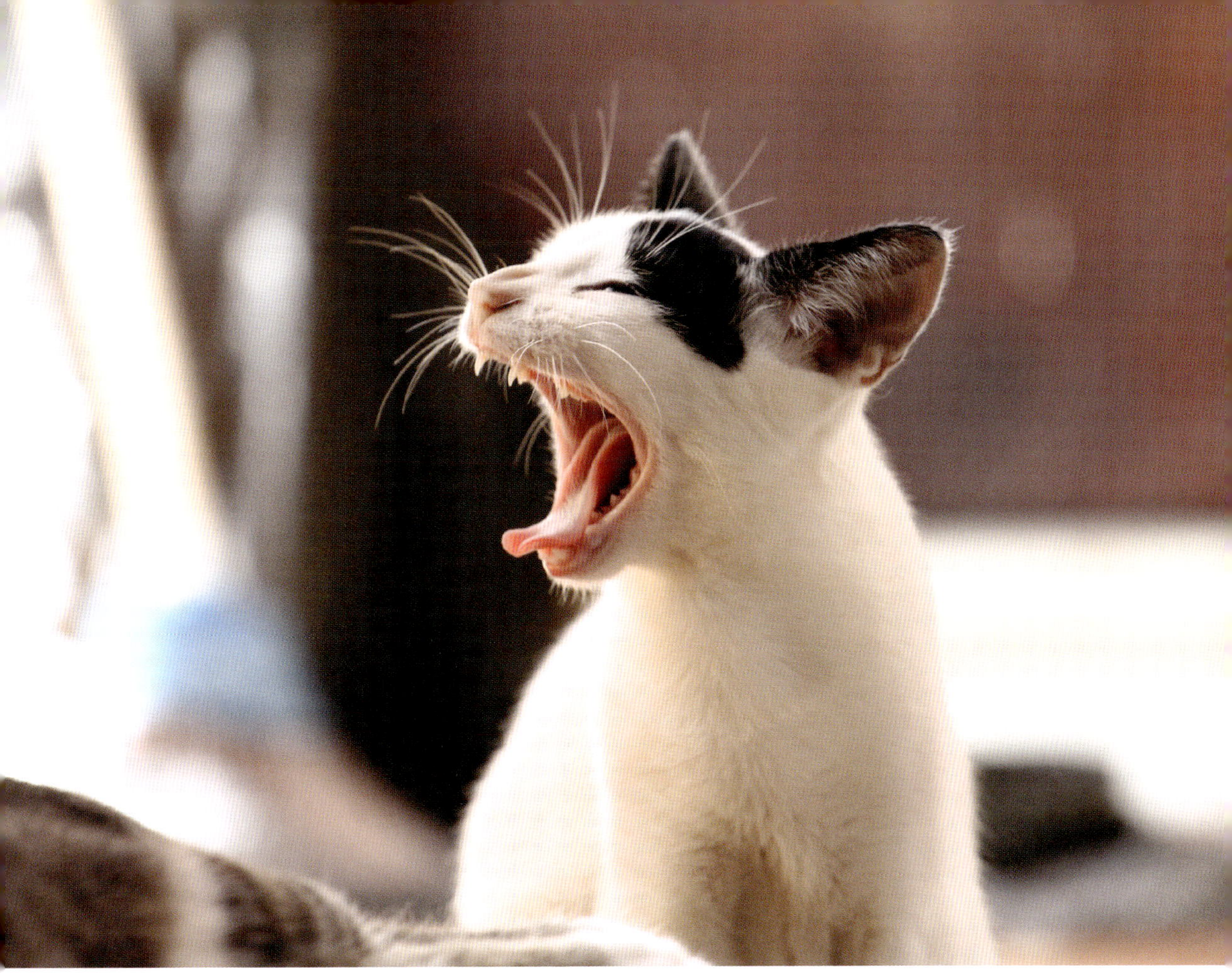

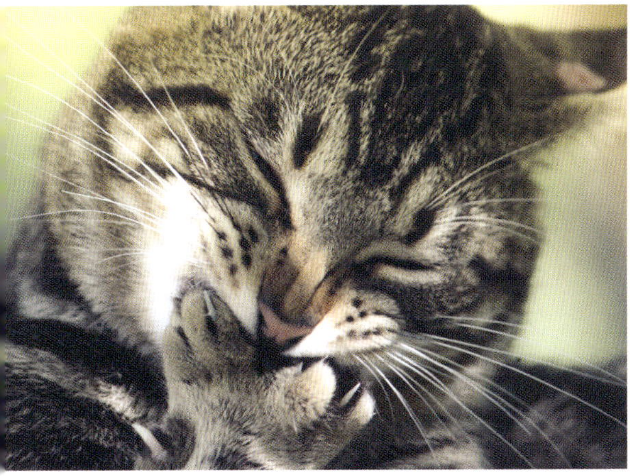

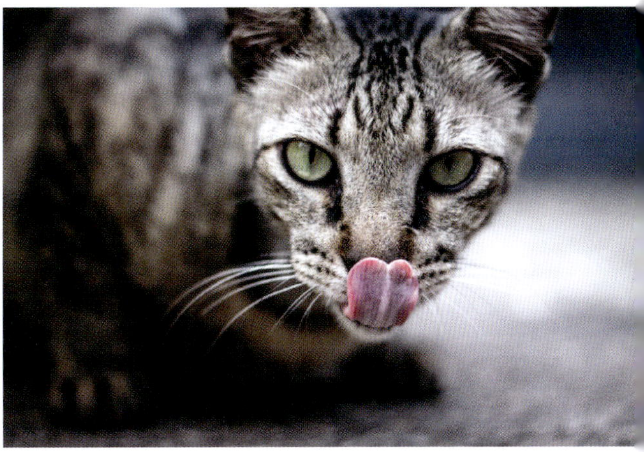

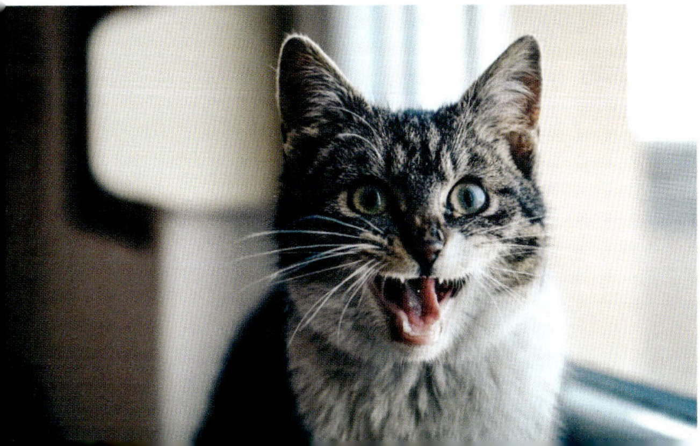

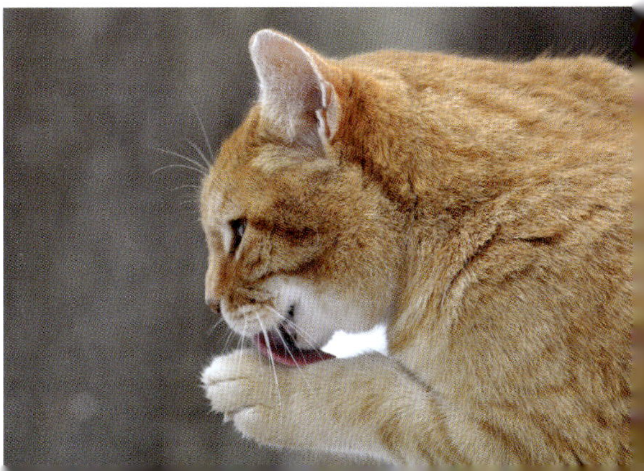

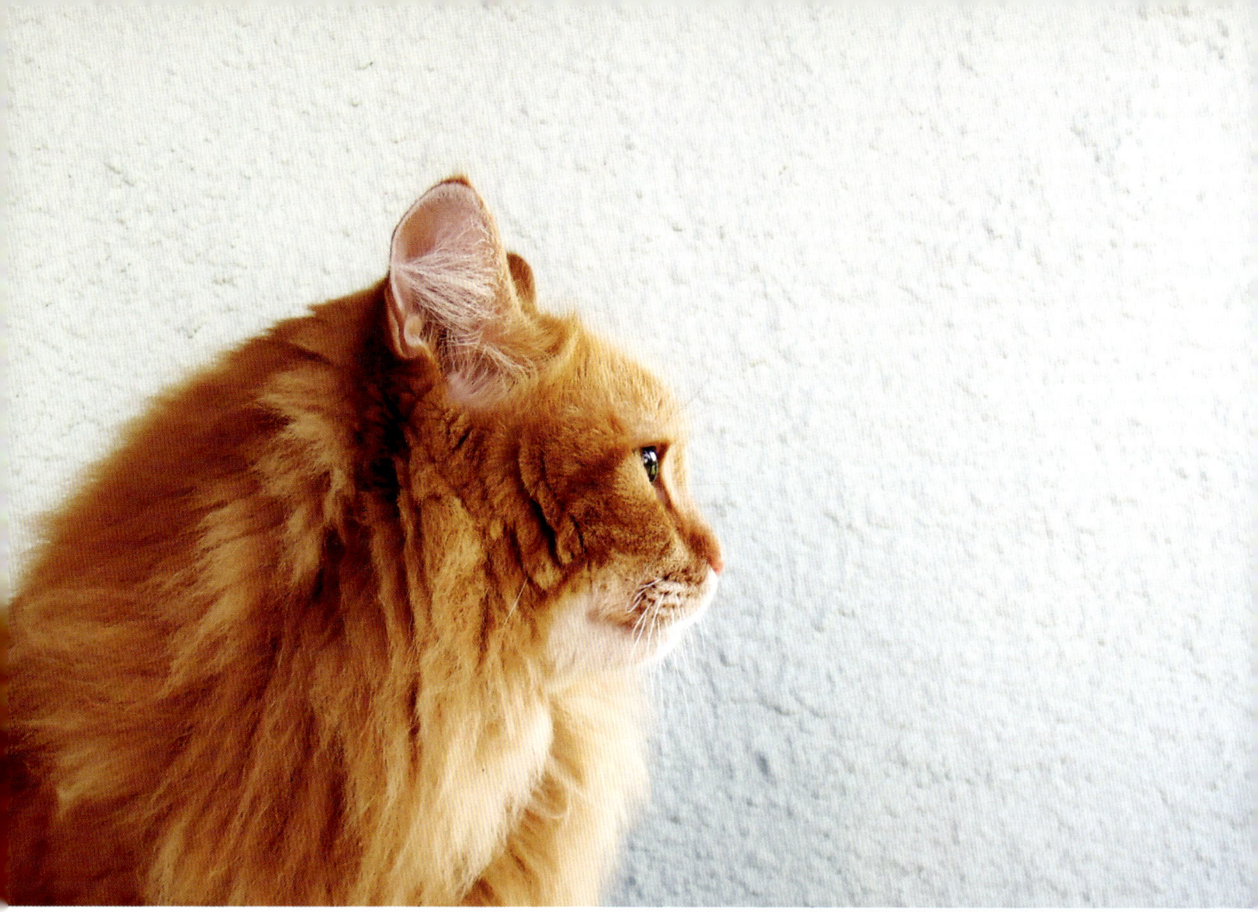
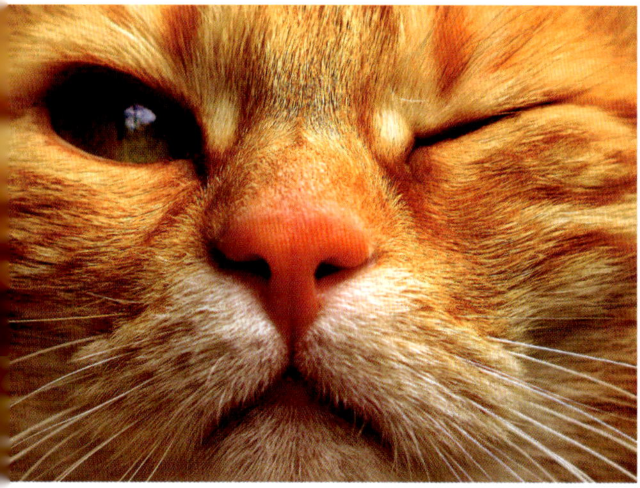
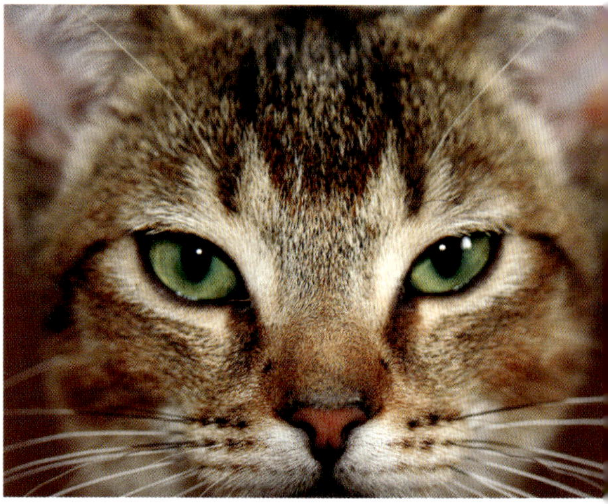
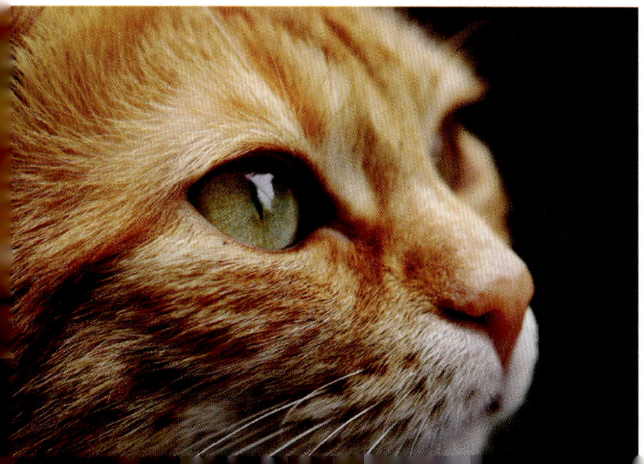
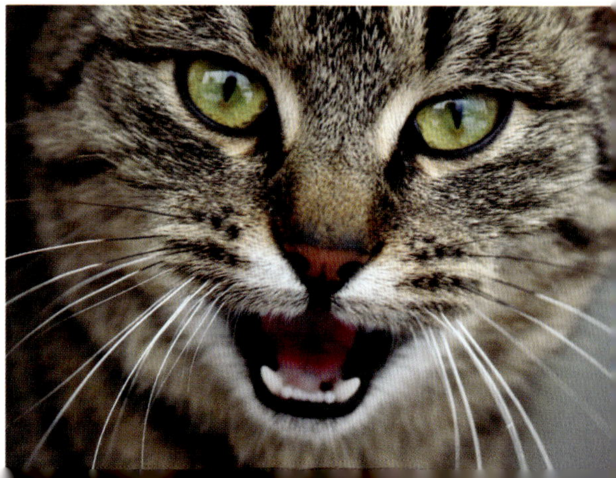

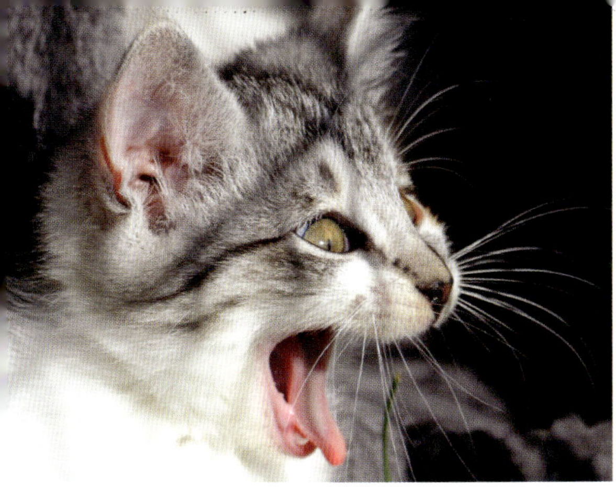
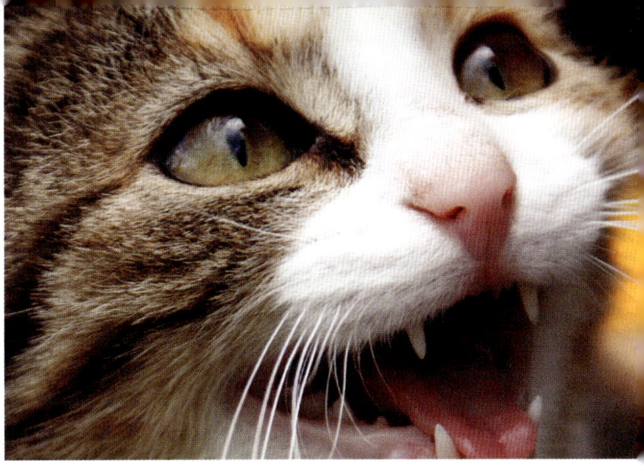
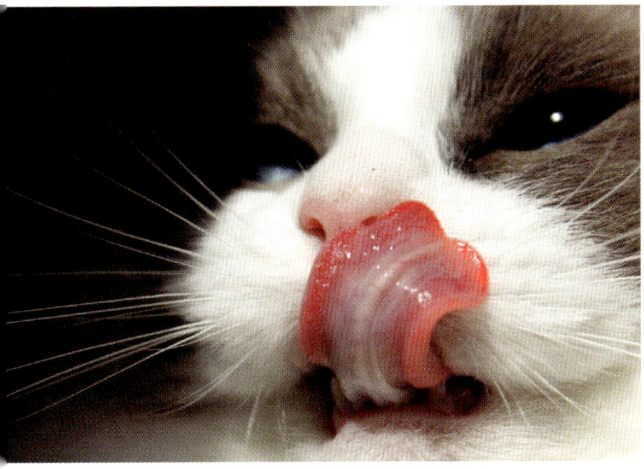
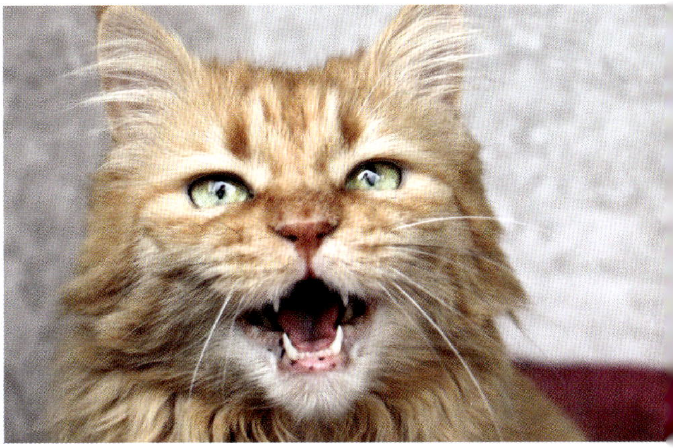
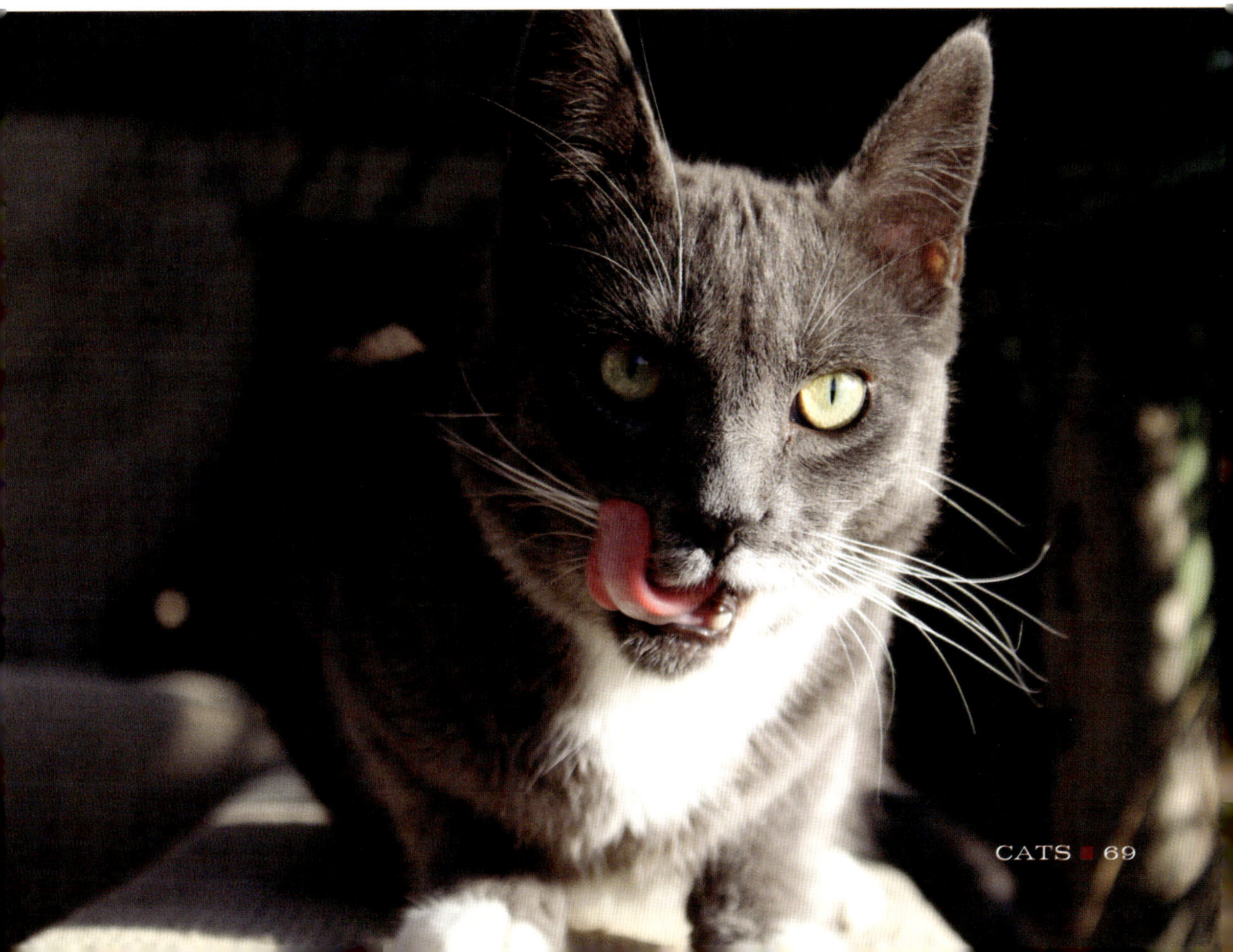

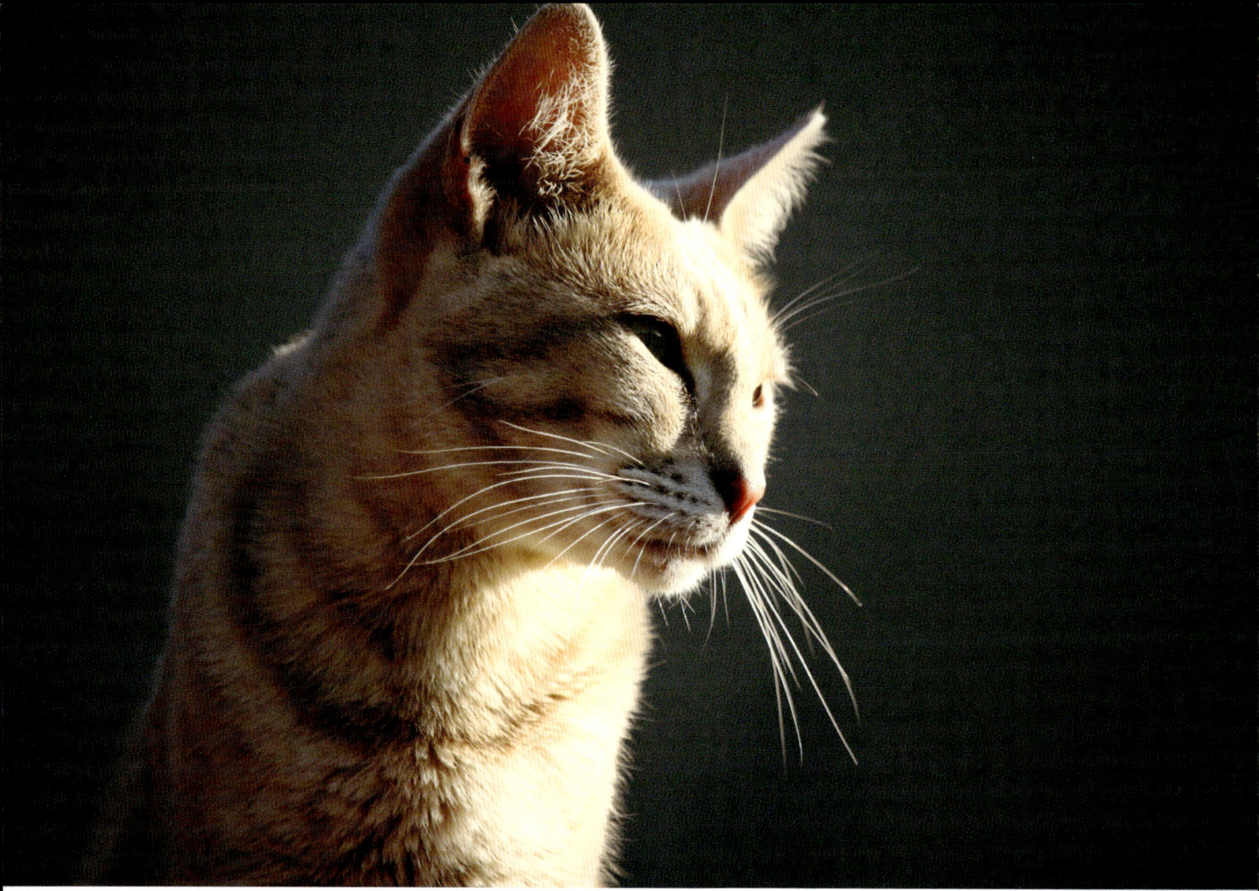
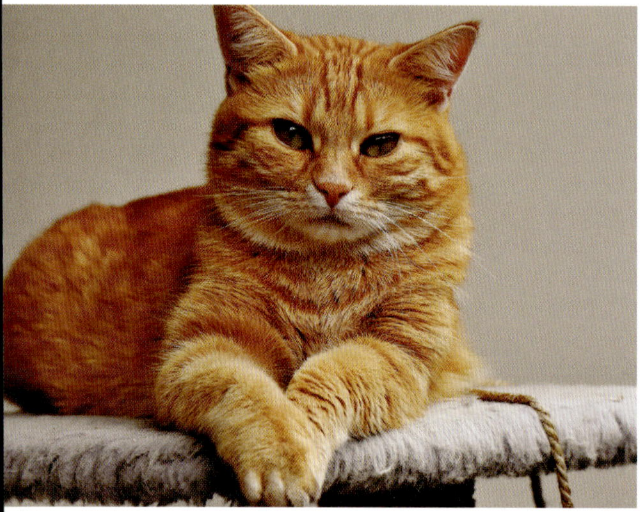
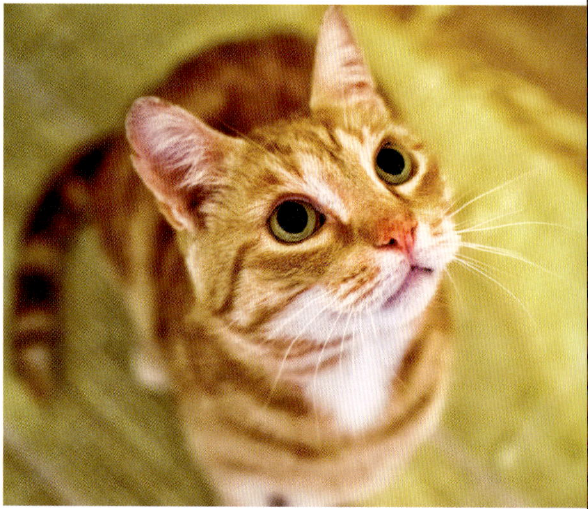
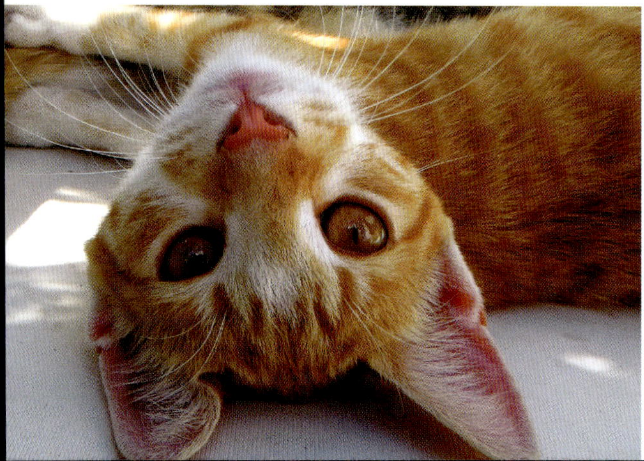
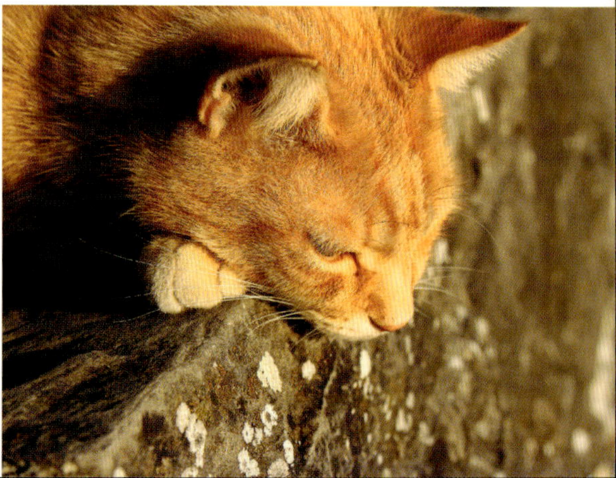

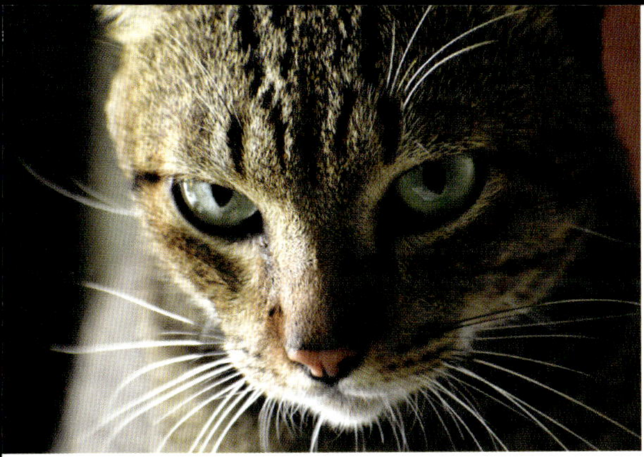

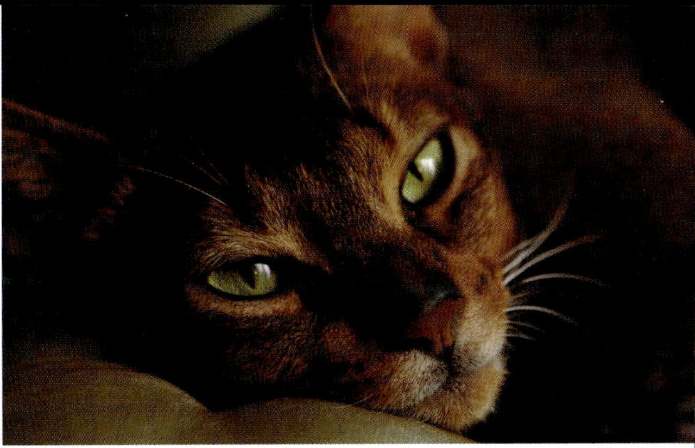

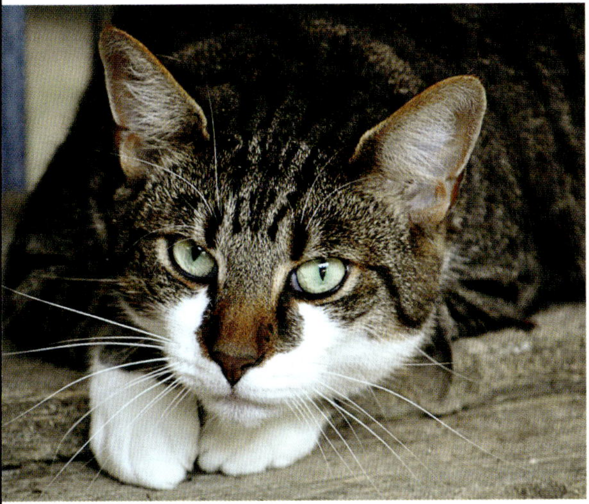

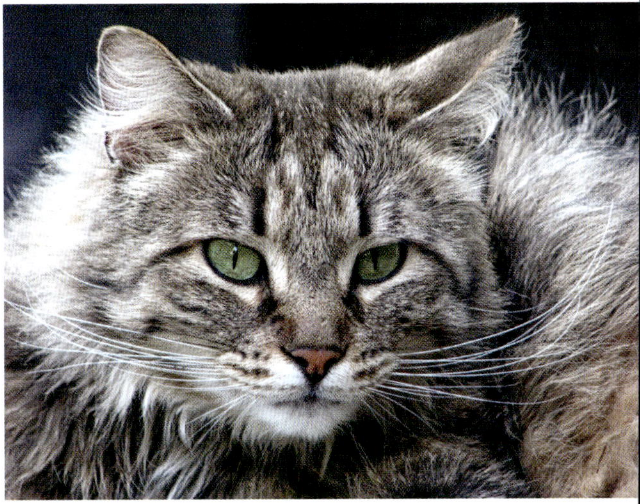

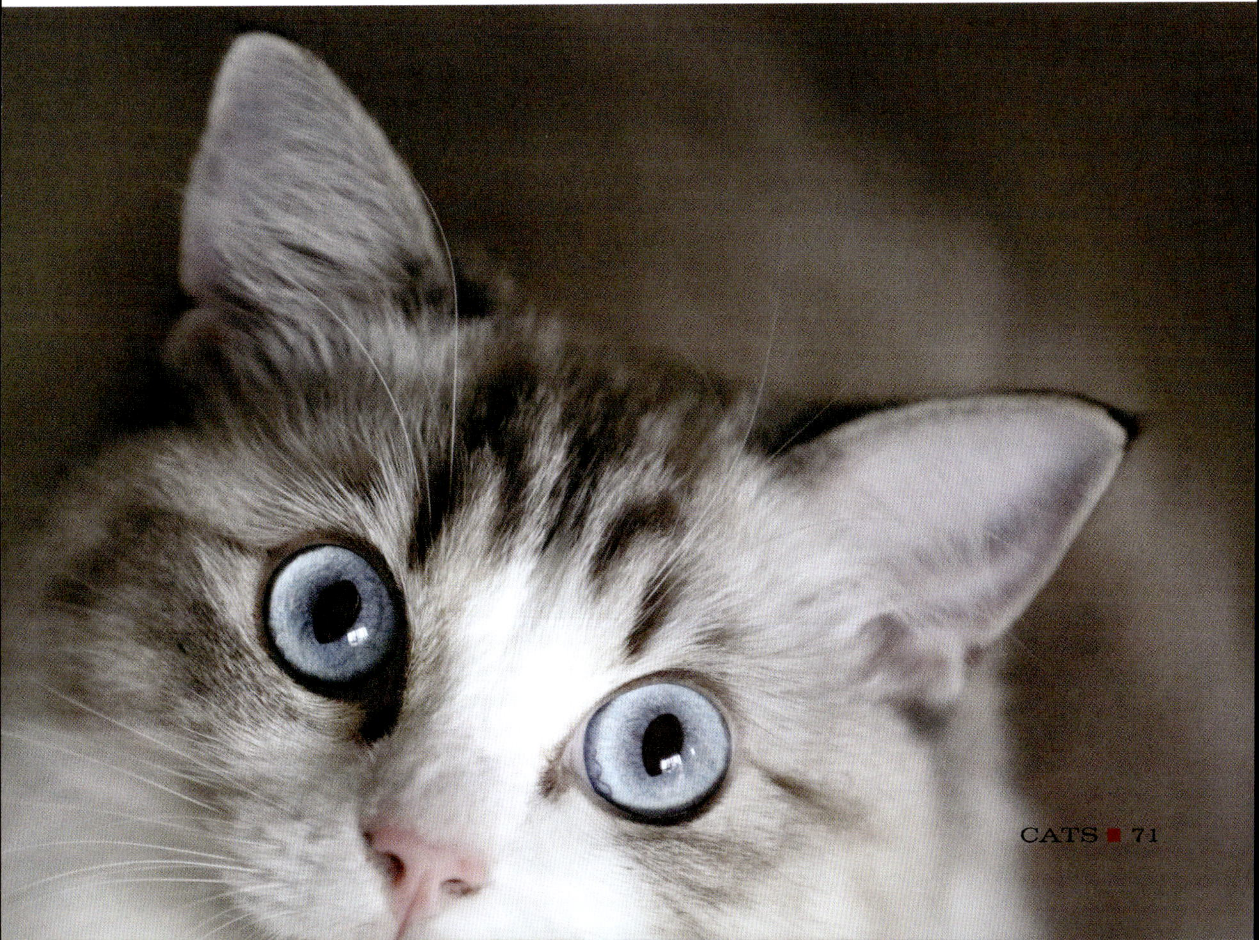

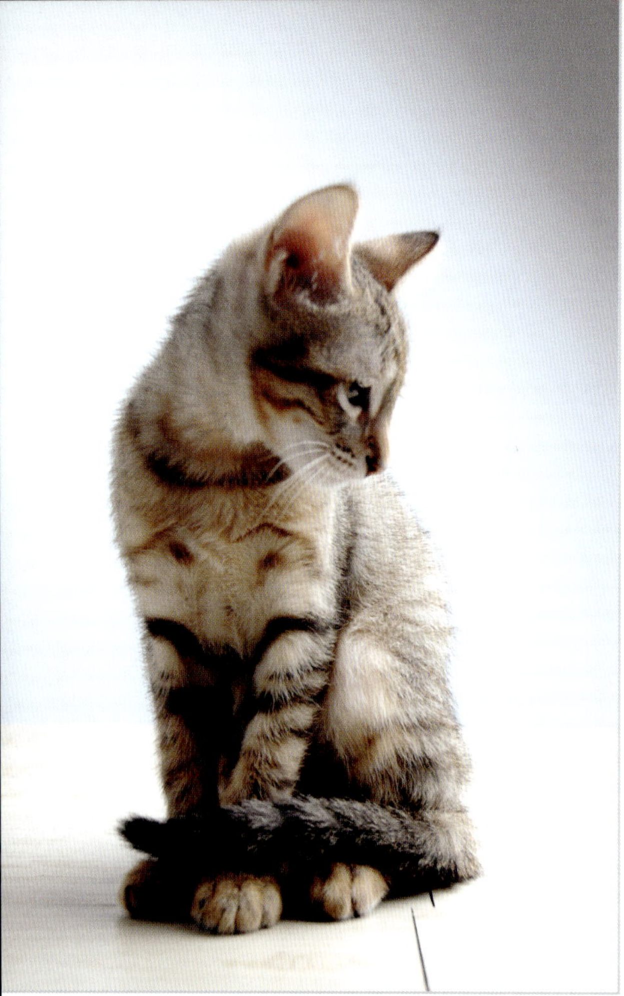
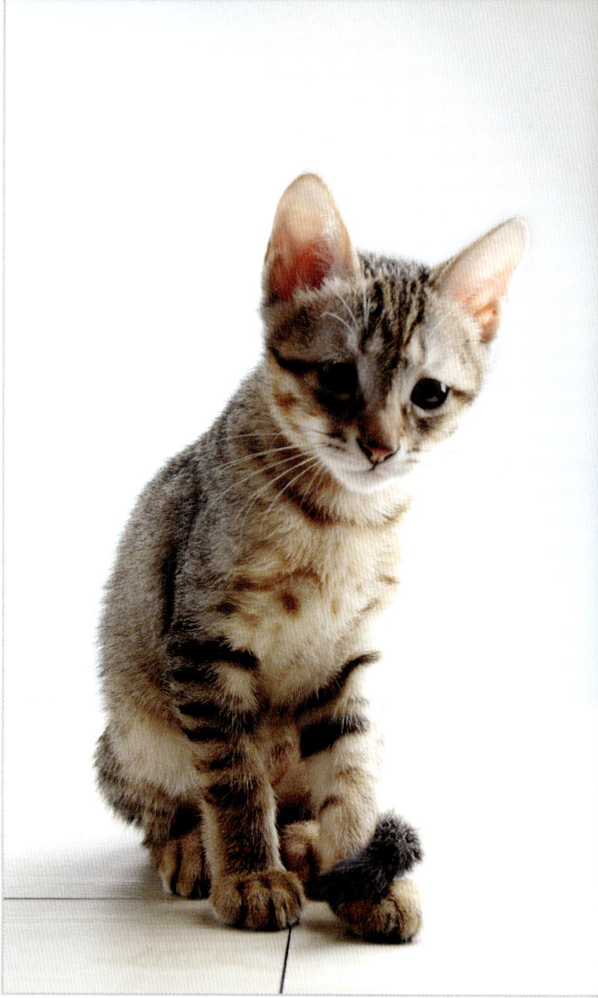
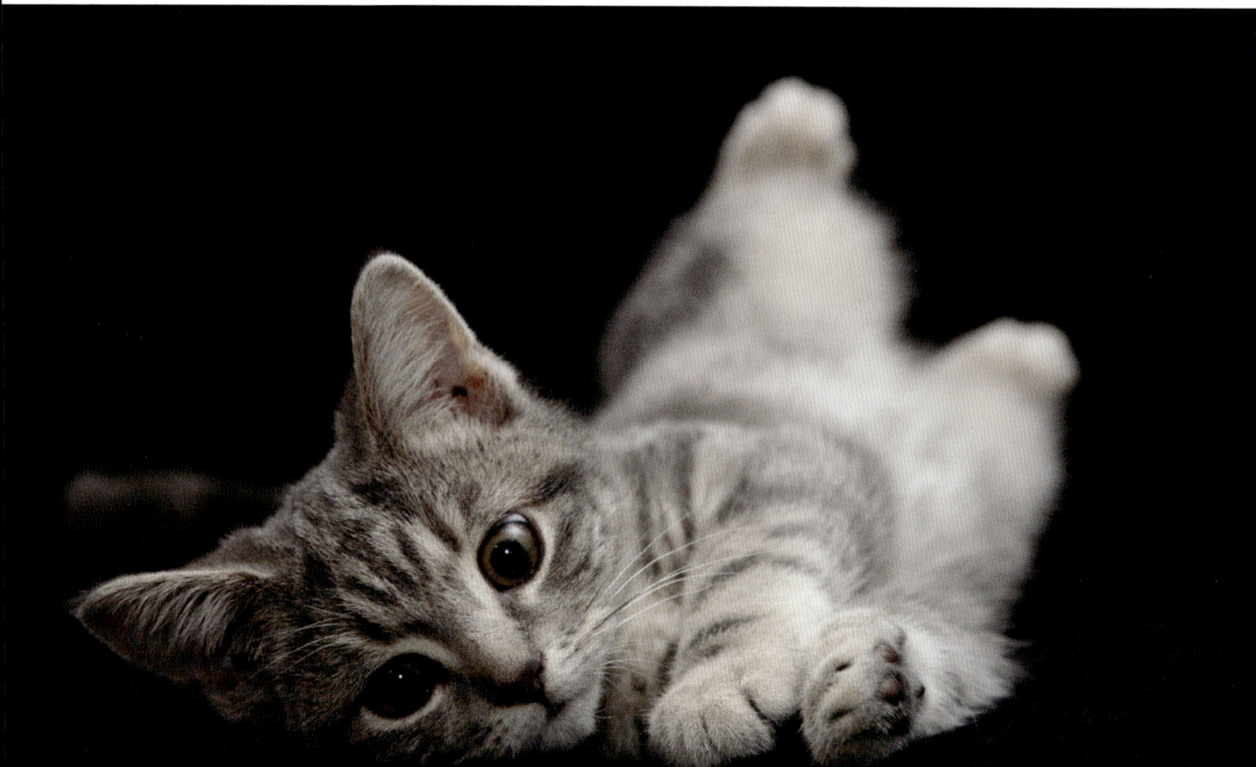

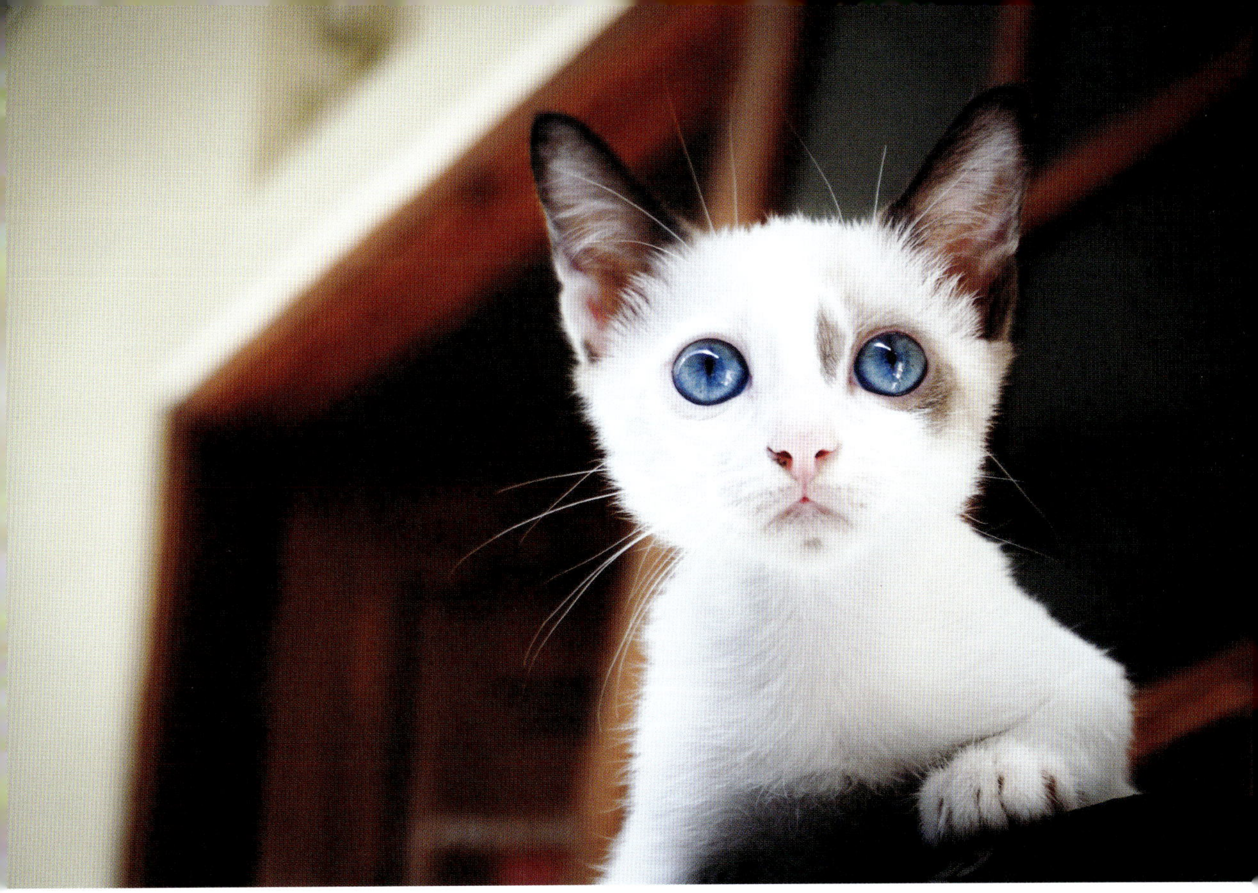
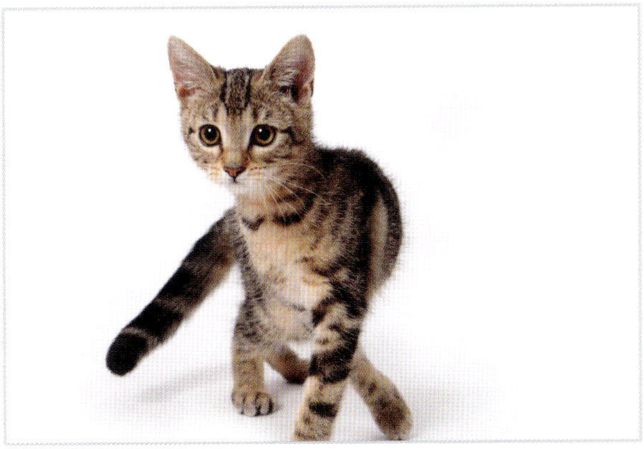
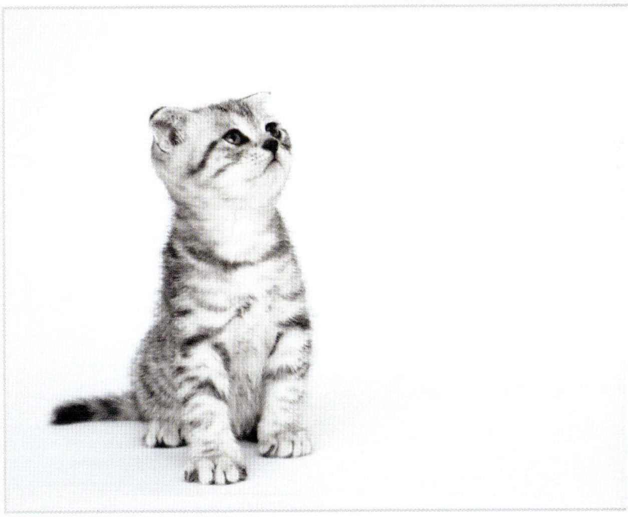
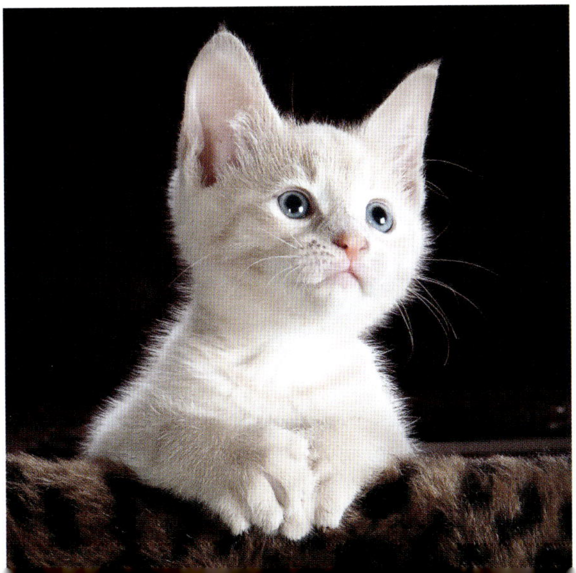
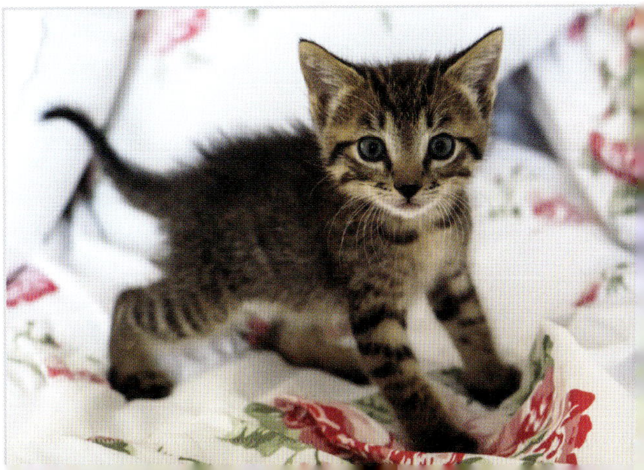

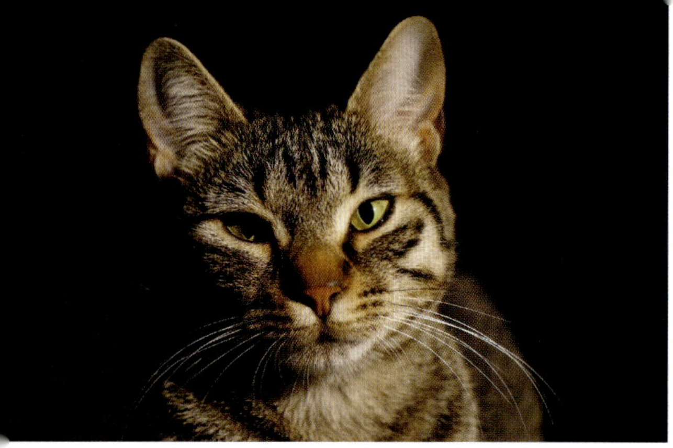
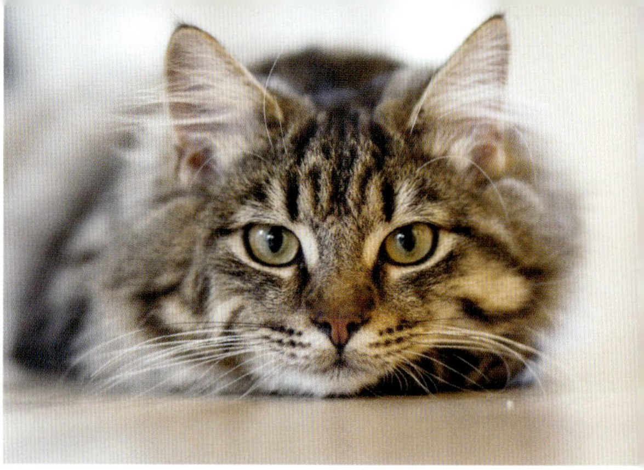
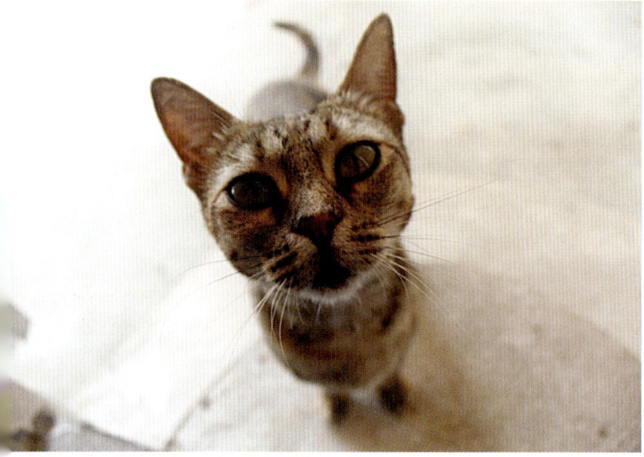
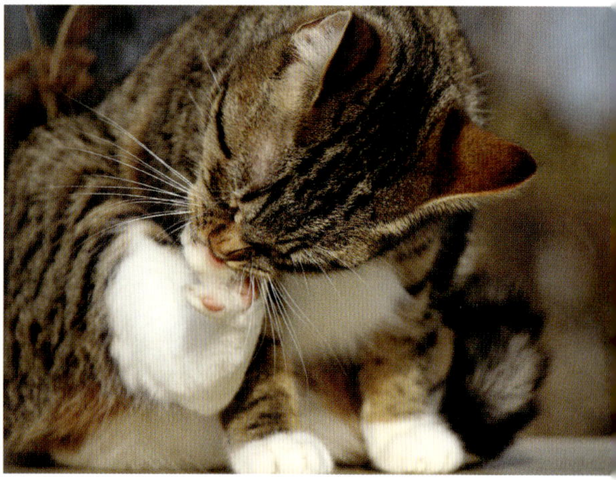
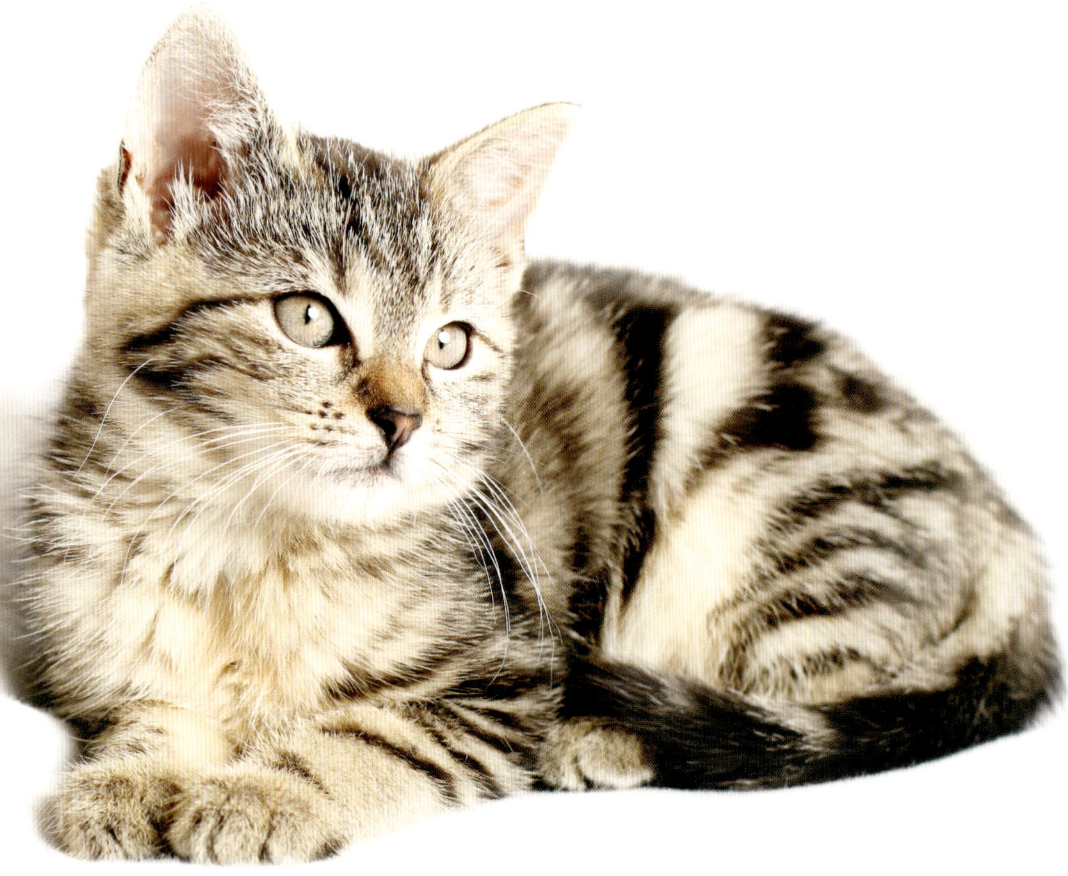

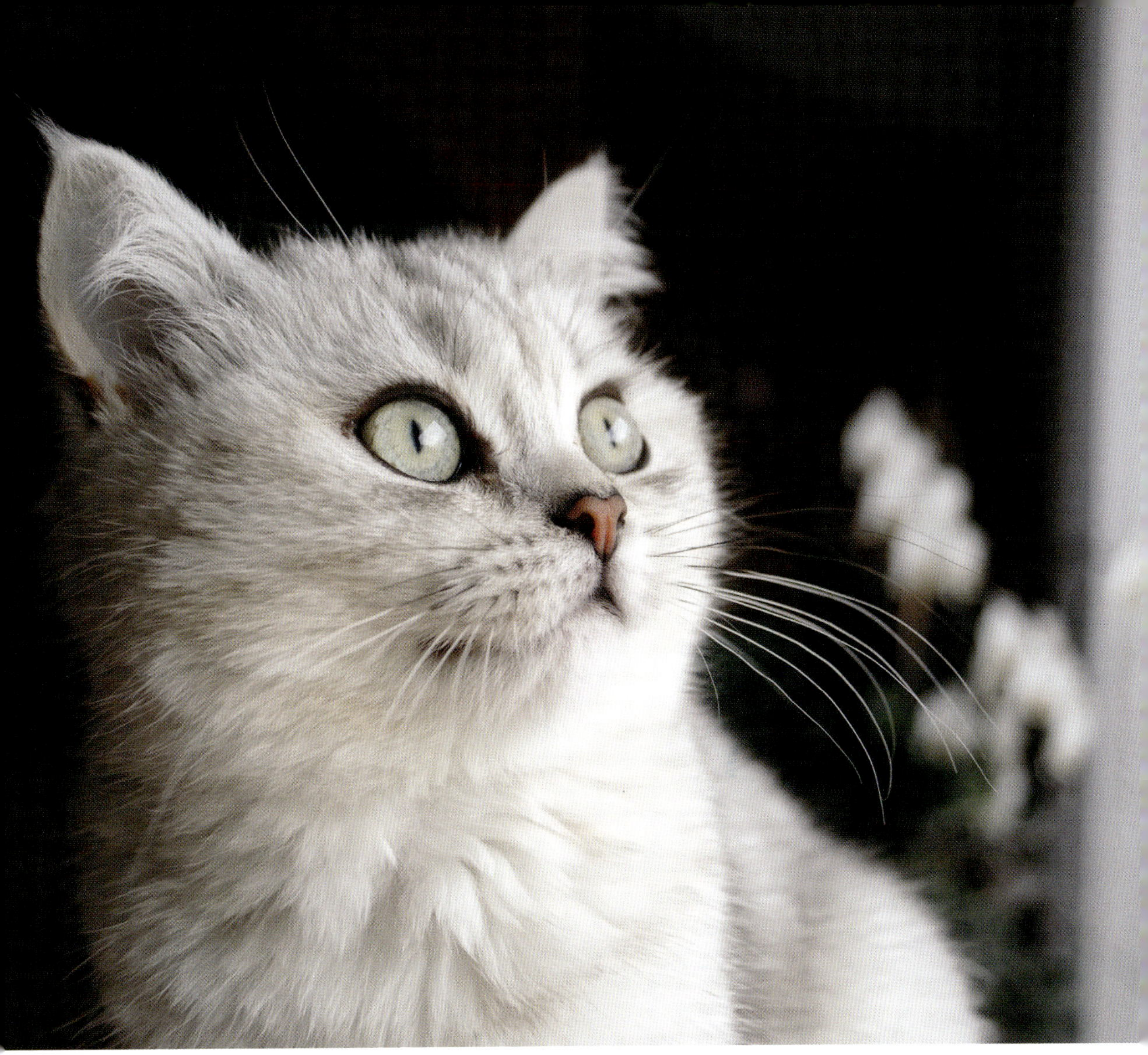
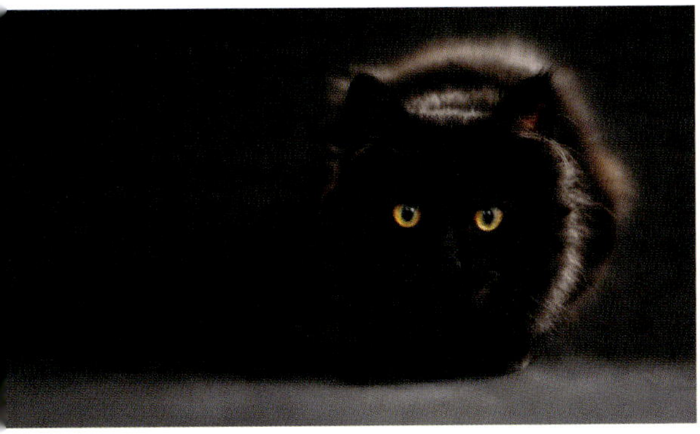
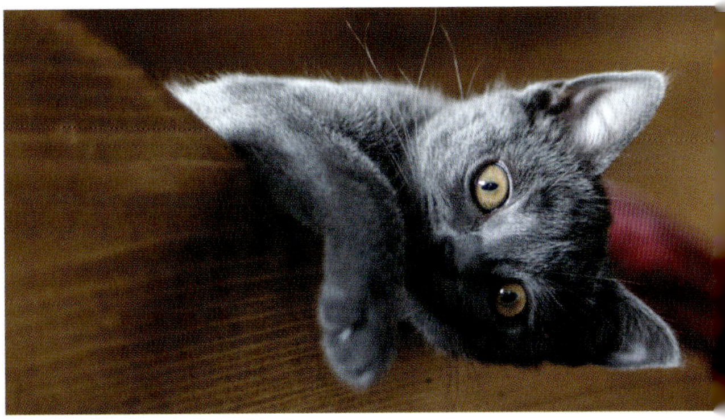
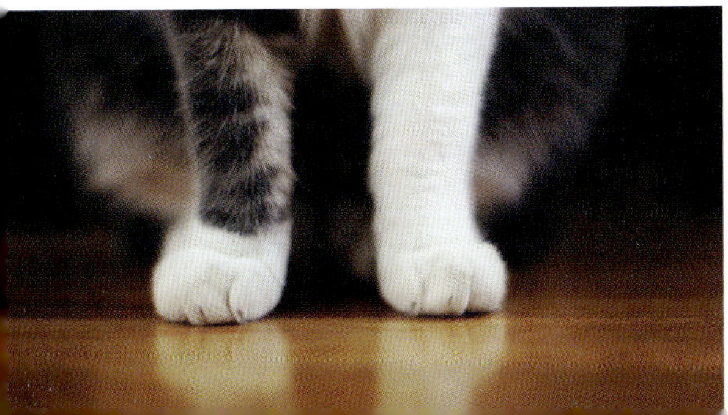
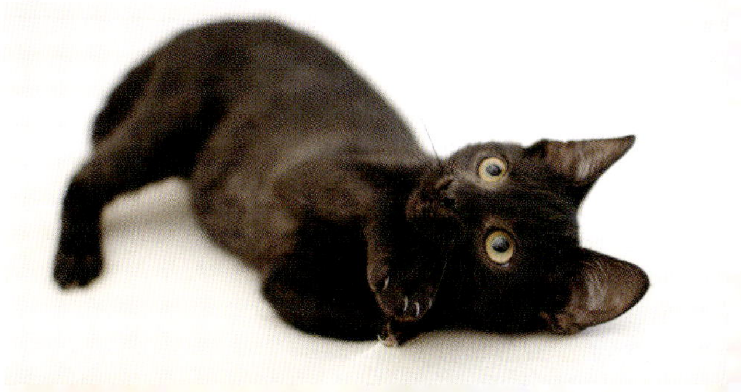

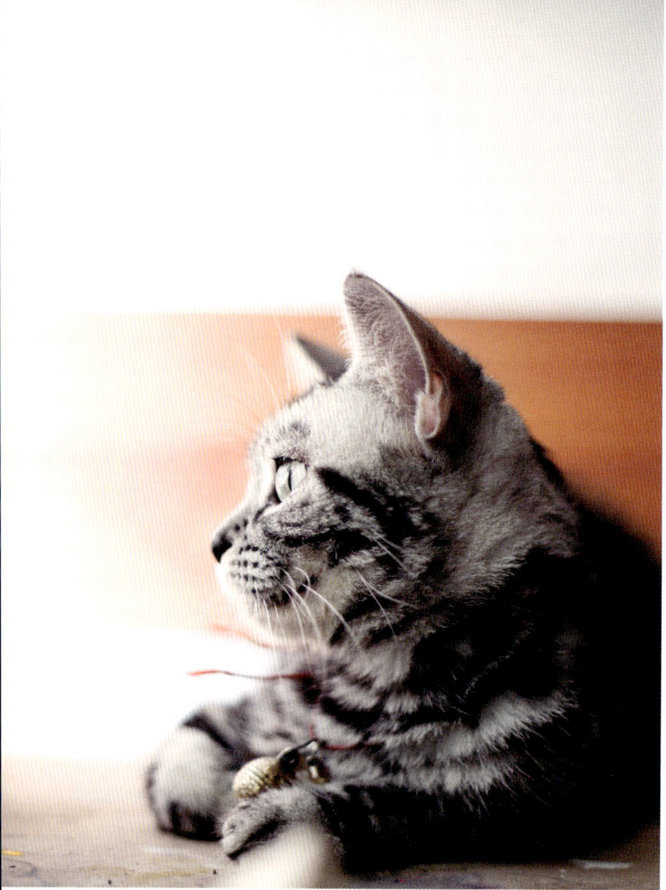
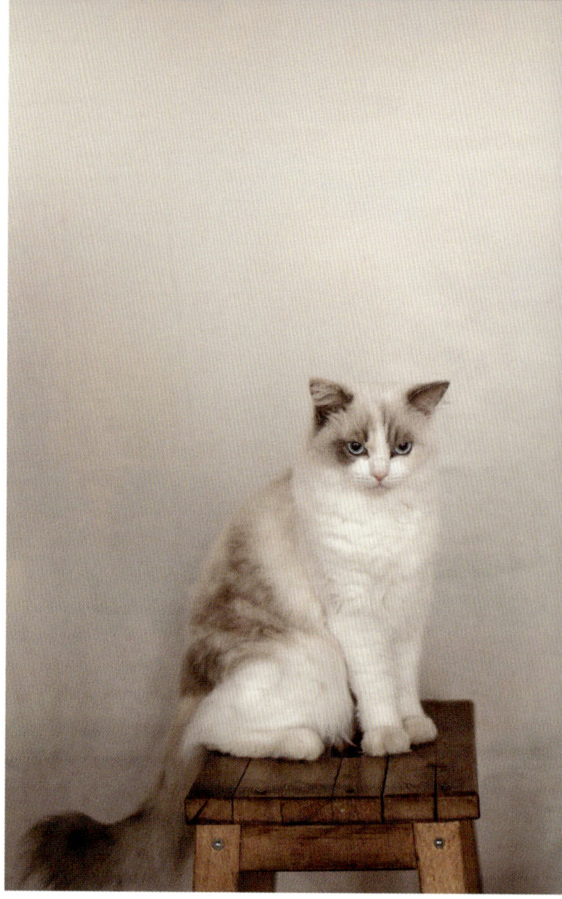
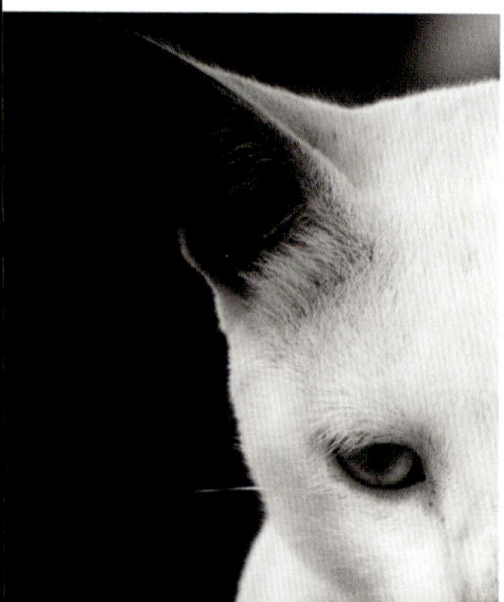
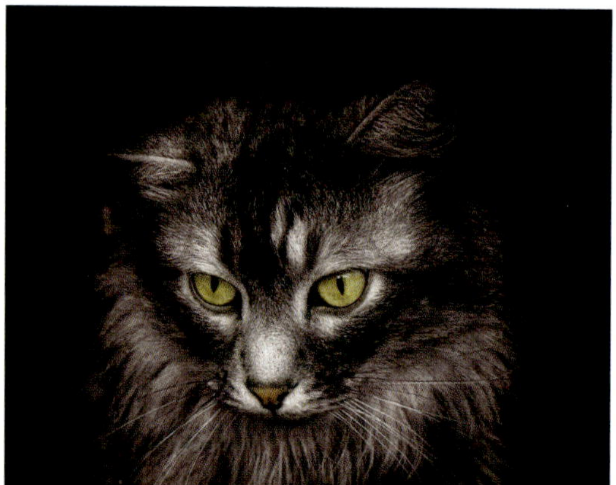
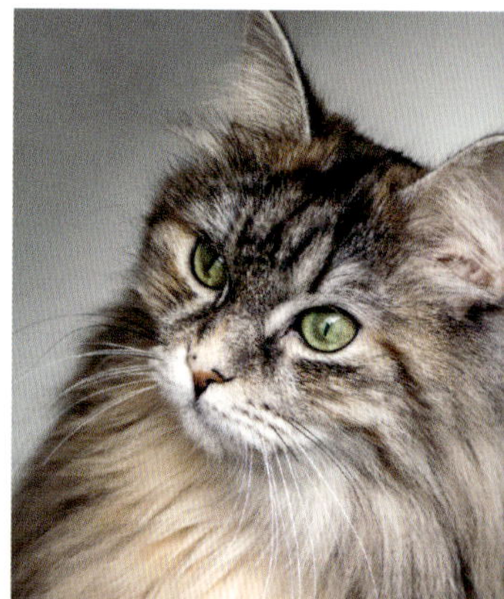
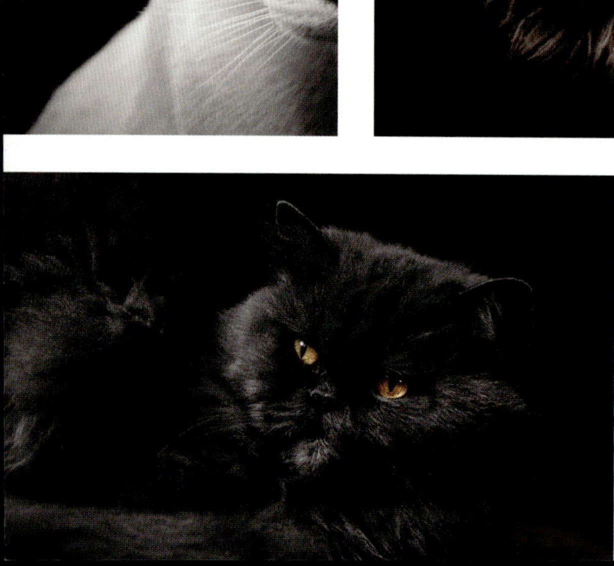
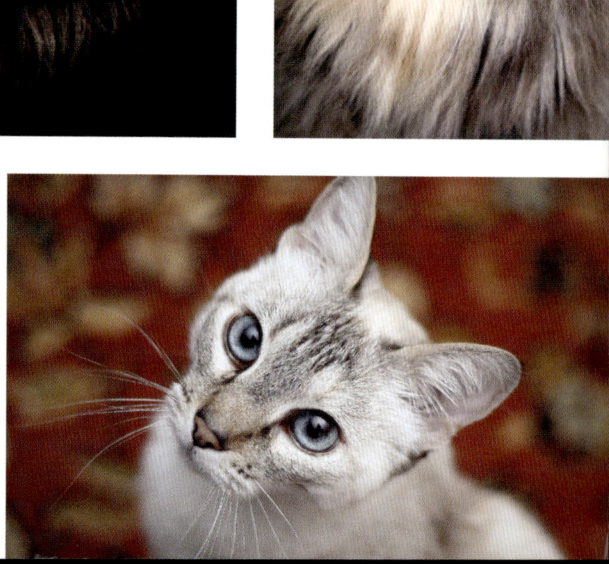

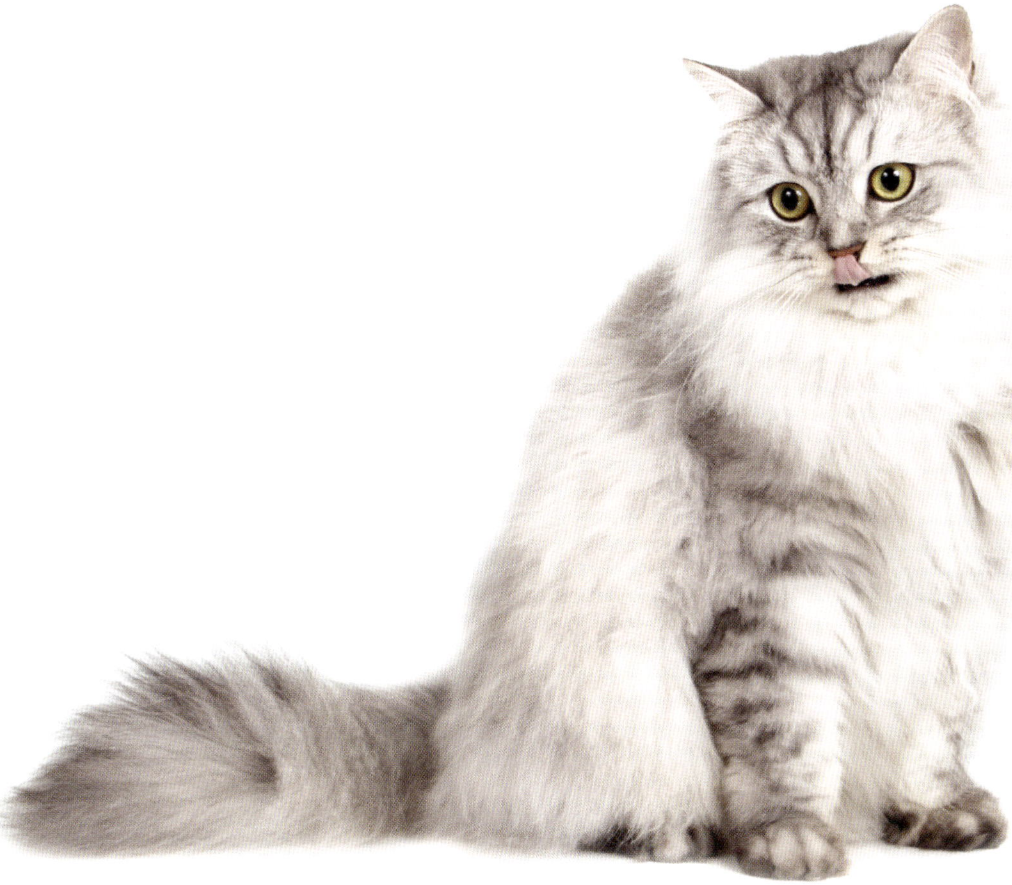

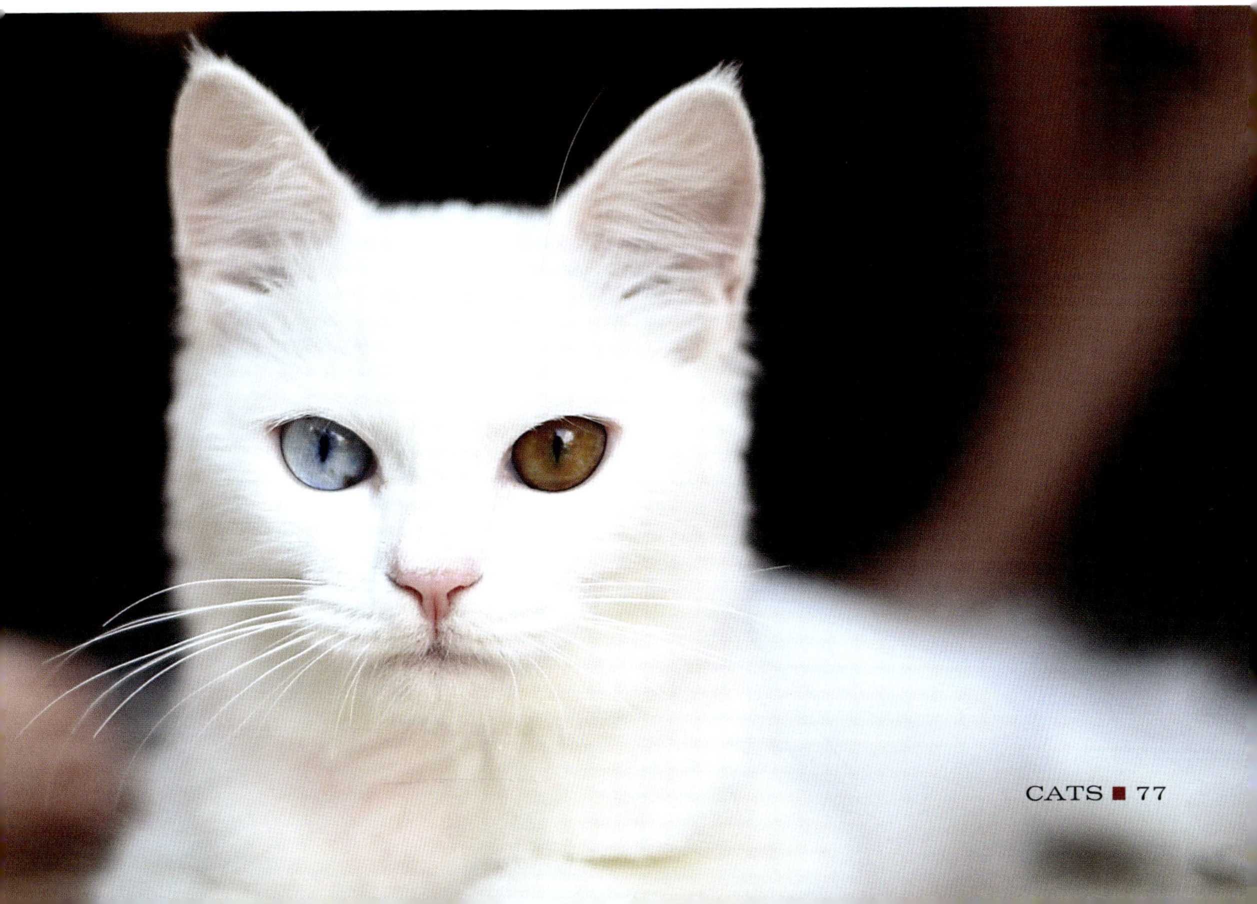

"Of all God's creatures, there is only one that cannot be made slave of the lash. That one is the cat. If man could be crossed with the cat it would improve the man, but it would deteriorate the cat."

—Mark Twain, author

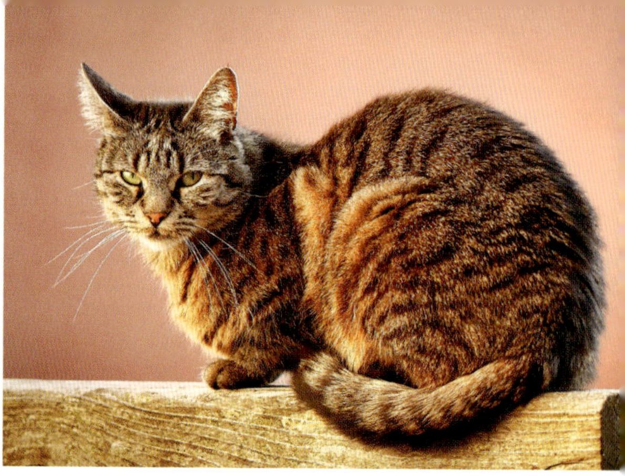

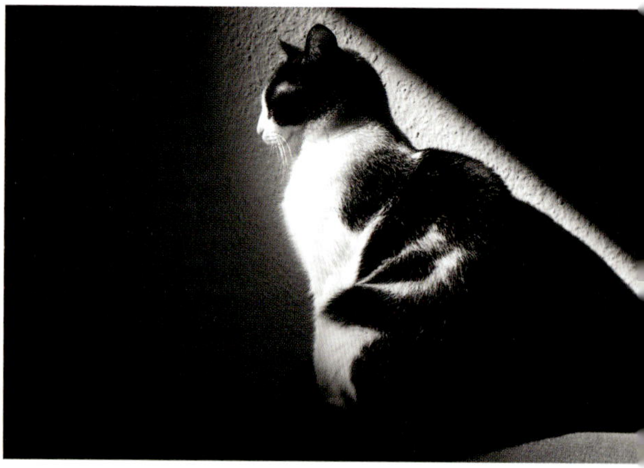

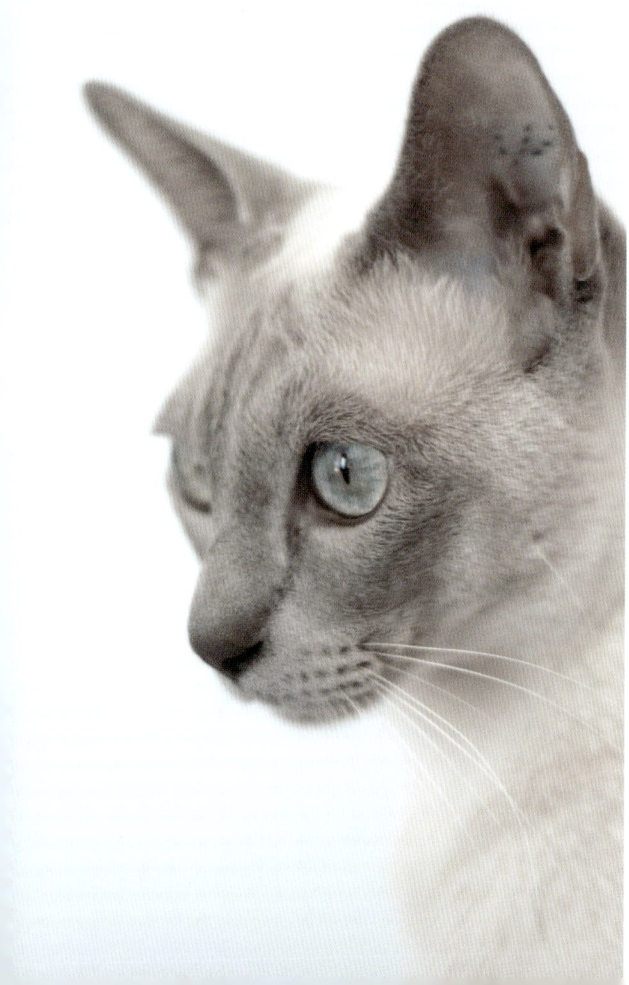

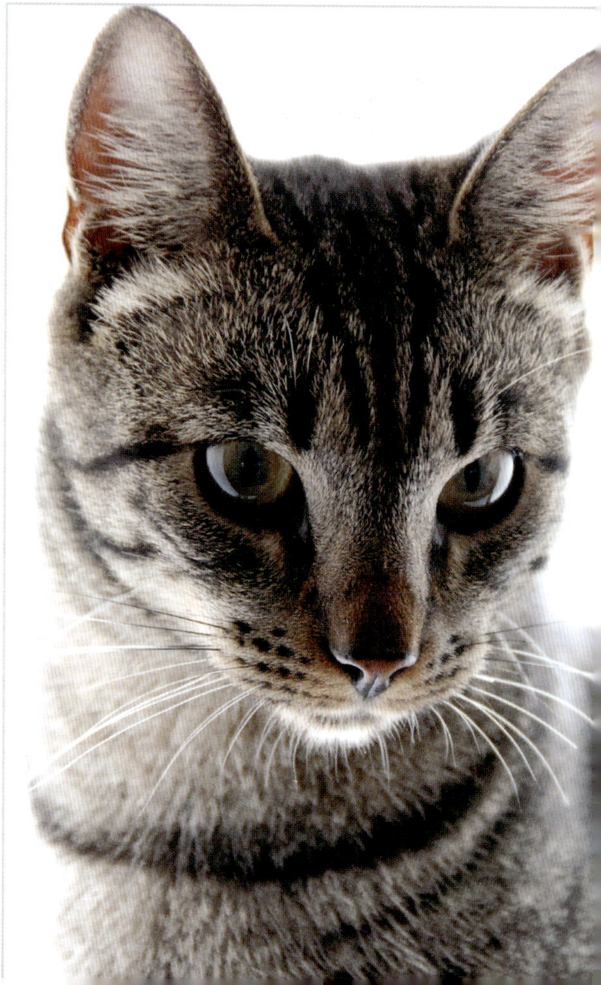

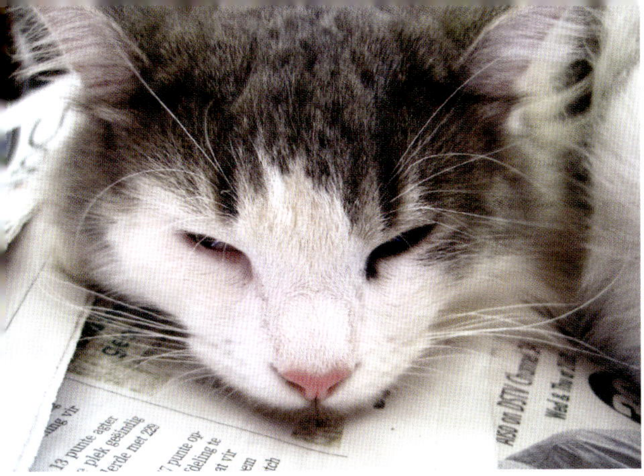
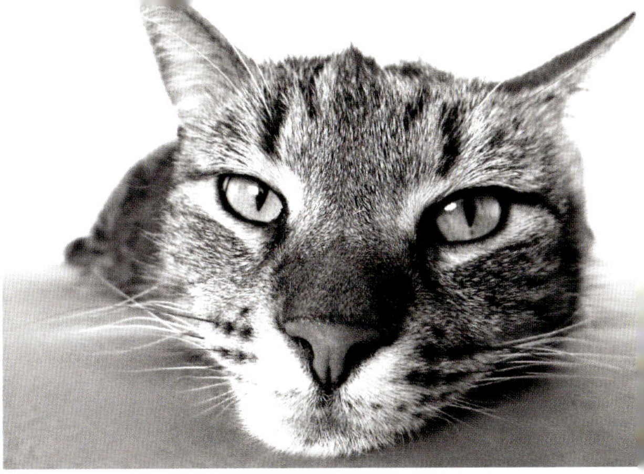
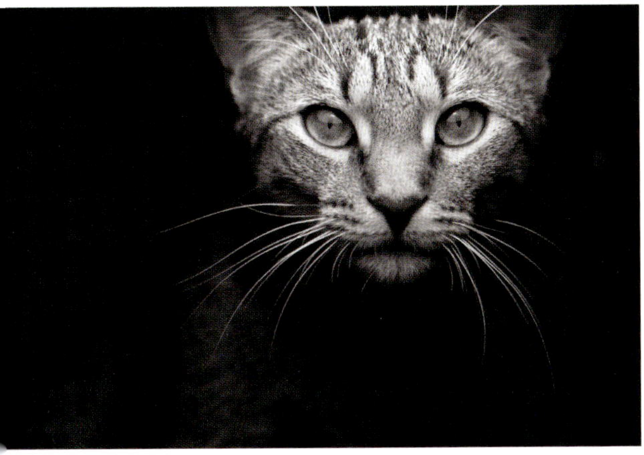
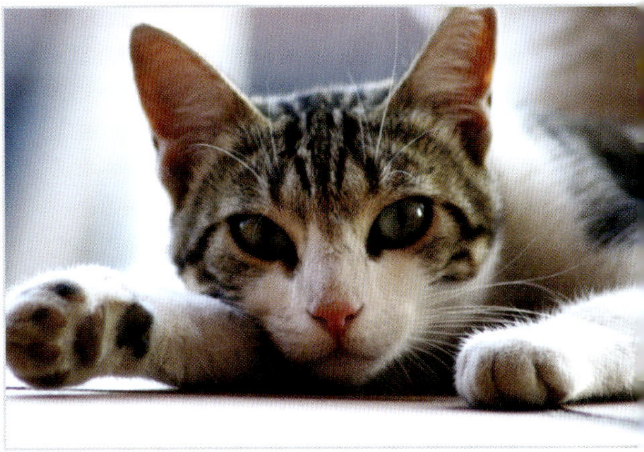
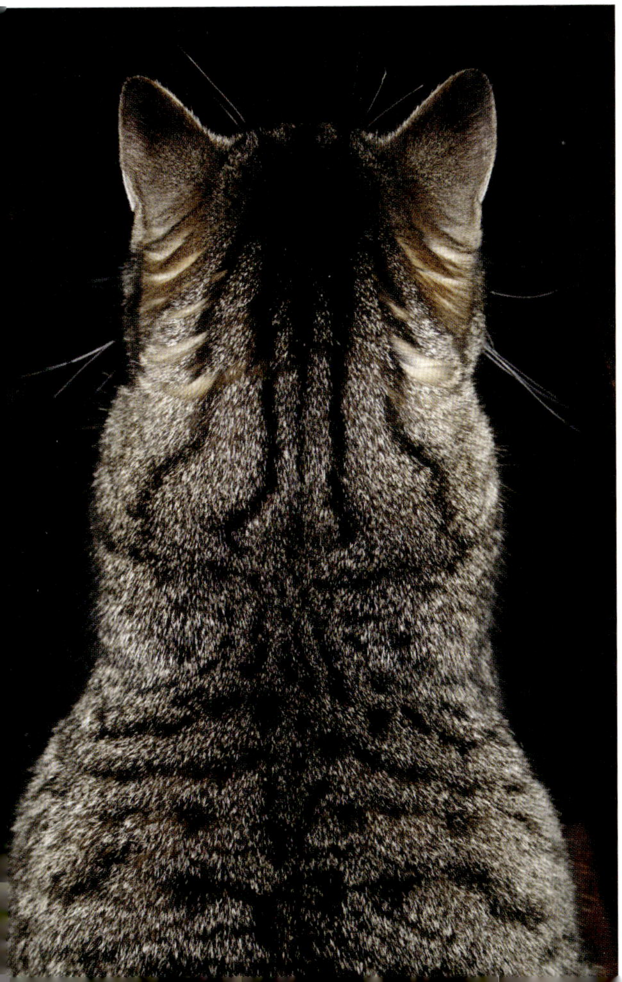
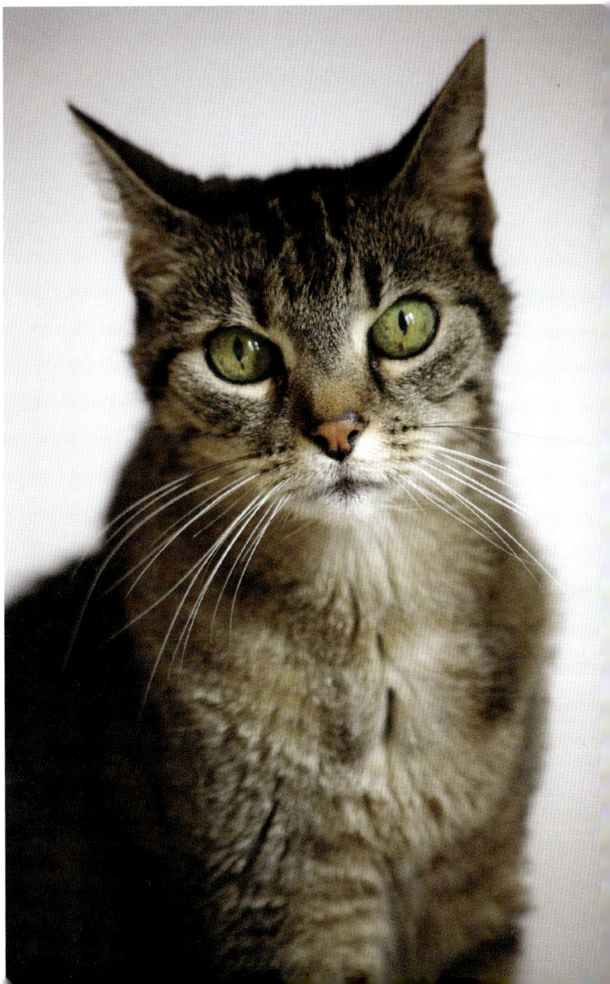

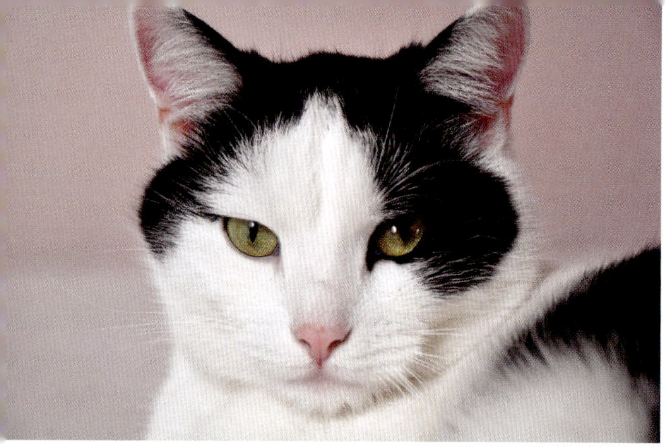
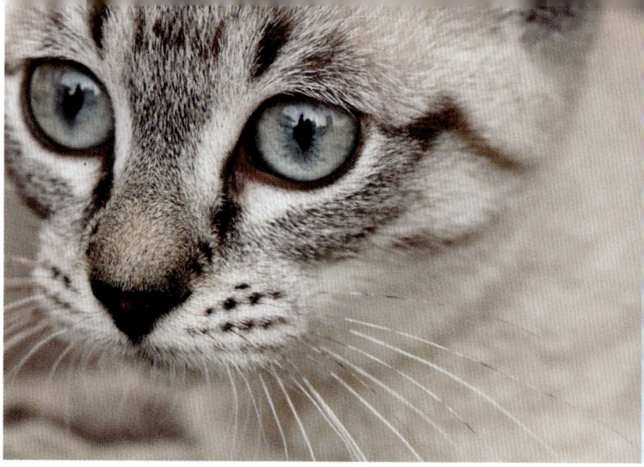
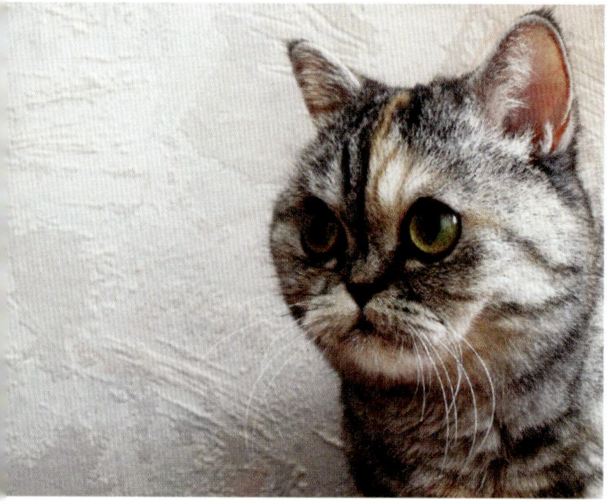
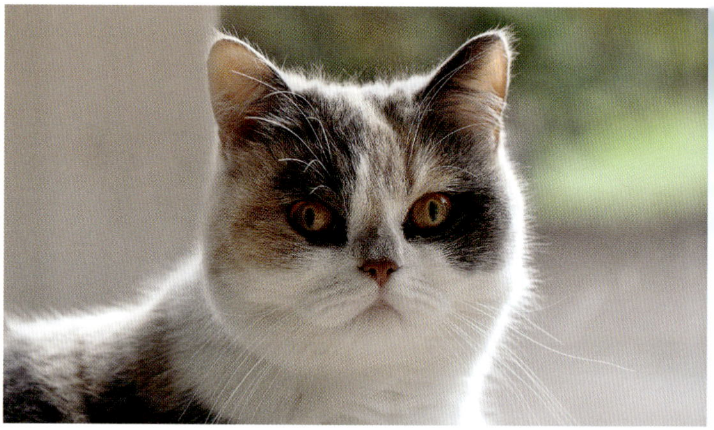
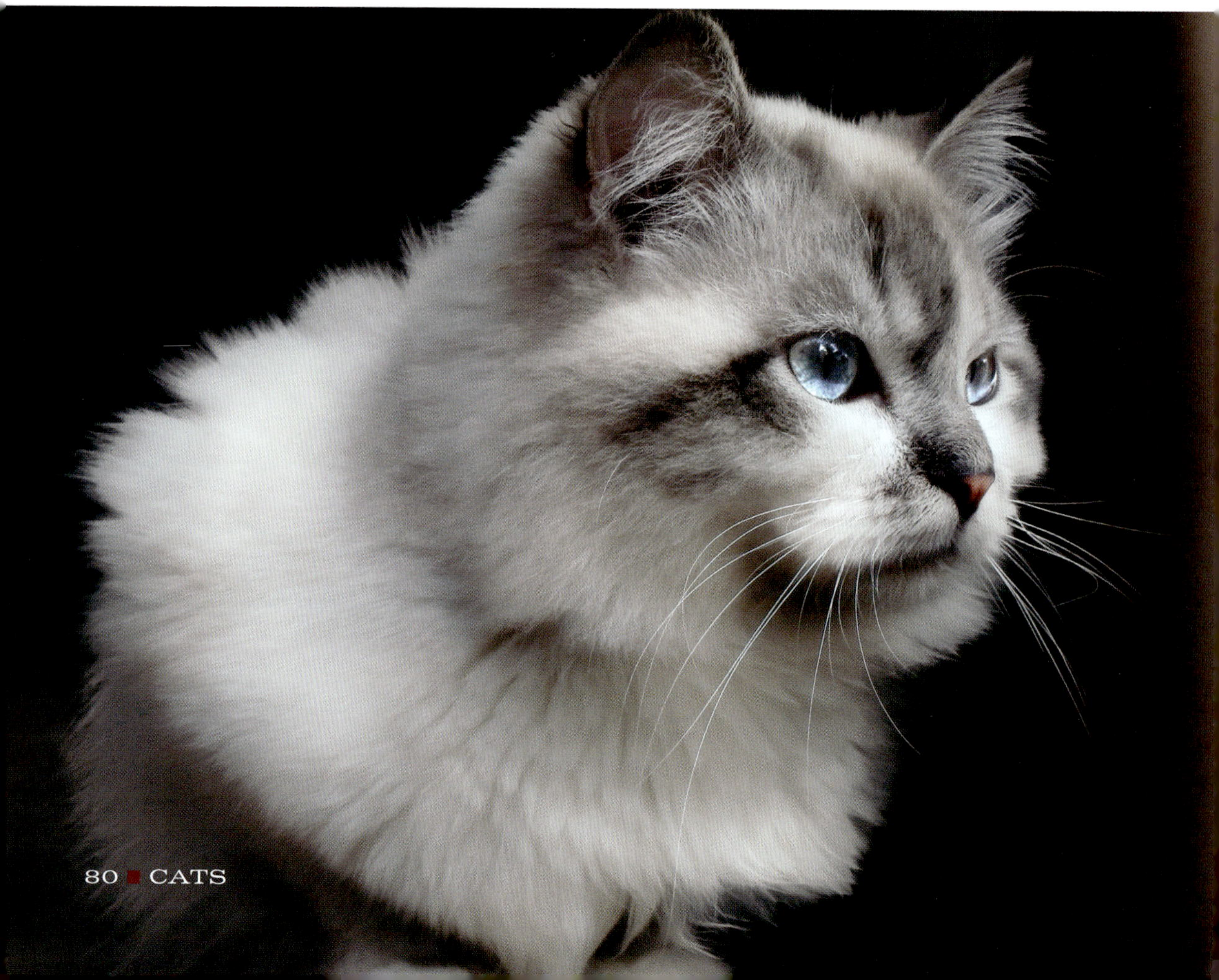

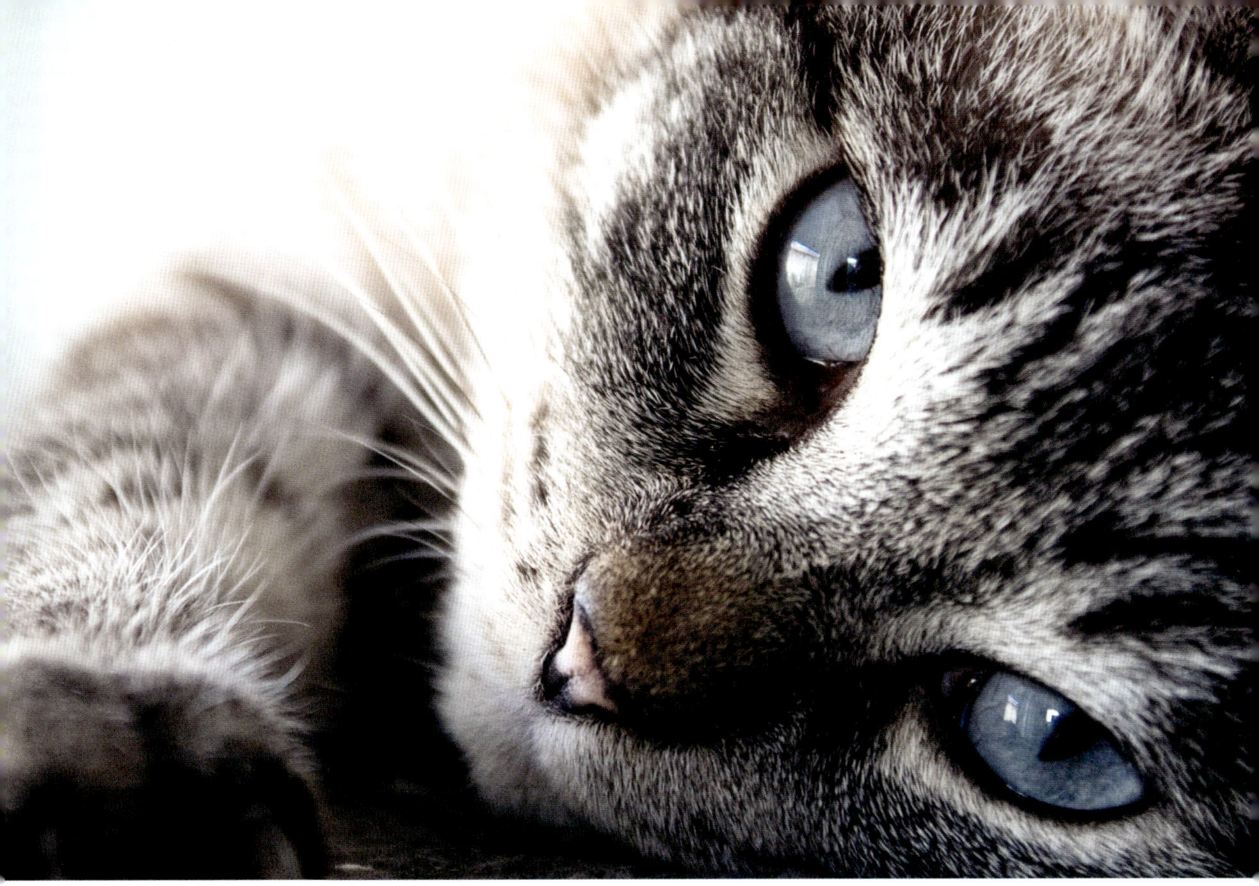
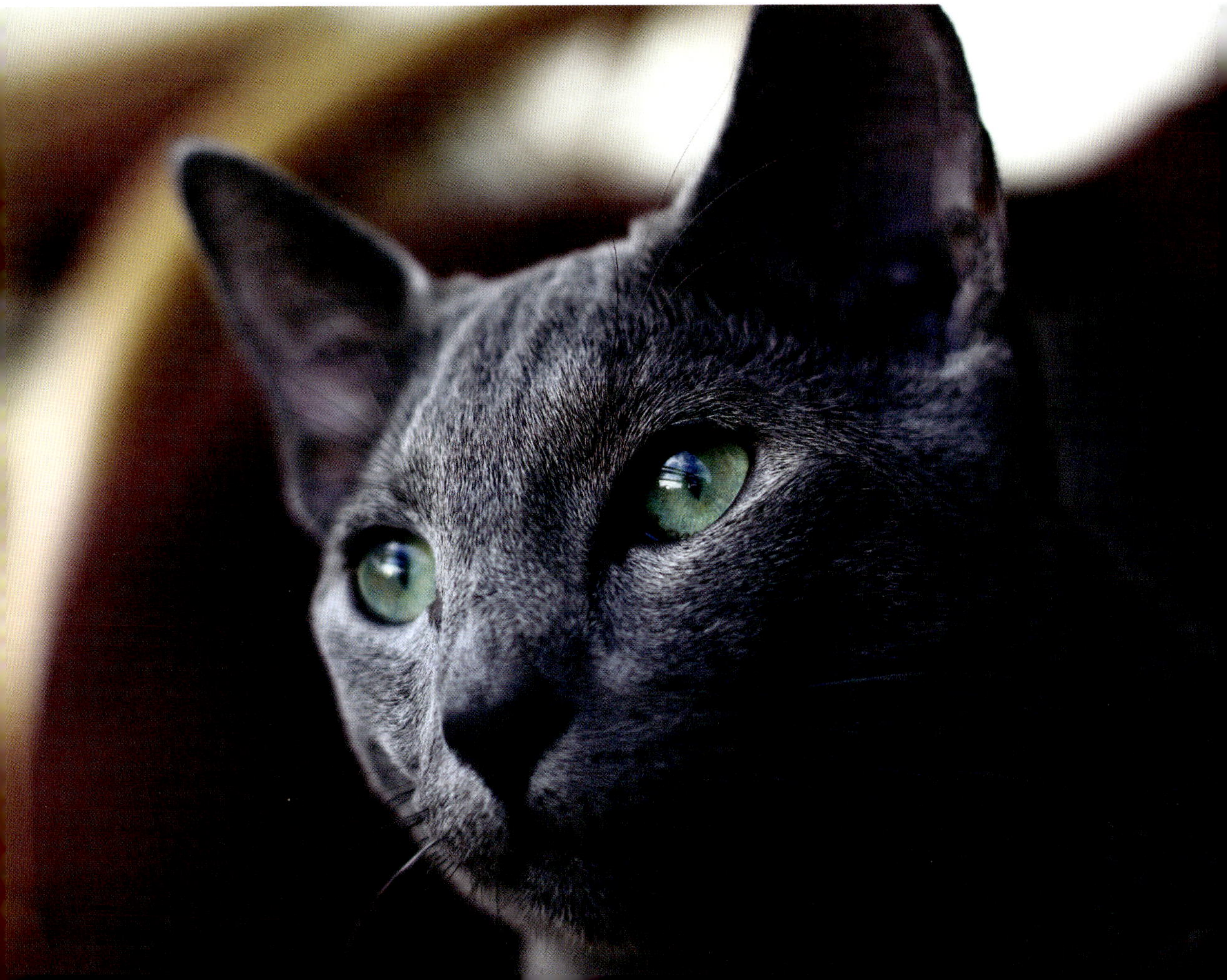

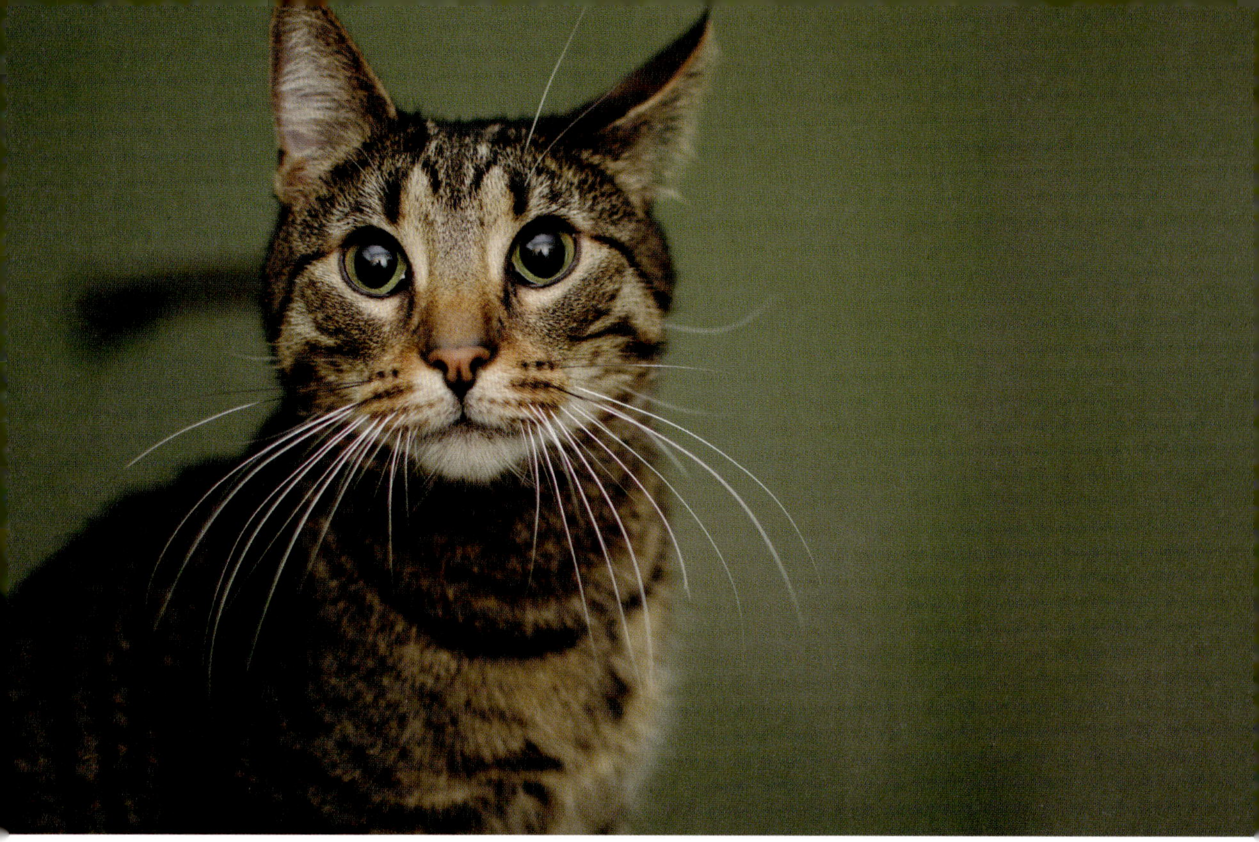
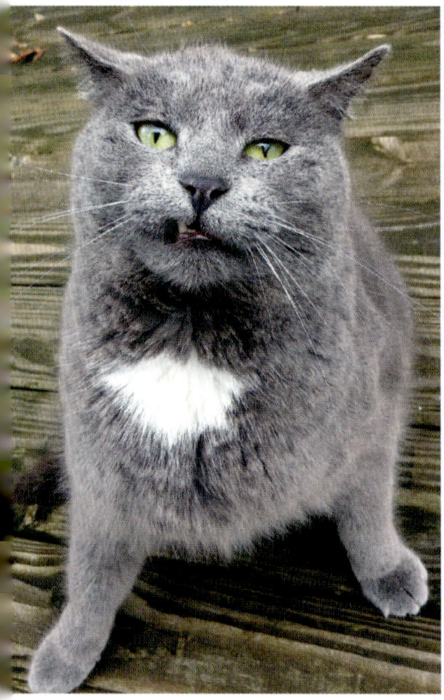
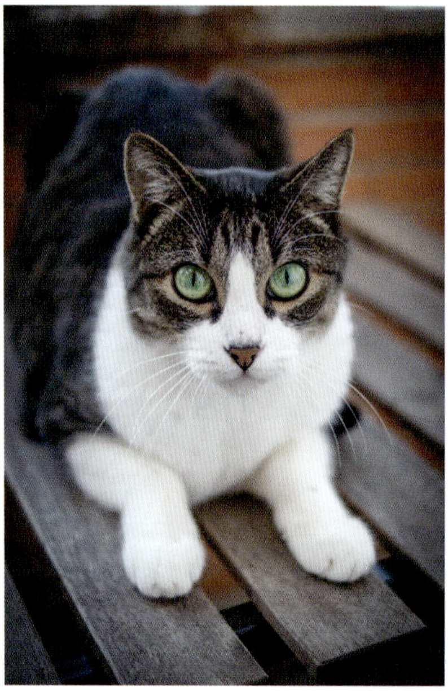
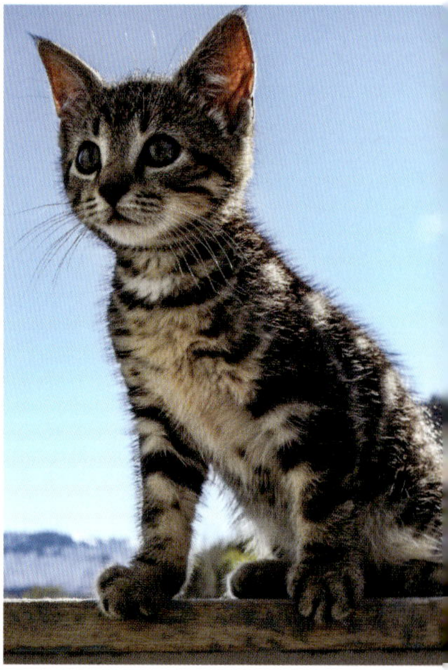
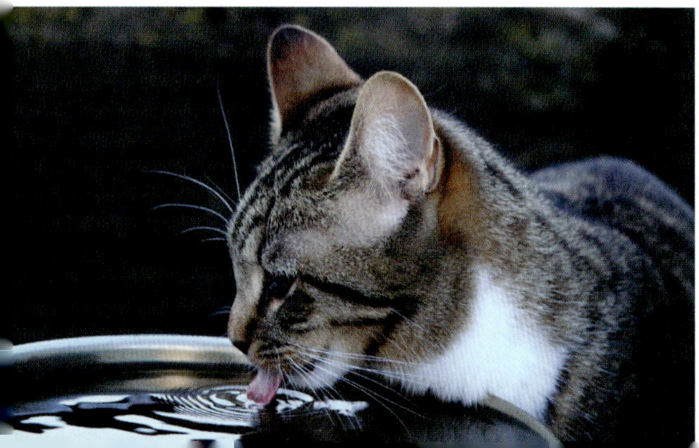
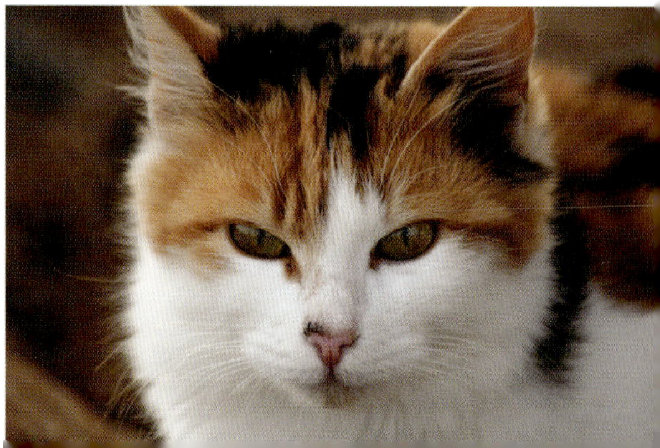

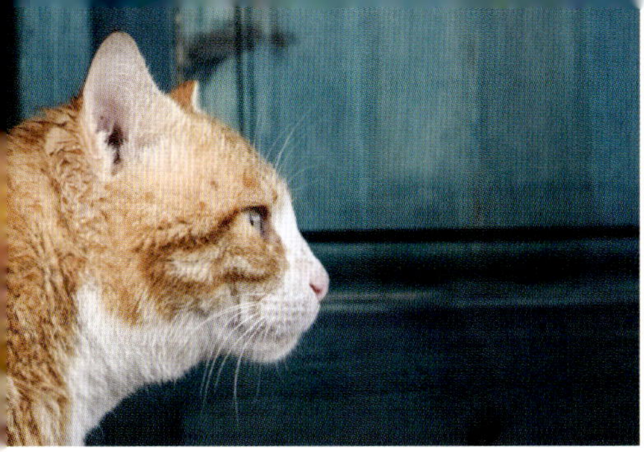

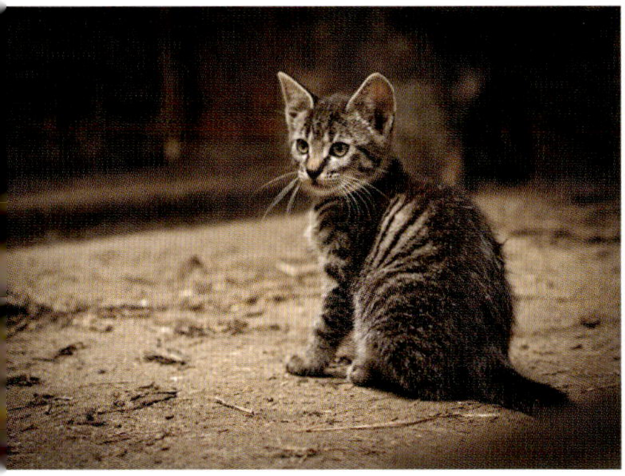

"A cat has absolute emotional honesty: human beings, for one reason or another, may hide their feelings, but a cat does not."

–Ernest Hemingway, author

"Like all pure creatures, cats are practical."

–William S. Burroughs, author

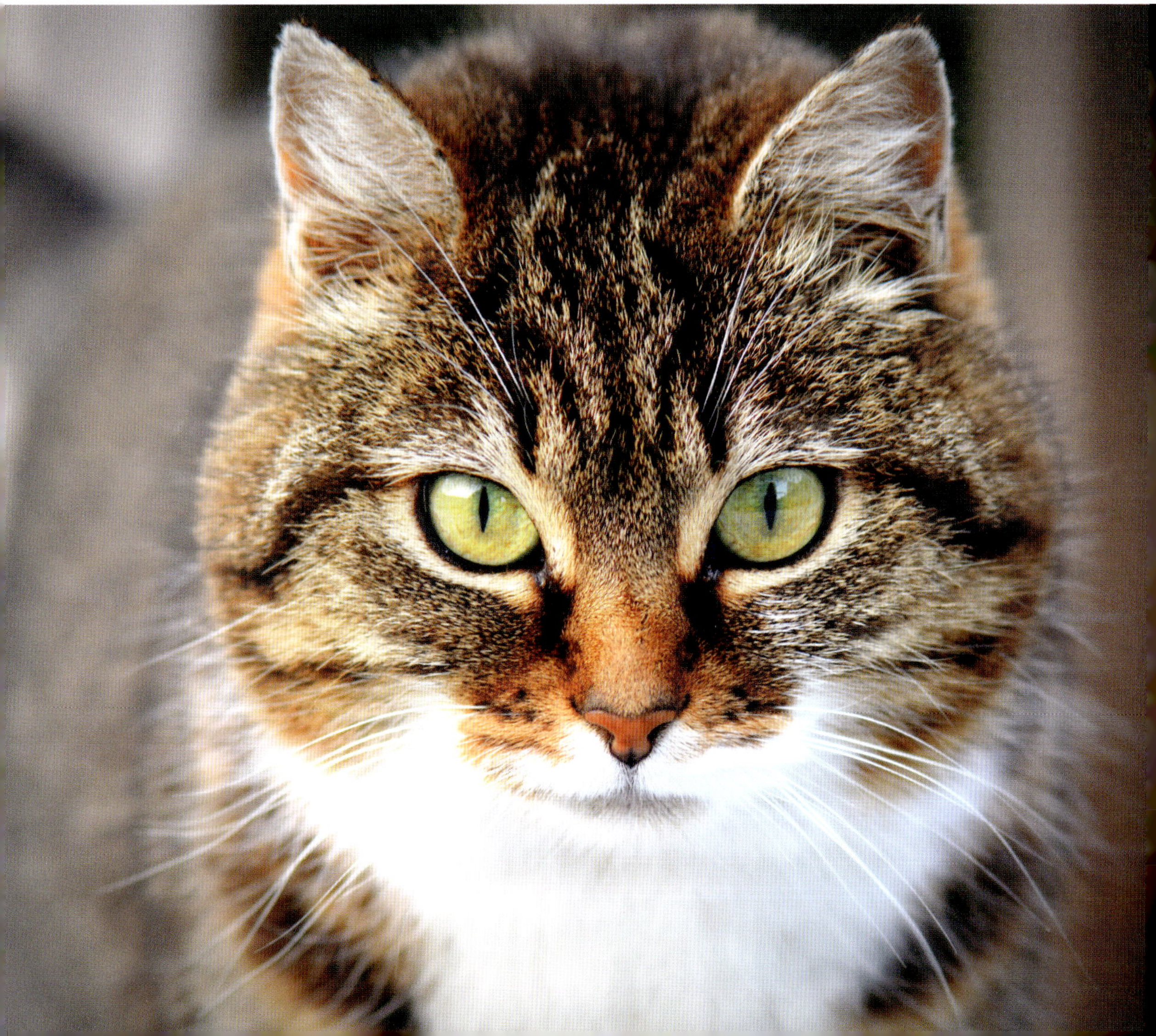

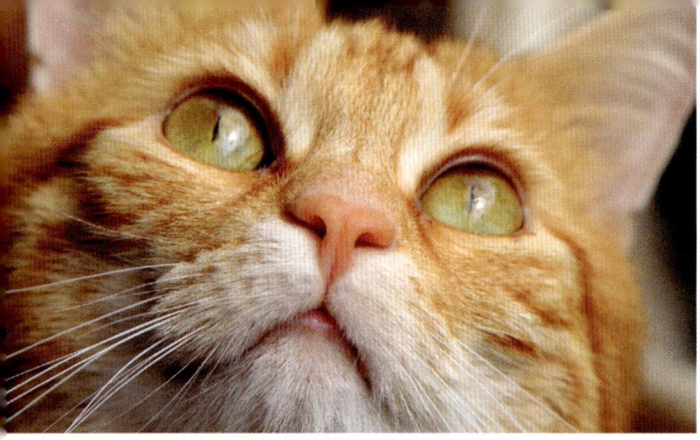
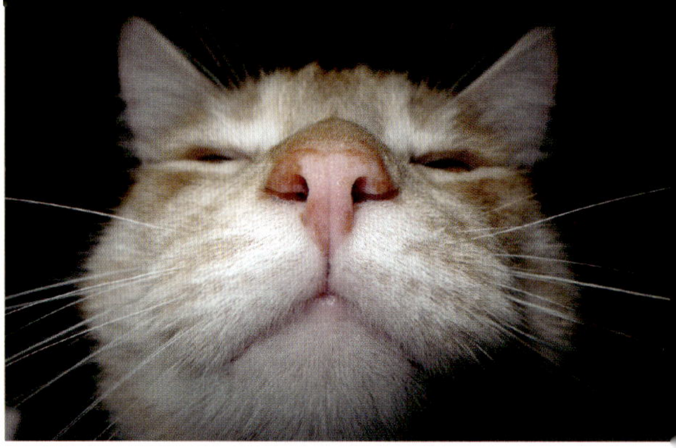
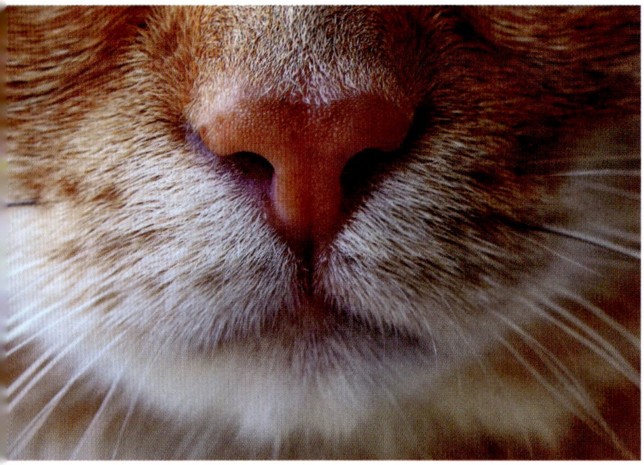
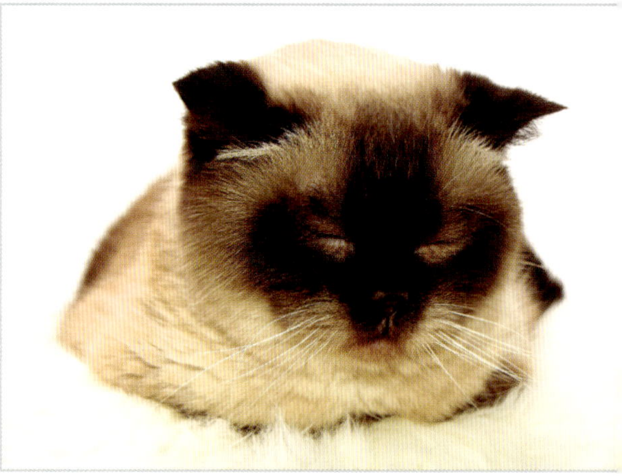
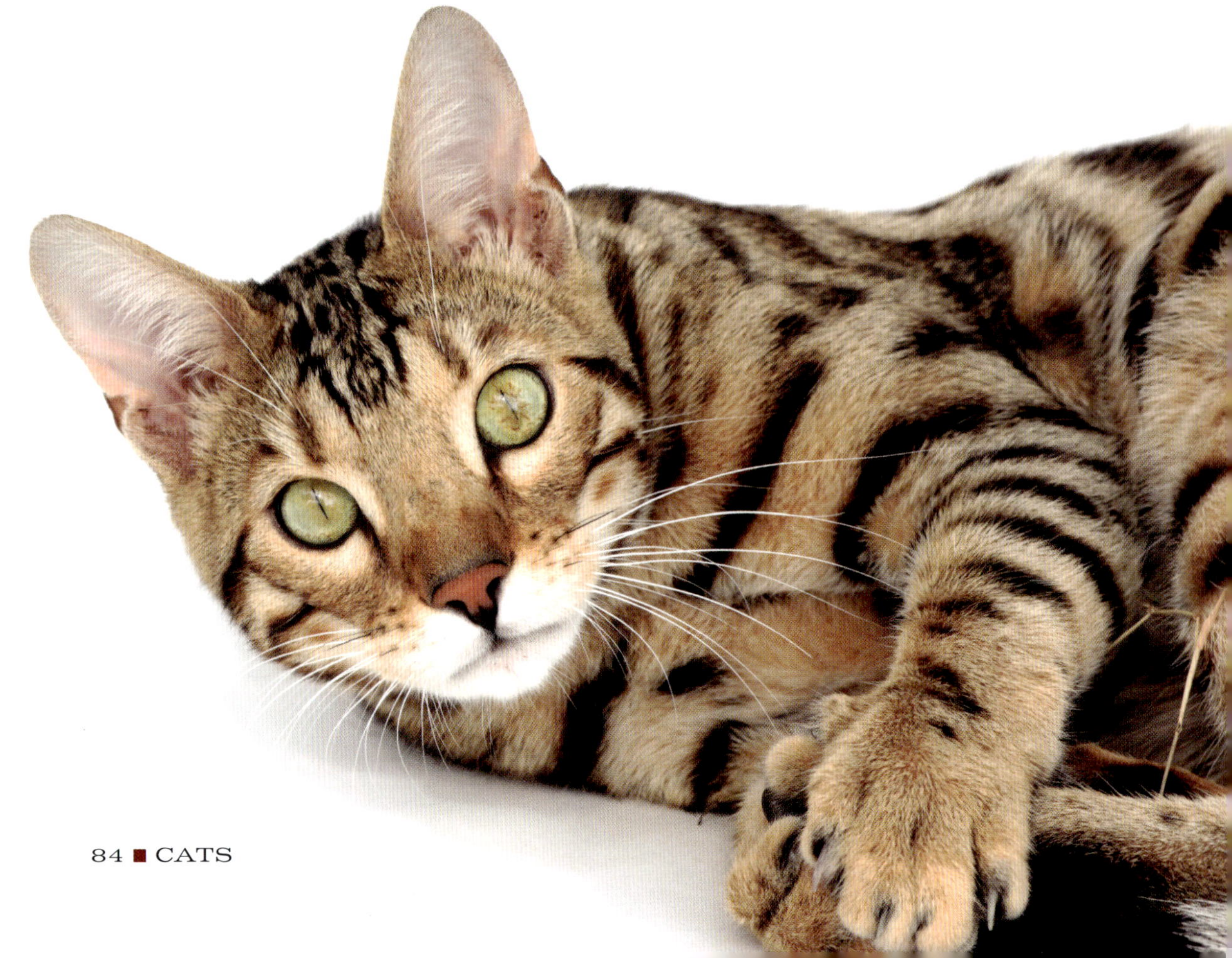

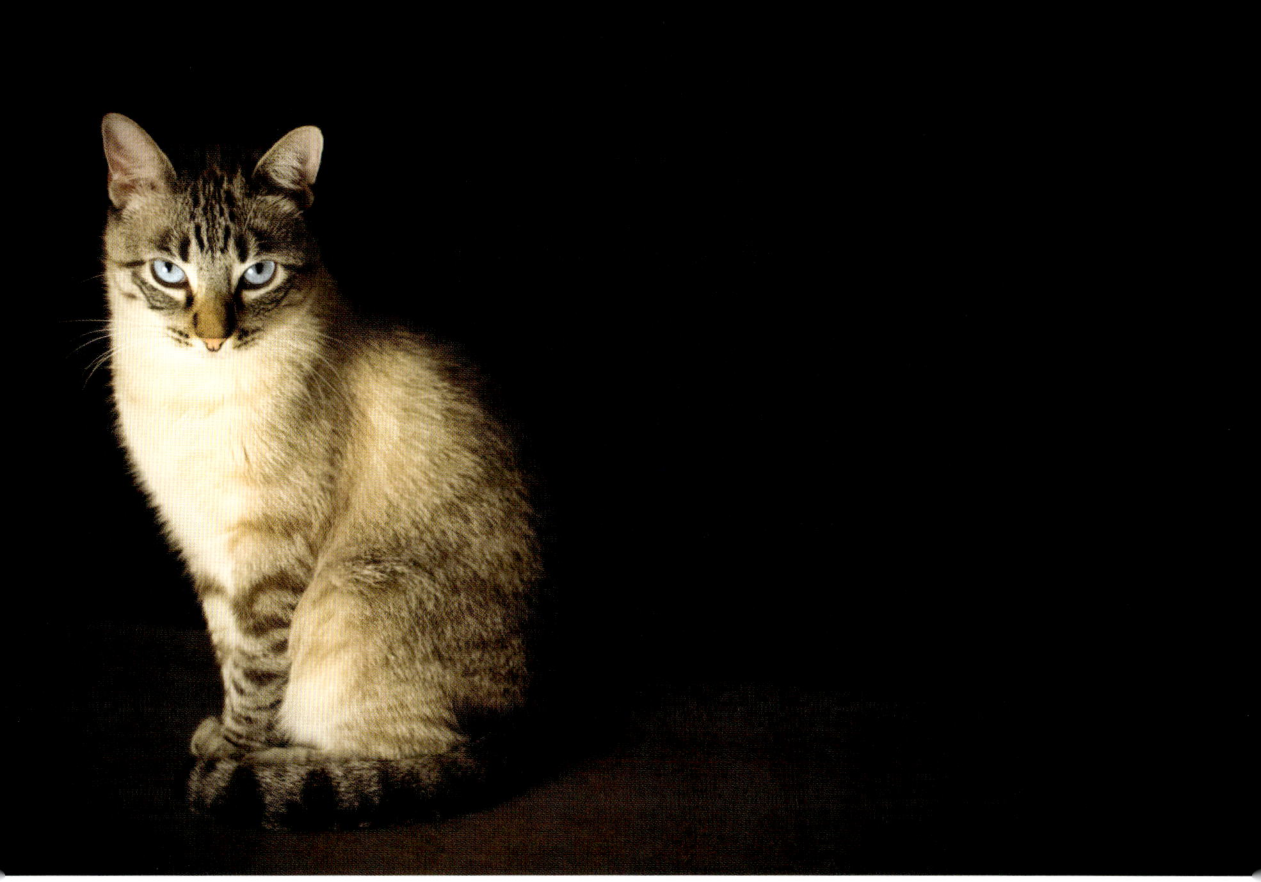

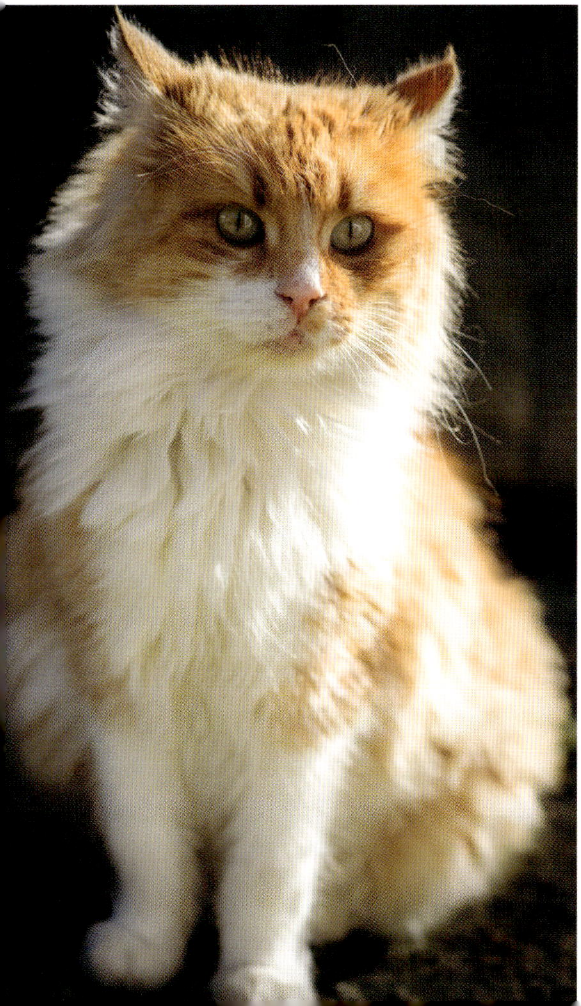

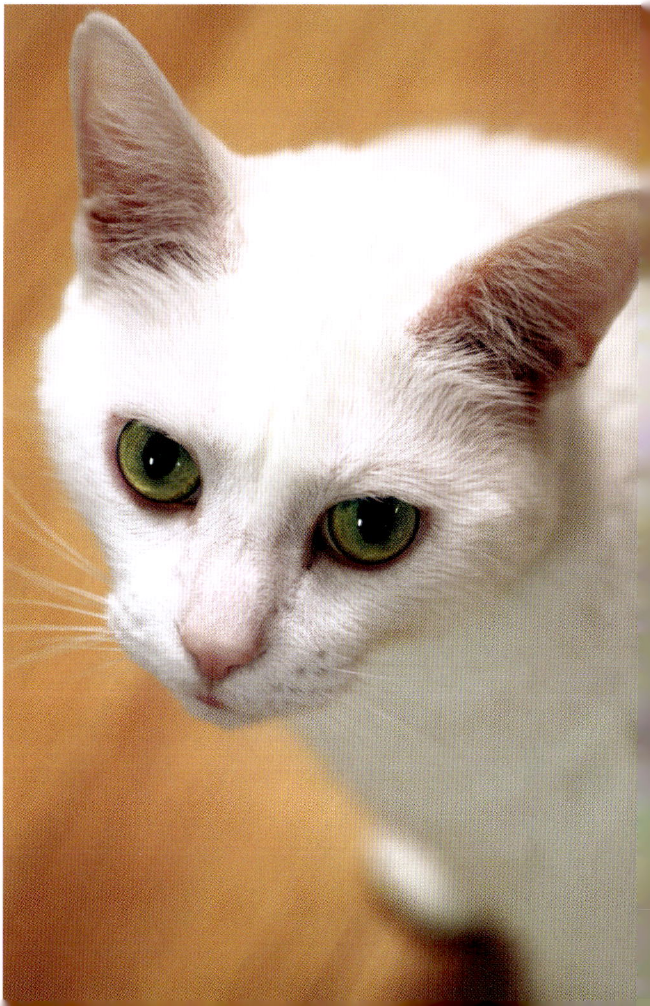

7. Kings & Queens of the Castle

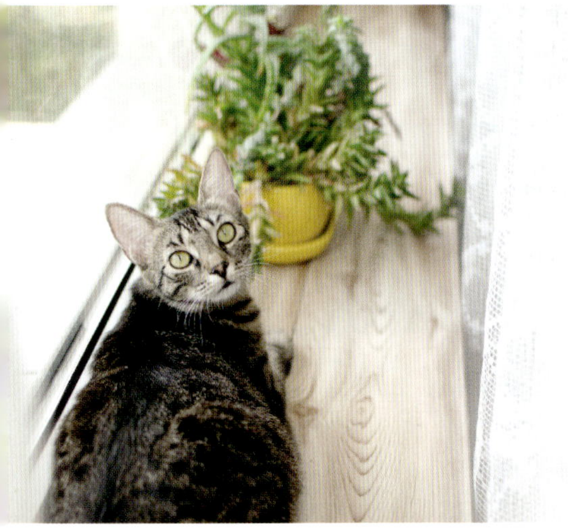

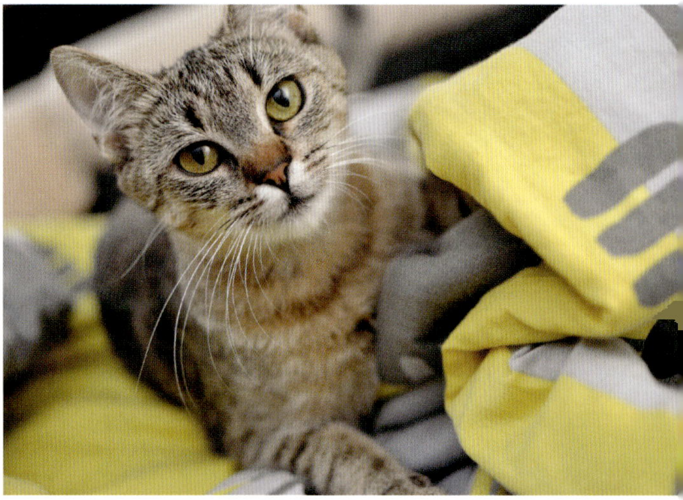

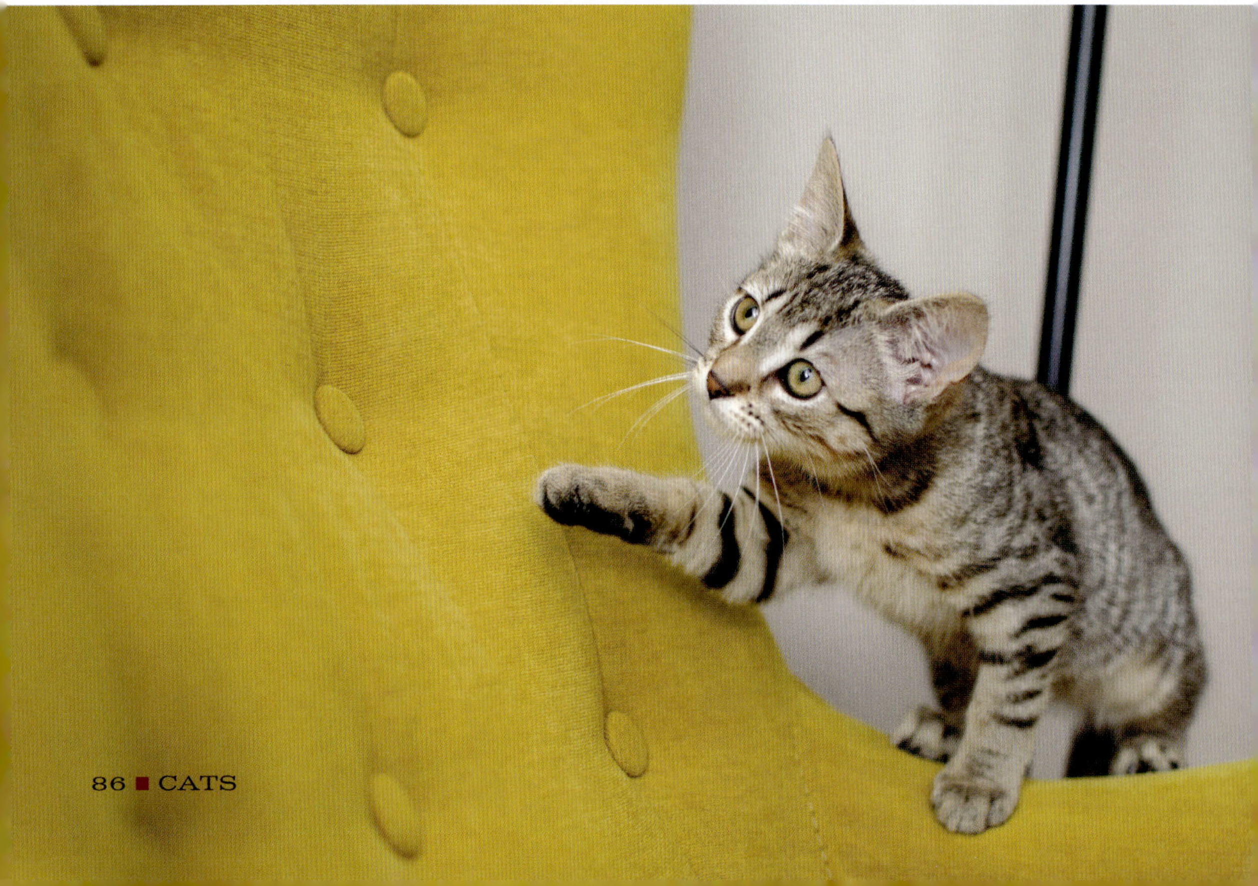

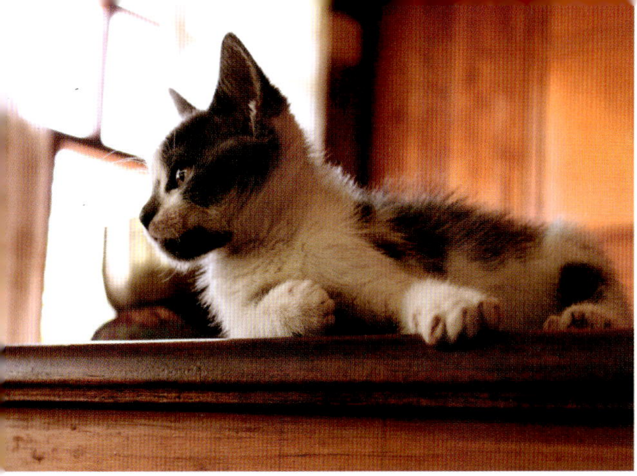
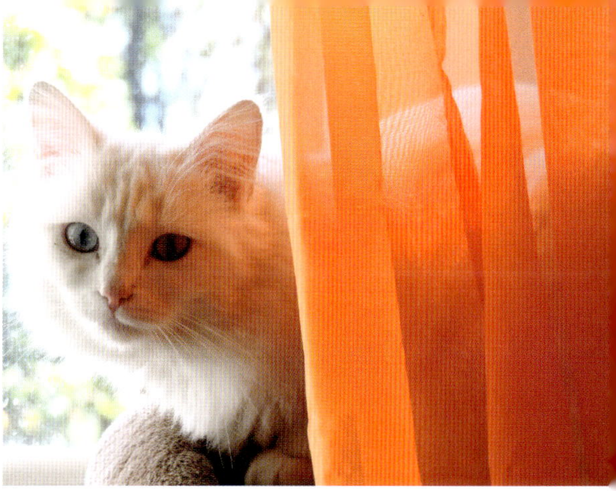
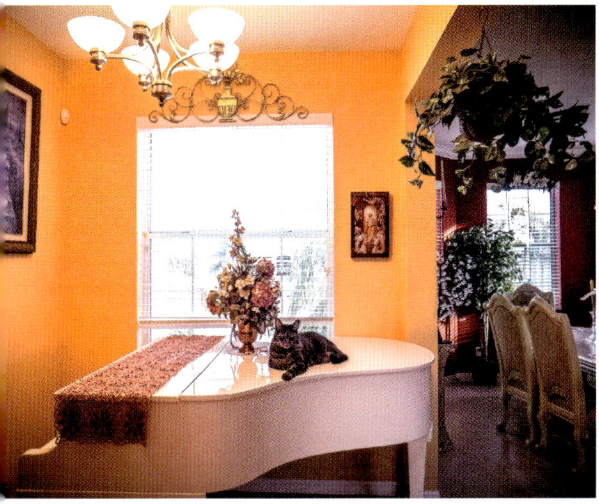
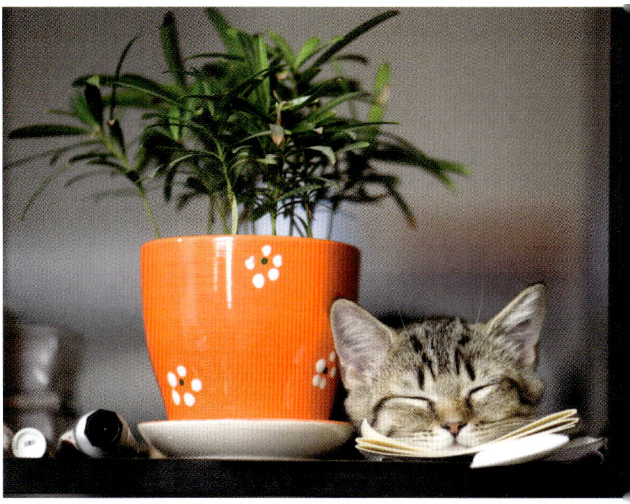
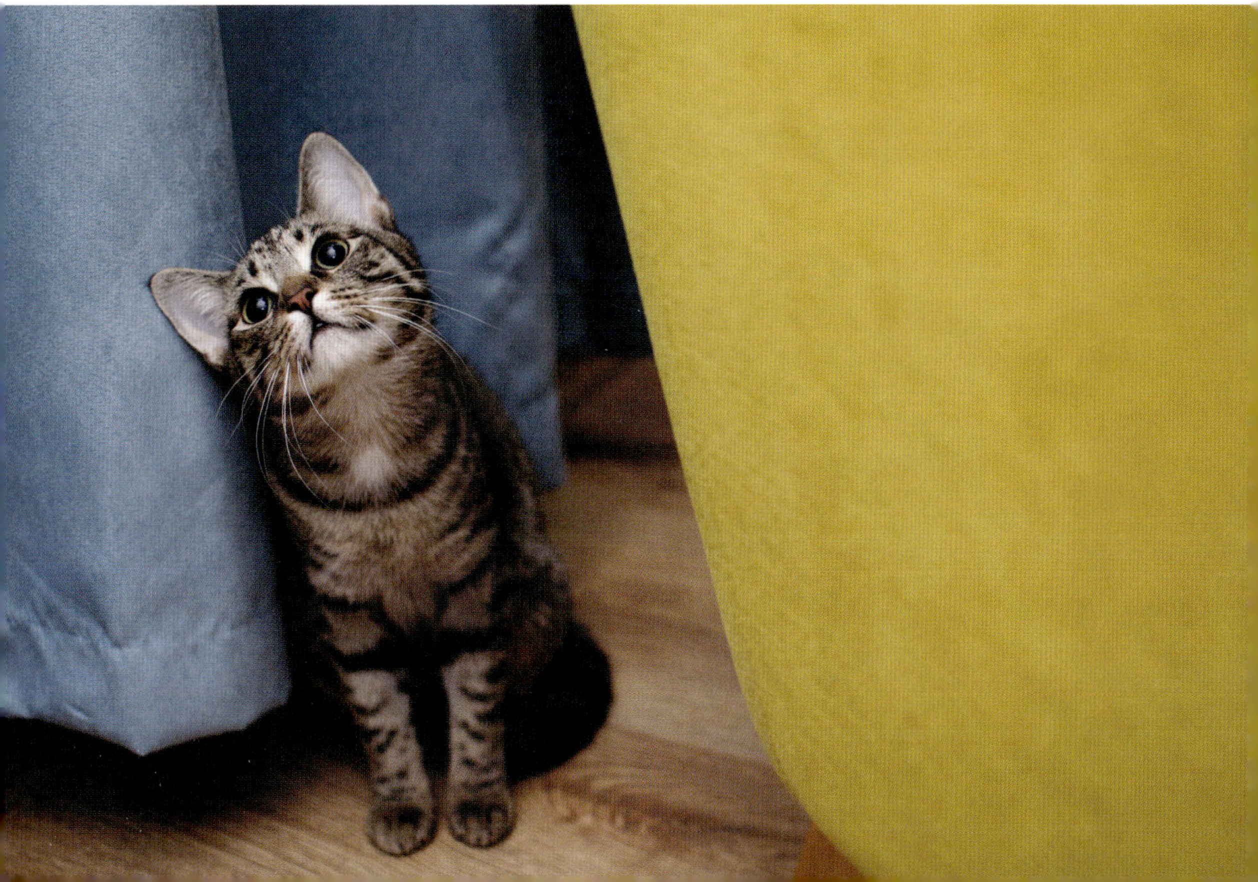

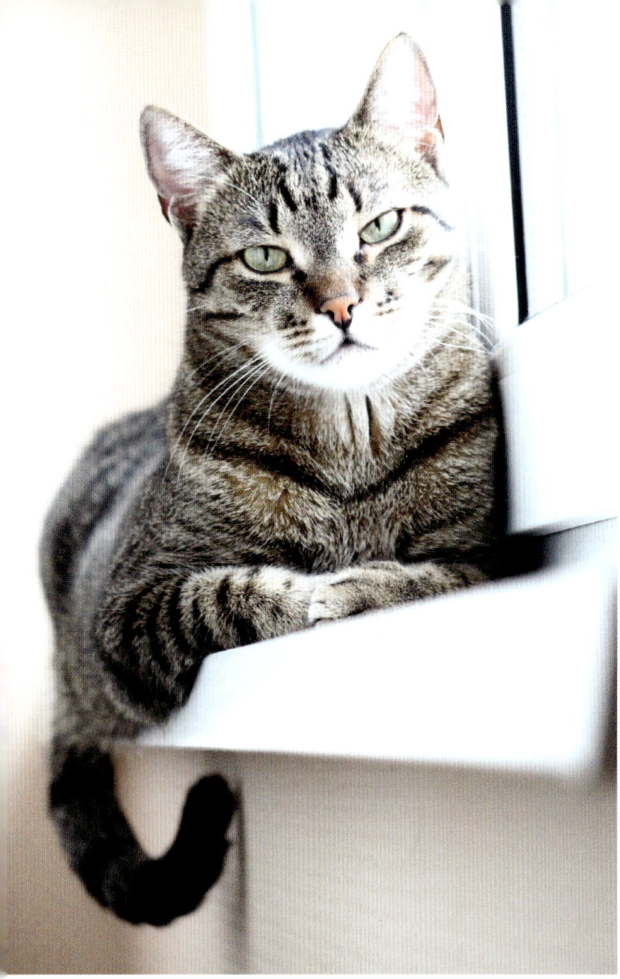
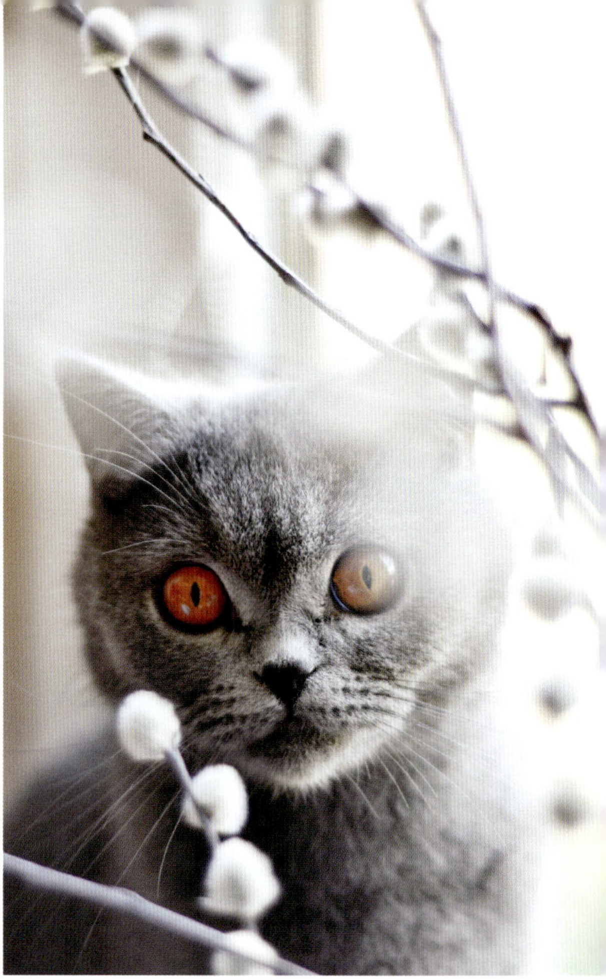
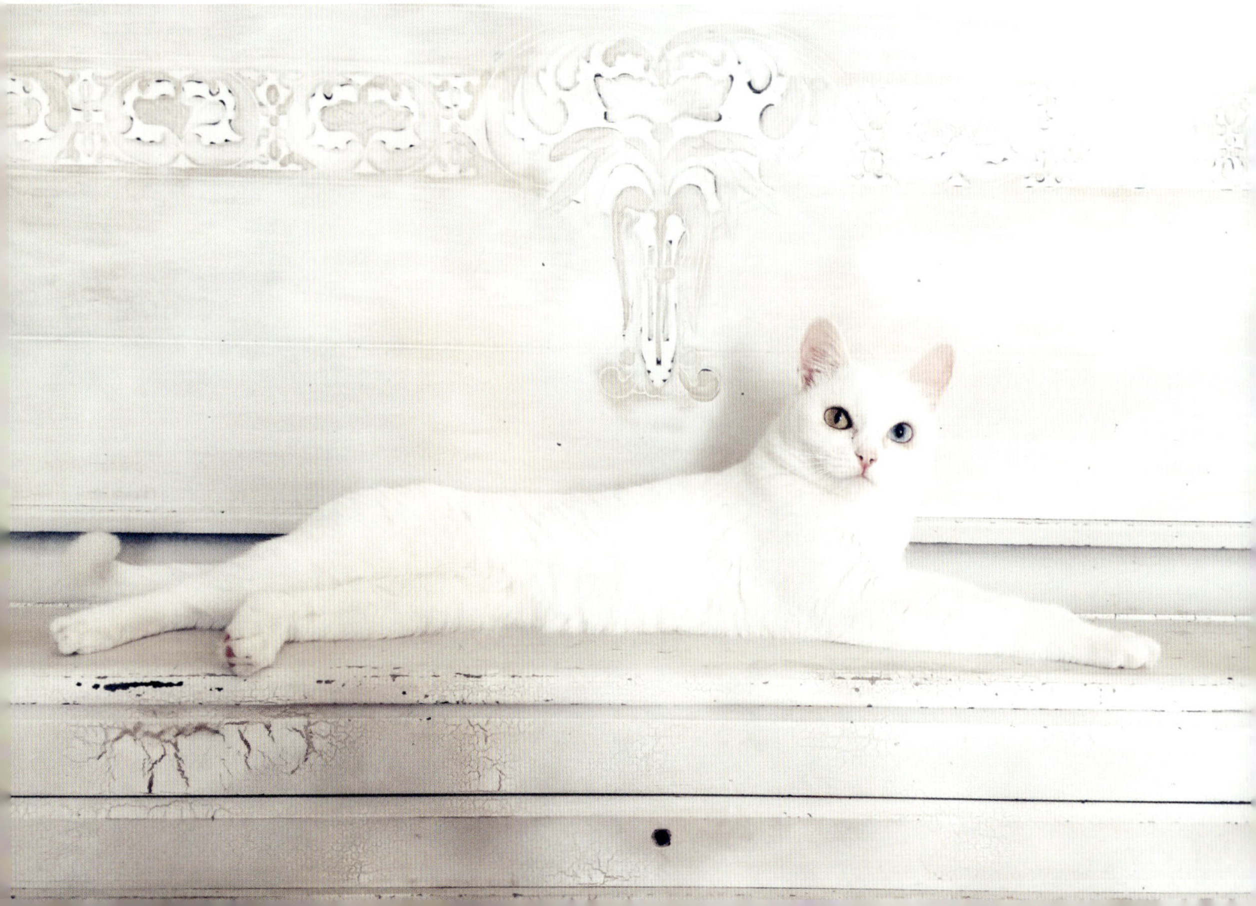

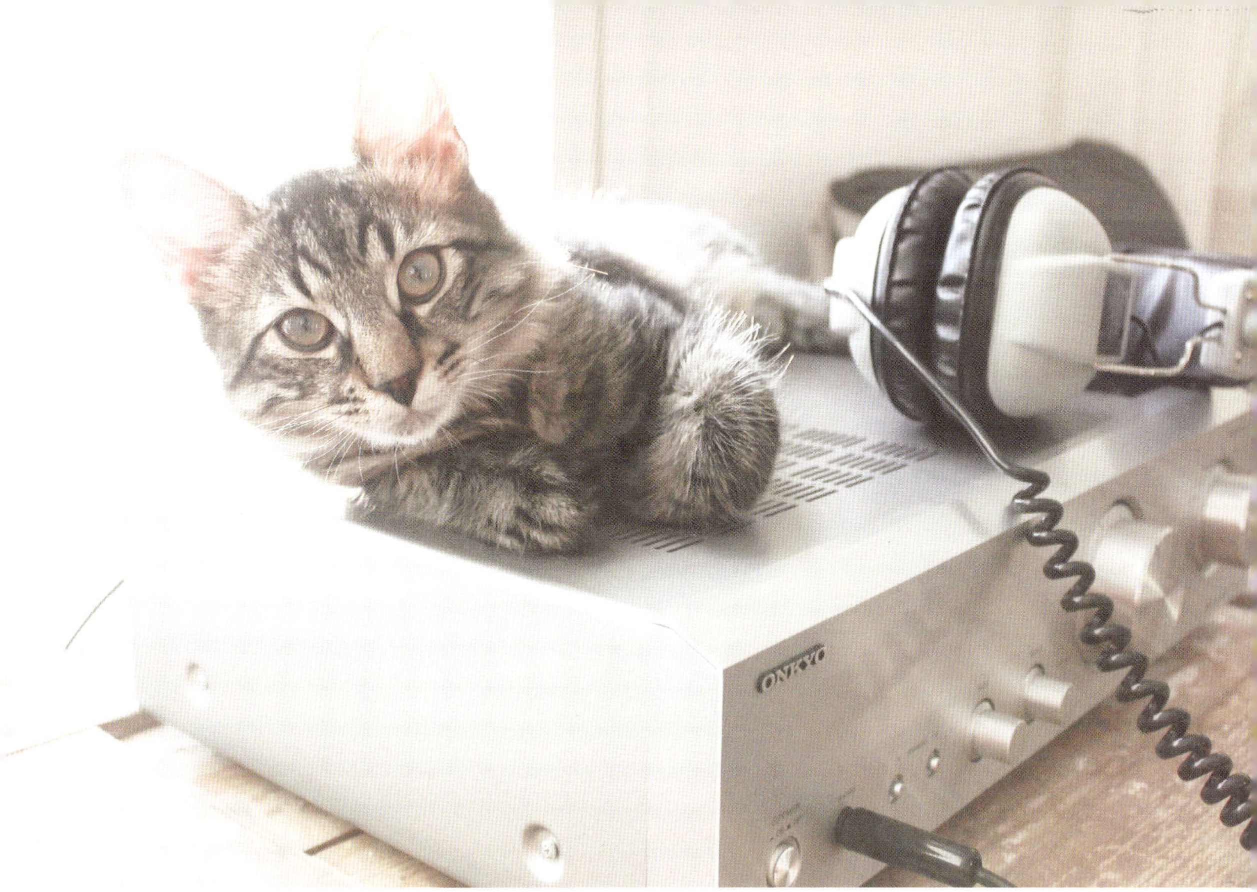
ONKYO

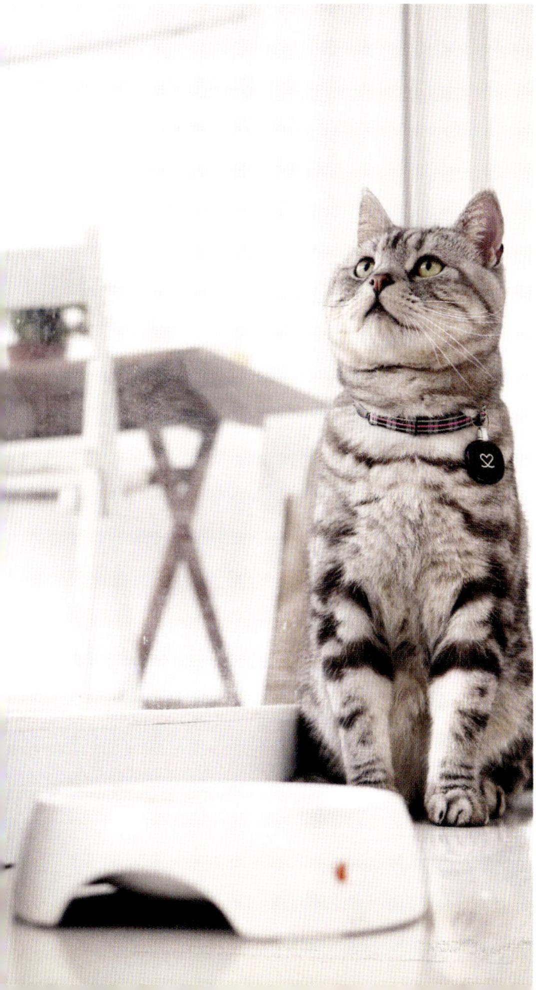

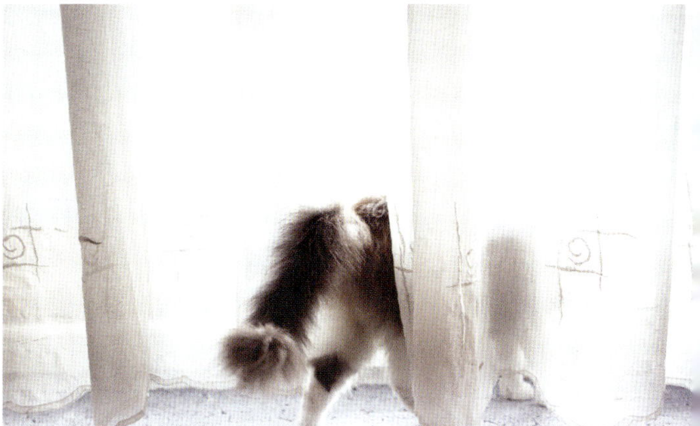

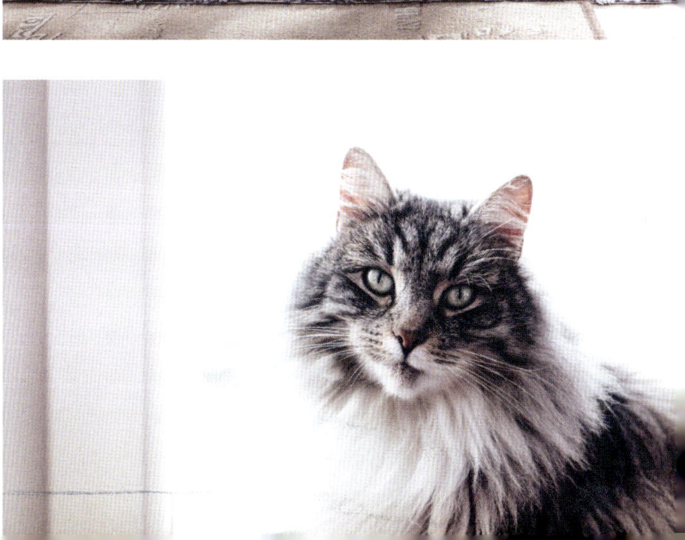

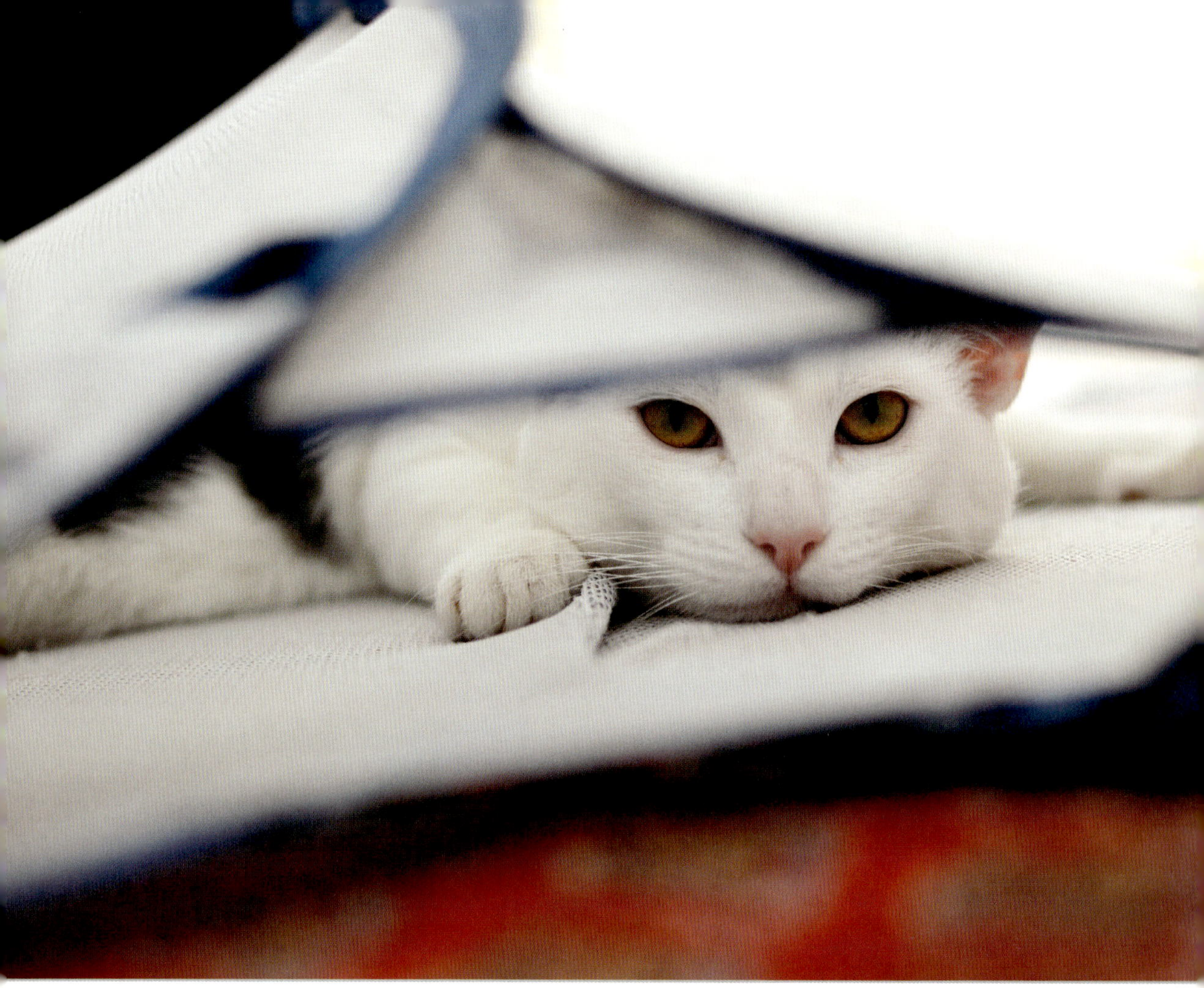

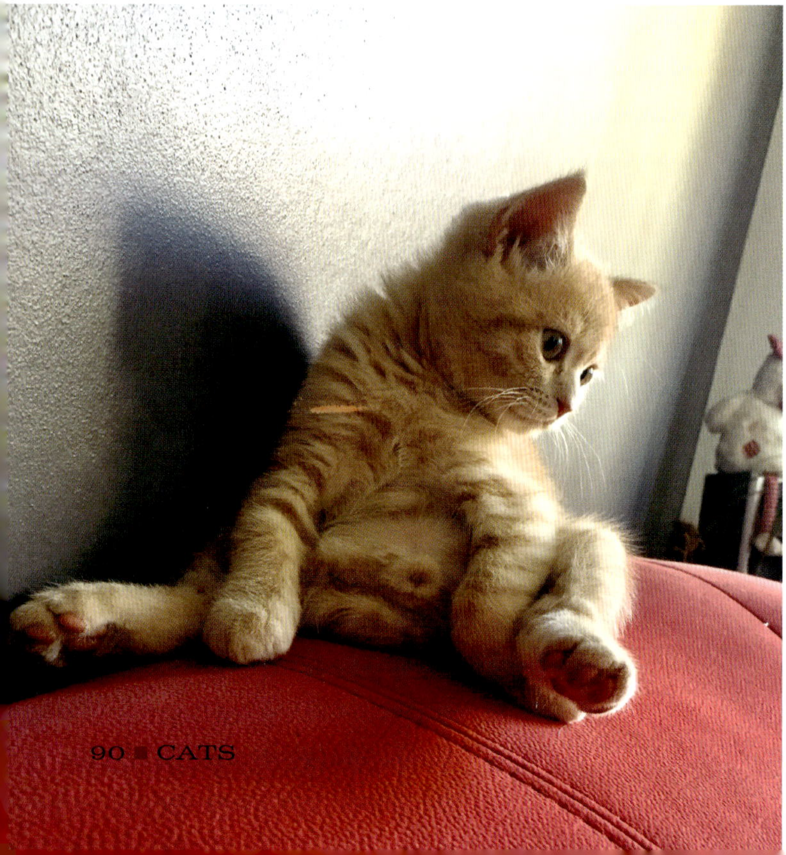

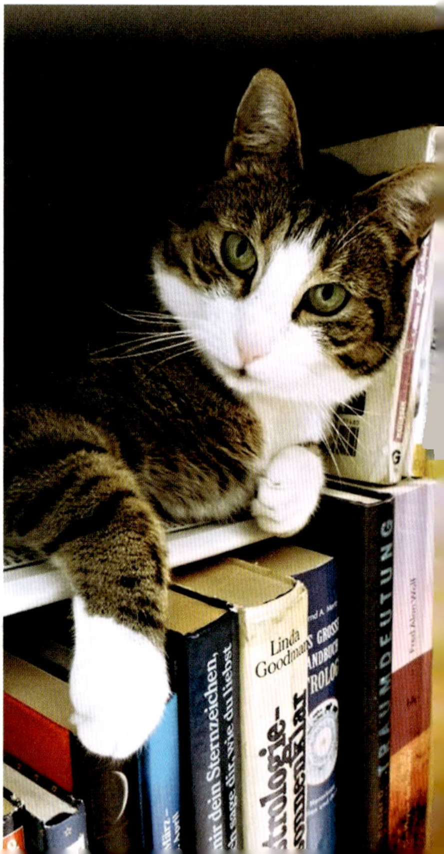
Linda
TRAUMDEUTUNG

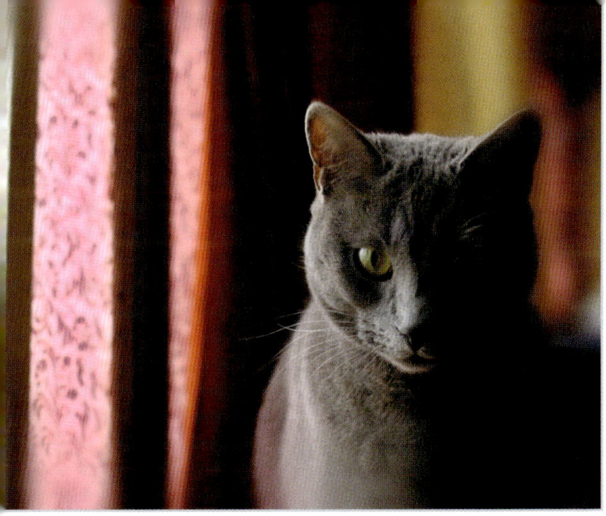
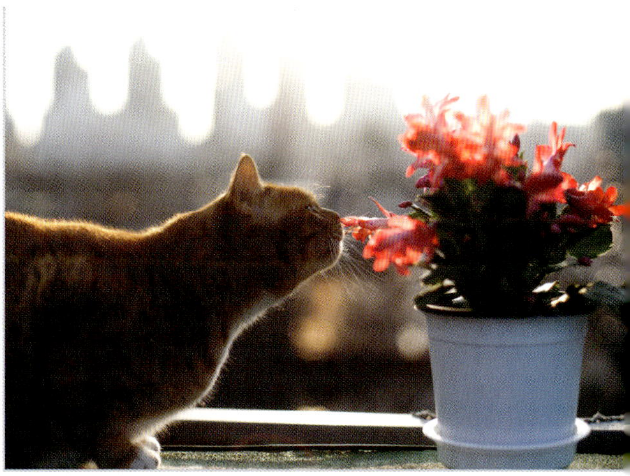
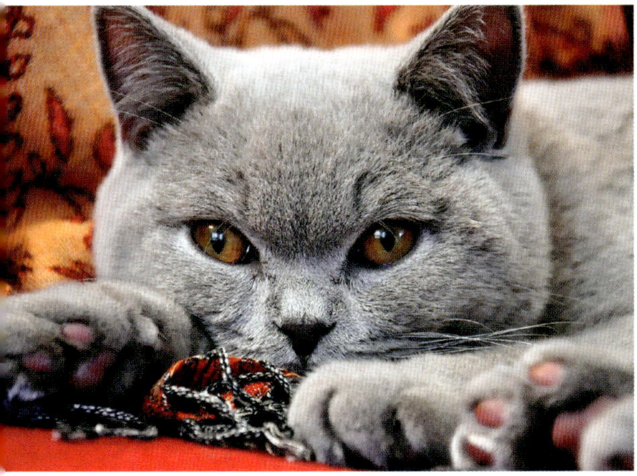
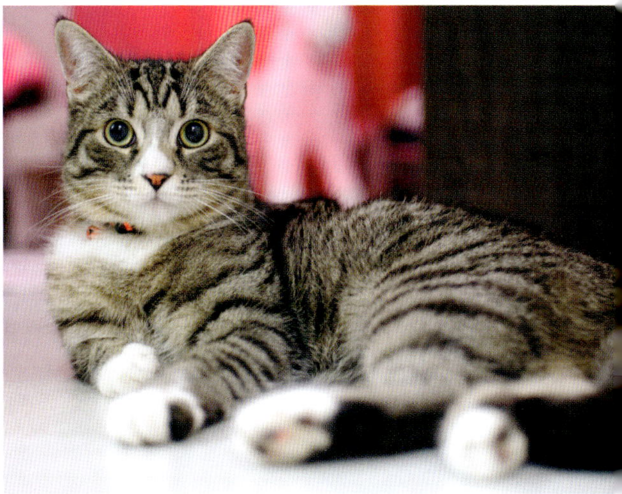
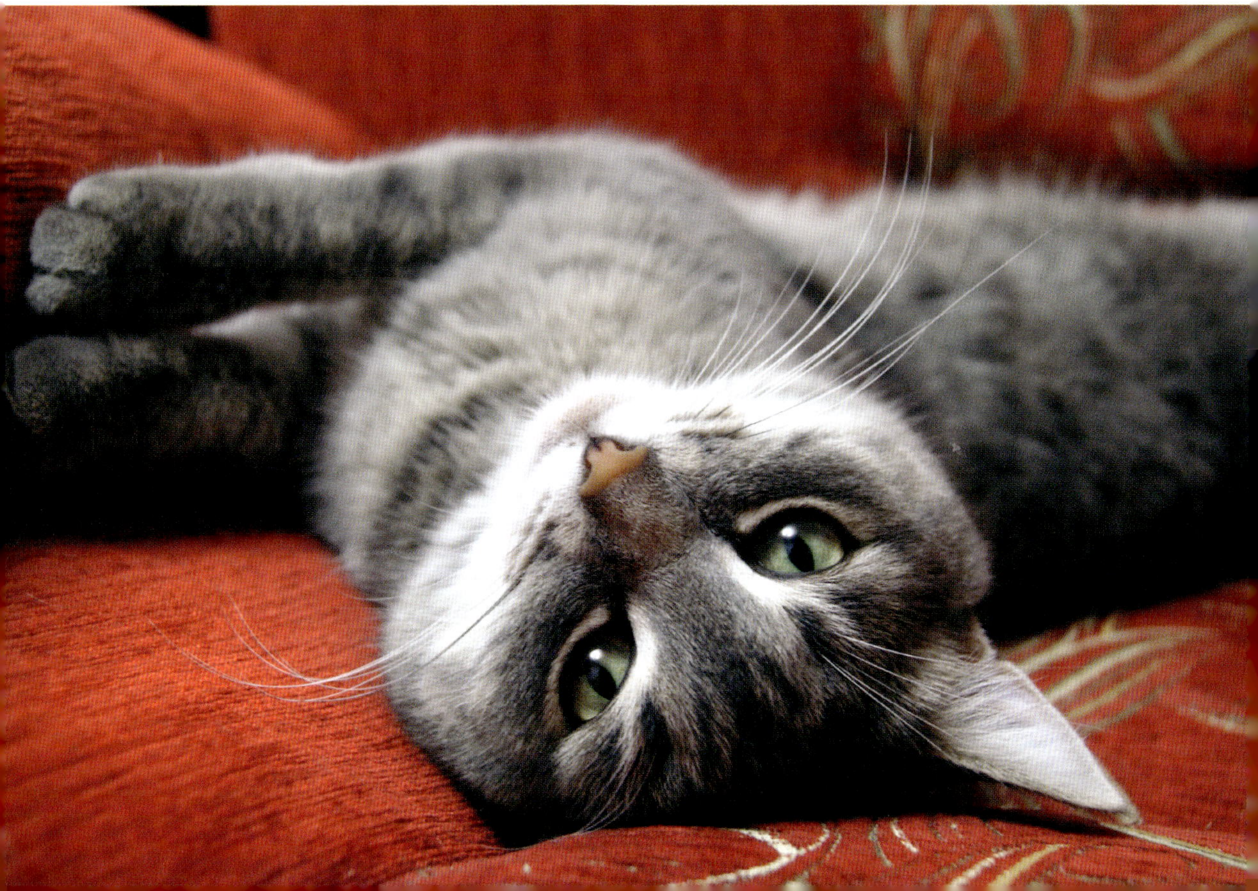

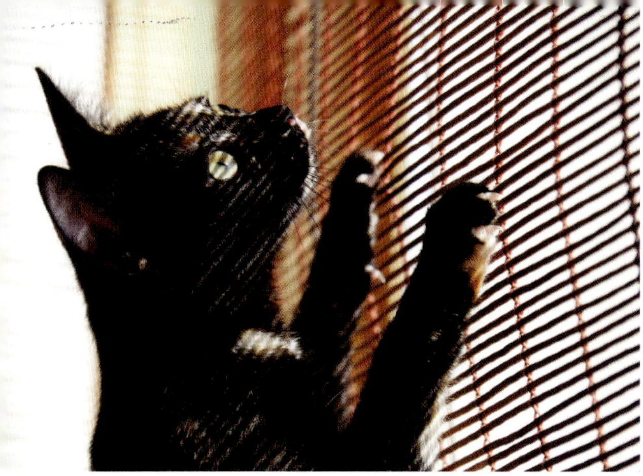
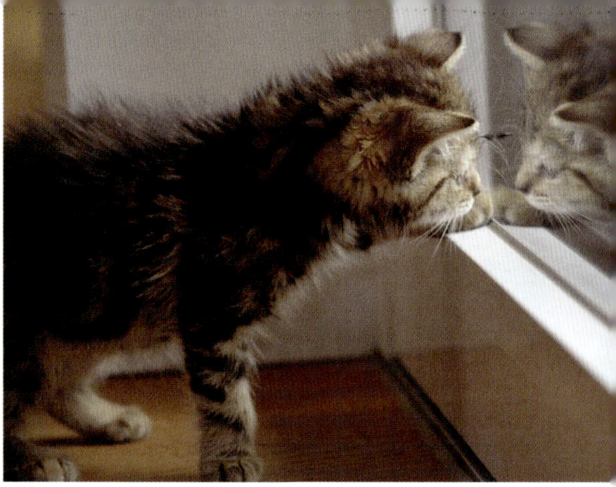
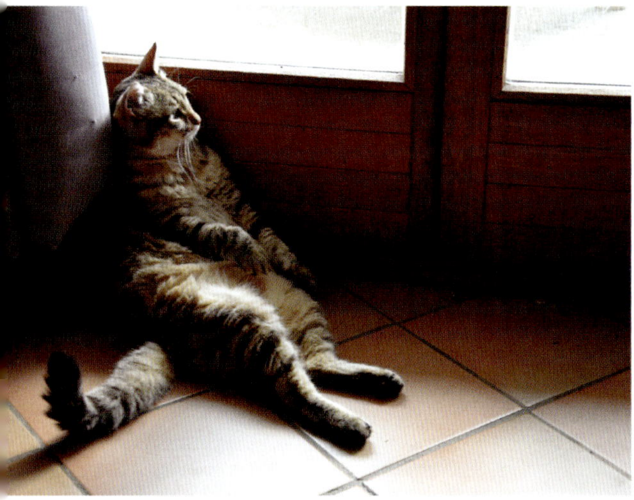
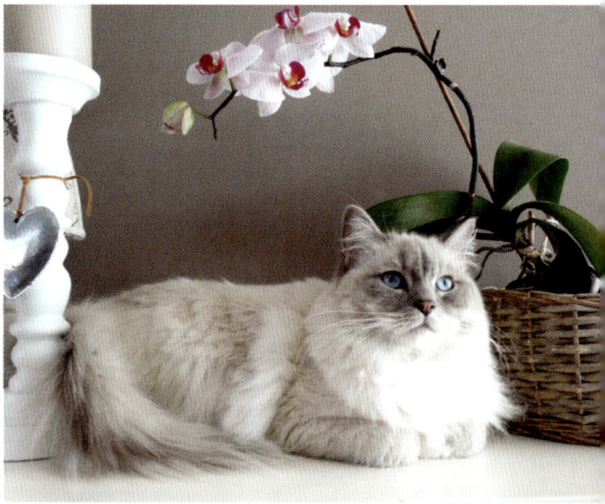
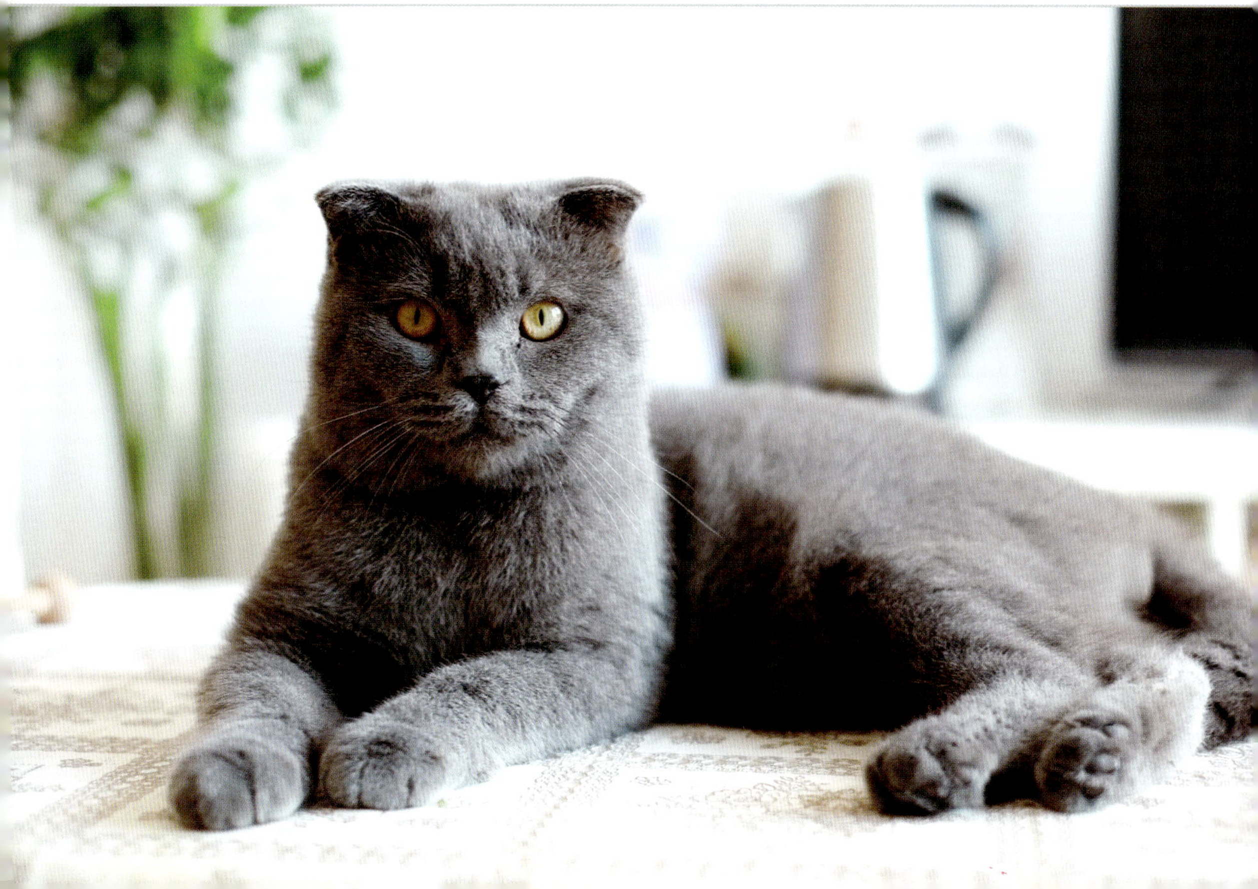

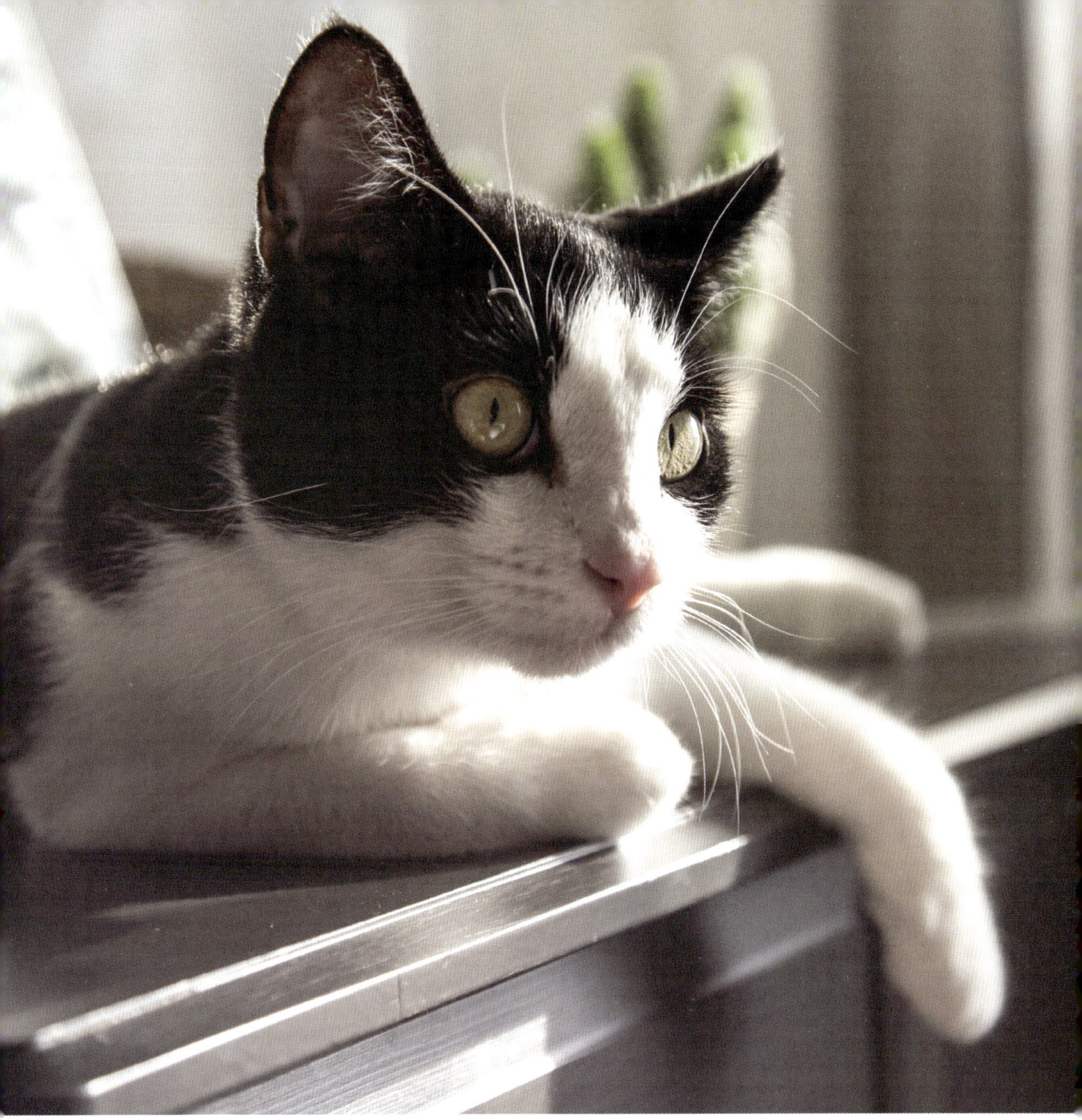

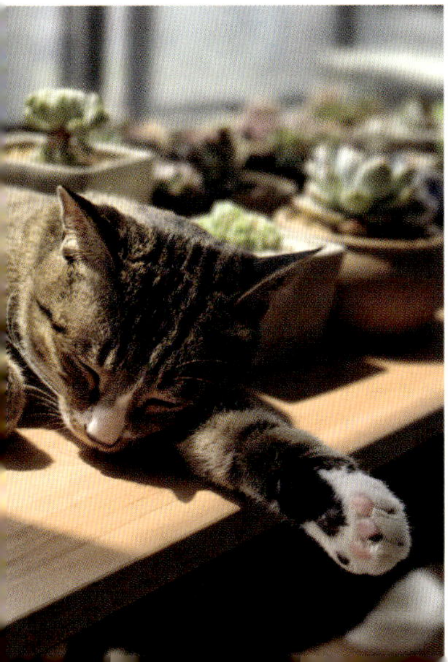

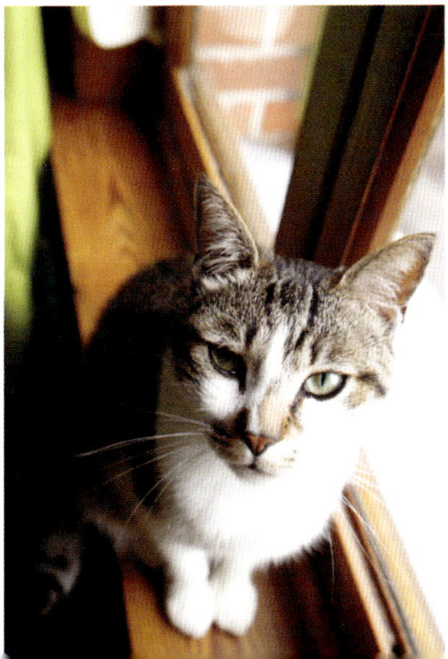

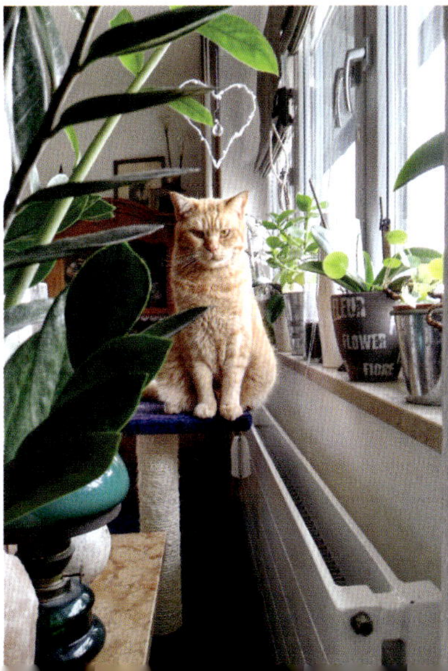

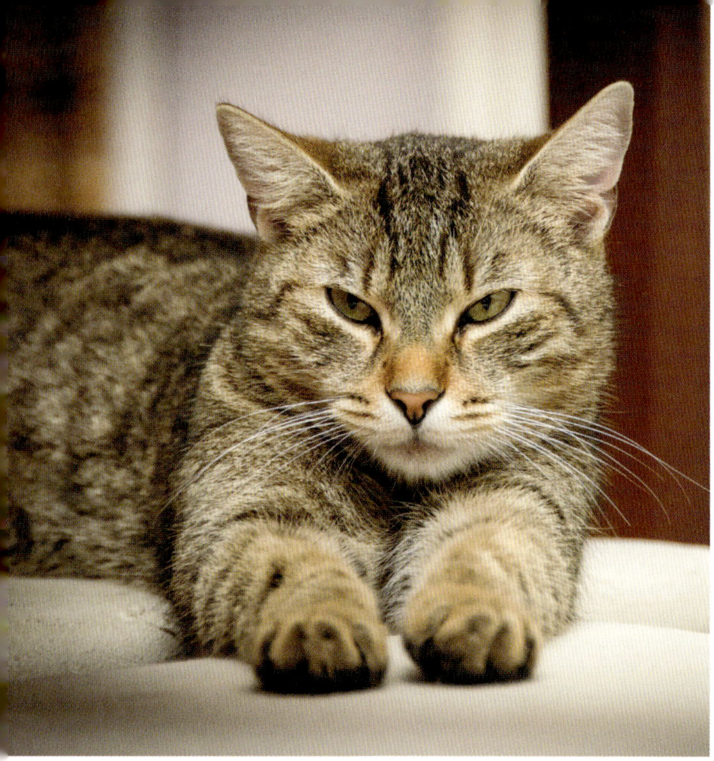

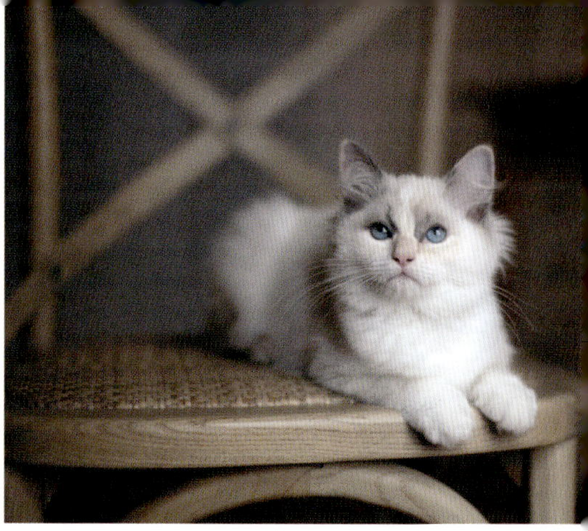

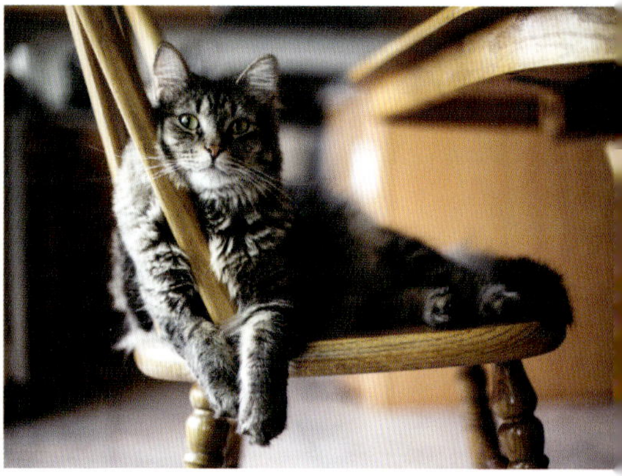

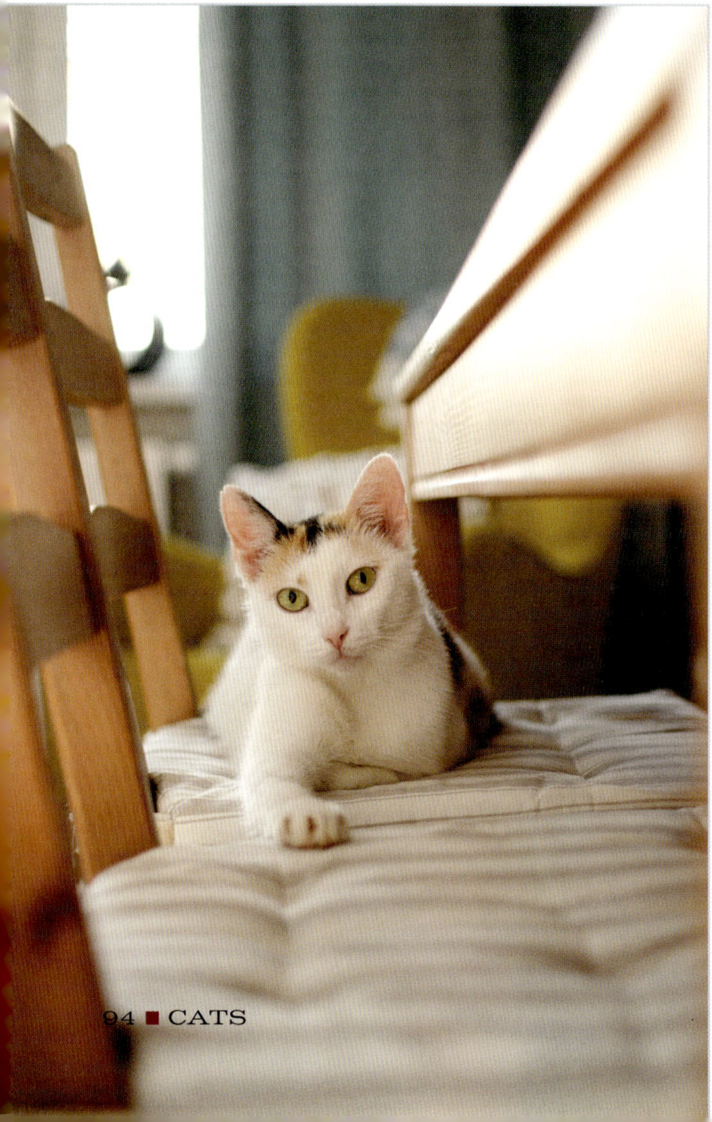

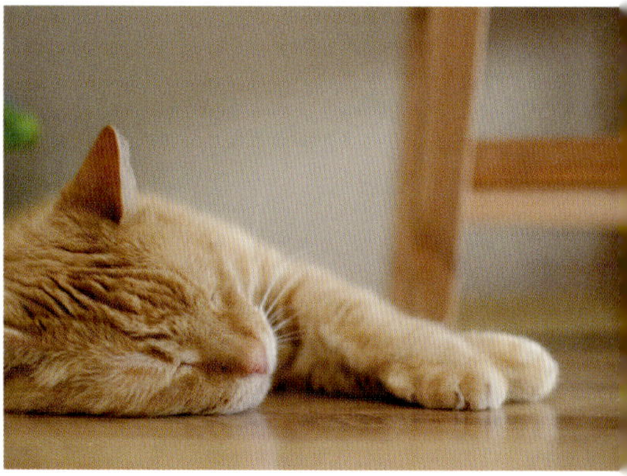

"A cat can be trusted to purr when she is pleased, which is more than can be said for human beings."

—William Ralph Inge, author

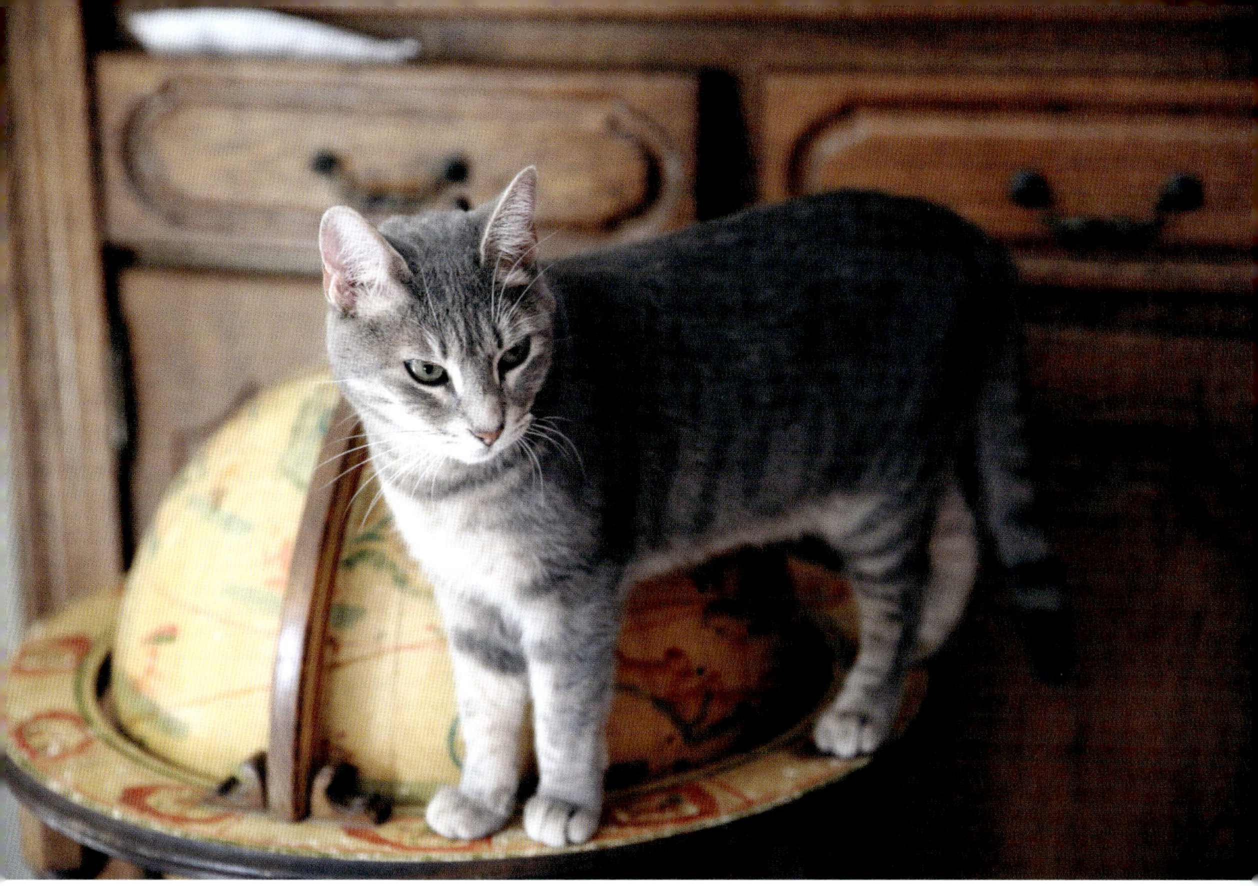
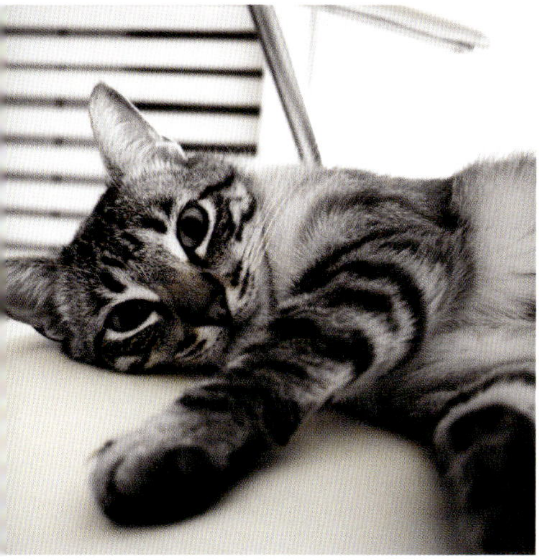
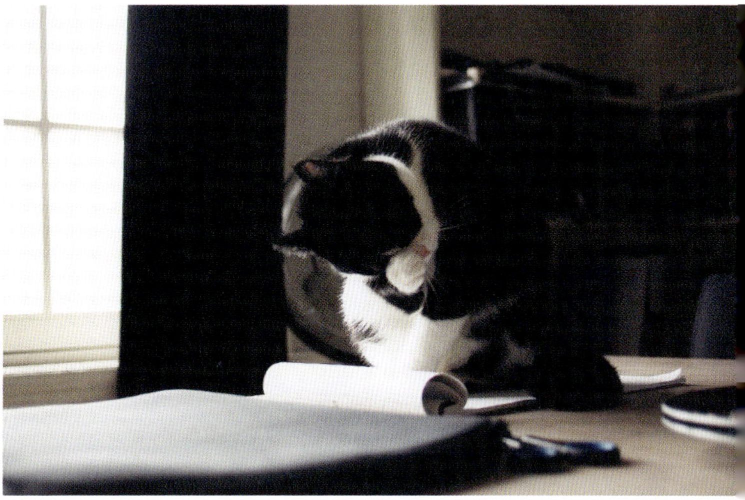
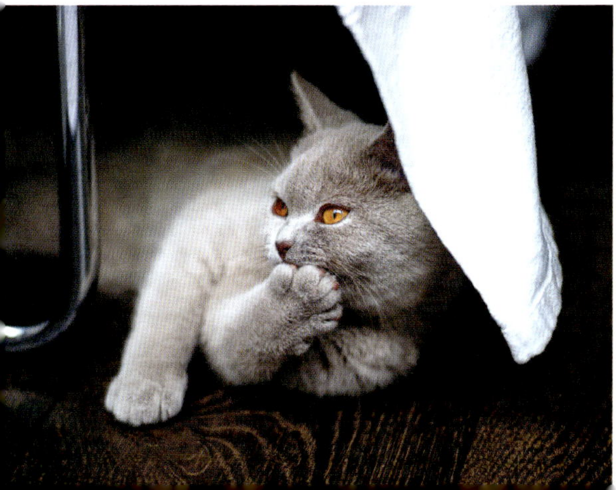
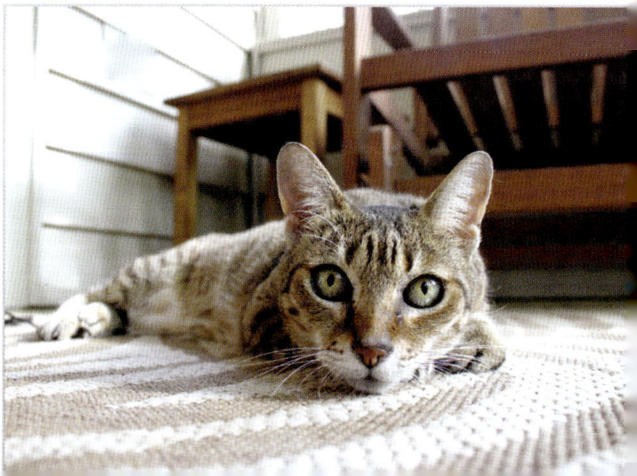

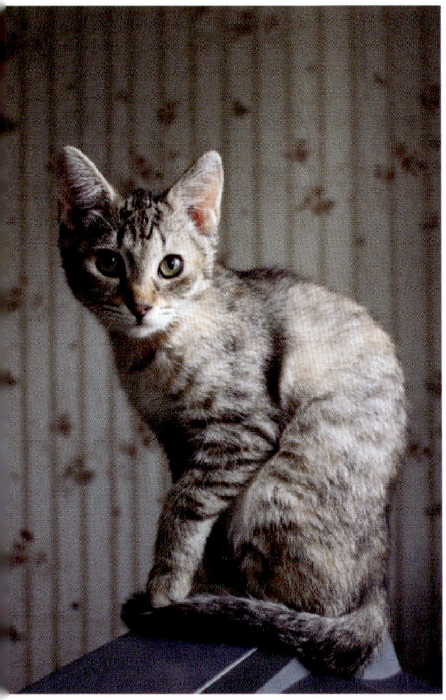
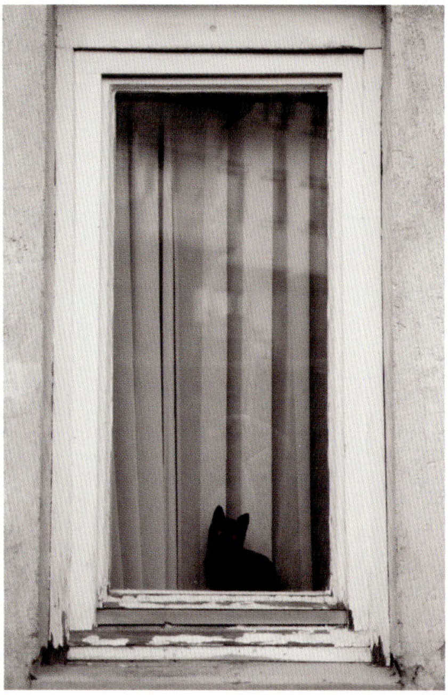
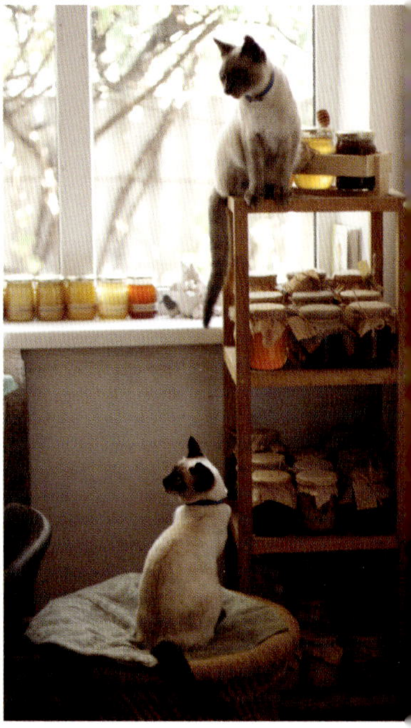
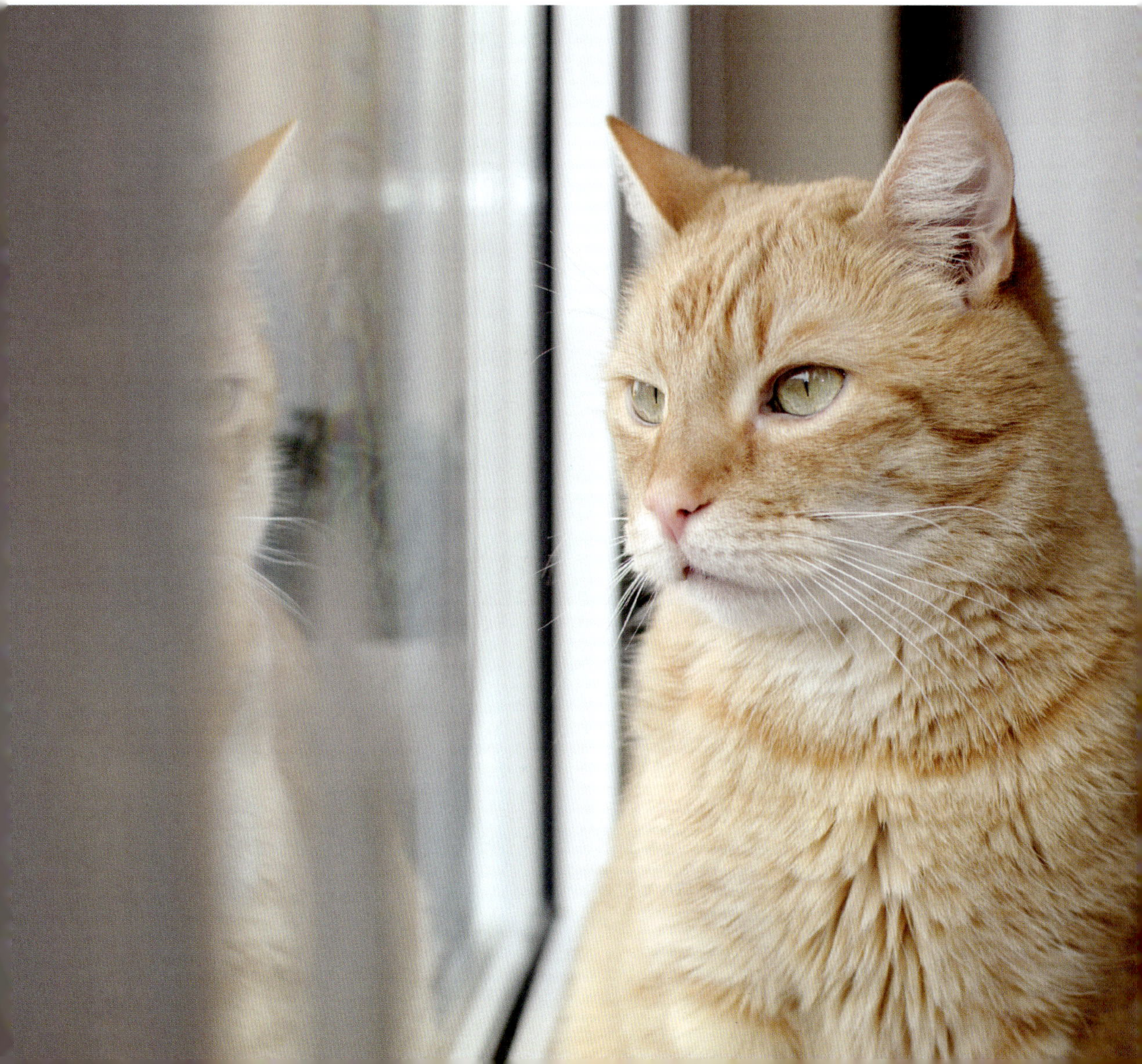

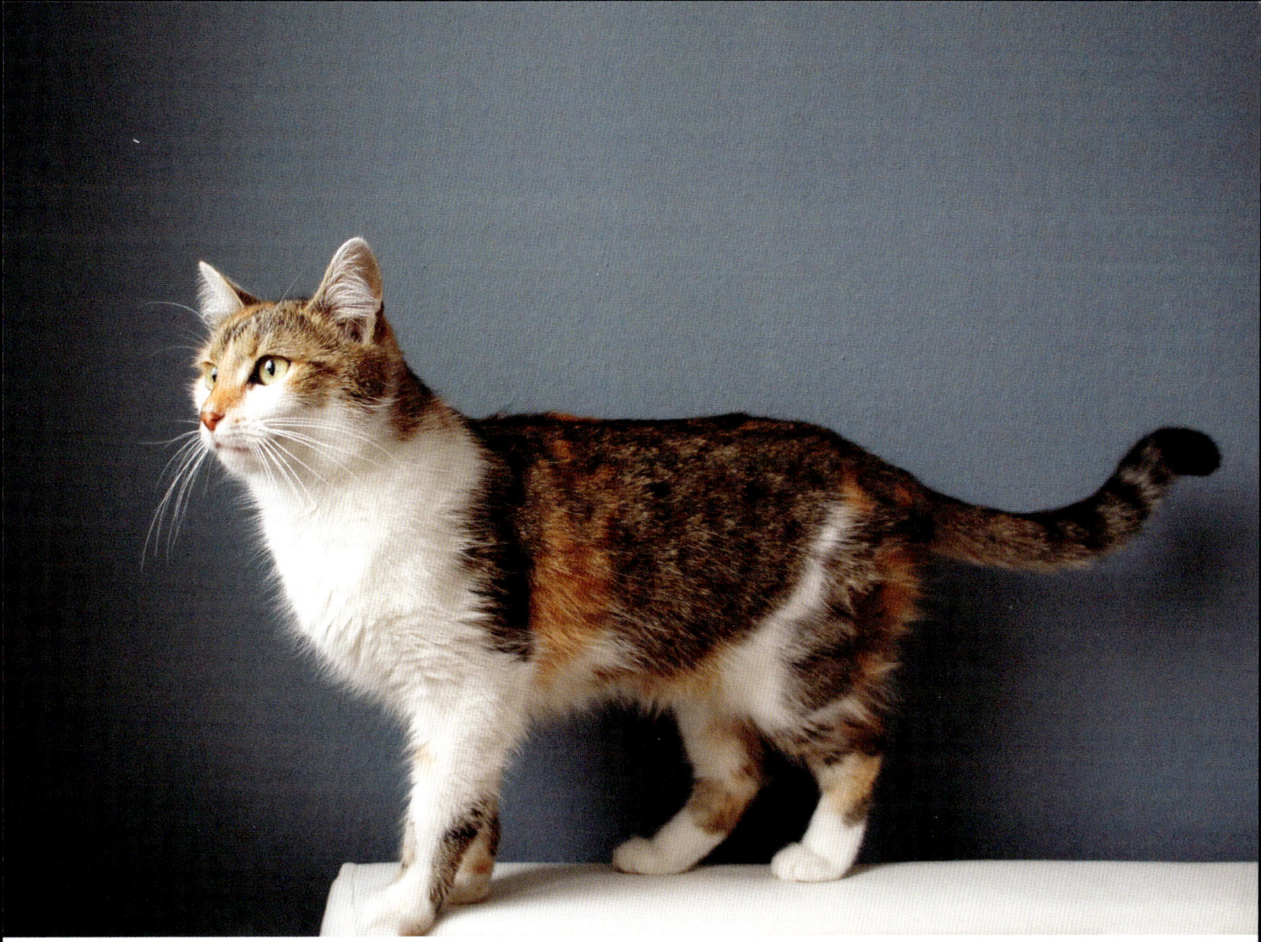
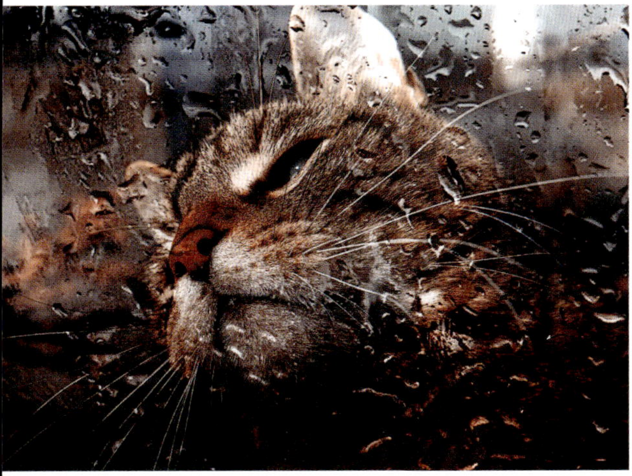
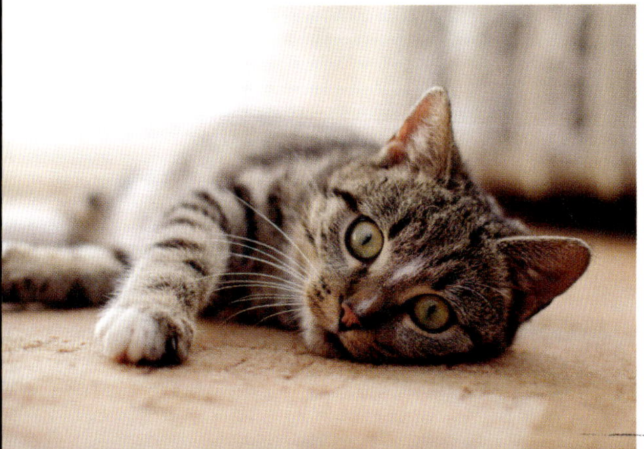
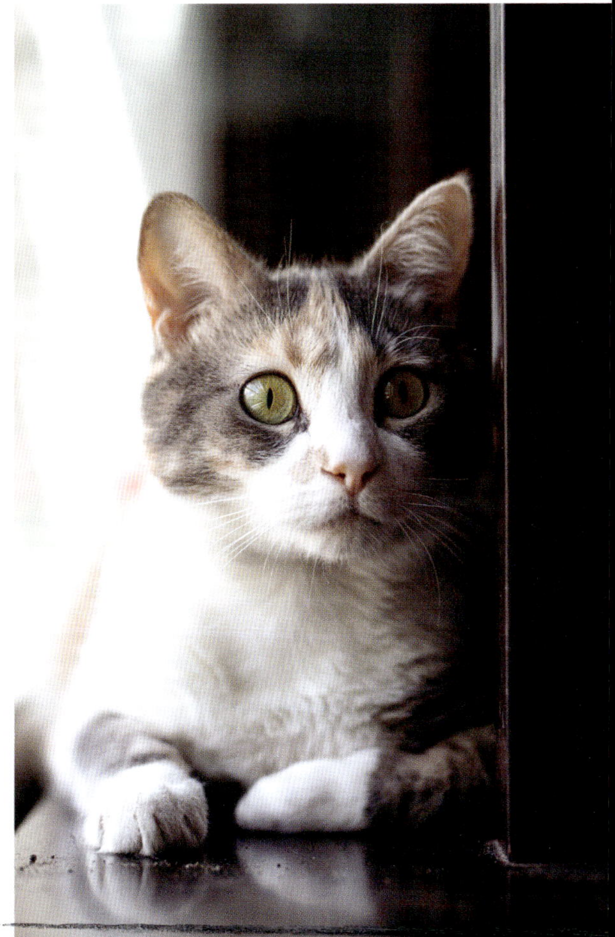

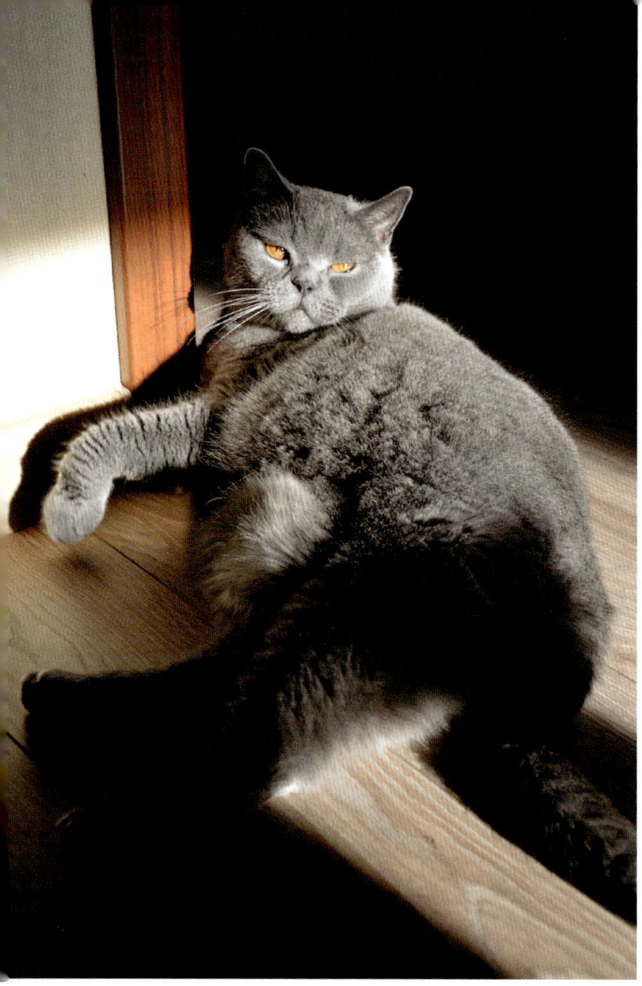
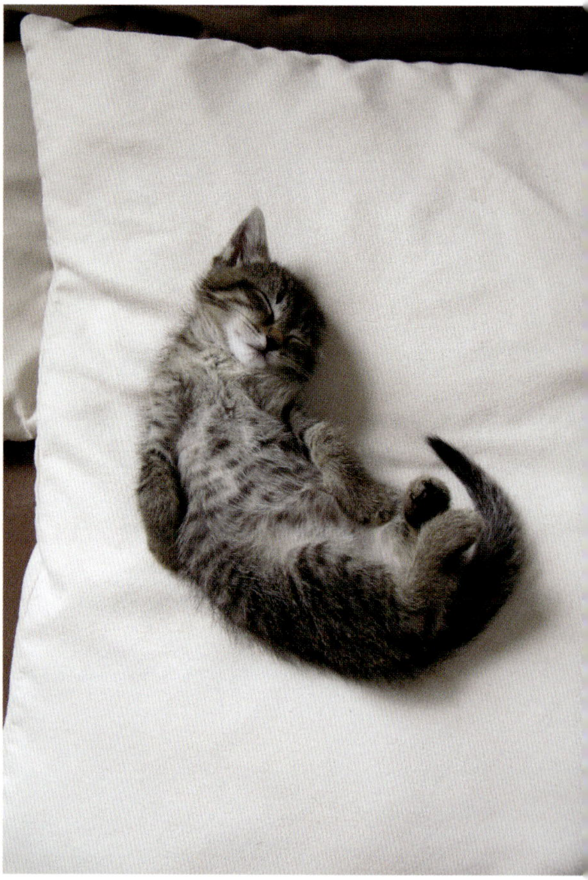
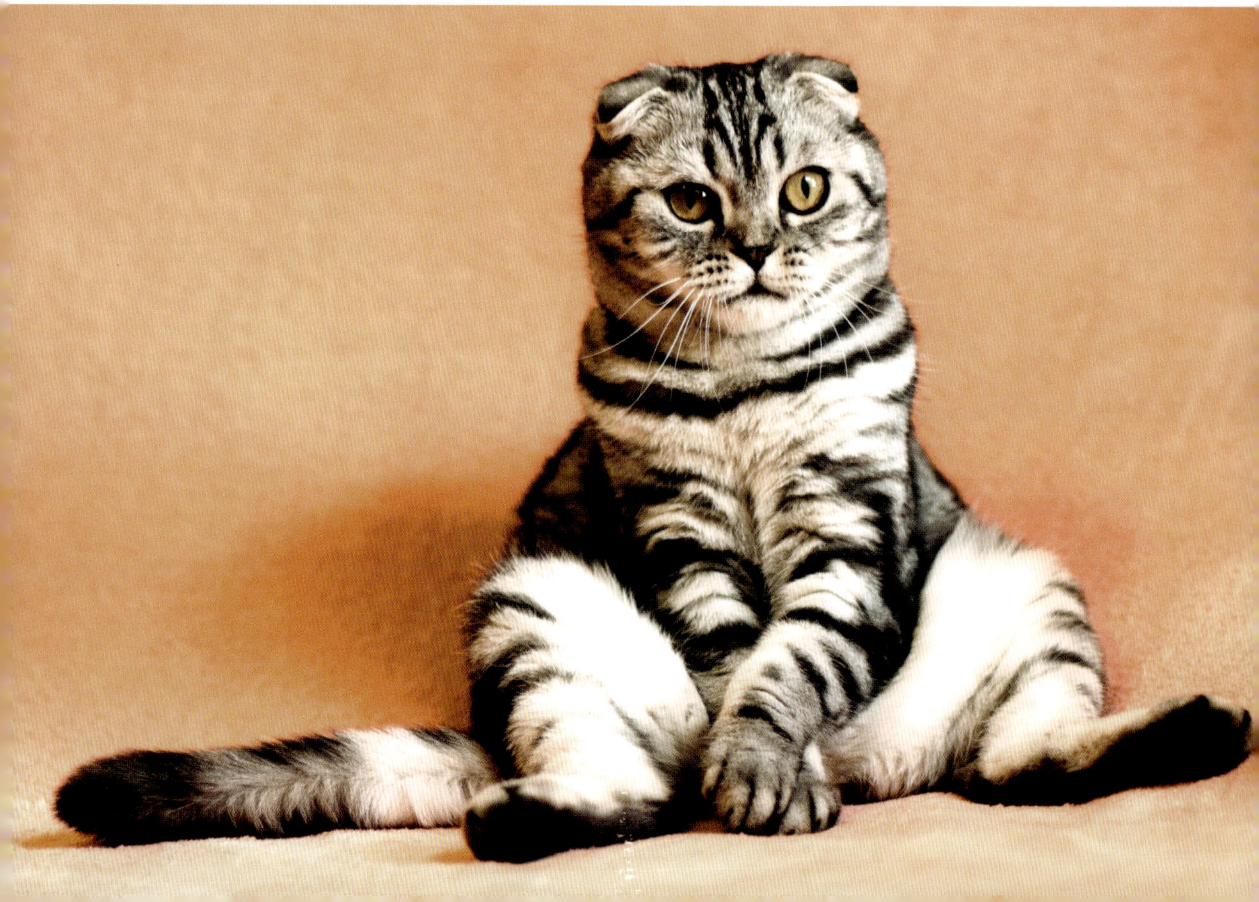

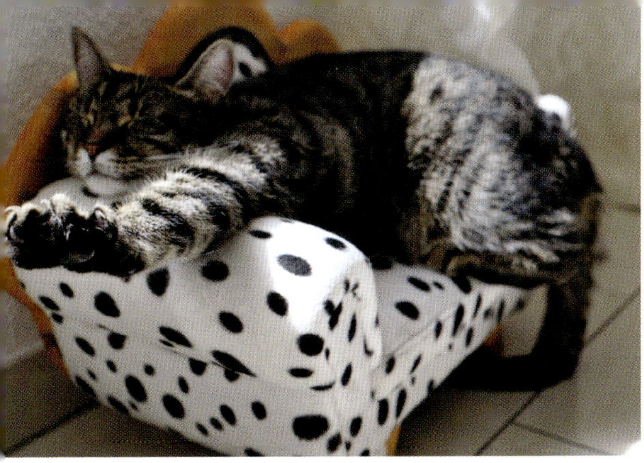

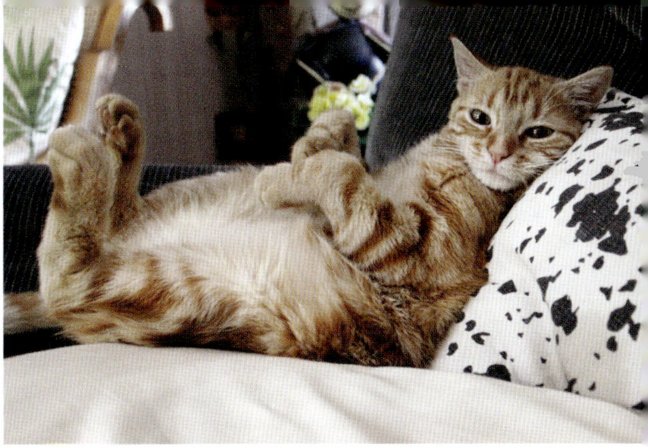

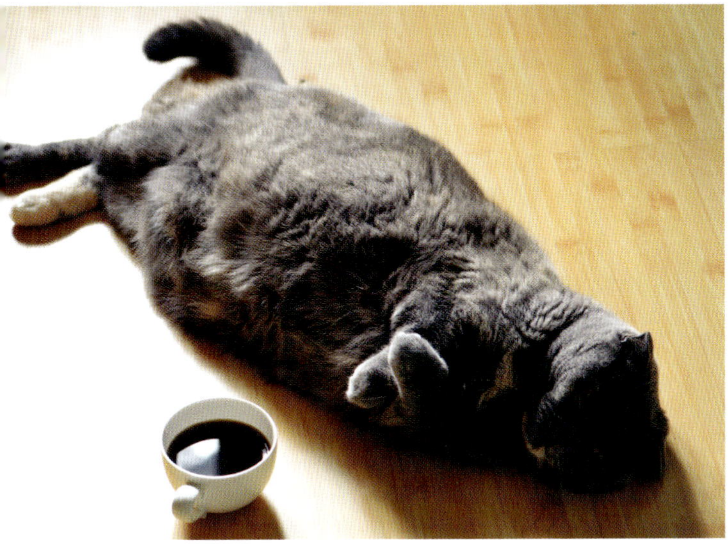

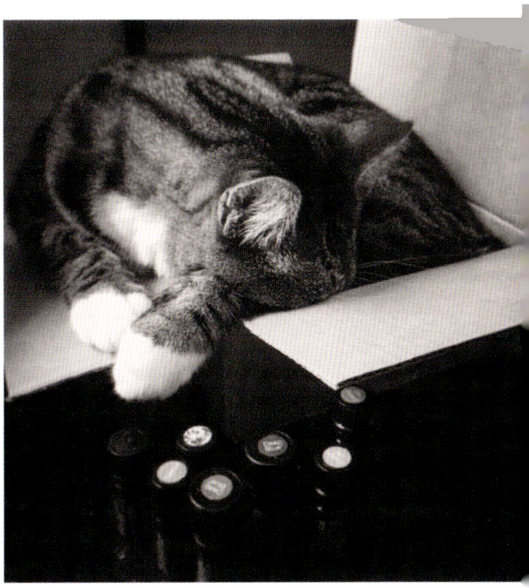

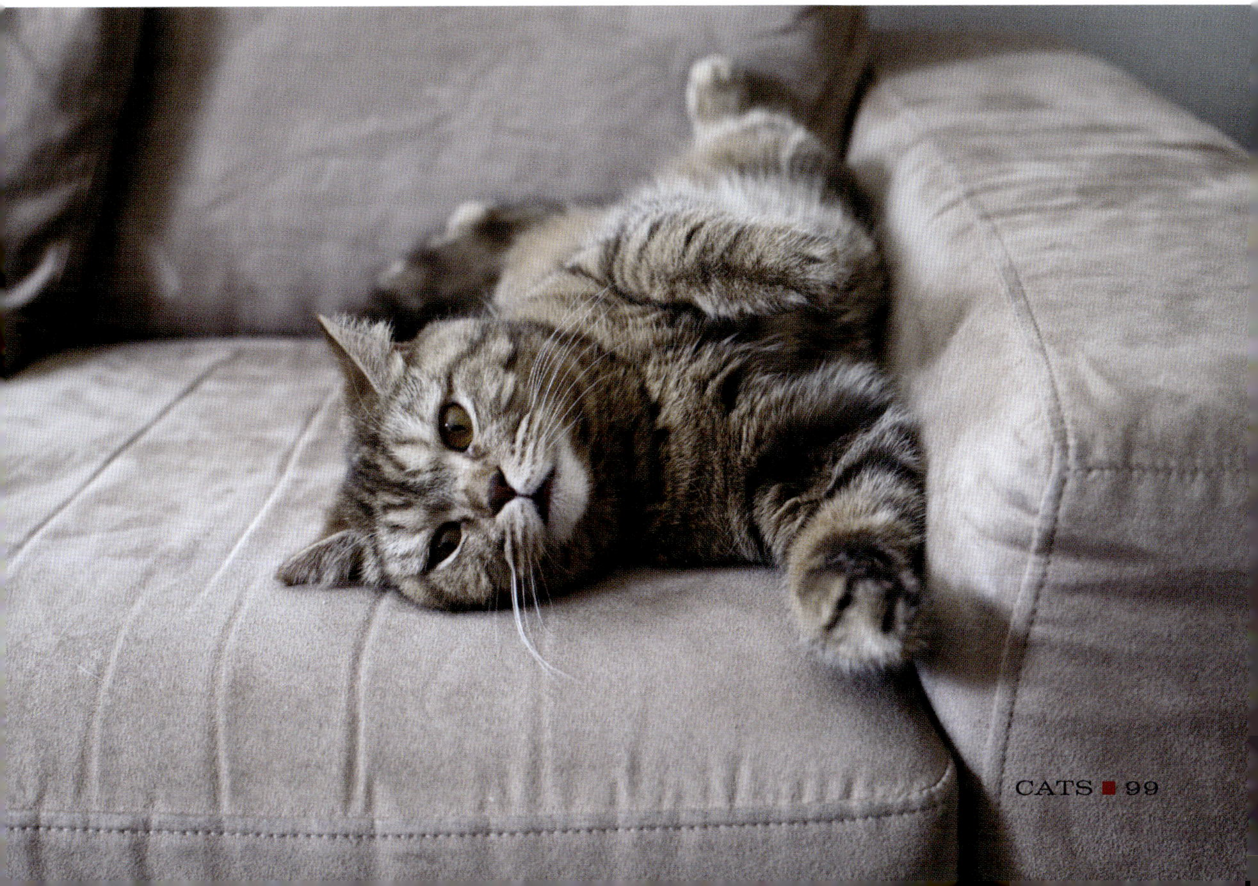

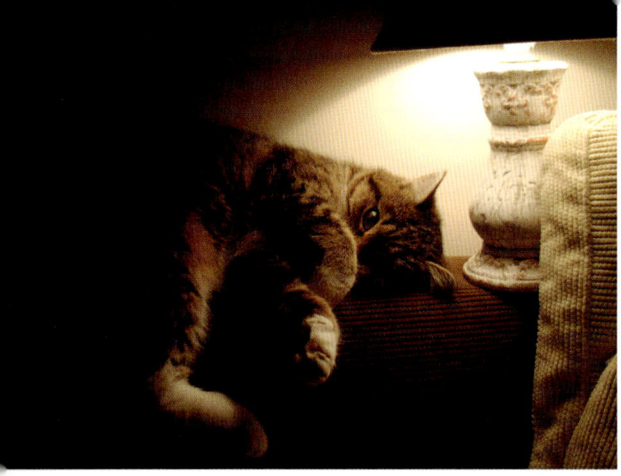
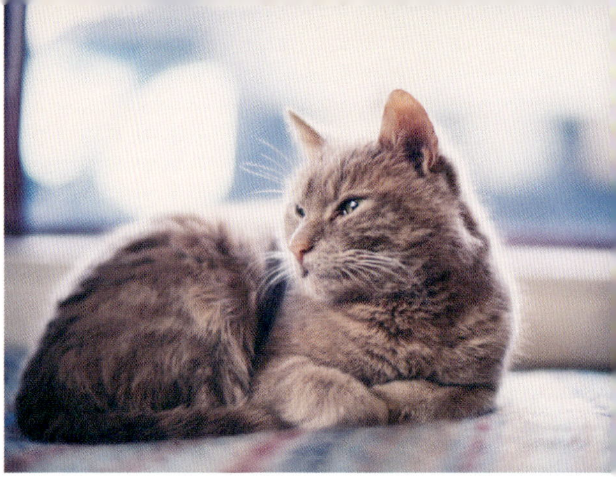
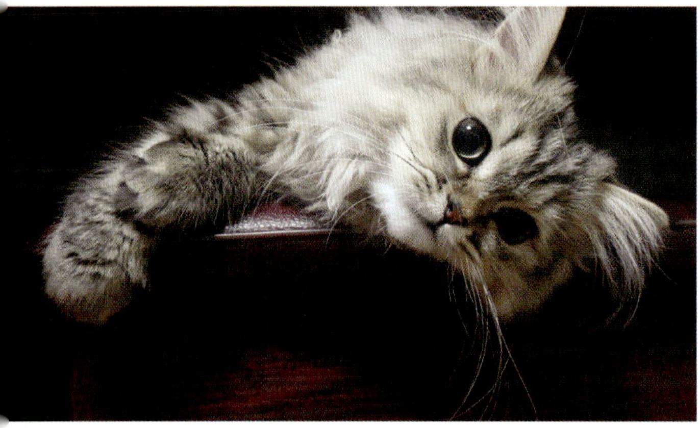
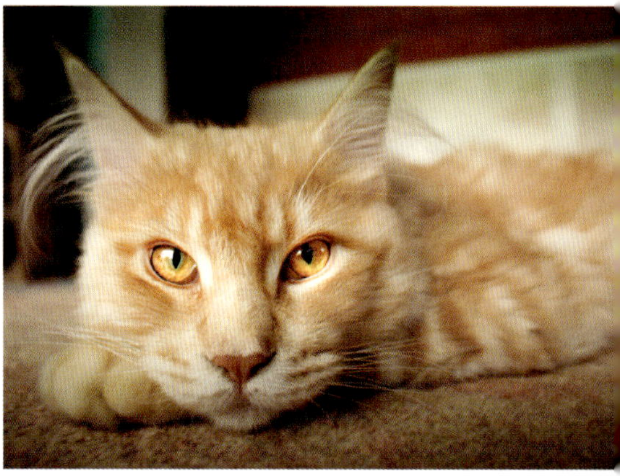
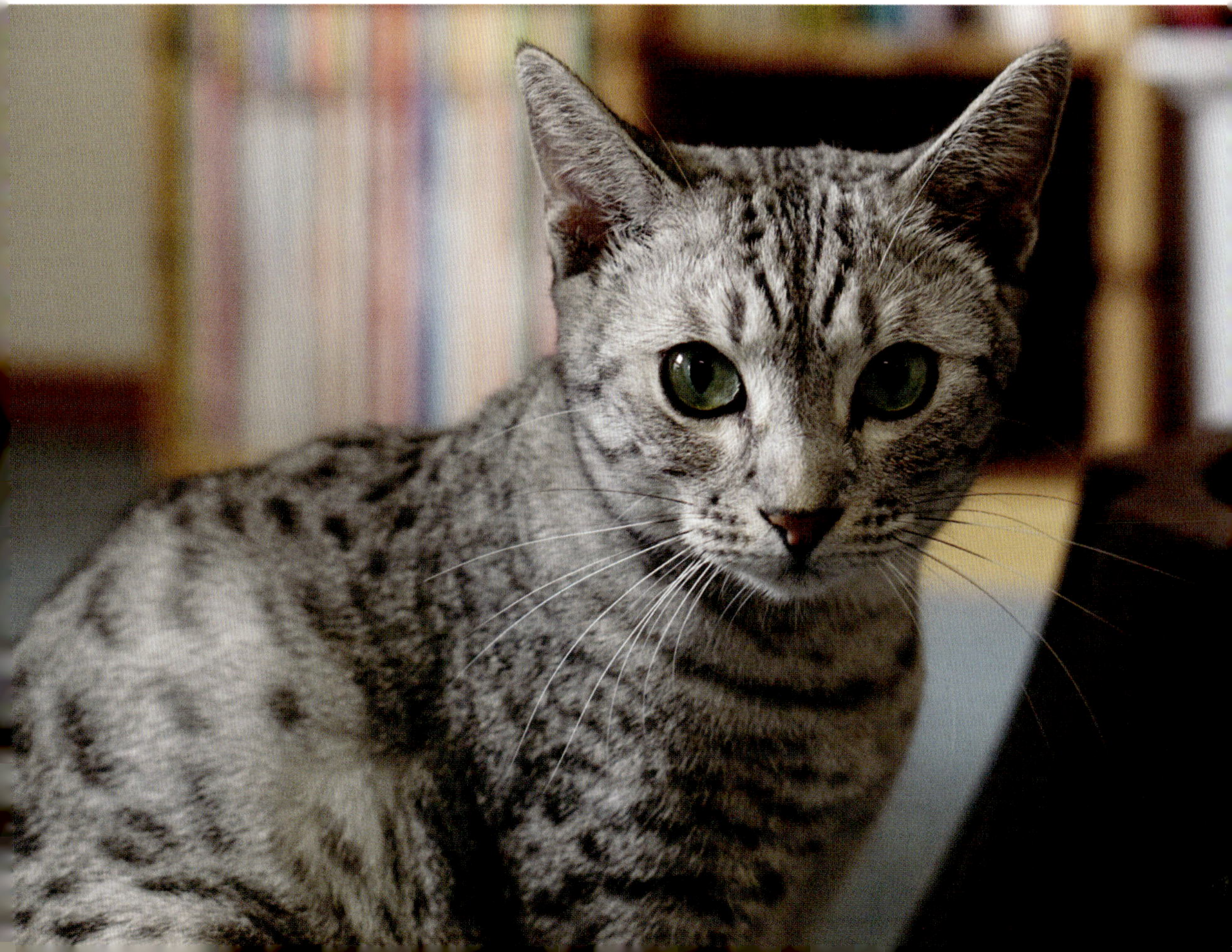

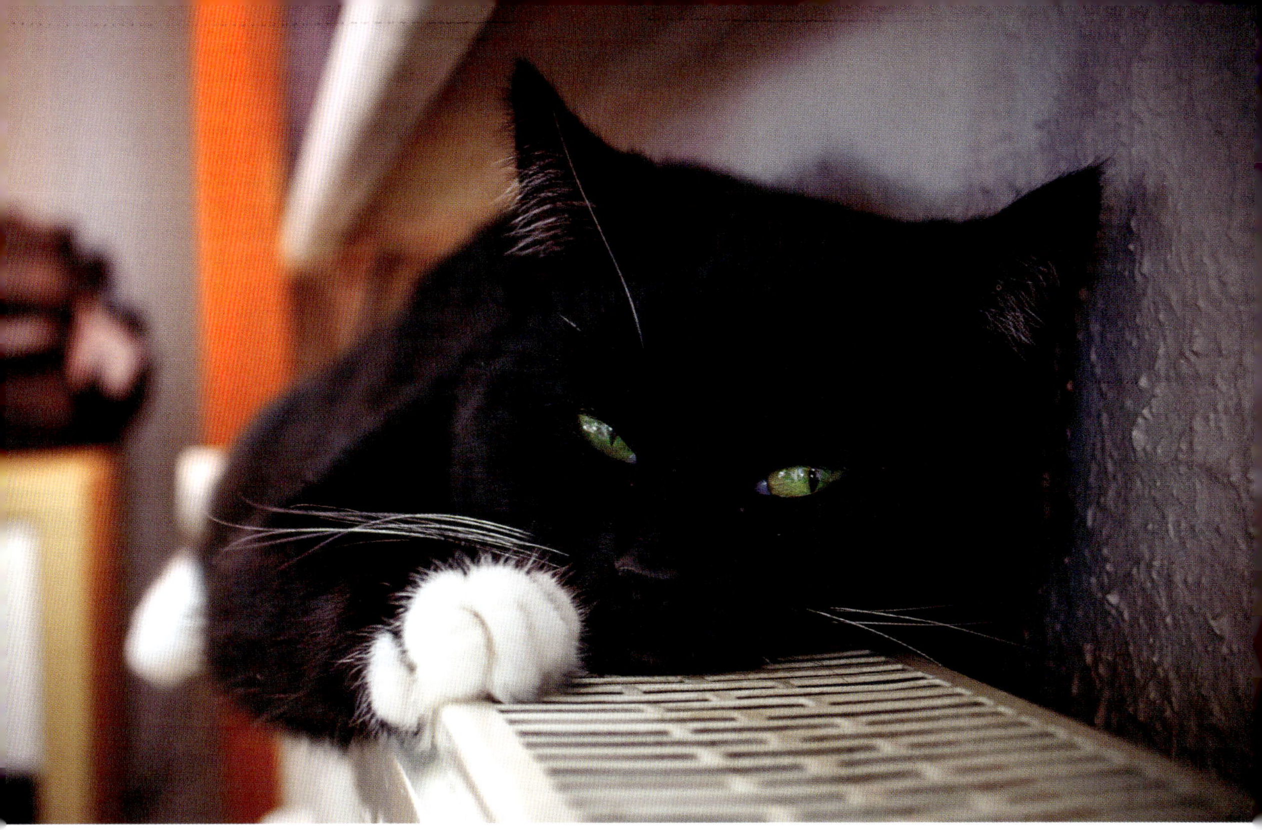

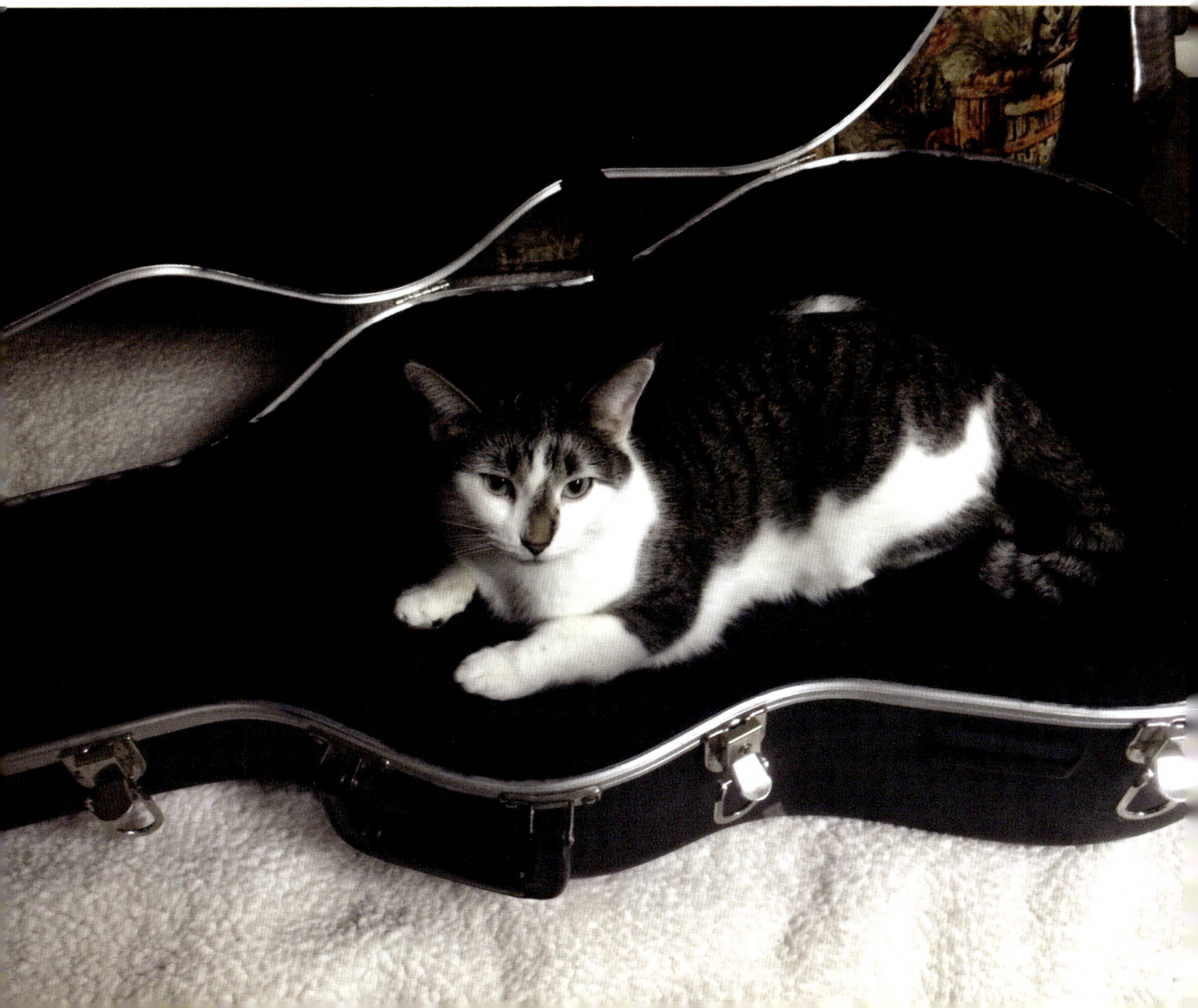

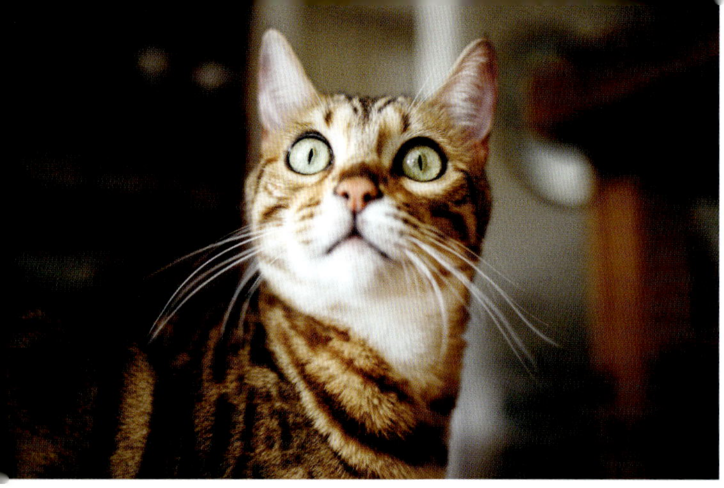

"Way down deep, we're all motivated by the same urges. Cats have the courage to live by them."

–Jim Davis, cartoonist

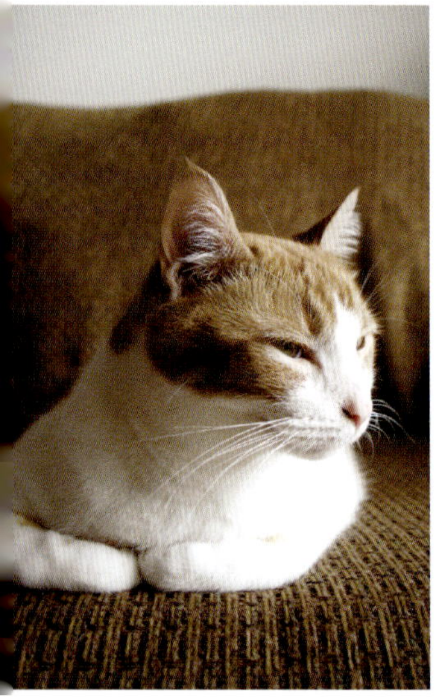

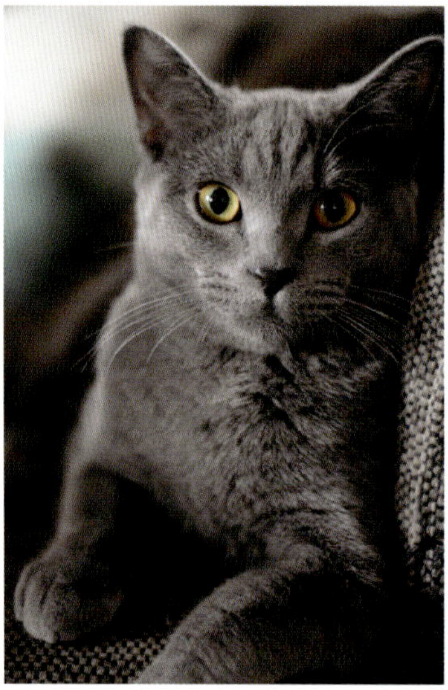

"Cats know how to obtain food without labor, shelter without confinement, and love without penalties."

–W. L. George, author

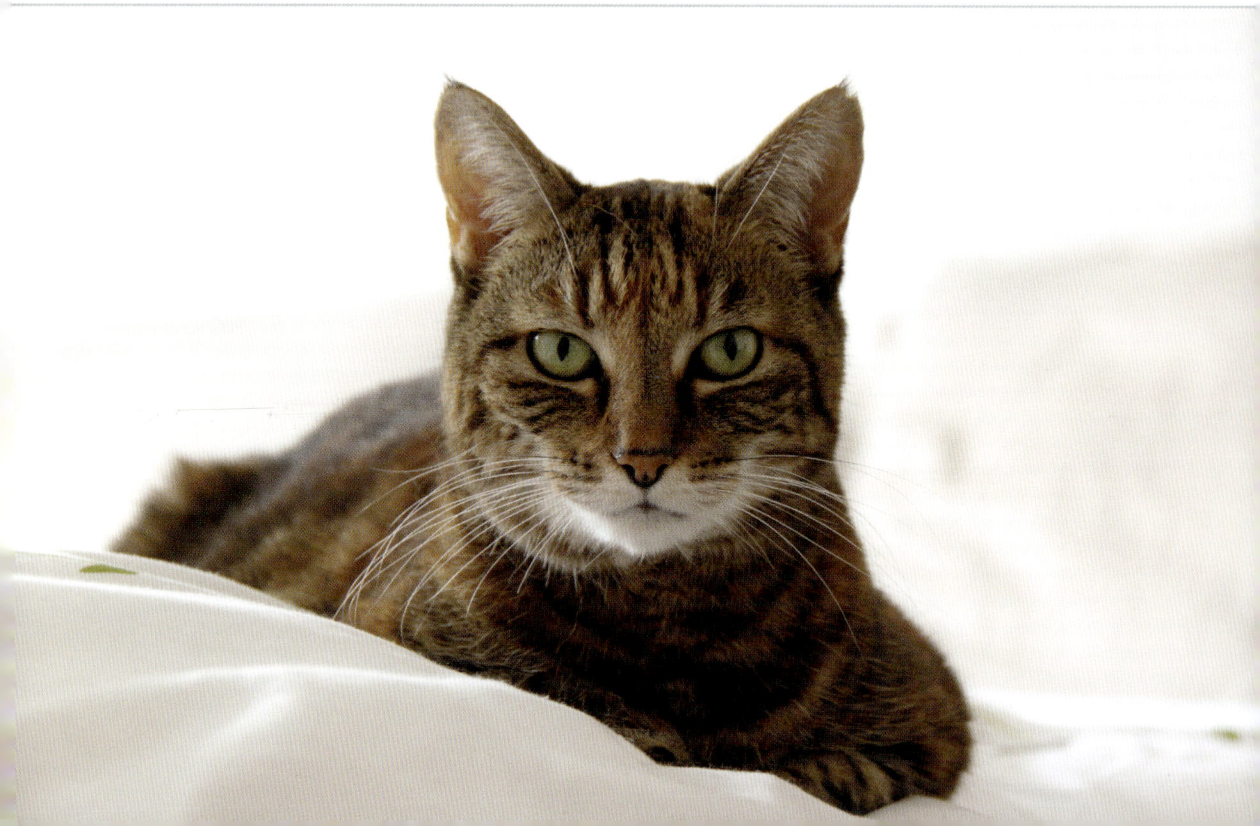

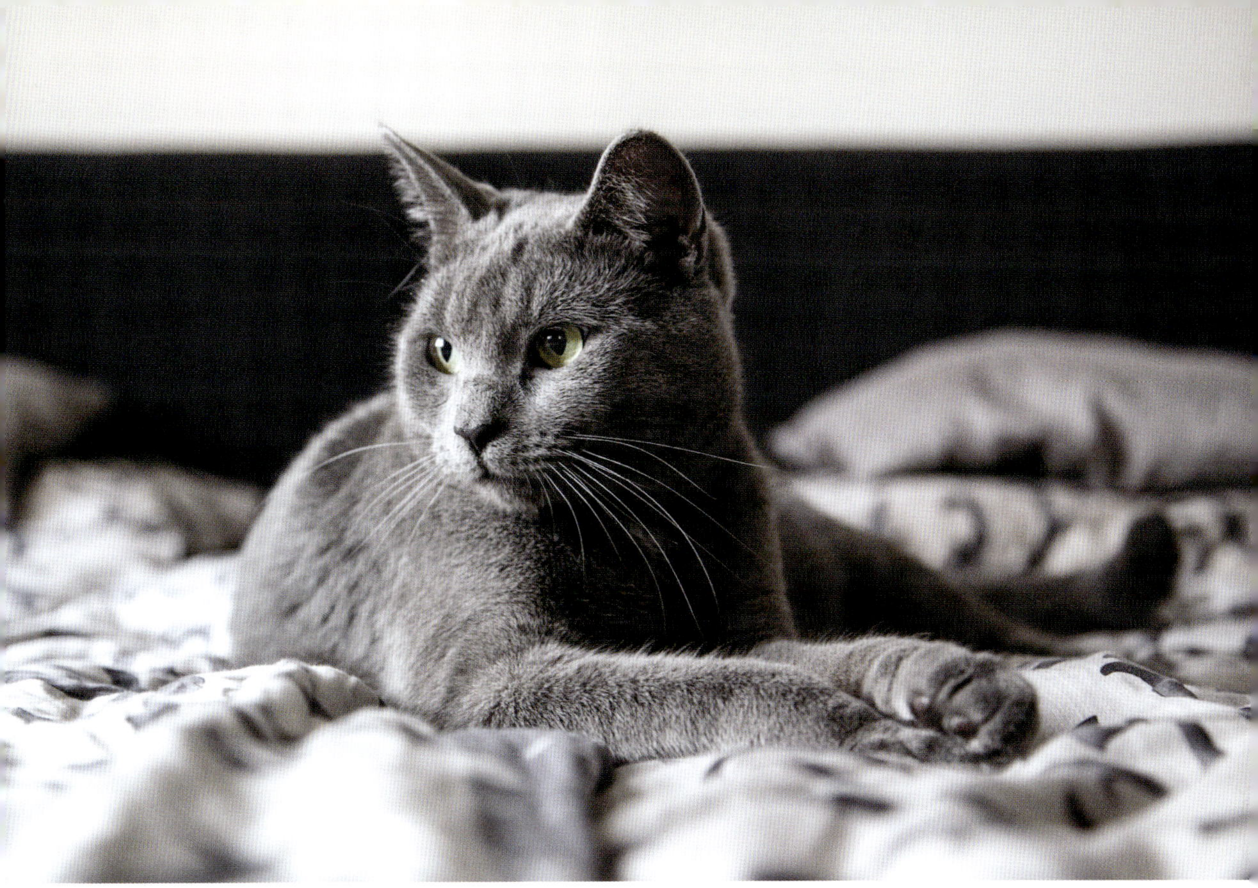

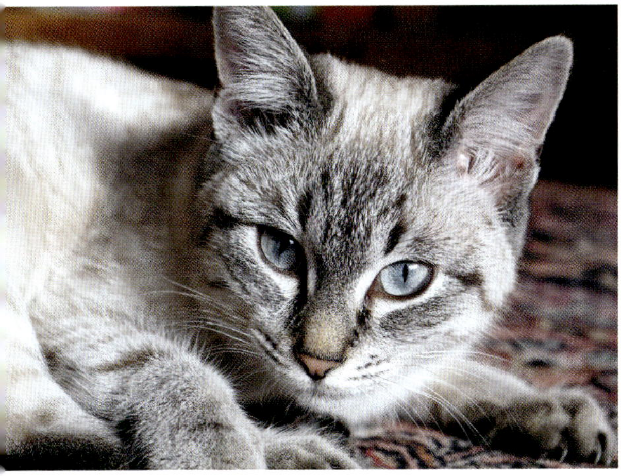

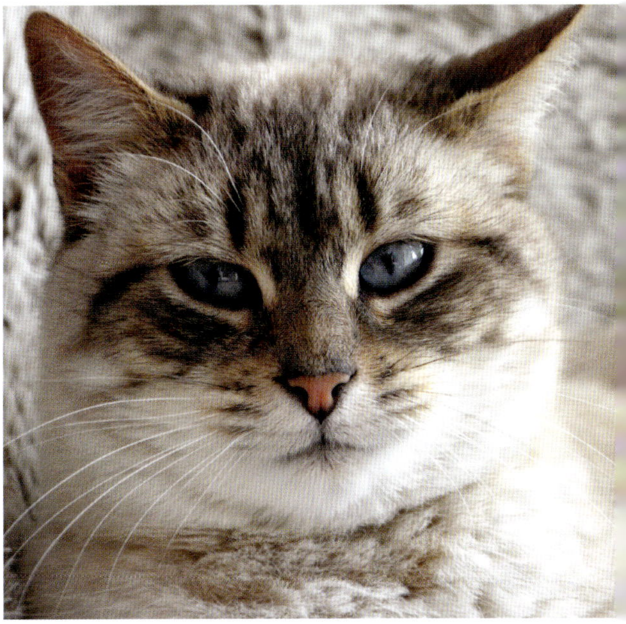

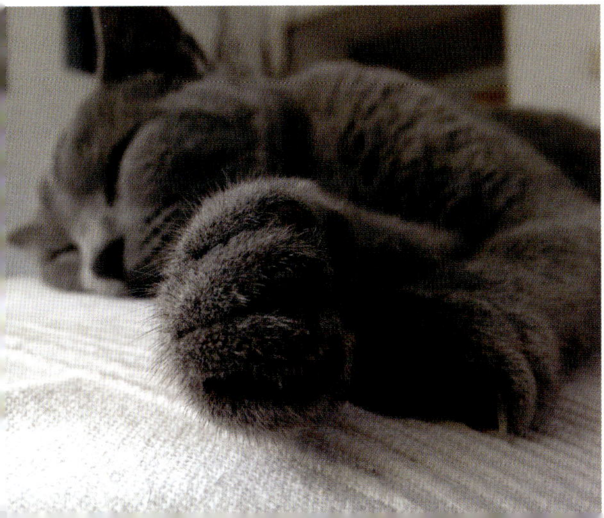

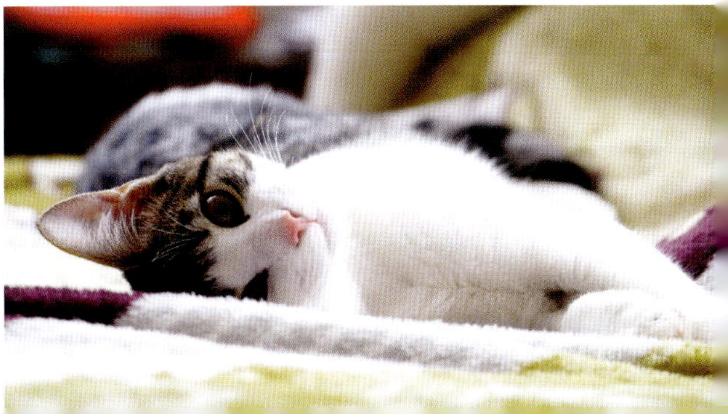

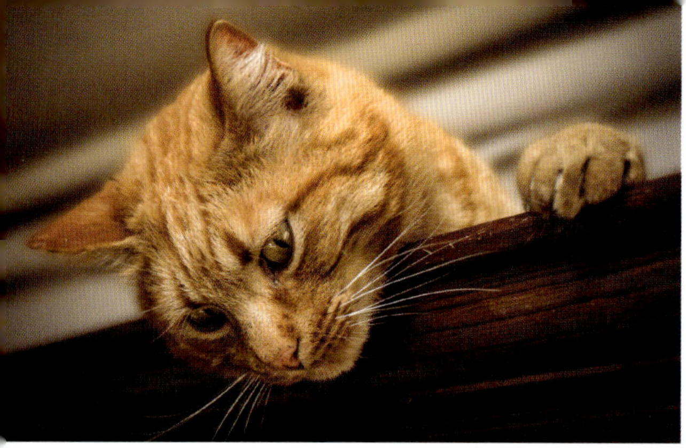

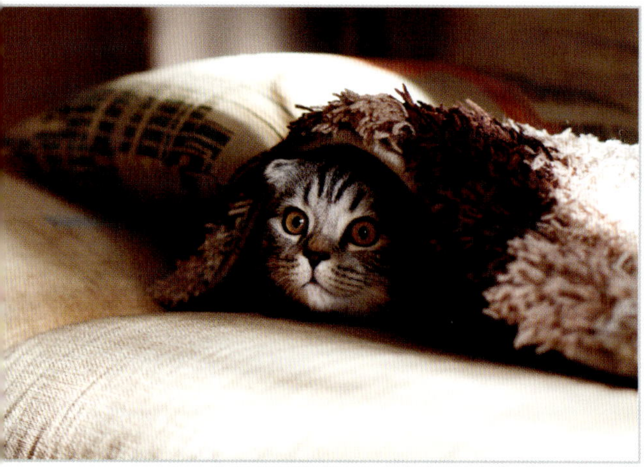

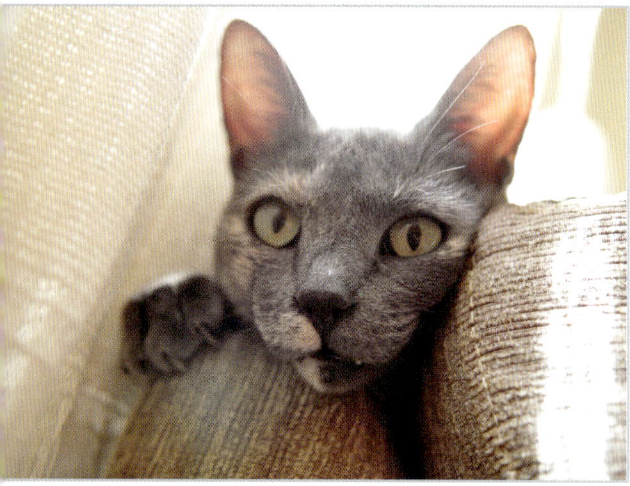

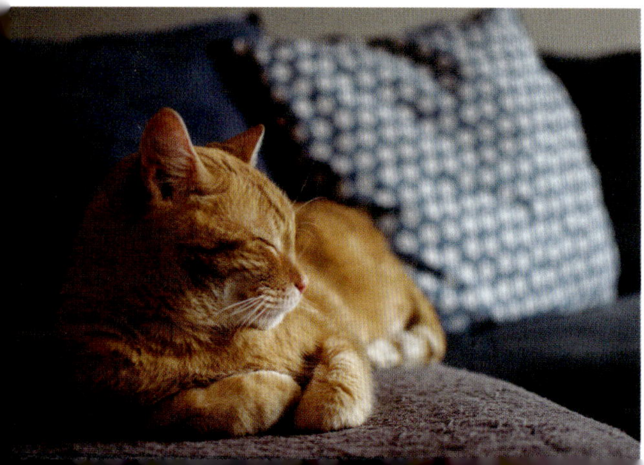

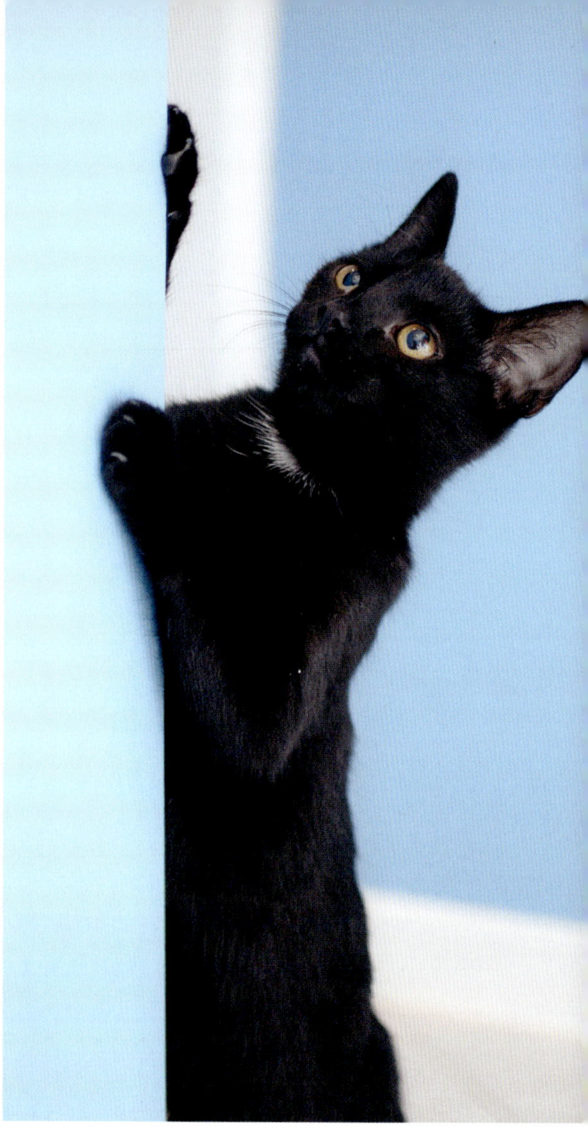

"I have felt cats rubbing their faces against mine and touching my cheek with claws carefully sheathed. These things, to me, are expressions of love."

—James Herriot, author and veterinarian

8. Nap Time

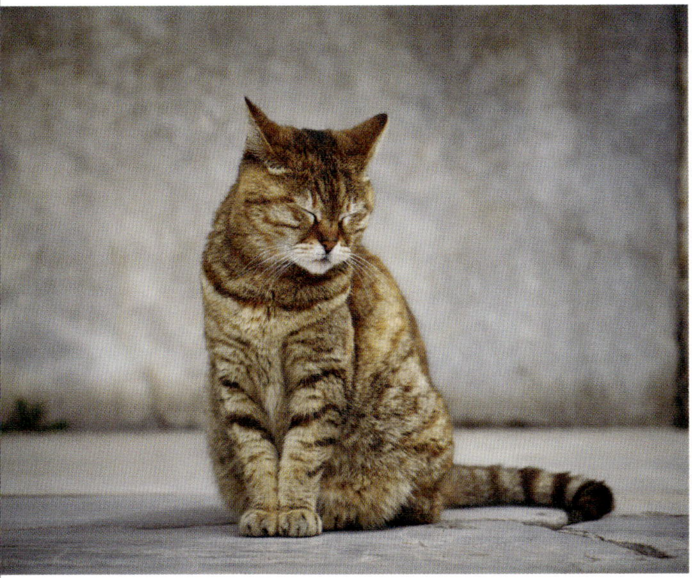

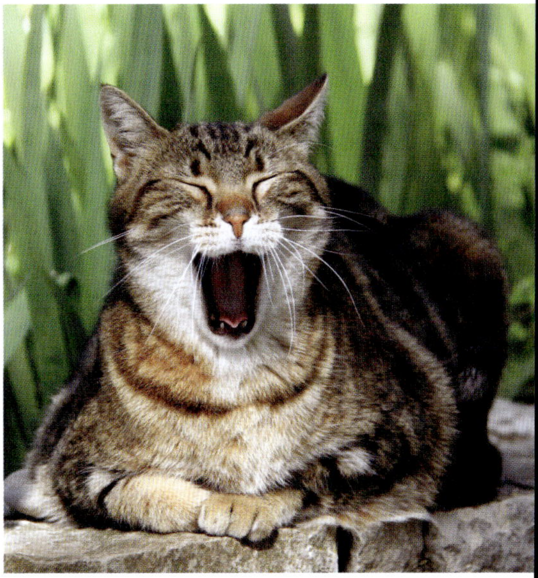

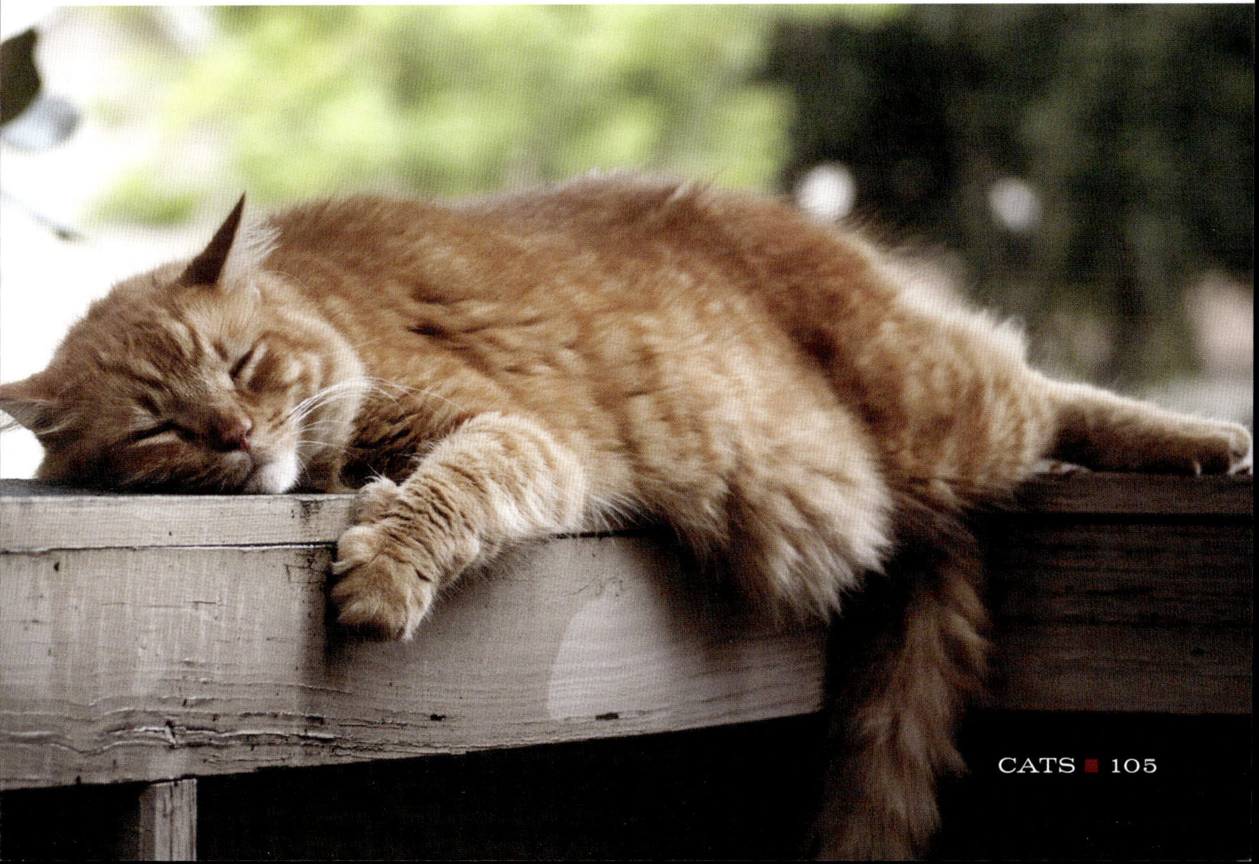

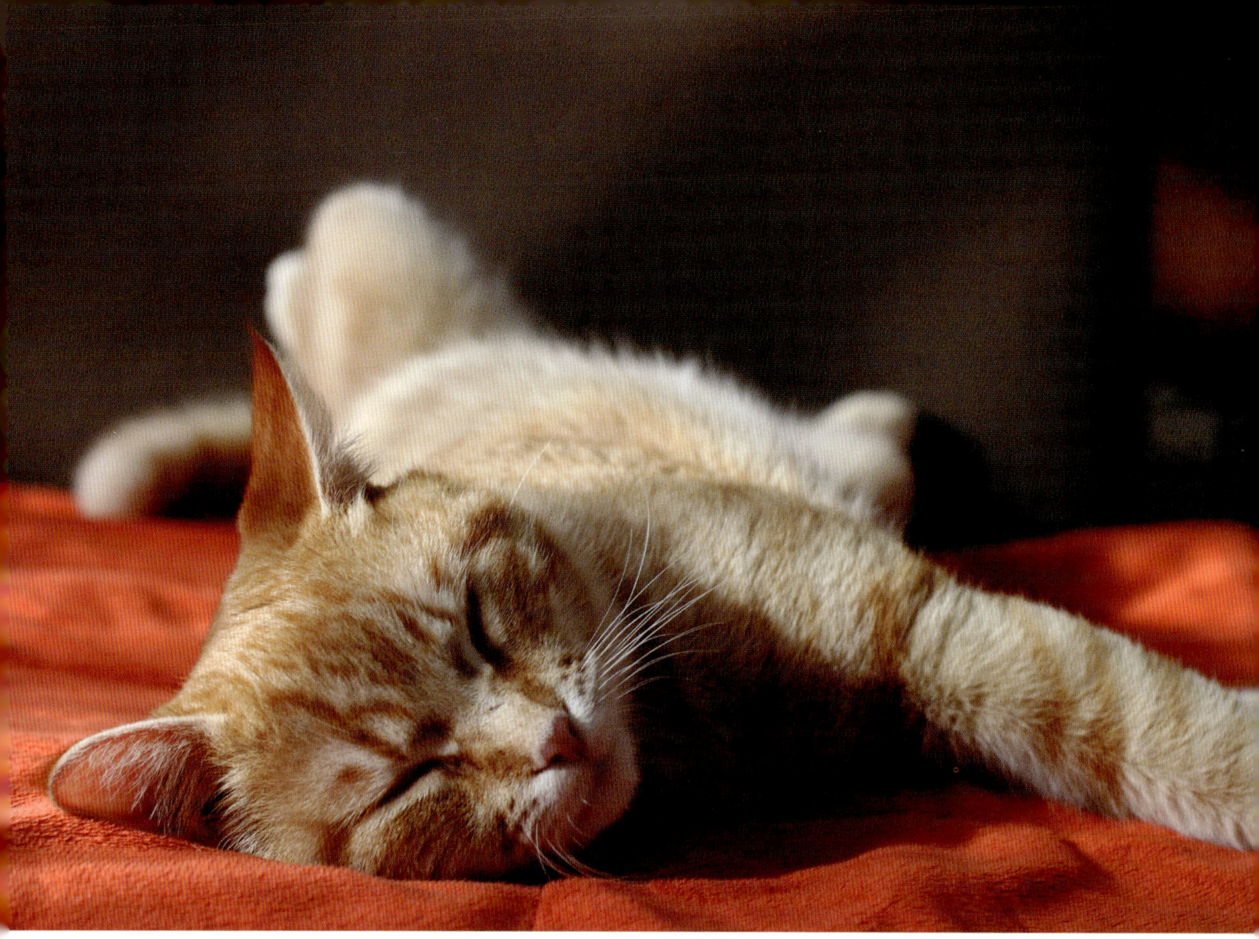
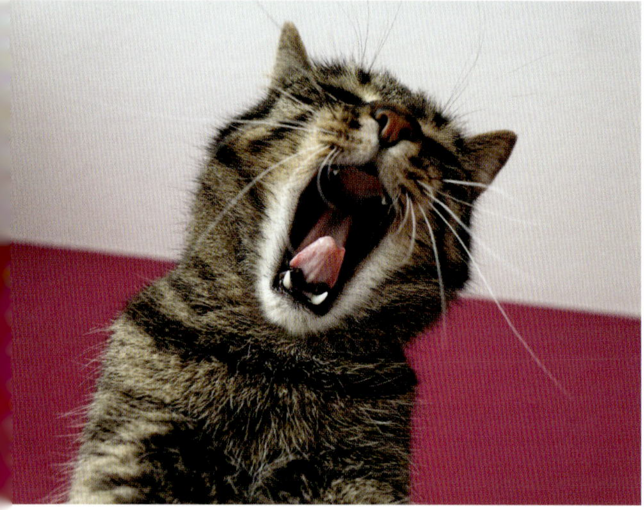
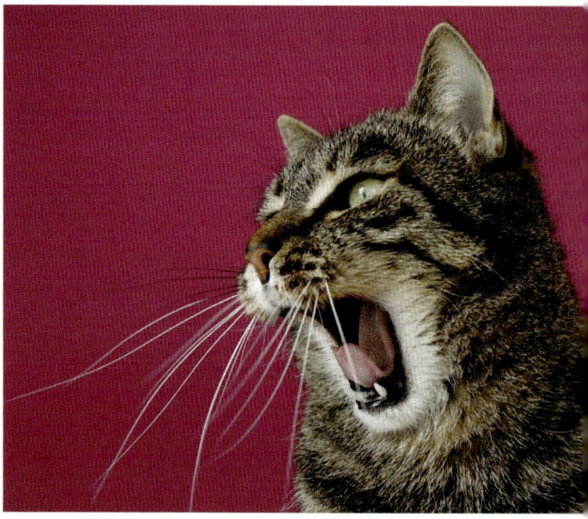
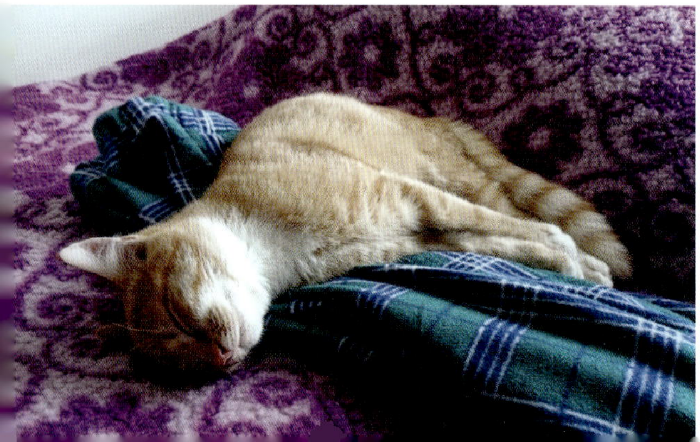
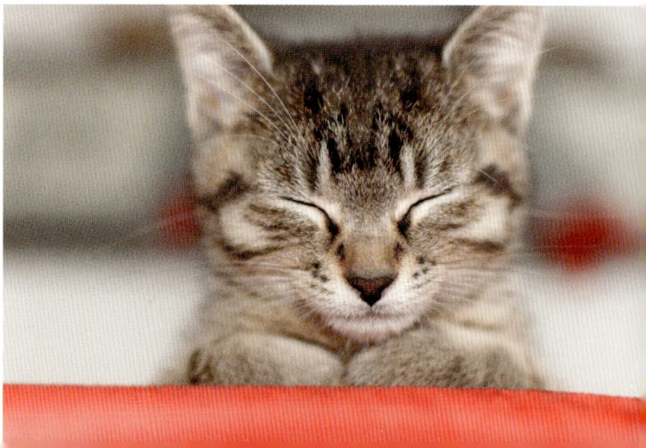

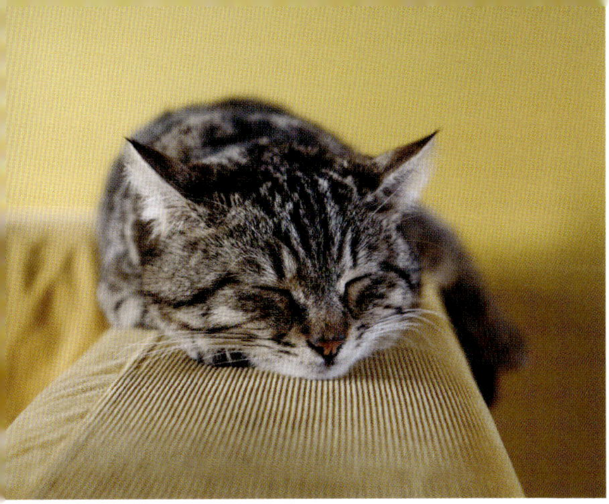
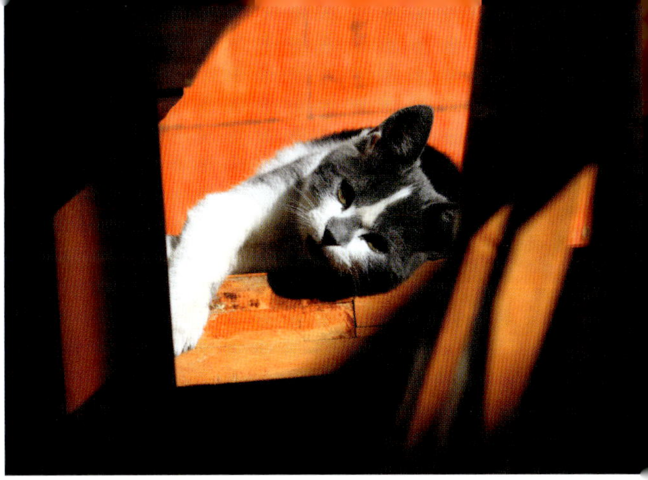
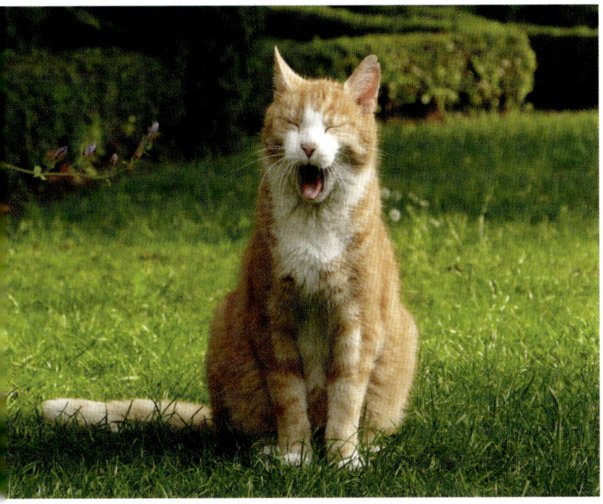
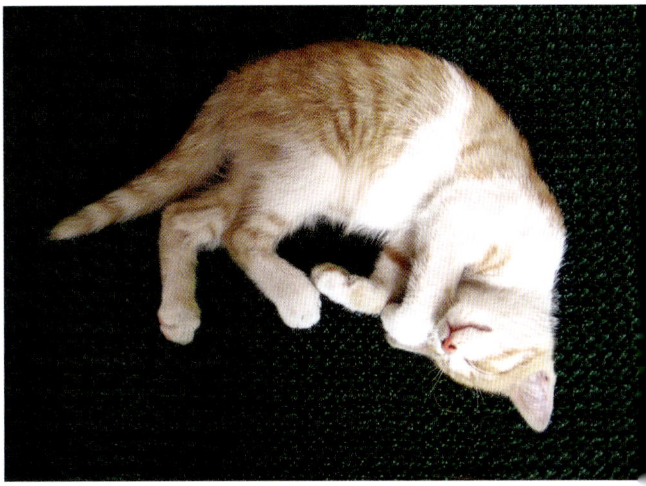
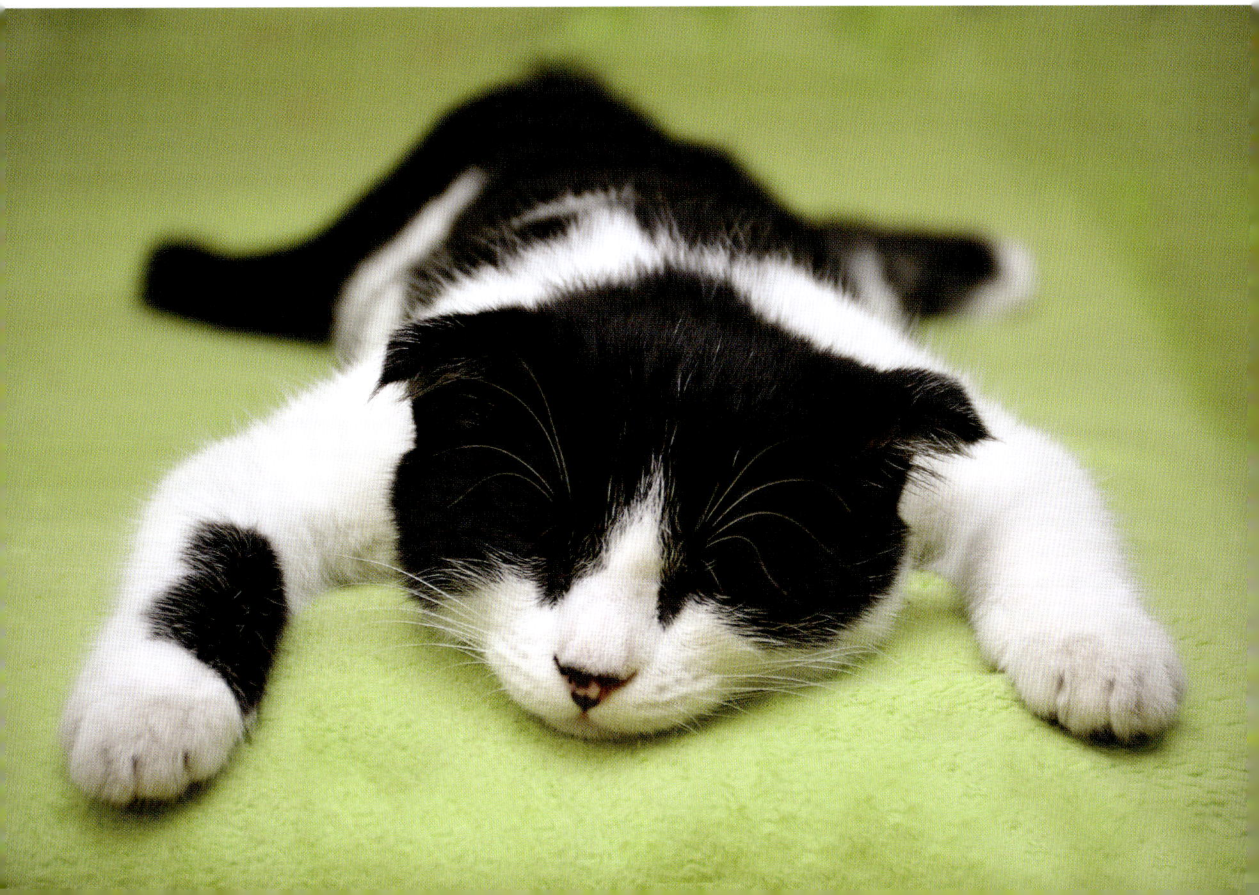

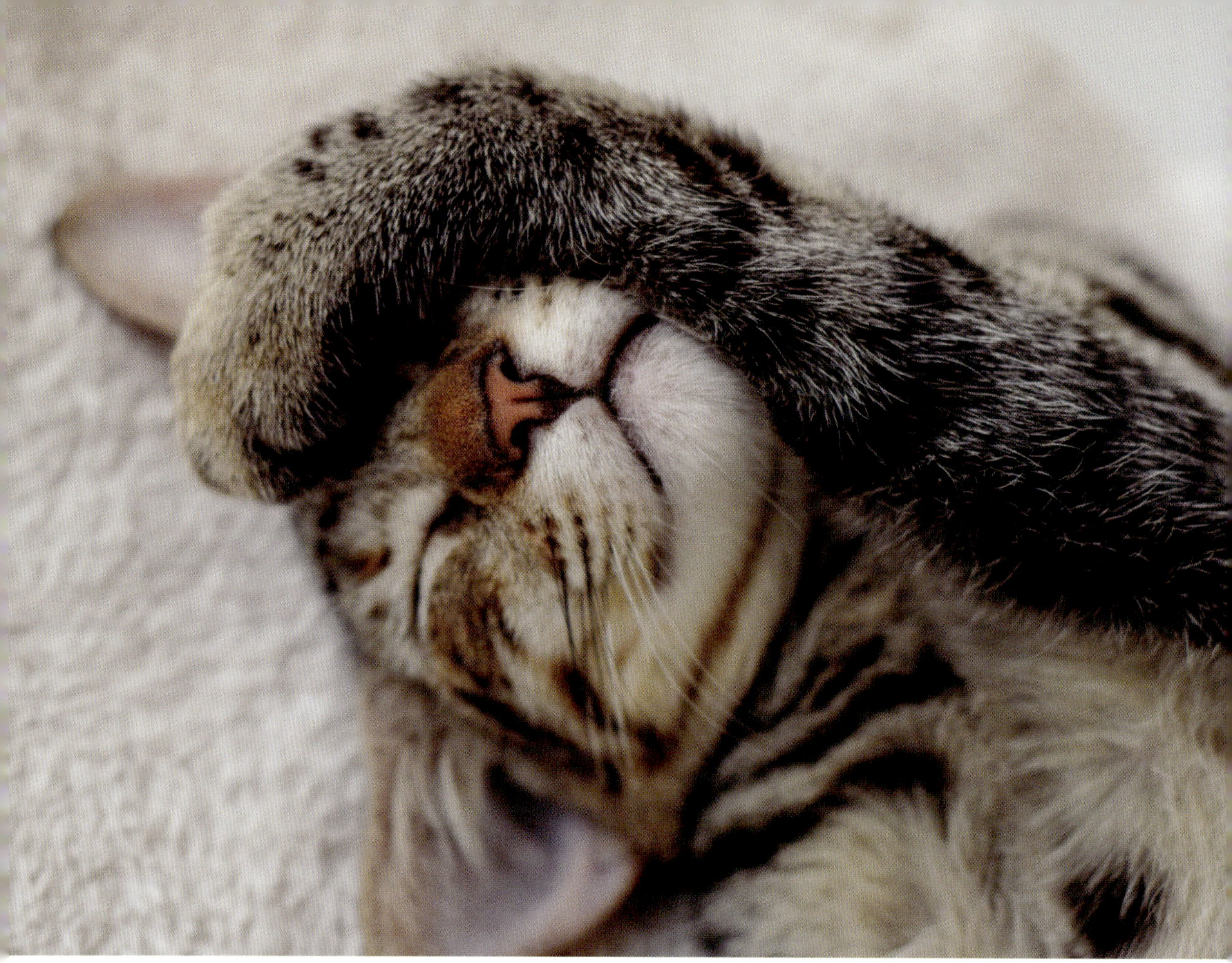

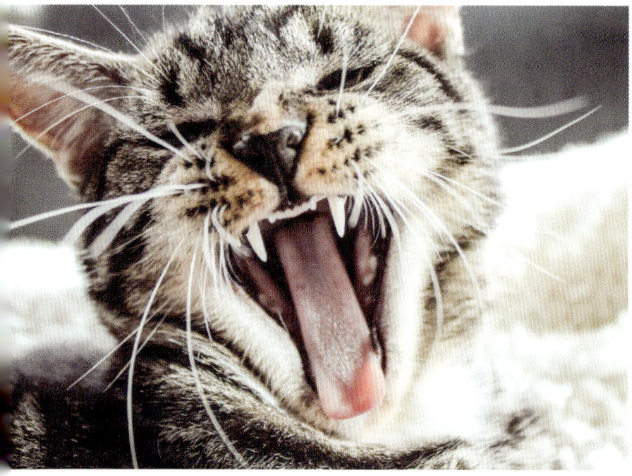

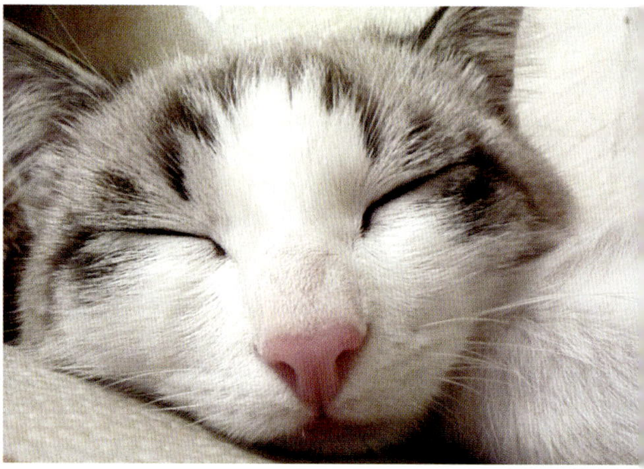

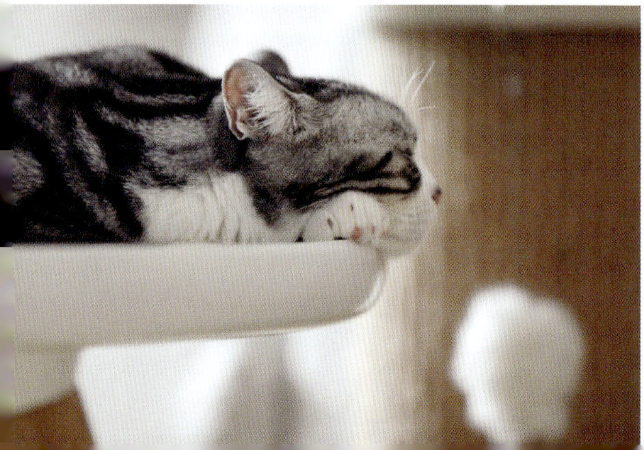

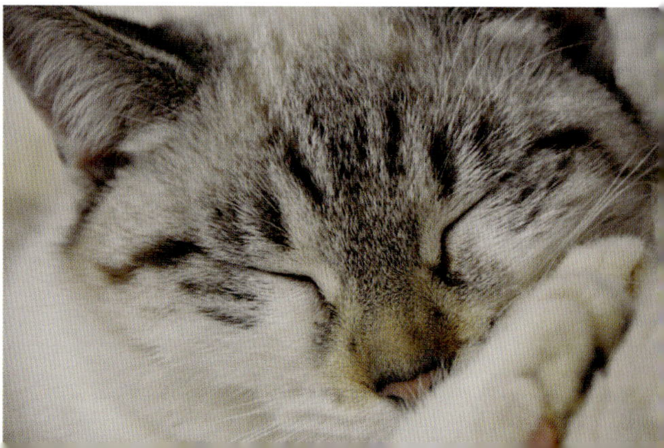

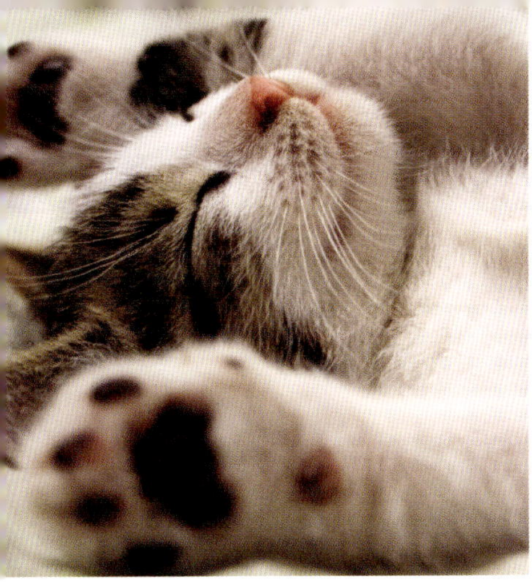
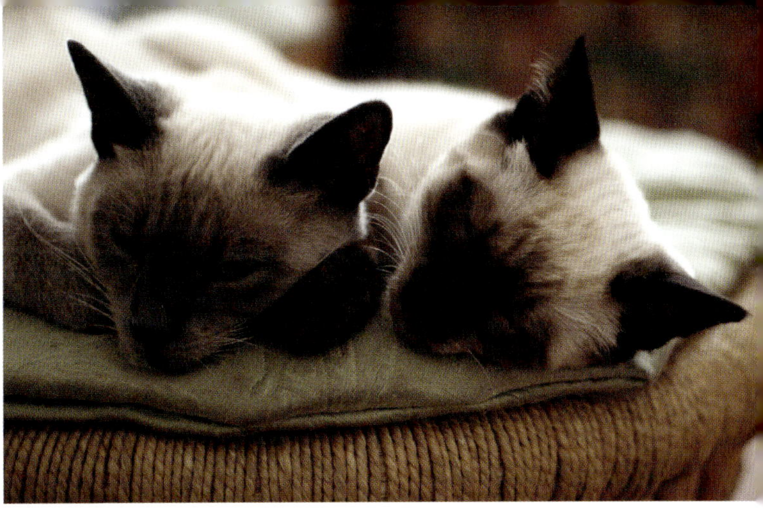
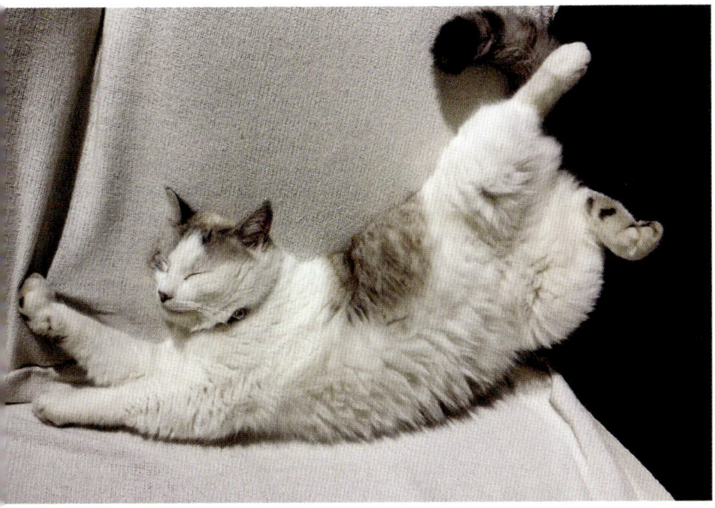
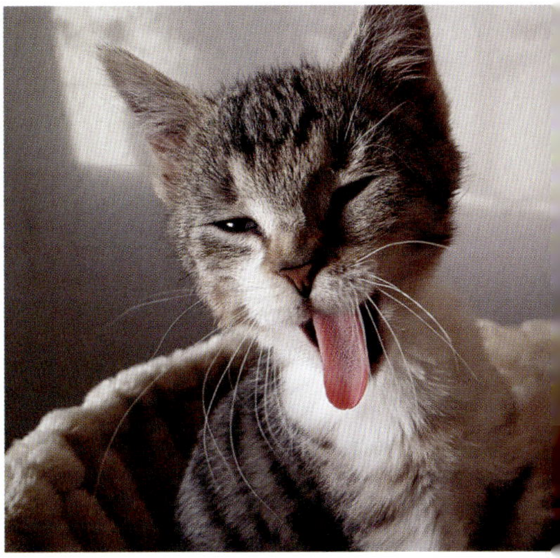
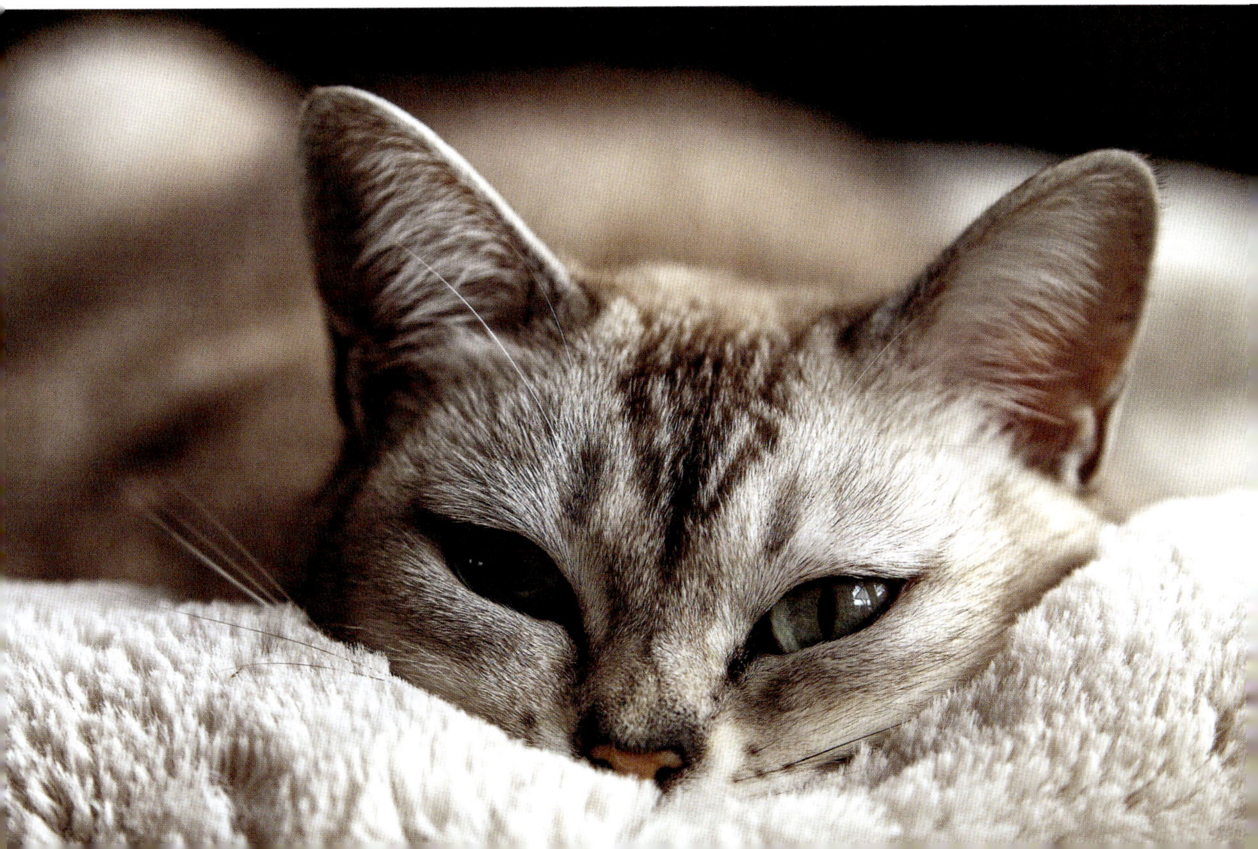

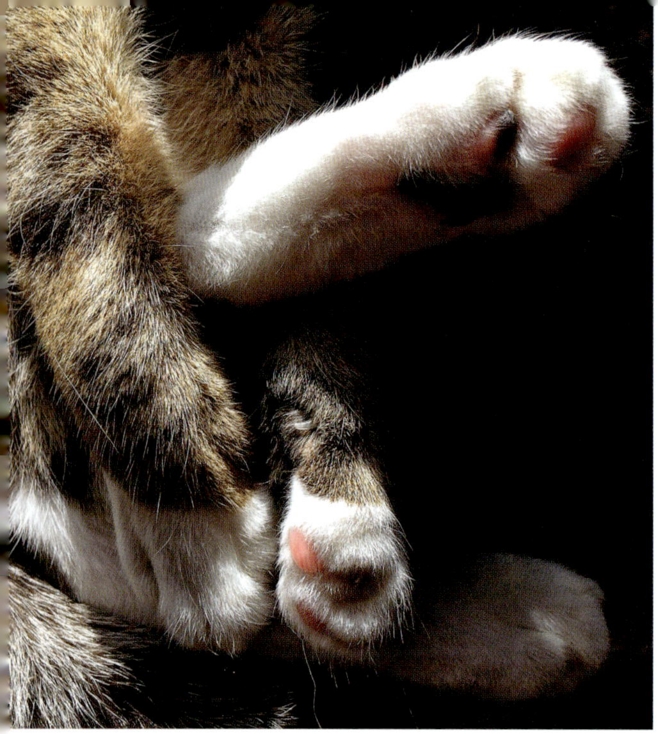

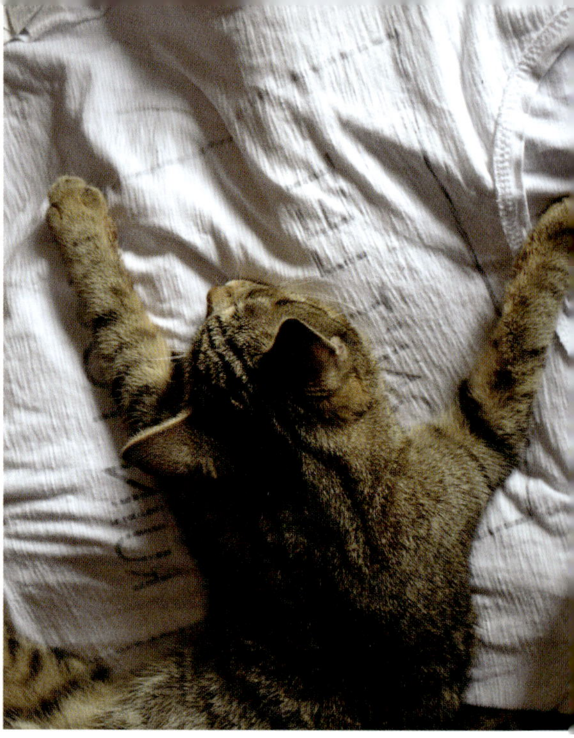

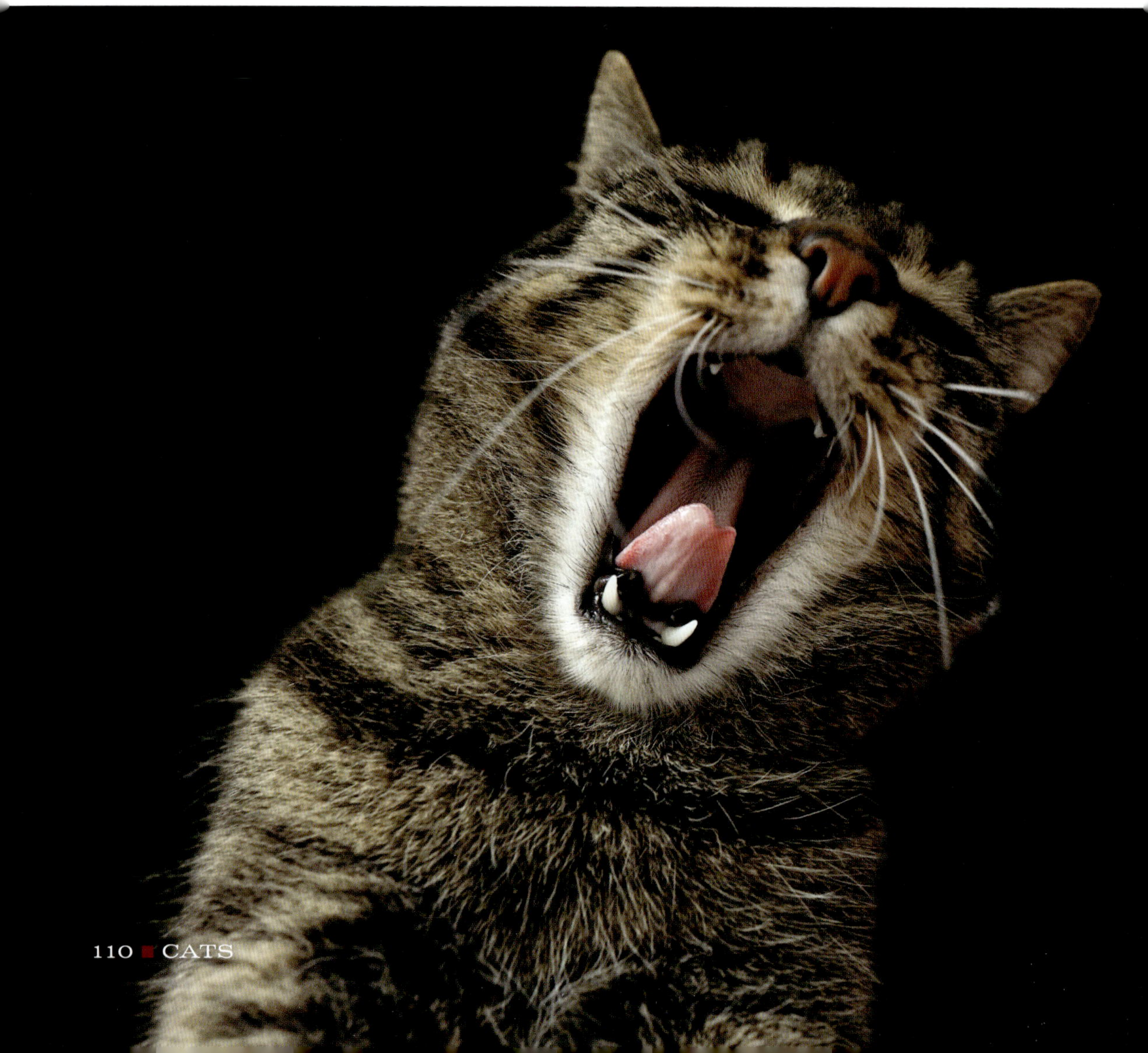

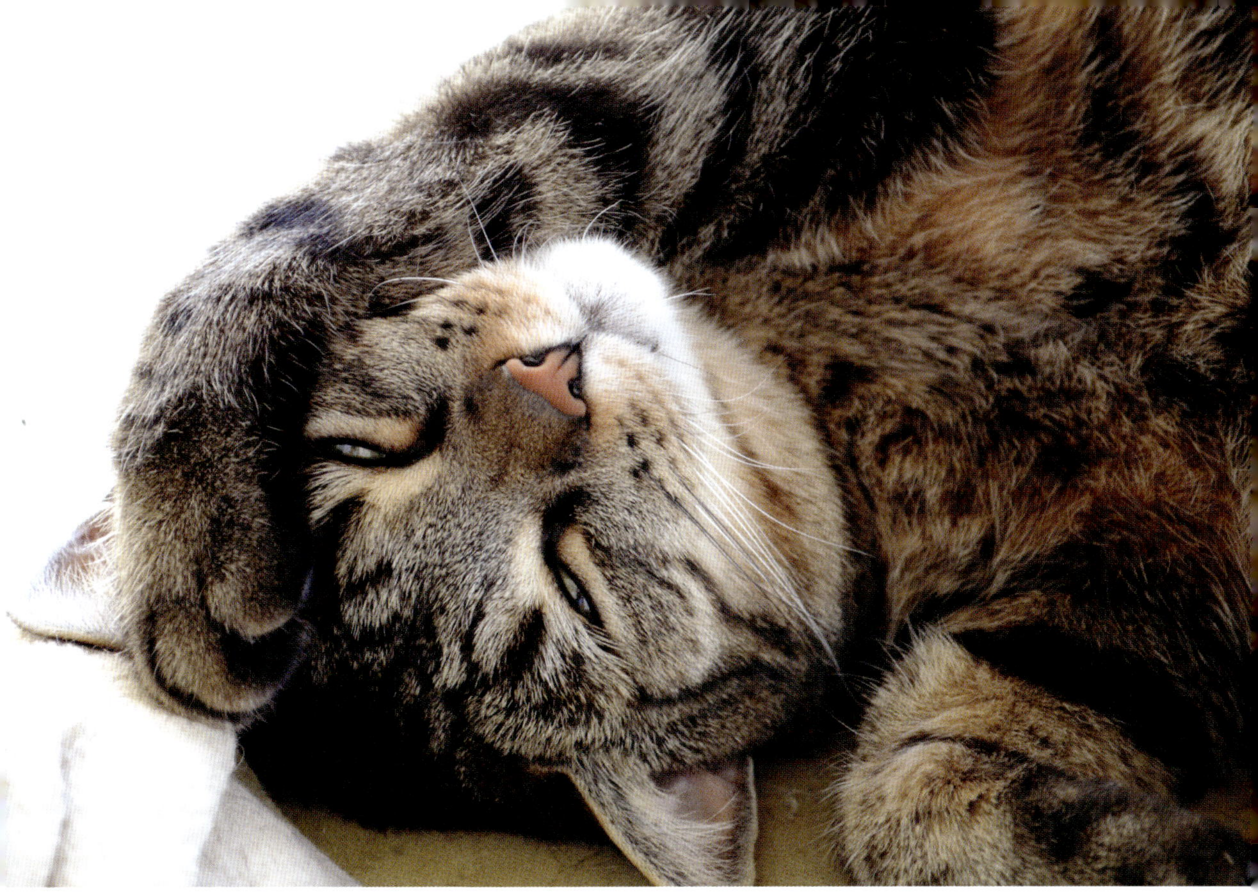

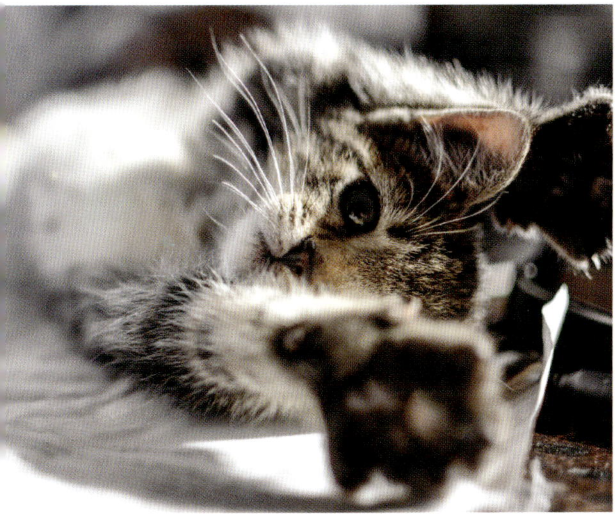

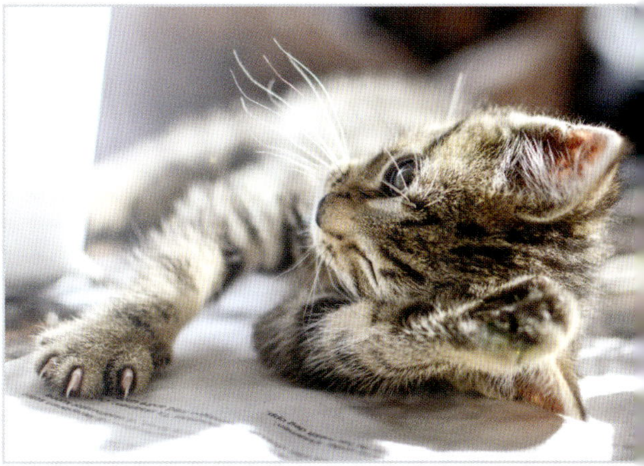

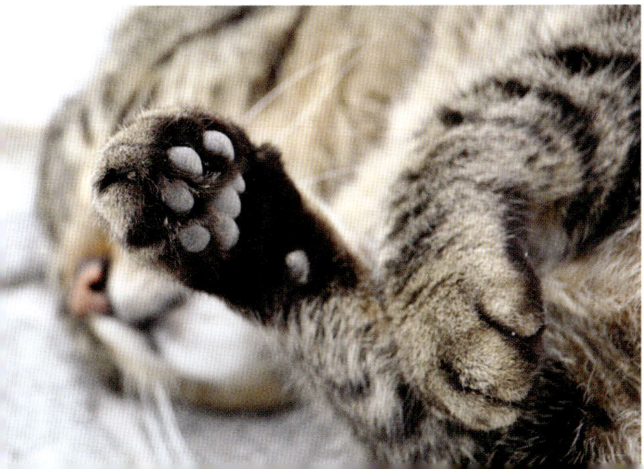

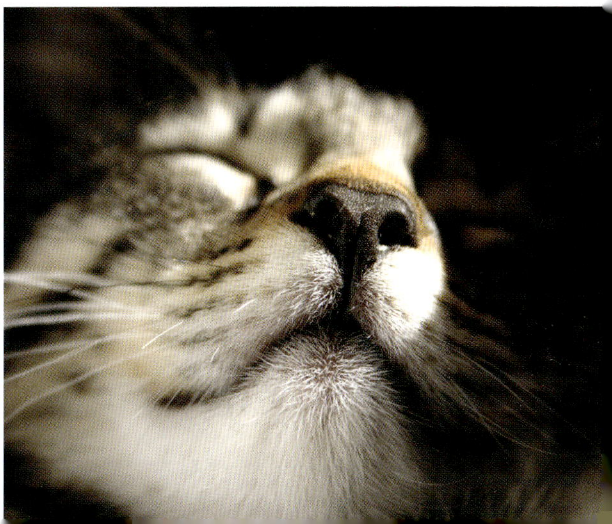

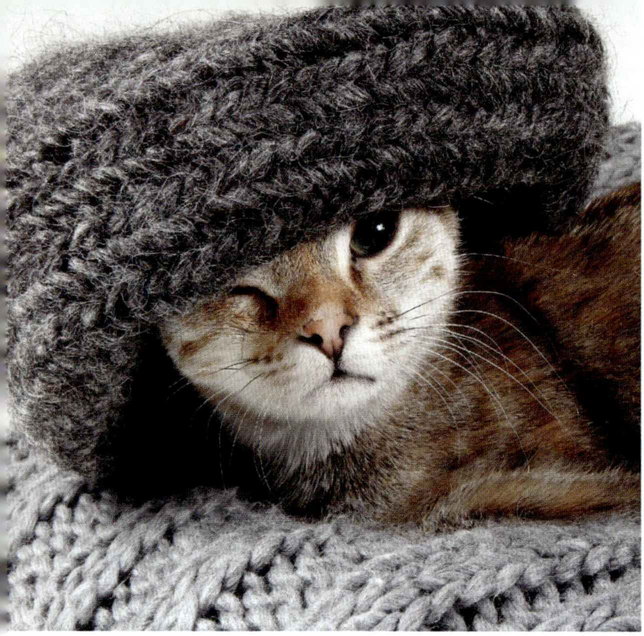
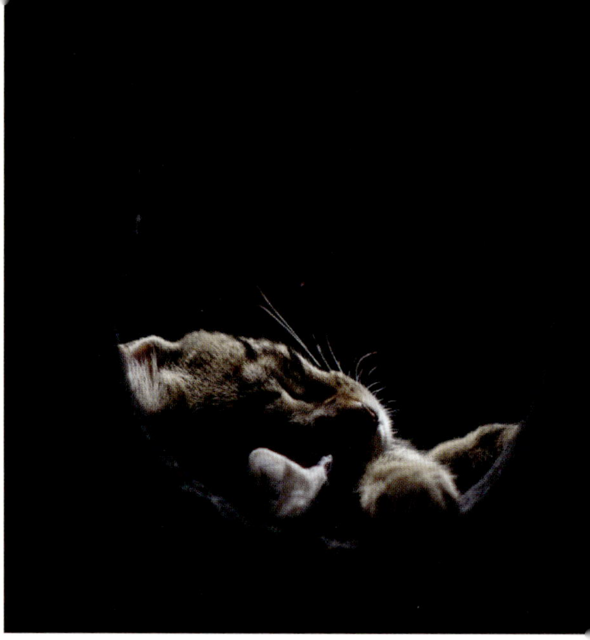
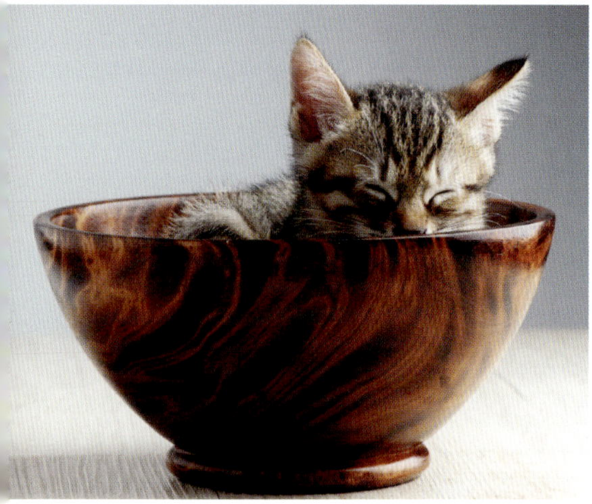
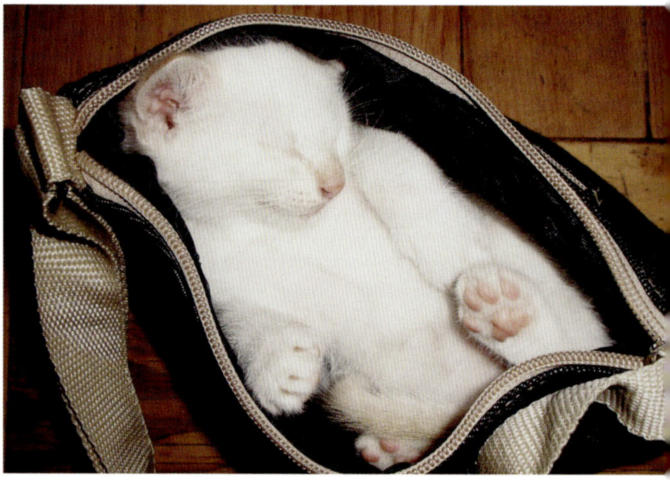
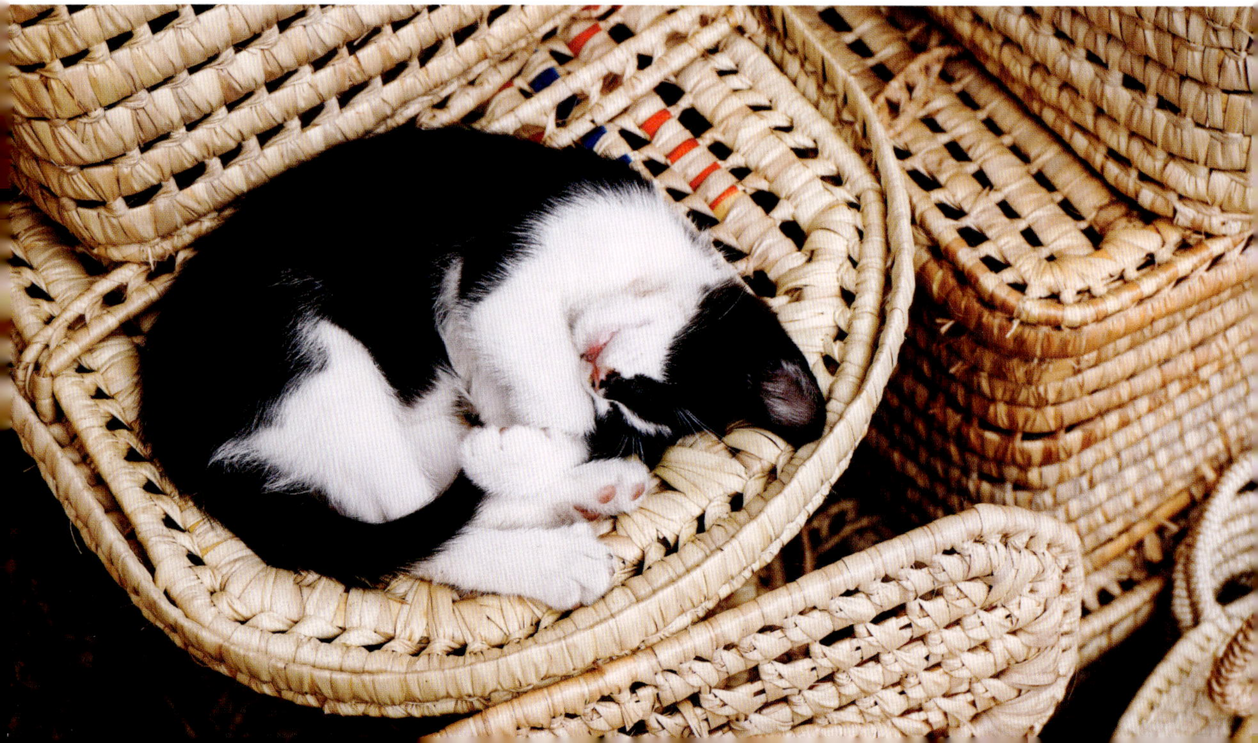

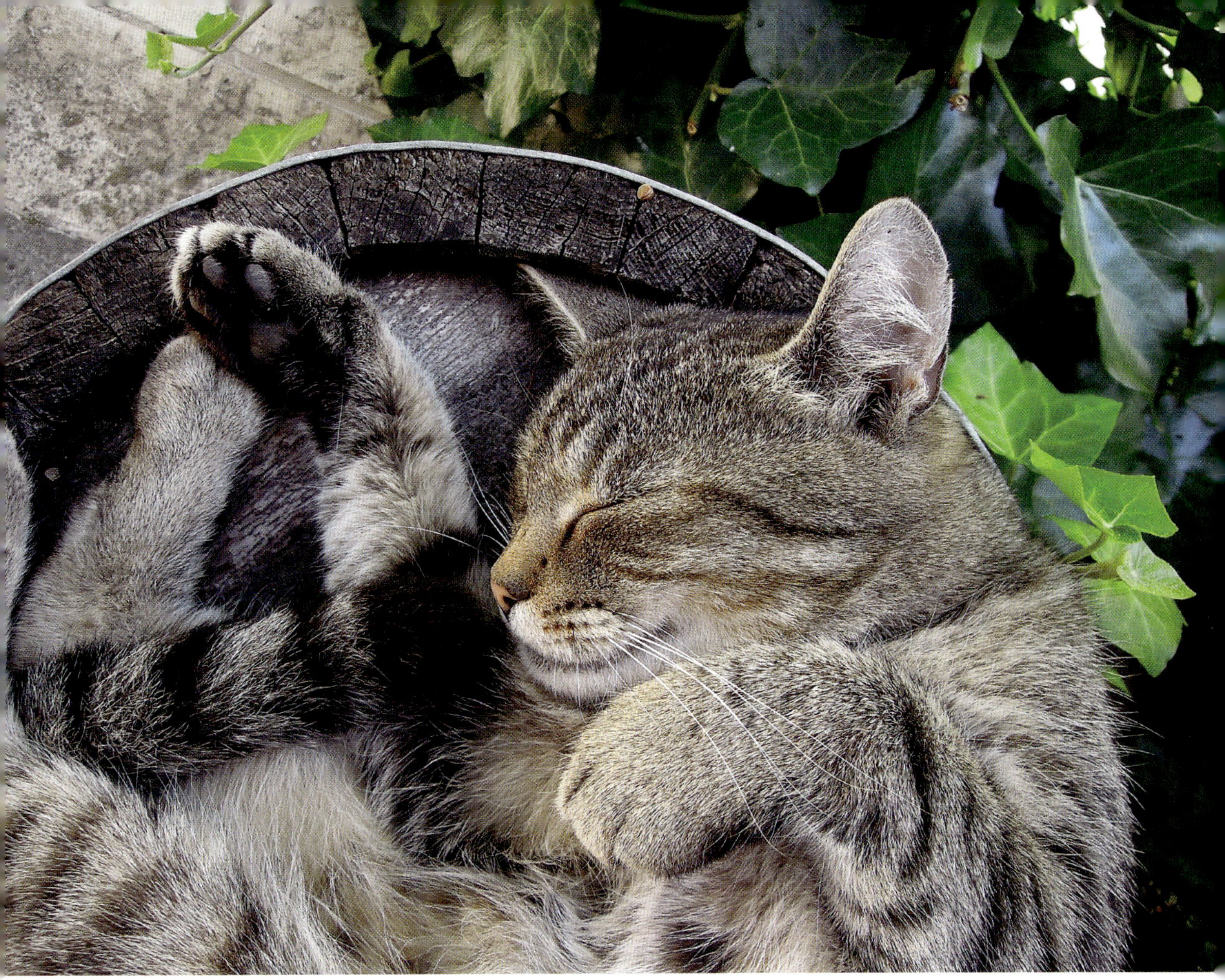
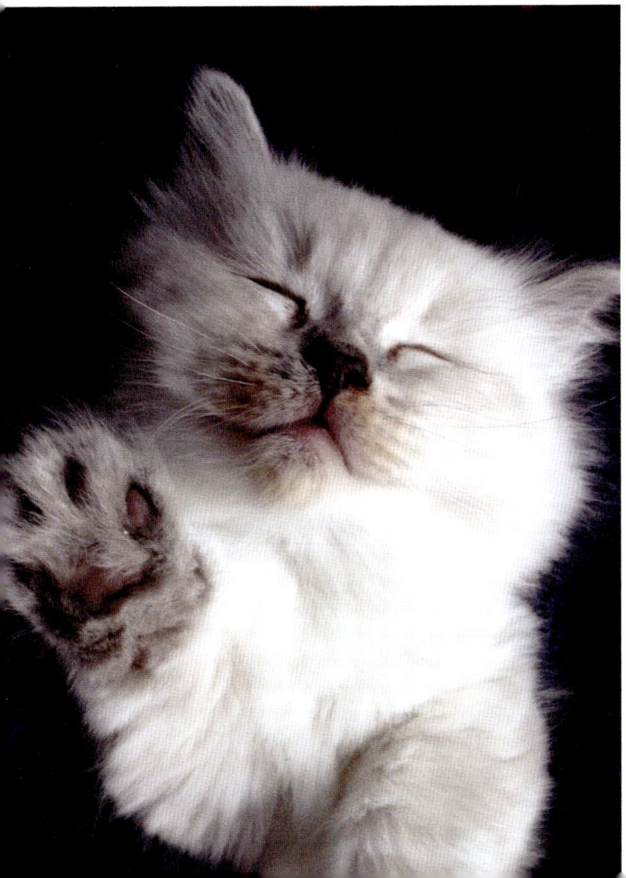
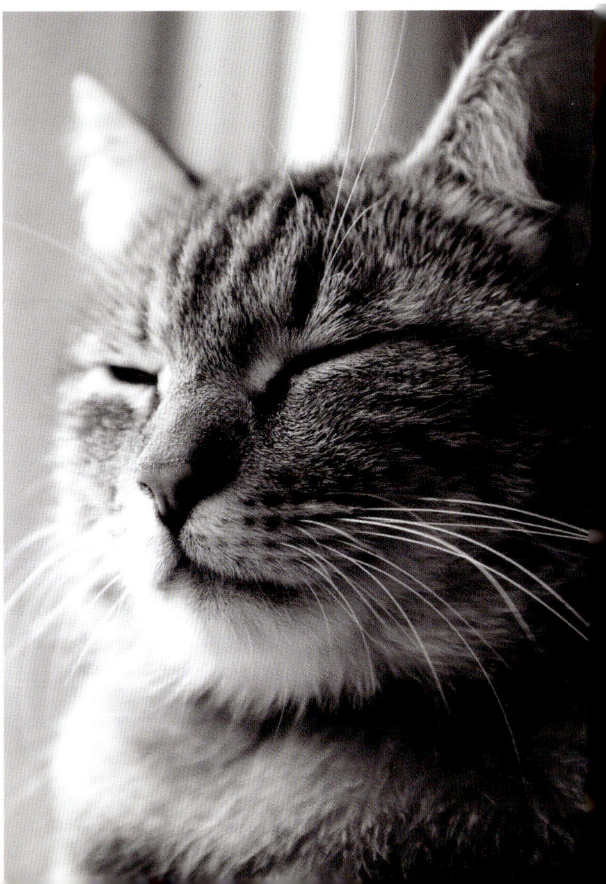

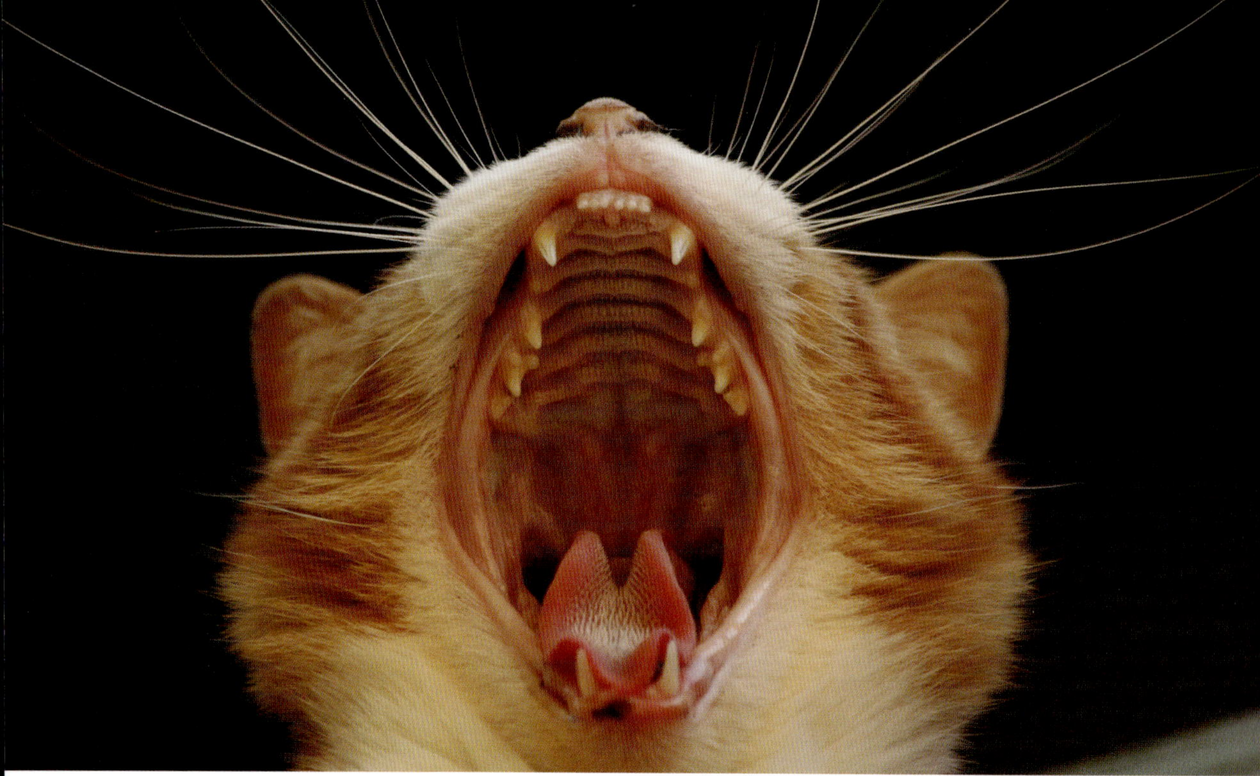
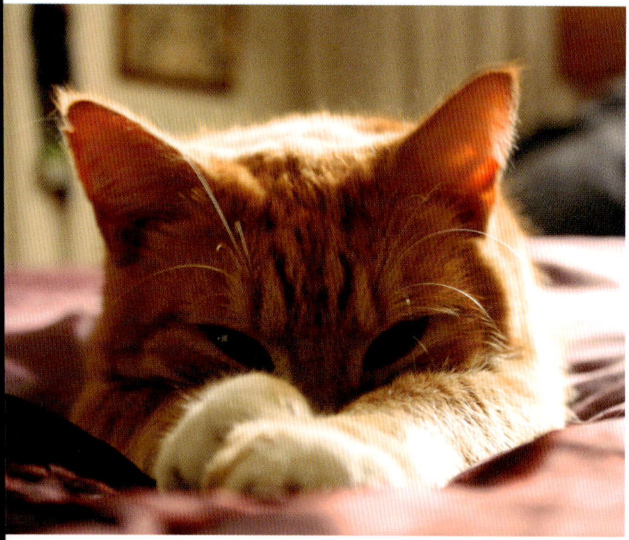
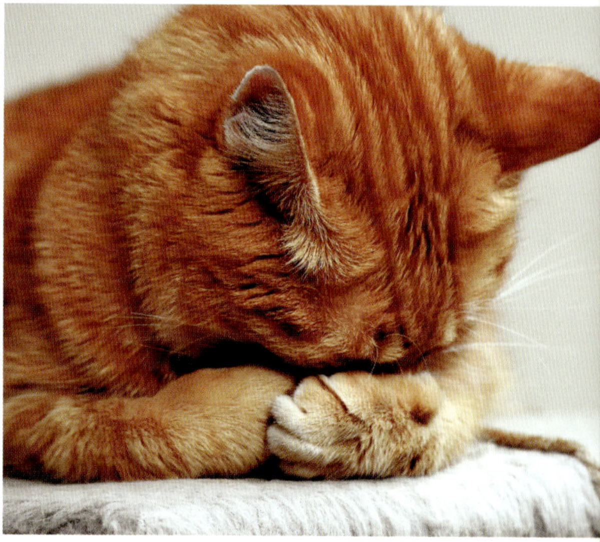
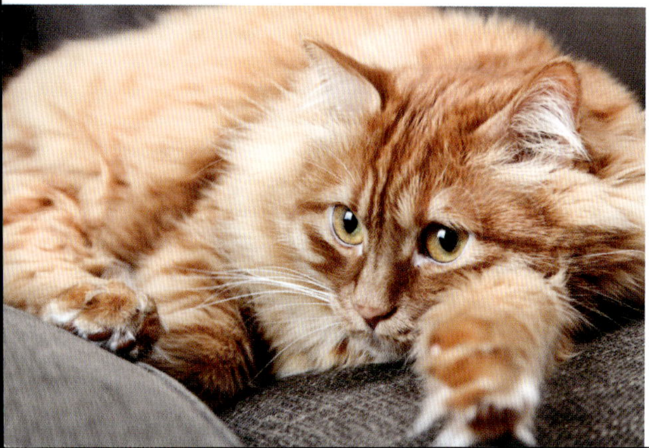
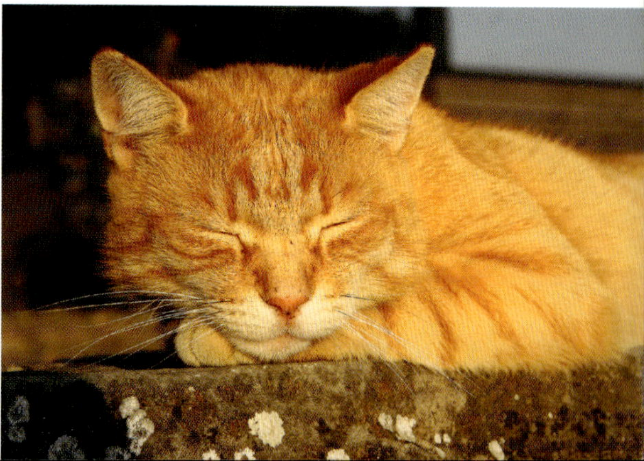

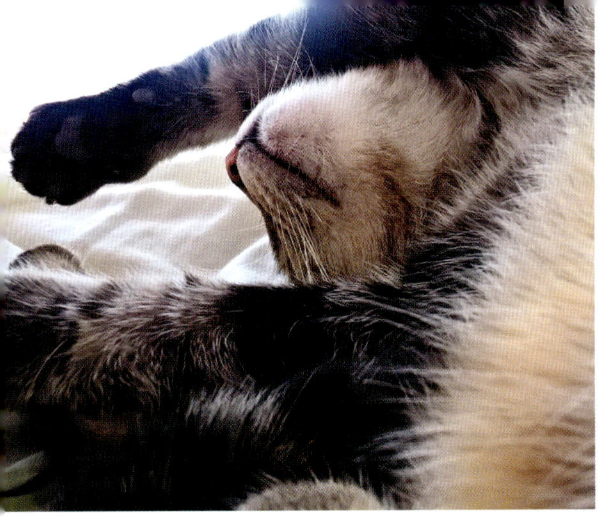

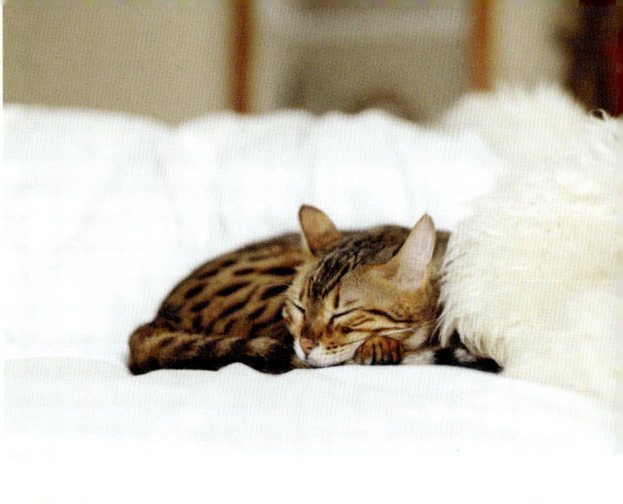

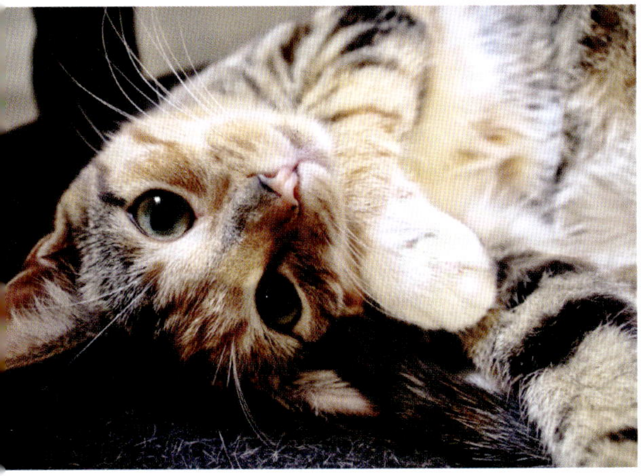

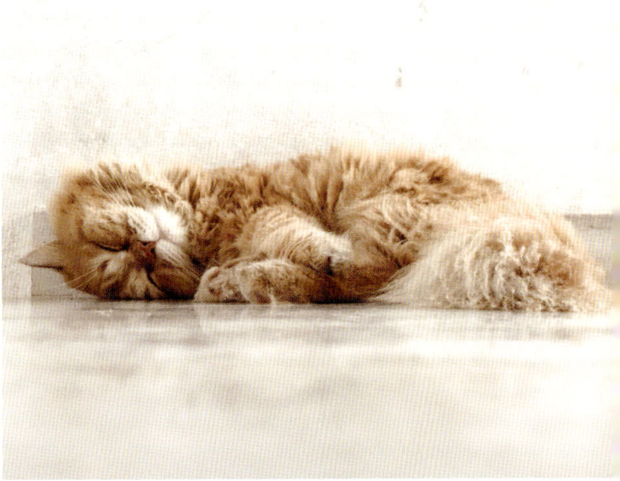

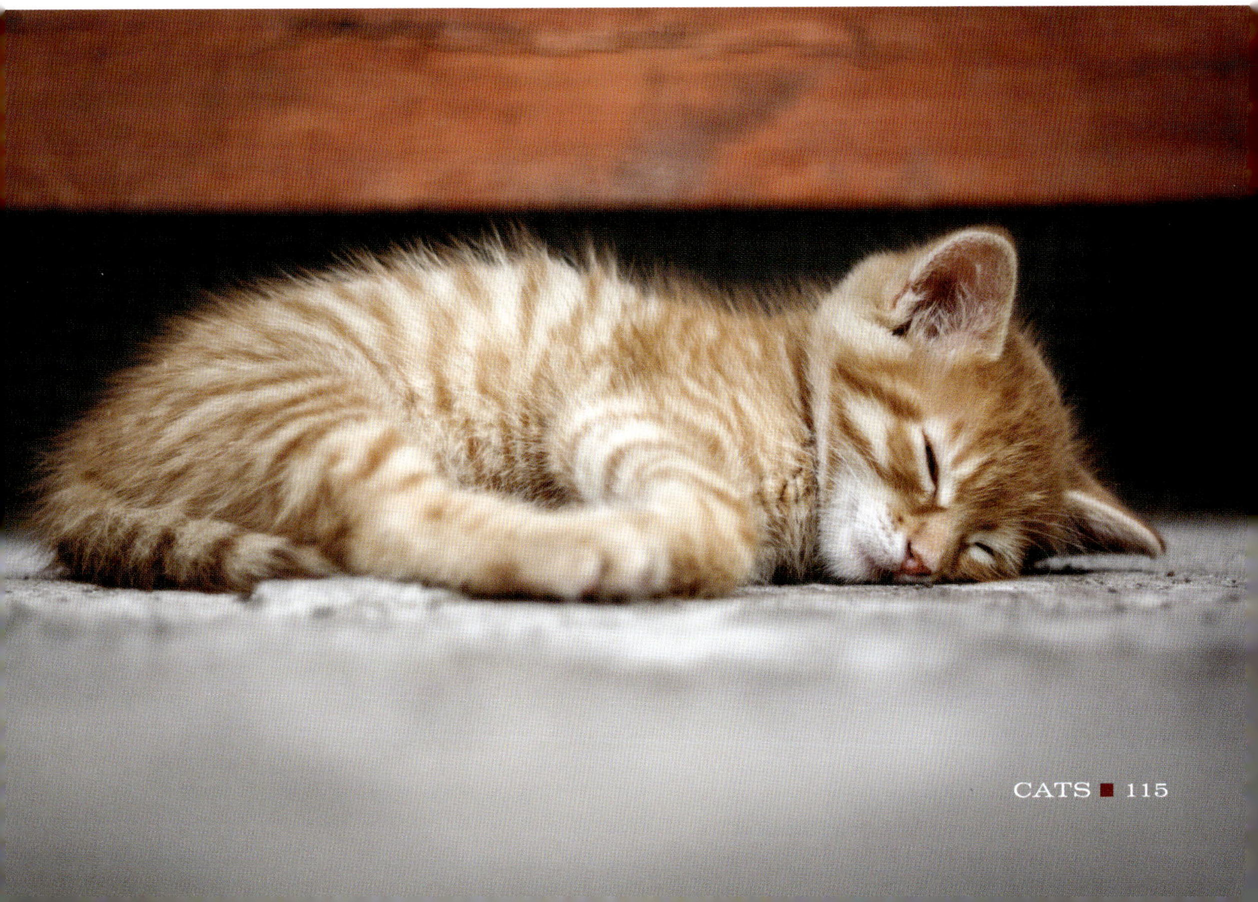

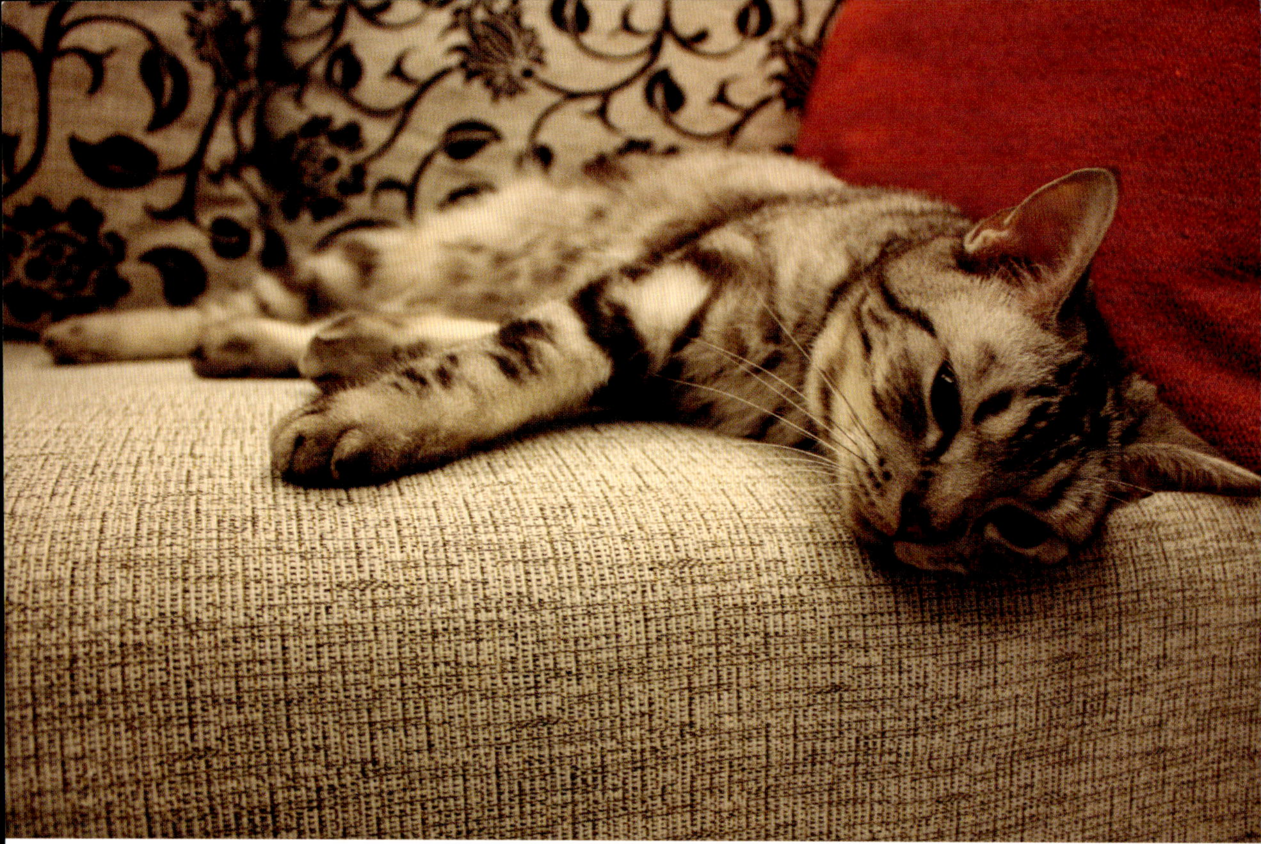
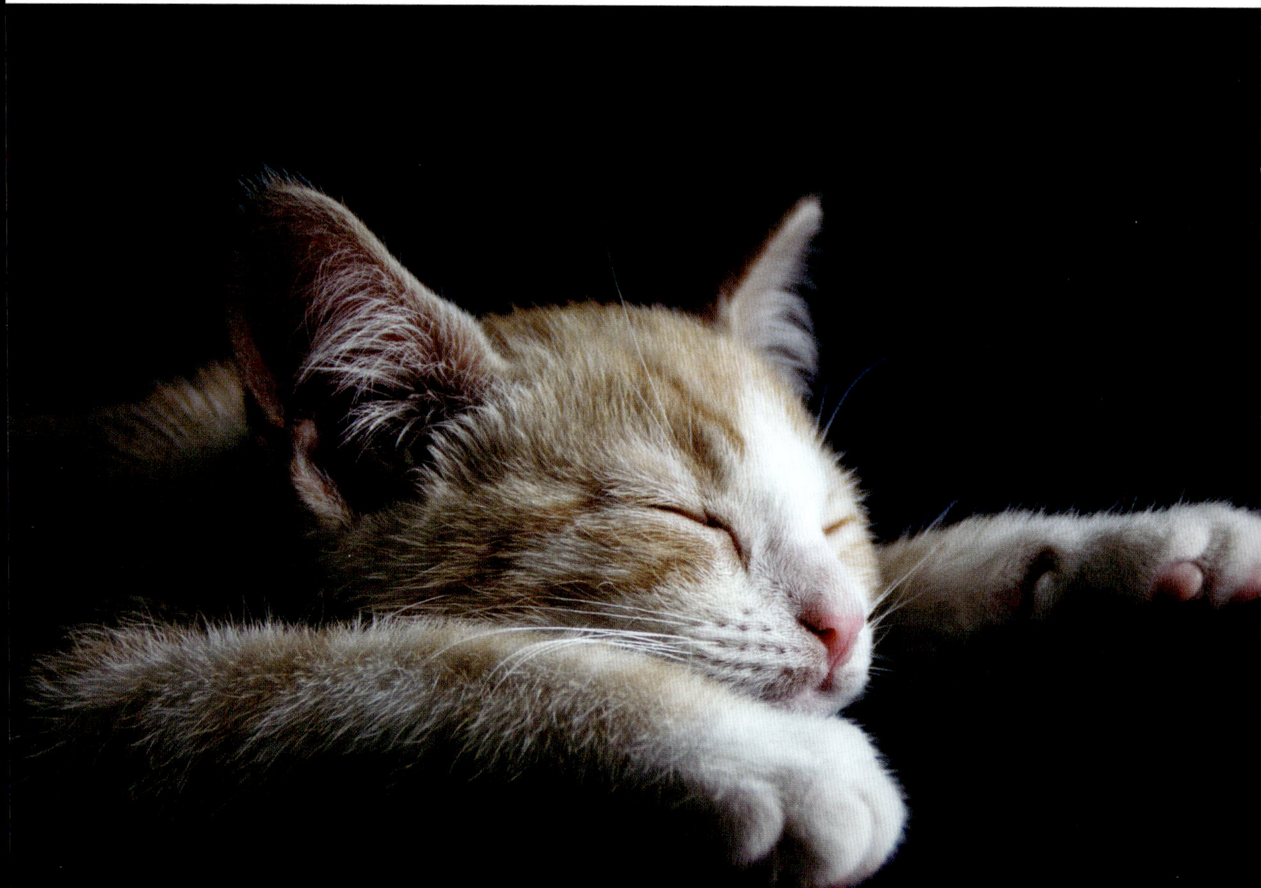

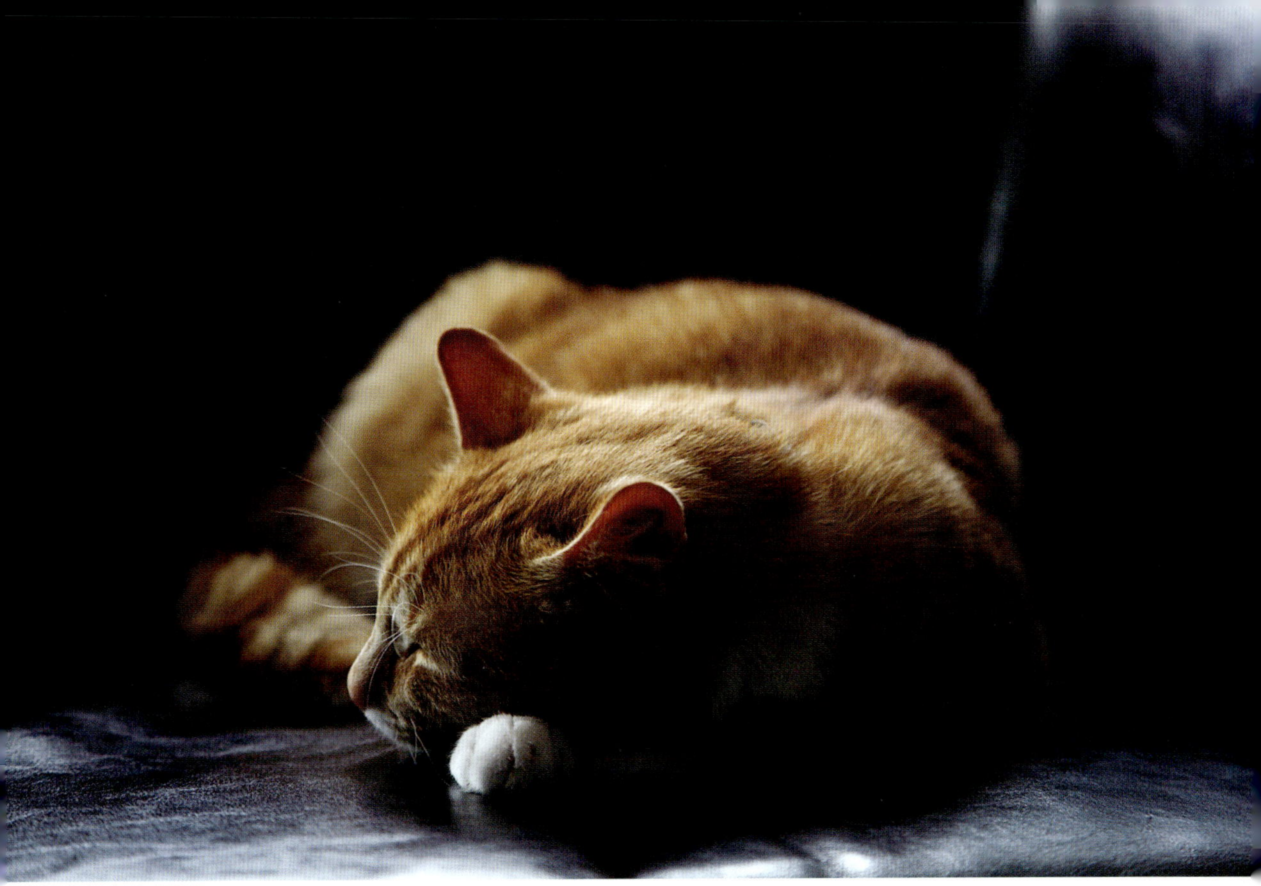

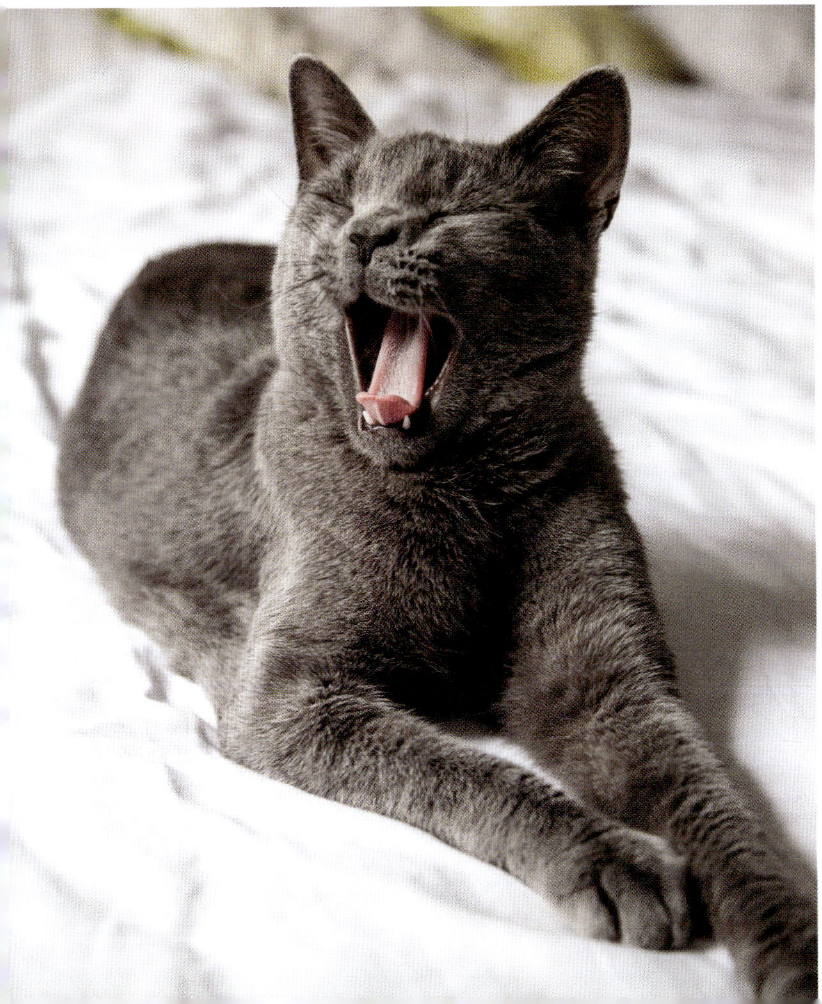

"I love cats because I enjoy my home; and little by little, they become its visible soul."

–Jean Cocteau, poet

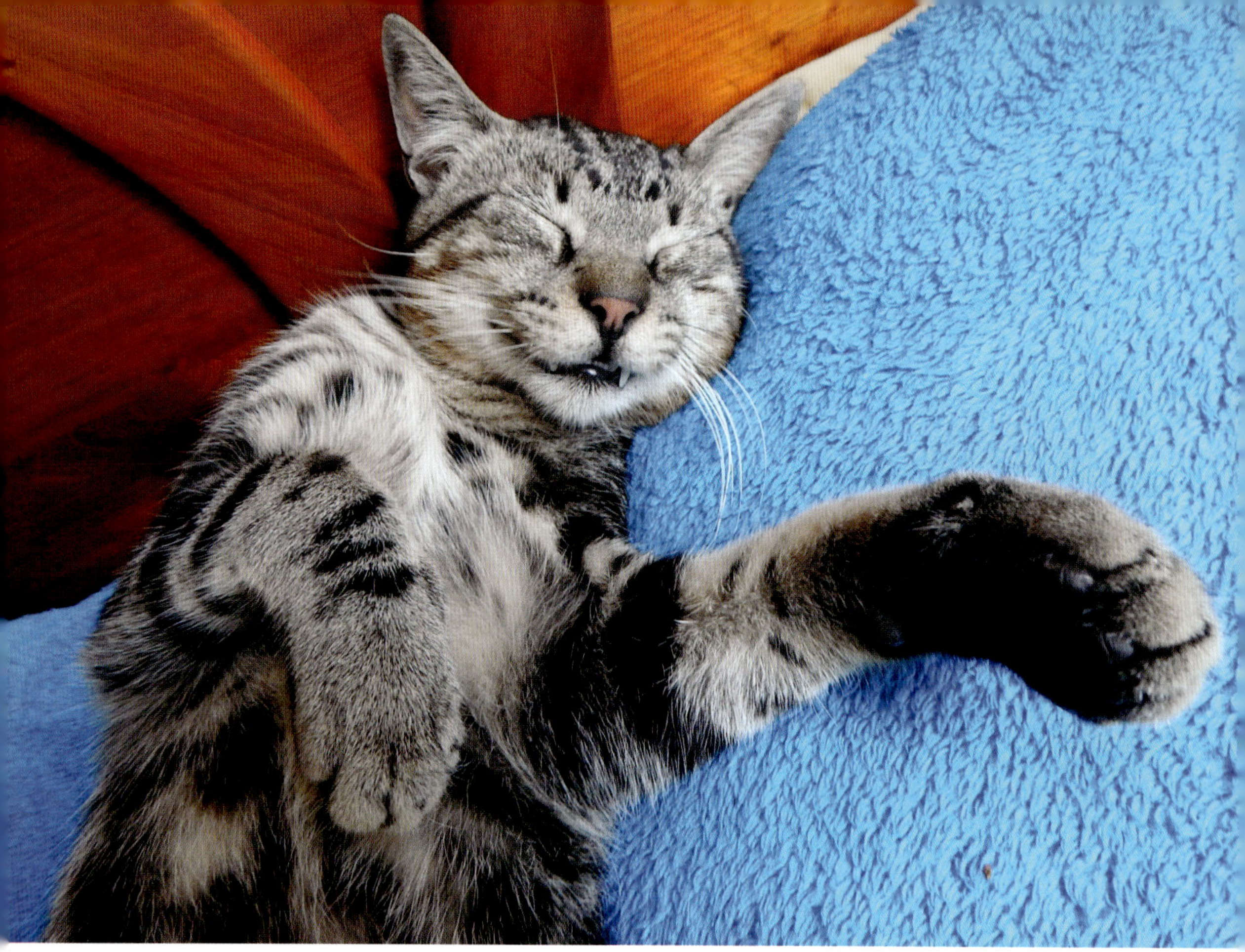
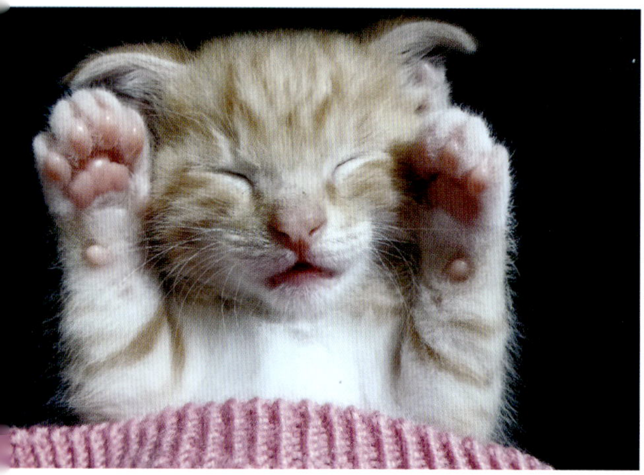
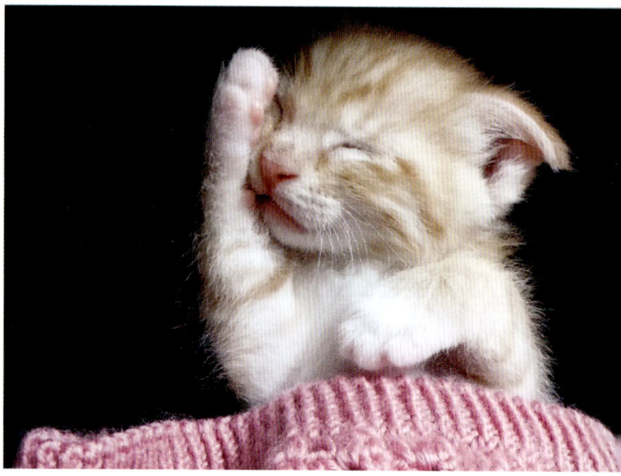
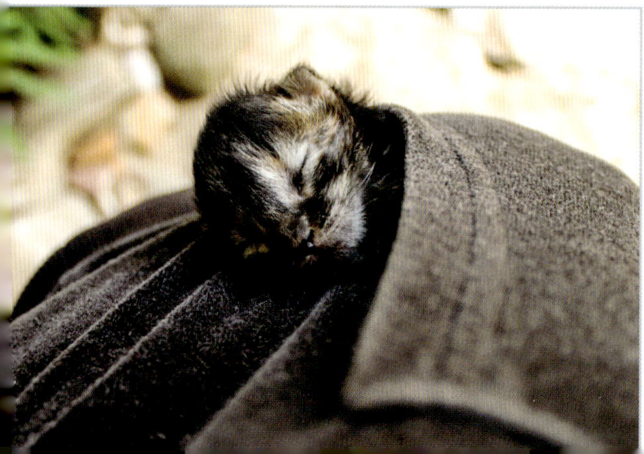
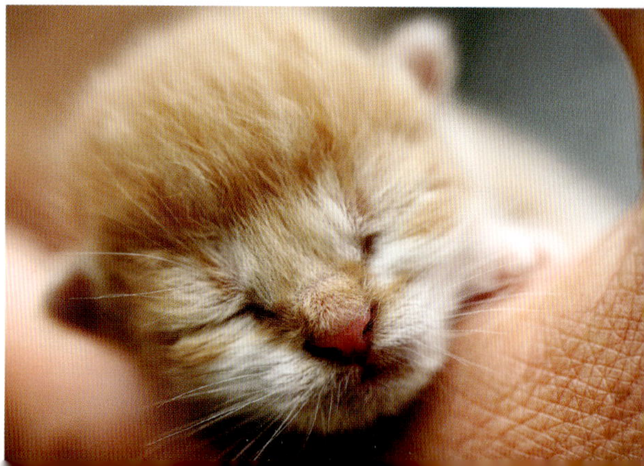

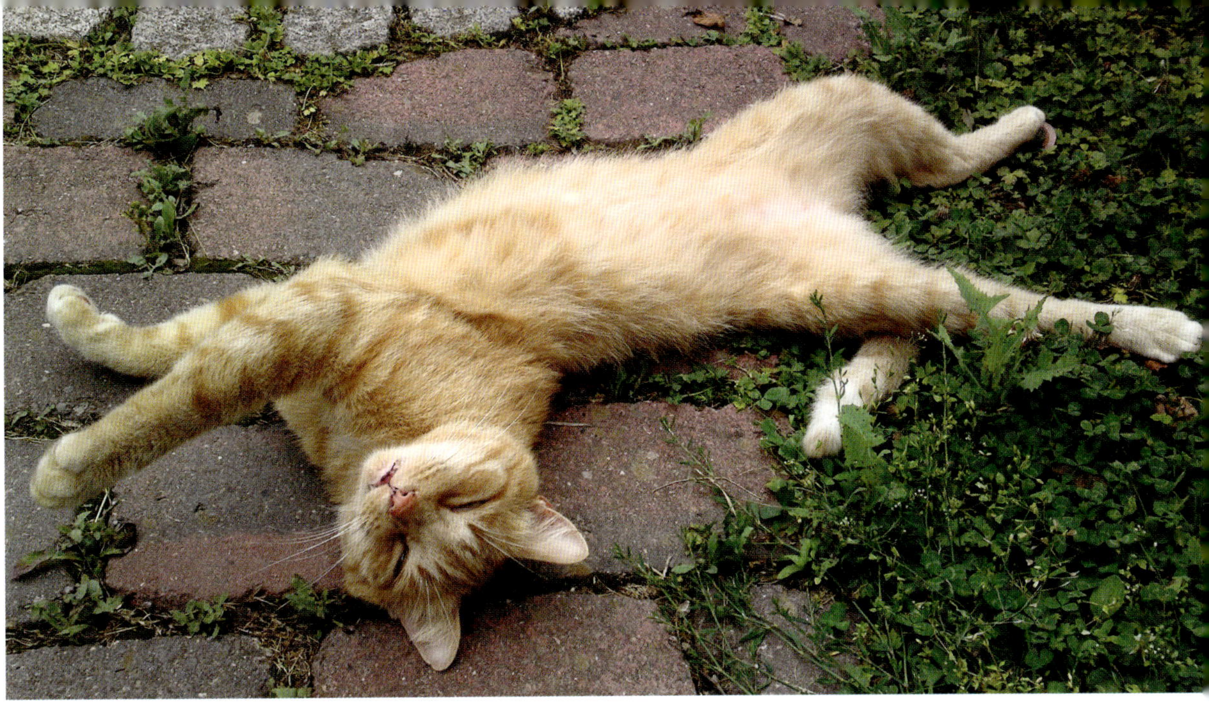

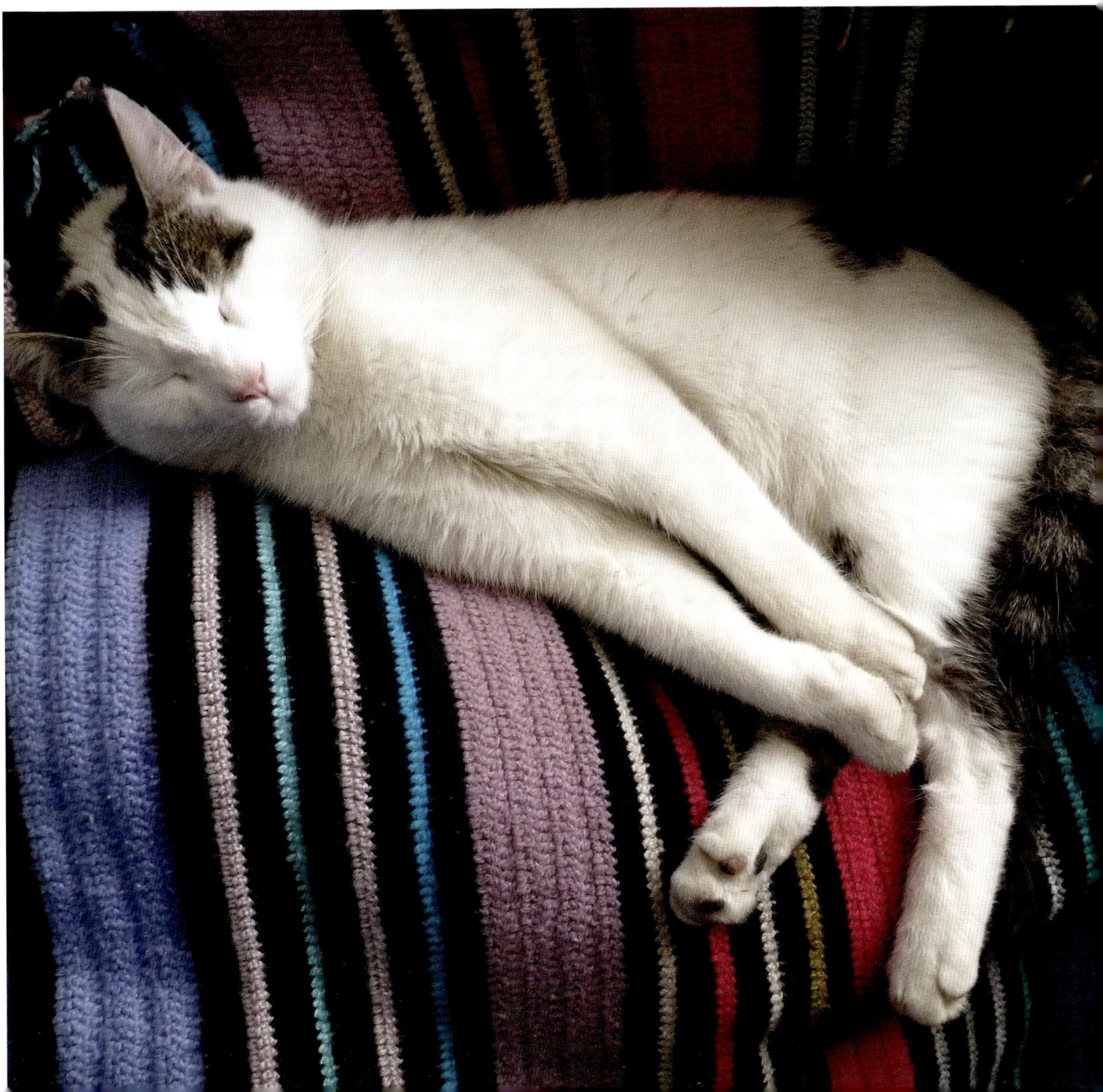

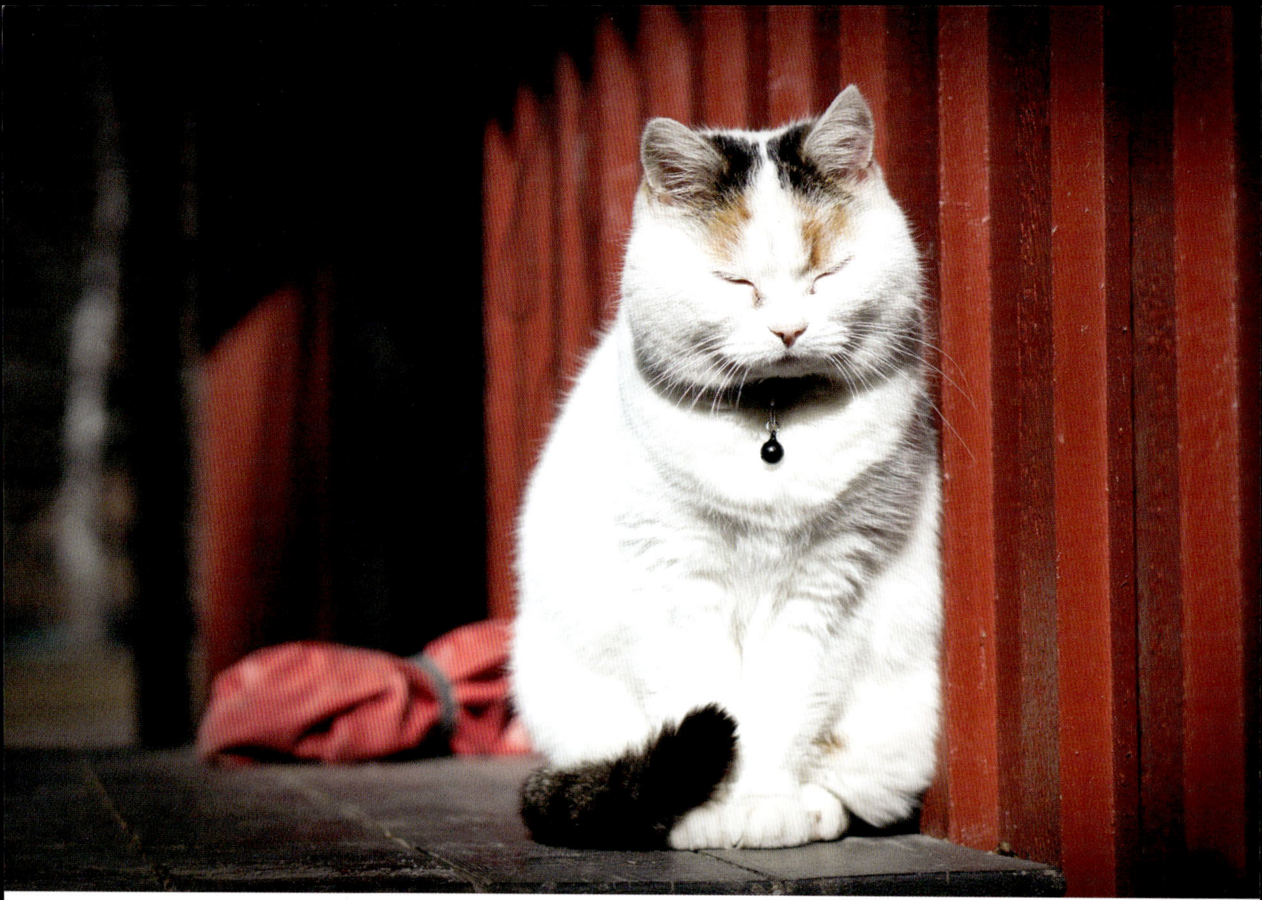

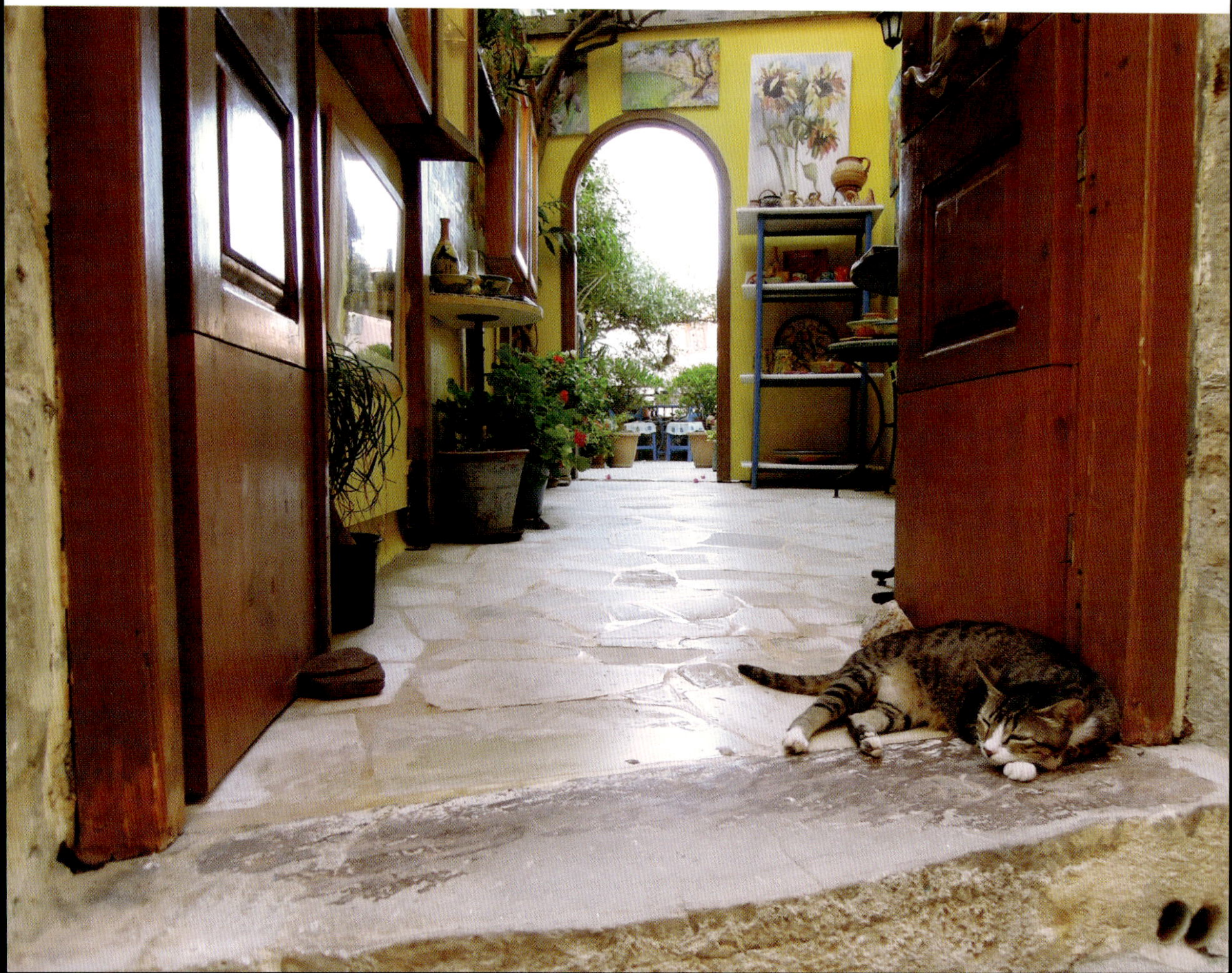

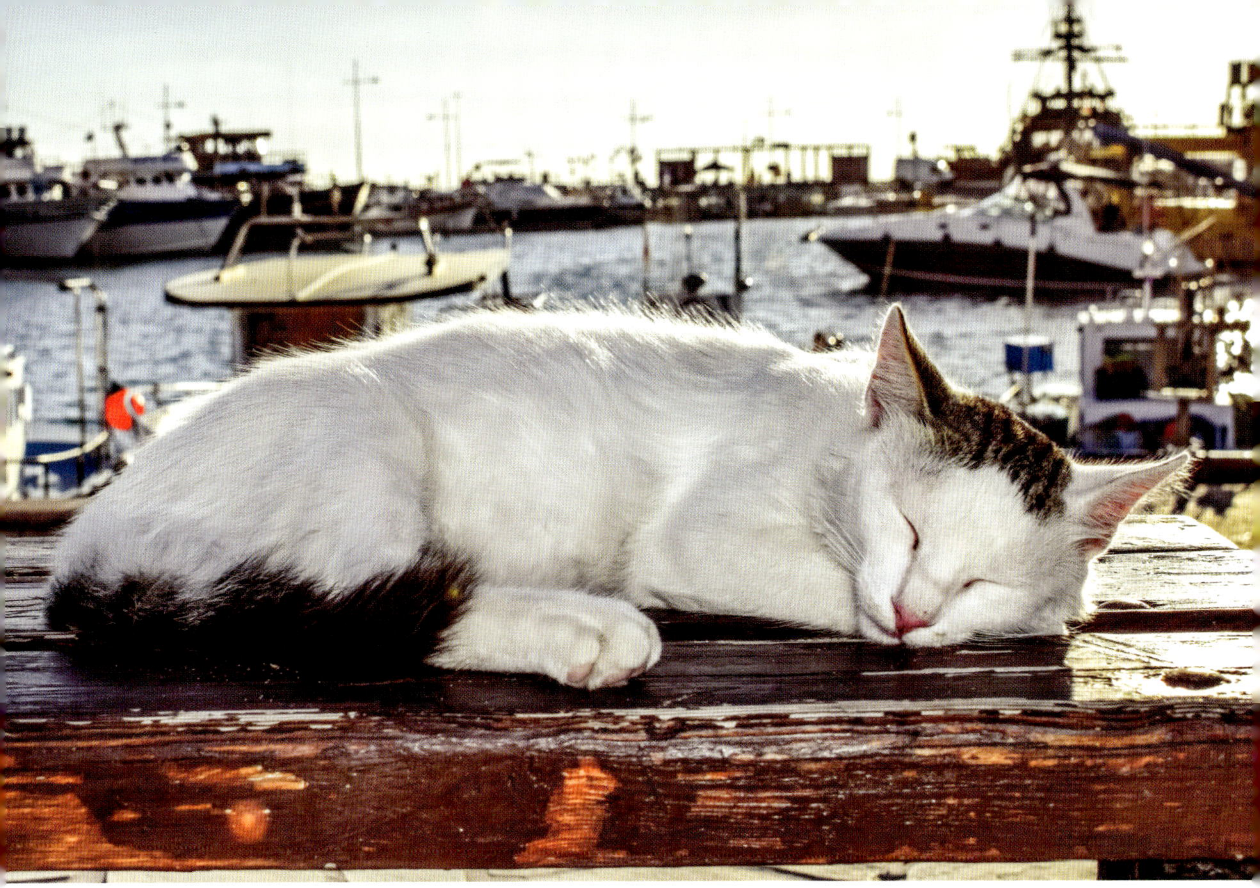

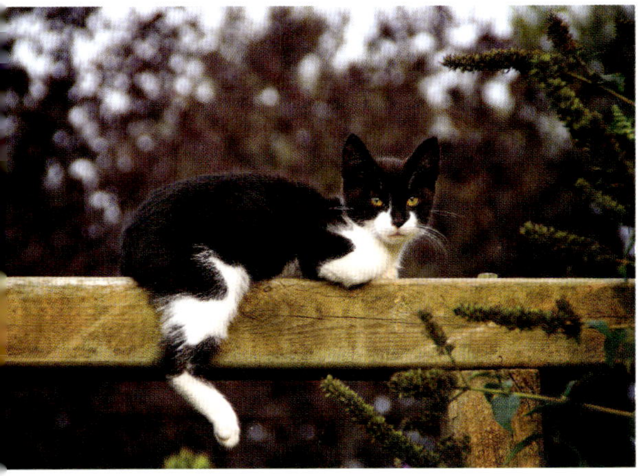

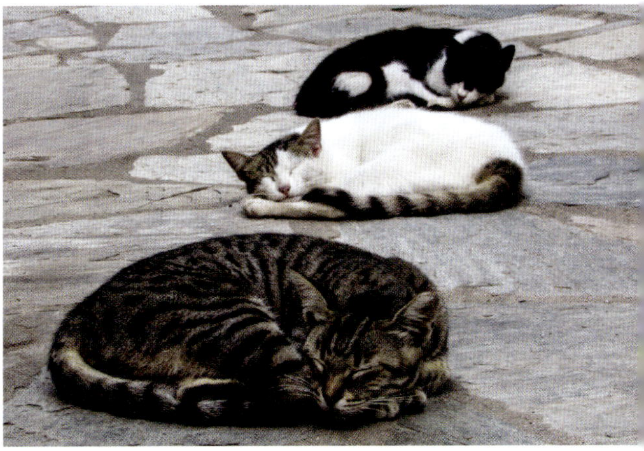

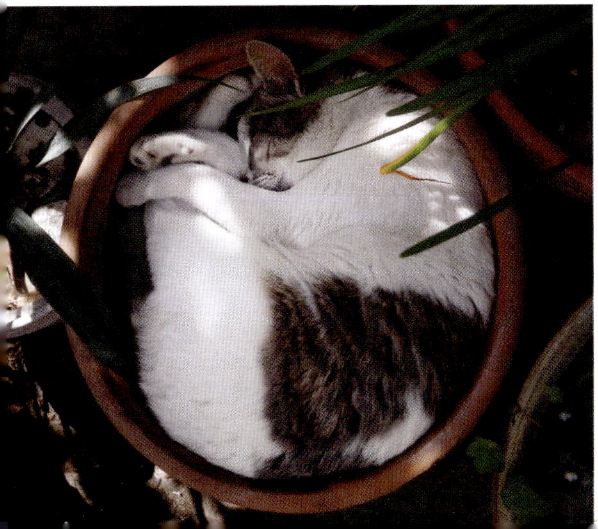

“In ancient times cats were worshipped as gods; they have not forgotten this.”

–Terry Pratchett, author

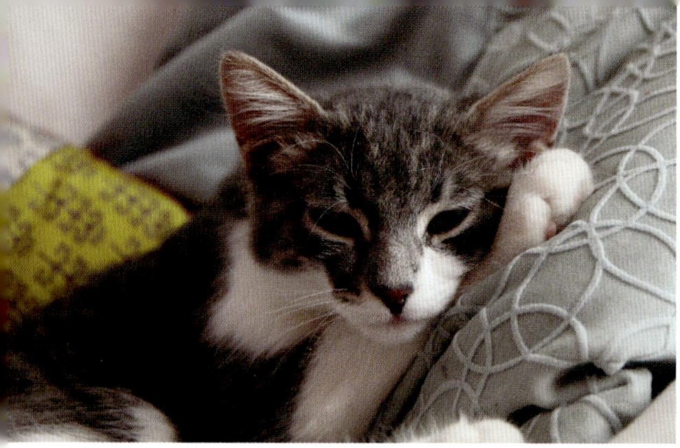
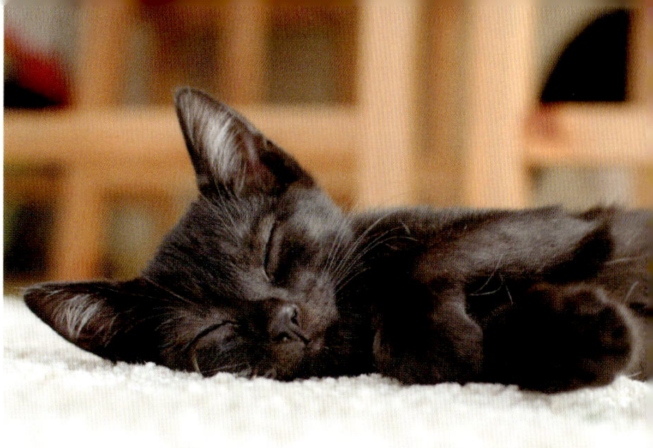
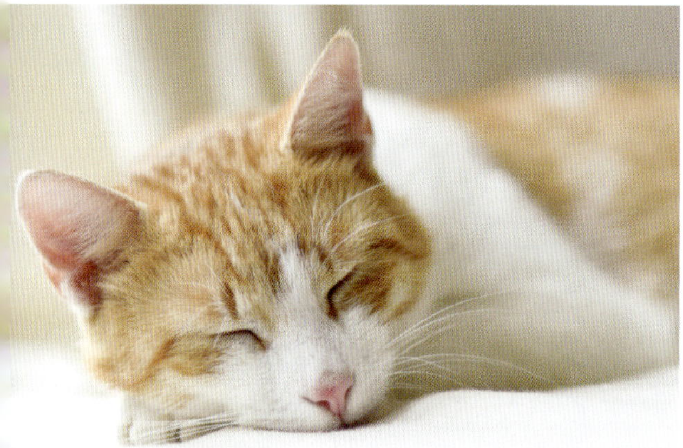
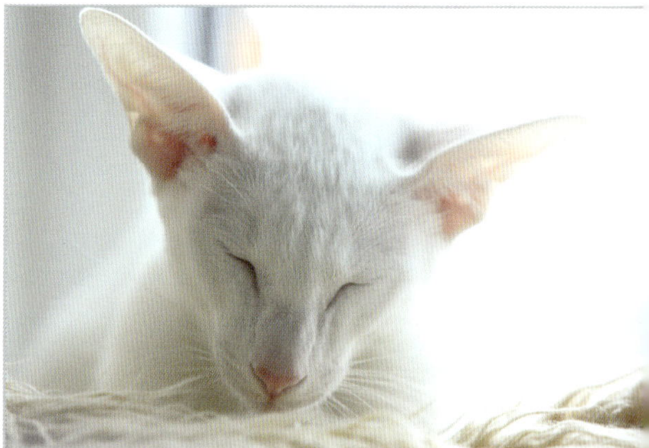
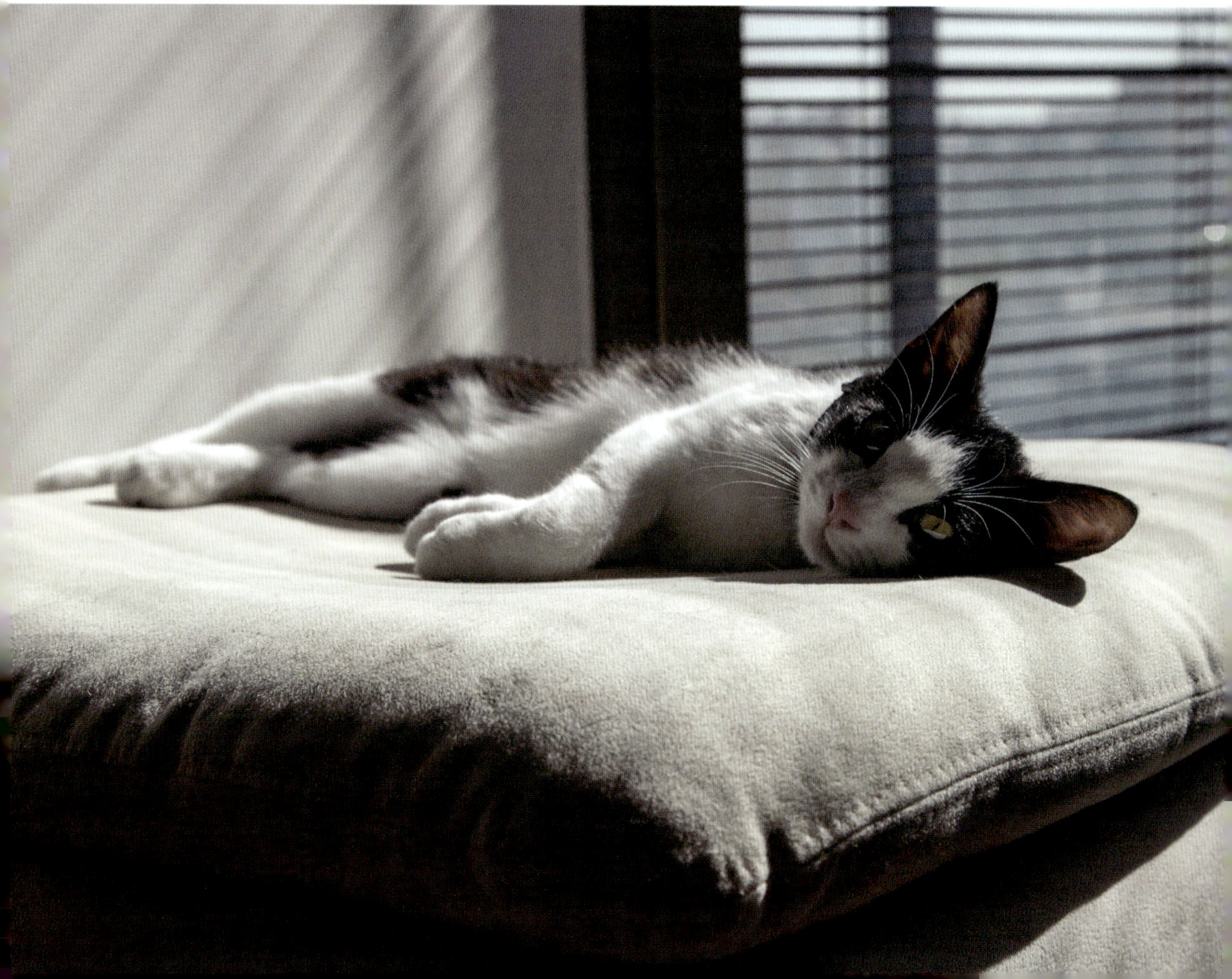

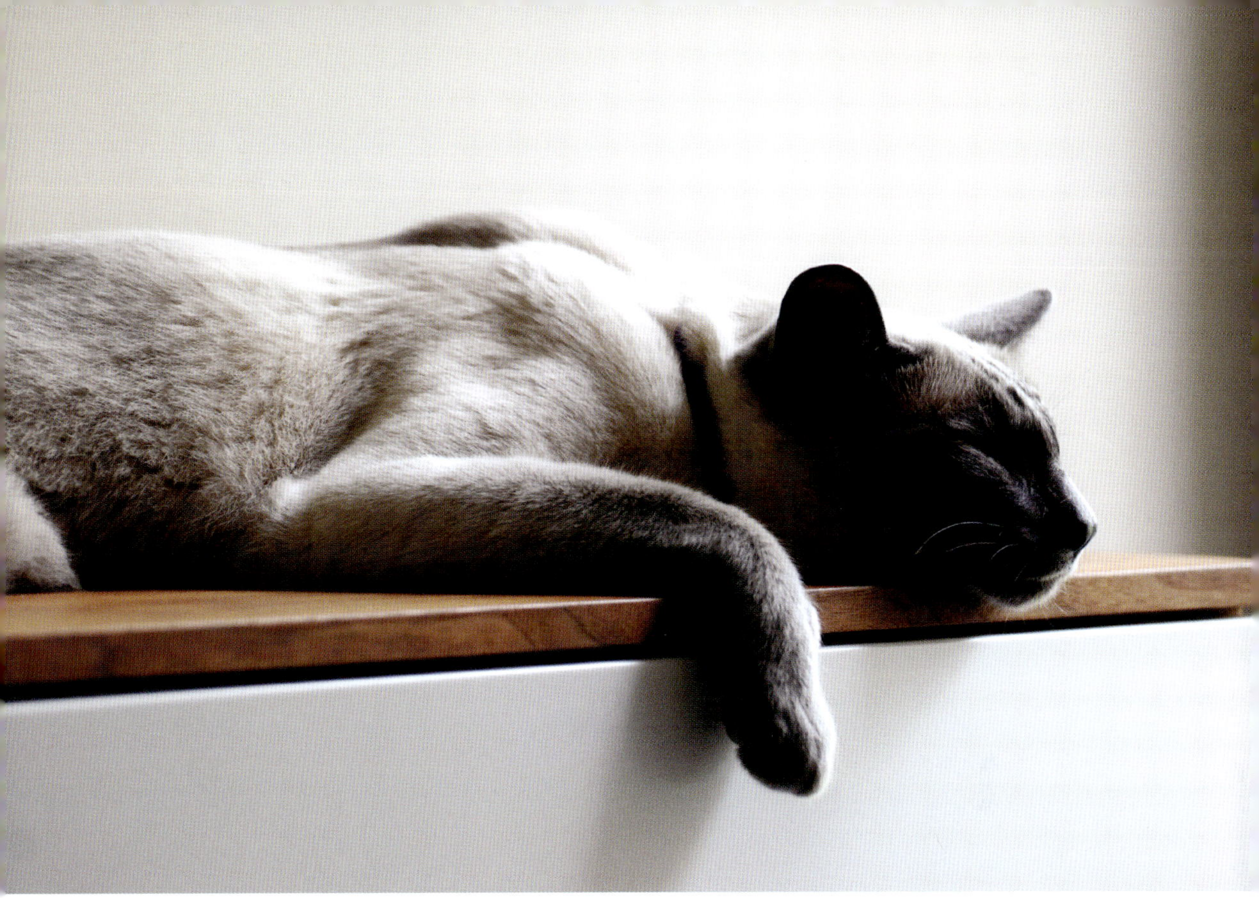
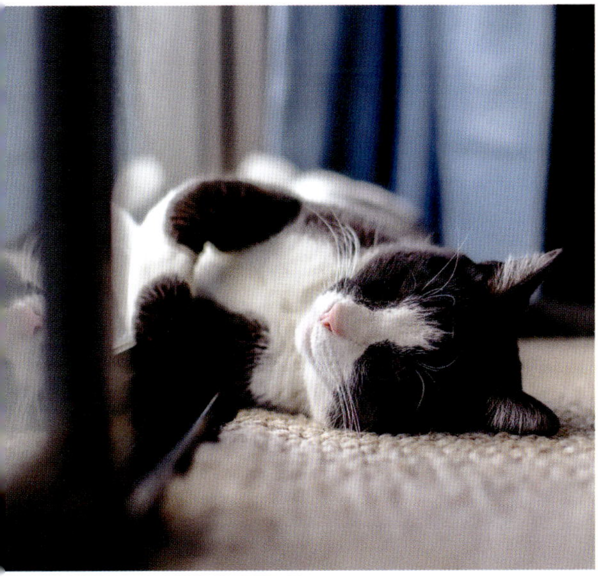
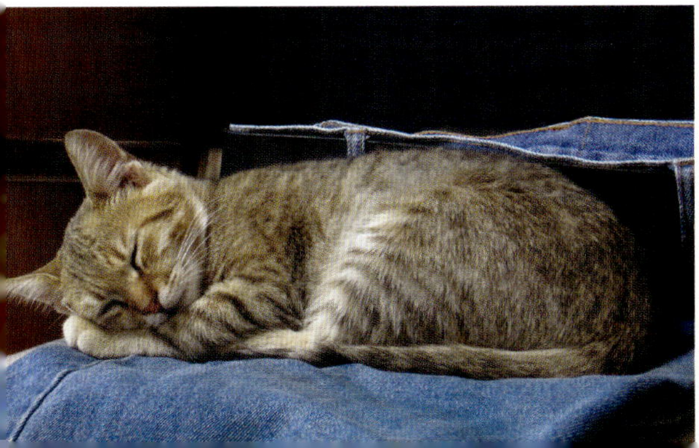
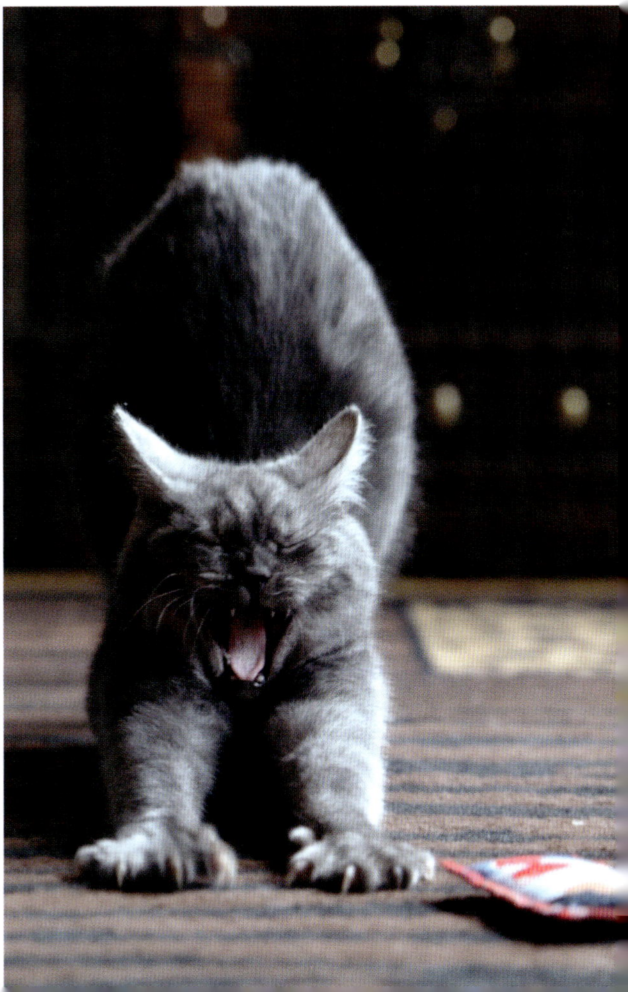

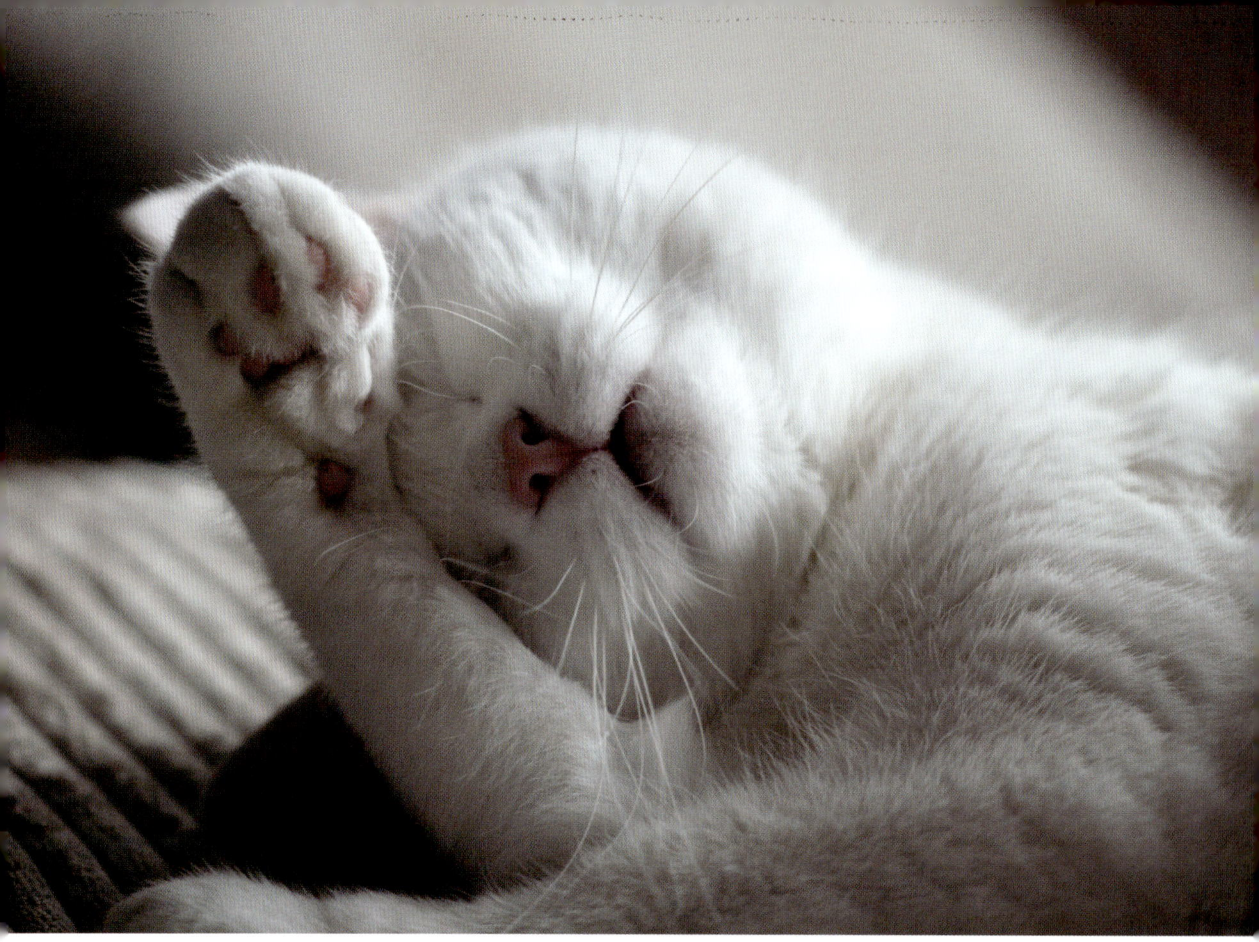

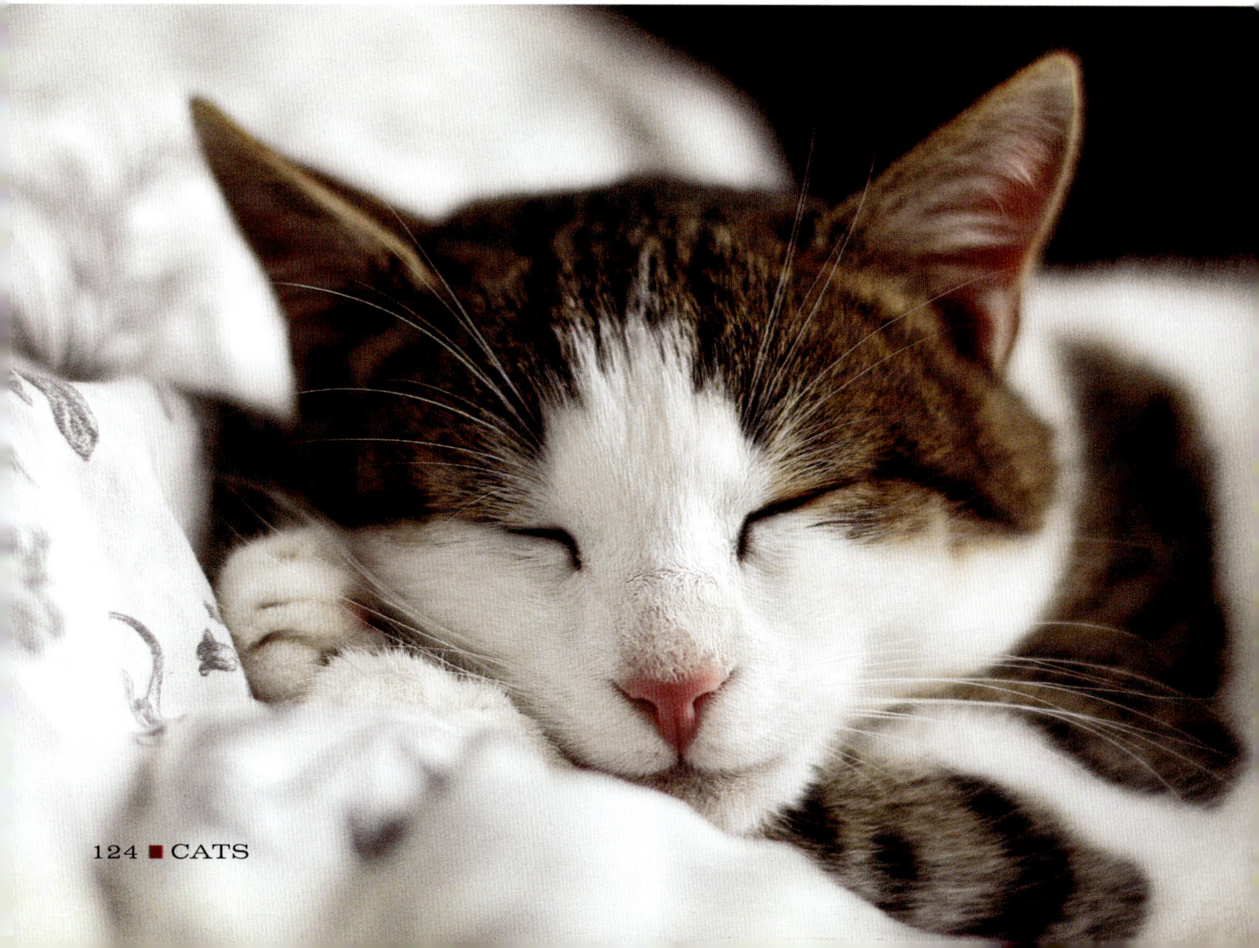

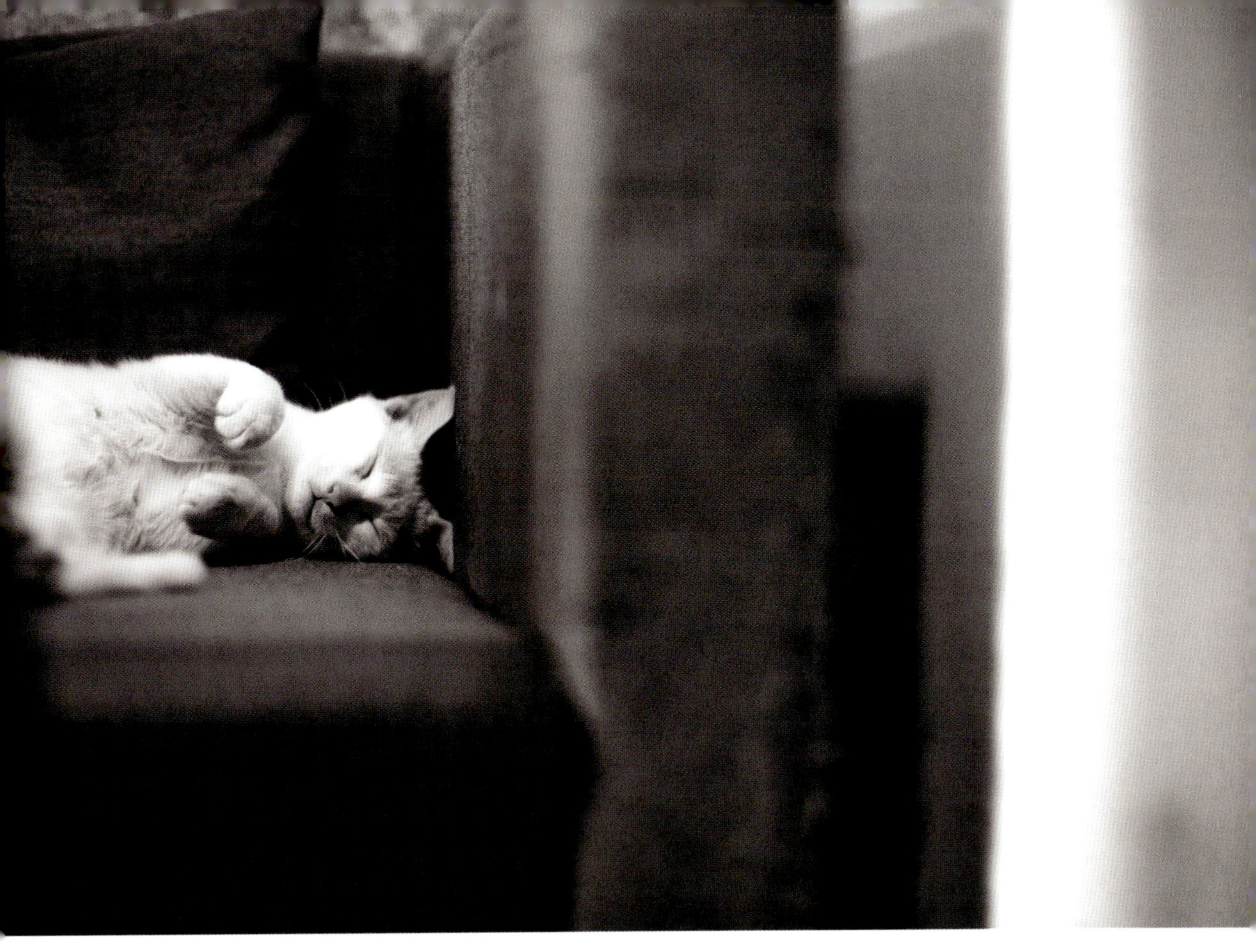

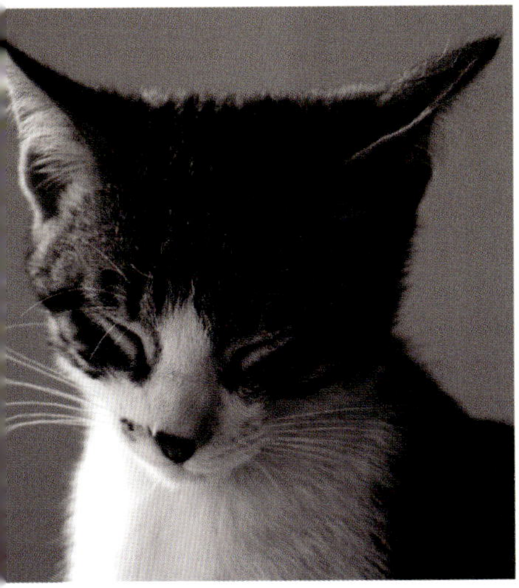

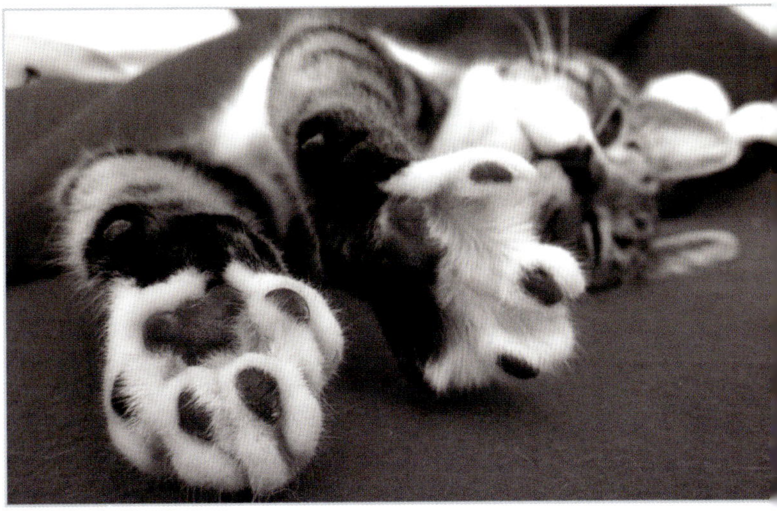

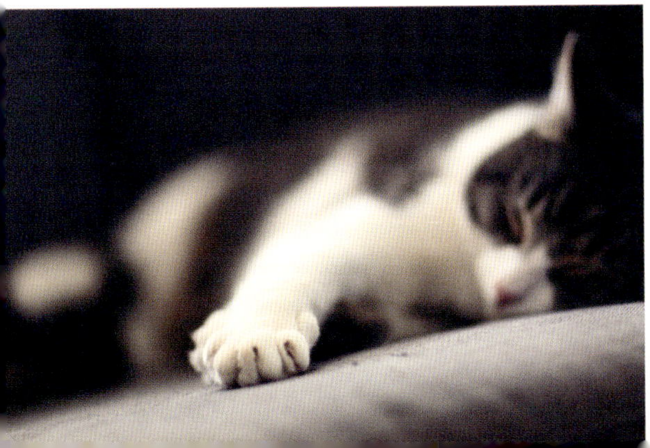

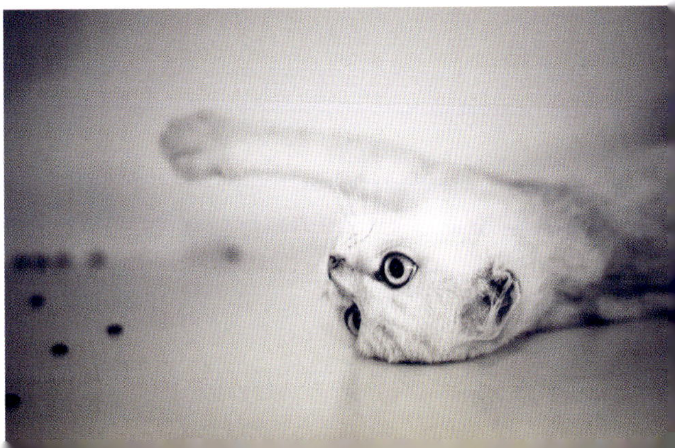

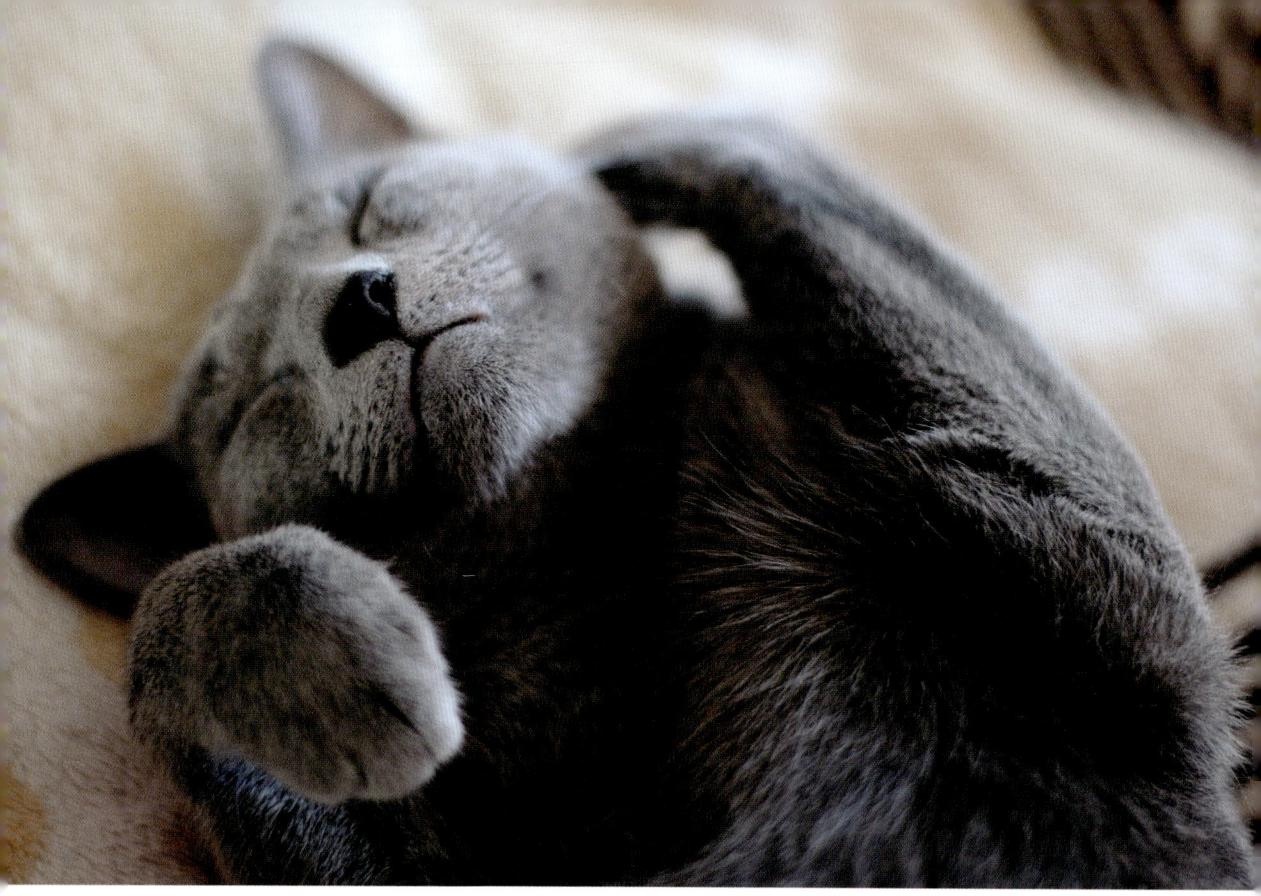
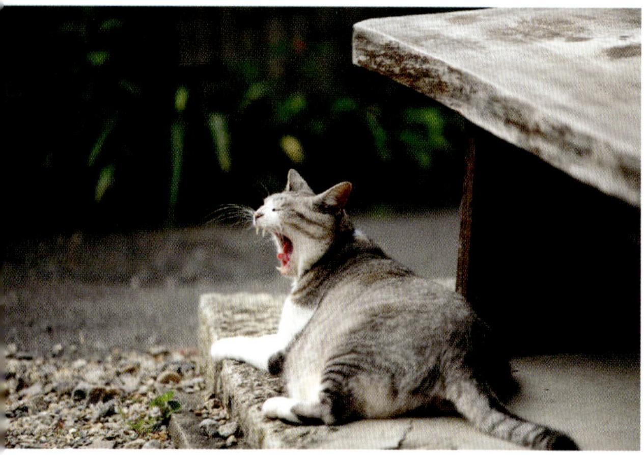
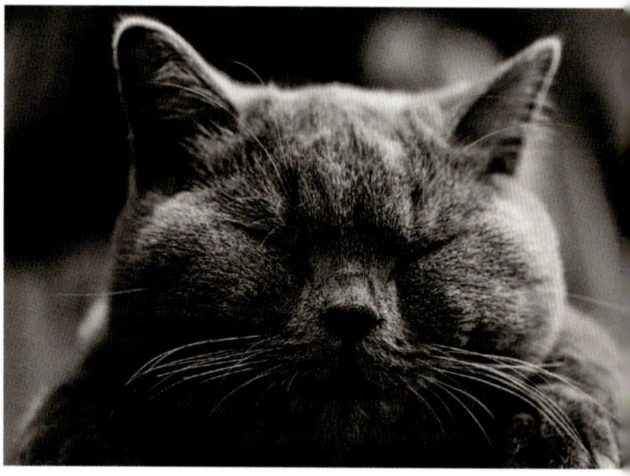
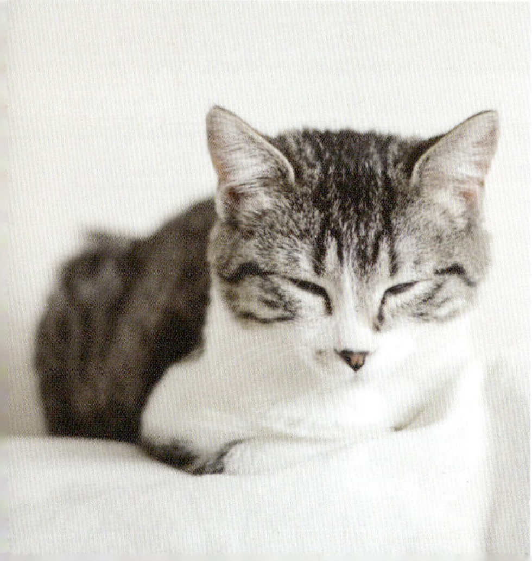
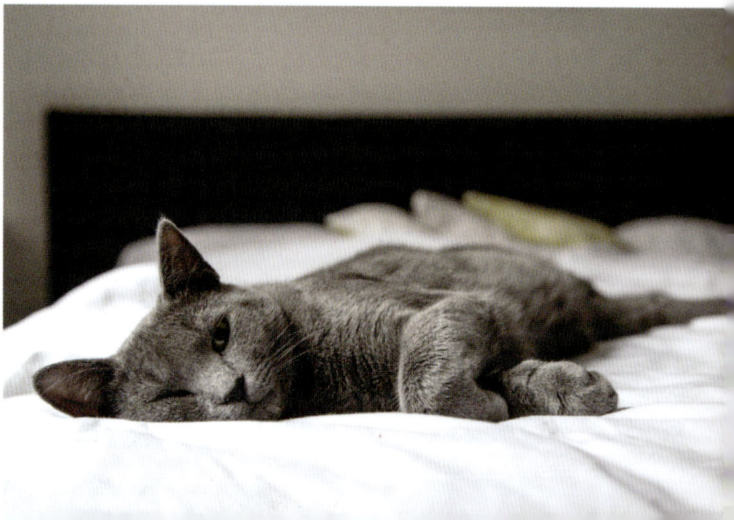

Conclusion

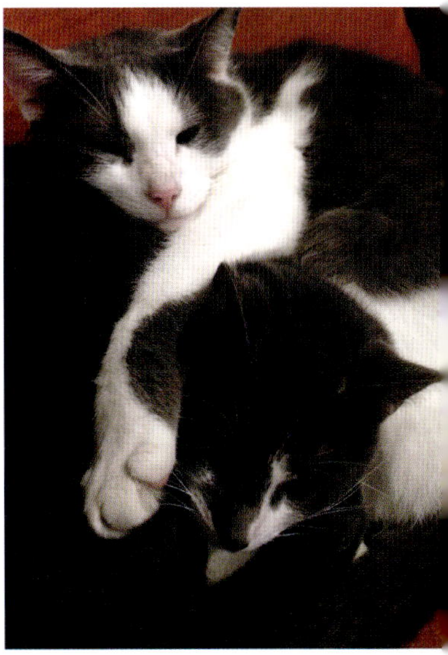

Hopefully, the sweet faces in these pages have brought a smile to your face! Now would be a great time to go hug your own pet—and, if you are able, consider donating to a rescue or animal care group in your area to ensure that all our furry friends have safe, happy lives. Finally, I want to send a shout-out to the fancy felines in my house, Clifton and Cleveland *(right)*. They were inseparable since they day they were born and have filled our house with love and laughter every day since.

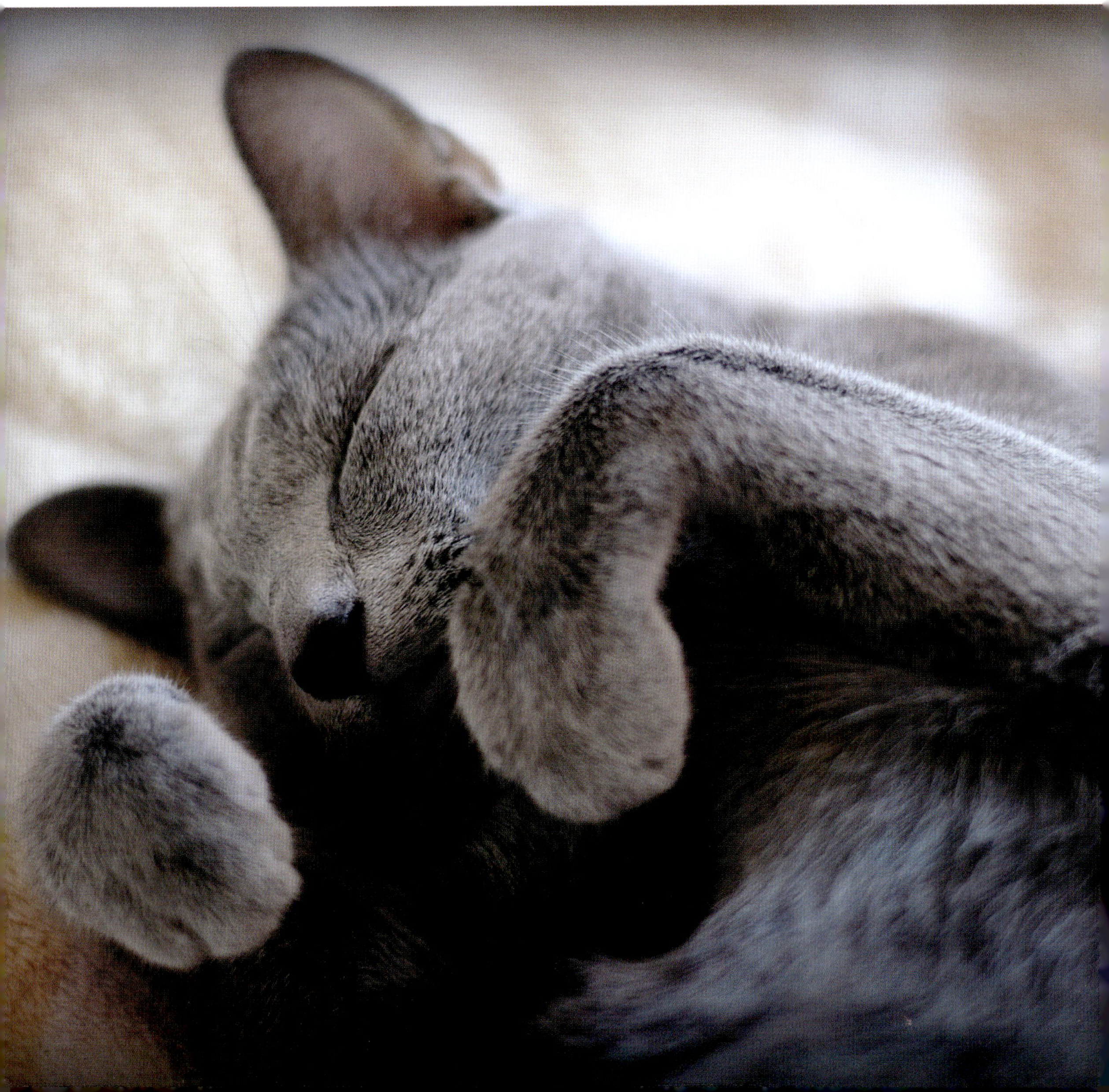